# Step Up to Writing

*Maureen Auman*

**Secondary Level**
Grades 6–High School

## Effective, Multisensory Writing Strategies

### Improves:

- **Writing**
- **Reading**
- **Listening**
- **Speaking**

Sopris West™
EDUCATIONAL SERVICES

A Cambium Learning Company

BOSTON, MA • LONGMONT, CO

Published and Distributed by

Sopris West™
EDUCATIONAL SERVICES

A Cambium Learning Company

4093 Specialty Place • Longmont, CO 80504 • 303-651-2829
www.sopriswest.com

**ILLUSTRATION CREDITS**
T17: toolbox ©2008 Jupiter Images. 276: dog ©2008 Jupiter Images. 439: baseball ©2008 Jupiter Images.

# Dedication

*To students, teachers, and administrators across the country who have been a part of the* Step Up to Writing *journey.*

*To trainers, current and former, who recognized the simplicity, power, and potential of the* Step Up to Writing *strategies and who then inspired educators everywhere to share them with their students.*

*To Cheryl Miller, my language arts coordinator and teacher mentor at Campus Middle School in Englewood, Colorado, for recognizing and appreciating the success that my students demonstrated once they learned and used explicit, visual, multisensory strategies to master reading and writing skills; for promoting the use of these strategies in all classes with students of all ability levels; for sharing her sense of humor, vision, and belief in the rights and talents of all students.*

## Acknowledgments

- A number of people worked with me at the Read Write Connection and helped make the third edition of *Step Up to Writing* a reality: John Auman, Dorothy Brock, Barbara Connaughty, Deana Hippie, Jill Yarberry-Laybourn, Bettye Lewis, Karen Miller, Joan Myer, Rodney Peffer, Janice Schwartz, Susan Smith, Claudia Styles, and Linda Archibeque Trimberger.

- I would especially like to thank Sharon Nealeigh and Caela Tyler for sharing their talents with technology and Lynn Utzman-Nichols for sharing her way with words.

- I would also like to thank the talented and dedicated staff at Sopris West Educational Services for their time and efforts.

- Most of all, I appreciate the support of my business manager, Jim Auman, whose work and organization made my work possible.

# TABLE OF CONTENTS
## Secondary Level

SECTION **4** Expository Paragraphs. . . . . . . . . . . . . . . . . . . . . . . . . . . . . **131**

**SECTION 5 — Accordion Essays and Reports** . . . . . . . . . . . . . . . . . . . . . . . . . . . . . . . . . 201

**SECTION 9** Specific Writing Assignments . . . . . . . . . . . . . . 359

**SECTION 10** Assessment and High Standards . . . . . . . . . . . 413

# Step Up to Writing

## ONE TEACHER'S JOURNEY

*My journey* with *Step Up to Writing* started in a classroom filled with eighth graders anxious to head to high school and nervous about passing their eighth-grade exit exams.

It was the 1985–86 school year—the year I moved from teaching in a small, private K–8 school to a large suburban middle school. My six years of teaching experience only partially prepared me for the challenges I faced. My biggest challenge, preparing students to reach proficient or advanced levels on district and state writing assessments, forced me to rethink the way that I taught writing.

Because of my competitive nature, my desire to keep my job, and my belief that all students can learn, I looked at the assessments as a challenge and took the role of a coach. With the right strategies, clear directions, encouragement, and lots of practice, I was certain that my second period students (identified as remedial) would do as well as my eighth period honors students and third, fifth, and seventh period "regular" students.

The assessments required students to write information/expository paragraphs or essays on a variety of topics (descriptive, persuasive, compare/contrast) in a short period of time. I analyzed the skills that students needed to master and broke my instruction into small steps. I taught the steps one at a time using direct, explicit instruction as well as a workshop approach.

Students participated in active, hands-on lessons as I explained and showed them how to organize information effectively, how to create topic sentences and introductions in only a few moments, and how to support their topics with facts, details, and elaboration. I gave them strategies for organizing that could be used when they had plenty of time to write as well as when they had to watch the clock. All strategies were visual and practical—easy to learn and easy to use.

We practiced each skill together. Students then worked in pairs or in small groups. I helped individual students, and they helped each other. They felt comfortable sharing their work with me—and with their classmates. I notice a dramatic improvement in all of my students' work.

We wrote on a variety of topics but mostly about what we were reading at the time and content that they studied in other classes. Along with the writing strategies, I taught students to be active readers. Over a period of time they learned a number of practical strategies for reading and writing. They then used these strategies to complete daily assignments and on their exams.

## The results were fantastic! 
Test scores validated the improvements that I had seen. Students and their families were pleased. Administrators and department leaders noticed. I, of course, was excited, but more importantly, I liked the fact that each day all students were on task and willing to write. Students liked the clear, simple directions that saved them time, provided a structure, and encouraged them to share their ideas.

Eventually, friends in my language arts department asked me to share the strategies that I had used with my students. Their enthusiasm and success with the strategies inspired teachers throughout the building. Math, science, social studies, health, art, and technology teachers joined us in an effort to improve the reading and writing skills of all students across content areas. The active reading, note-taking, summarizing, essay, and paragraph-writing strategies became the basis for a common language about literacy. Together we set high standards and high expectations for work from all students.

Later I was asked to share the same strategies with other teachers. Kindergarten as well as high school science and history teachers attended workshops sponsored by my district. Teachers at all grade levels left the workshops inspired to try the strategies. It soon became obvious that elementary teachers were experiencing the same kinds of success that I had with my middle school students.

Teachers working with hearing-impaired students, special education teachers, and those working with students identified as gifted and talented all adapted the strategies to meet the needs of their students. The strategies, educators realized, produced immediate improvements, were flexible, and could be use to meet district or state standards. The word spread: practical, visual, hands-on, kinesthetic strategies help students learn and master important academic skills.

*Then word spread* beyond my district and even more teachers wanted to learn the strategies, so I designed a graduate-level course open to all who were interested. The rest, as they say "is history." Teachers spread the word. Principals whose students had great success on district and state exams spread the word. Parents and students themselves spread the word.

*Step Up to Writing*, originally called *The Read Write Connection*, started as a simple effort to give eighth graders the skills and confidence they needed to pass a district exam. Thousands of teachers, in and out of the United States, now use *Step Up* strategies every day in K–12 classrooms.

My hope is that *Step Up to Writing* 3rd Edition will inspire even more teachers to make all lessons active and multisensory—guaranteeing the academic success of students everywhere.

*Maureen E. Auman*

# What is Step Up to Writing?

## Visual, Multisensory, and Practical Strategies

*Step Up to Writing* can be used quickly and applies to all subjects. Students use the strategies throughout the day for all kinds of assignments. Students learn to visualize each academic task through multisensory instruction, such as color-coding the parts of a paragraph or report or using paper folds to visually separate information on a page. The focus of these approaches is to promote the goal of all good writing: clear communication.

## Effective Instruction Techniques

*Step Up to Writing* instruction is part of an ongoing process of frequent demonstration, guided lessons, and practice opportunities. This ensures that students have the skills they need to become successful, independent readers and writers.

- **Demonstration and explicit instruction:** Teachers demonstrate each strategy in interactive, hands-on lessons, explaining all steps so students can learn and master the skill.

- **Guided lessons using models of good writing:** Teachers work with students or show them examples to model the kind of work expected. These whole- or small-group lessons give students a chance to get feedback and ask questions.

- **Frequent practice and application:** Students practice (independently and with peers) what they have learned and continue to receive feedback. They are encouraged to apply strategies to content-area assignments. They learn to self-evaluate their work using models, checklists, and scoring guides.

## A Step-by-Step Approach

*Step Up to Writing* breaks complex tasks into small, easy steps. Students learn these steps individually and then practice putting them together. As they master these processes, they are encouraged to ask questions and, ultimately, to make the methods their own.

One step-by-step approach is the *Step Up* writing process. Students follow eight steps that guide them from brainstorming and planning to creating a final, polished composition. Students learn how to follow the process when time is limited and how to use longer periods of time to create their very best work.

Revise · Draft · Edit

## Numerous Models and Reference Materials

*Step Up to Writing* provides numerous models of good writing and reference lists of words, phrases, and examples to build skills and promote thinking. Reading, analyzing, and marking examples of good writing help students understand the expectations for their own writing. Students also use these examples as guides when they write, or they may assess examples using the same scoring guides that teachers use to evaluate students' work. Students use lists to jumpstart their thinking or writing. The lists help with word choice, idea development, and sentence variety. As students add to these lists, they become a helpful reference in their writing notebooks.

## Comprehensive Tools for Students and Teachers

*Step Up to Writing* gives teachers useful Tools that help students complete a wide range of important academic tasks. These Tools combine the strategies explained in this Teacher's Guide with reproducible pages that match the strategies. Tools can be used to teach, practice, or assess a skill. Teachers use Tools throughout the day to facilitate learning and can adjust the Tools as needed to fit their teaching styles and class goals.

## Success for Students

Teachers and administrators help students by prioritizing literacy skills and monitoring student progress. Students learn to track their success by working to reach the proficient and advanced levels on all assignments. They use scoring guides and quick check forms to help monitor their progress. These guides give specific information about what is needed to move from below basic or basic to proficient and advanced levels. Teachers, administrators, and families use the scoring guides and quick checks to monitor progress and to give students the help they need.

## A Common Language

By developing a common reading and writing language across grade levels and classes, *Step Up to Writing* helps students quickly learn and understand what teachers mean by specific writing terms and assignments. For teams, schools, and districts wanting to improve students' daily work and increase scores on high-stakes assessments, this consistency is a real help. A common language improves the writing skills of all students because they apply the same concepts and skills in all classes and grade levels. They receive instruction from a number of teachers and support from peers who have learned the skills.

## Support for Other Programs, Methods, and Materials

*Step Up to Writing* works well as the primary or only language arts program for a school or district. However, these strategies are also an excellent way to enhance and support other programs, methods, or materials like the following examples.

### Six Traits

*Step Up to Writing* supports and teaches the writing skills used with Six Traits assessments. With *Step Up*, students learn many strategies for **organization** that help with **idea development**. They build strong vocabulary skills, which help with **word choice** and **voice**. They also learn and frequently practice different sentence structures. This knowledge empowers them to write with the kind of **sentence variety** that Six Traits suggests. When student writers combine good sentence variety with careful word choice, they begin to develop a style and voice of their own. Finally, *Step Up* teaches students proper **conventions** for editing and revising their work to make it the best it can be.

*Step Up to Writing* gives students the skills they need to become proficient, independent writers; Six Traits gives students a way to assess and think about their writing. The *Step Up to Writing* four-level assessment guides (Section 10) help prepare students for Six Traits and high-stakes writing assessments.

### Writers Workshop

*Step Up to Writing* gives teachers resources that fit many different teaching and learning styles. Some teachers use *Step Up* in a readers or writers workshop setting, whereas others present strategies in whole-group, structured lessons. In both cases teachers demonstrate and give explicit instructions. Either way students are given time to write and to confer about strengths and weaknesses in their writing. They also can ask questions and share insights about what they have read.

*Step Up* strategies and activities promote two important parts of learning to read and write:

- Students use a variety of materials and resources and have many opportunities to read and write.
- Students learn from their teachers and from each other as they share strategies and discuss various kinds of writing; they have frequent opportunities for individual and small-group work sessions with teachers and classmates.

### Textbooks and Reading Programs

*Step Up to Writing* strategies make using textbooks easier for teachers and students. The active reading strategies empower students to tackle and comprehend material in content-area textbooks. Students learn to create useful study guides and to take notes quickly and effectively. They also learn to answer questions accurately in a way that saves time and prepares them for tests.

Teachers use *Step Up to Writing* strategies to help students complete writing assignments included in textbook chapters and reading selections. For example, a teacher could use the informal outline, topic sentence, and organization strategies to help students with a persuasive writing assignment. That same teacher could use the quick sketch strategy to help students retell a story and the IVF summary topic sentence to check for comprehension.

### Core Knowledge

*Step Up to Writing* strategies support teachers and students as they tackle a wide variety of reading and writing tasks. Active reading and listening strategies help students read with comprehension and remember more of what they have read. They empower students to ask and answer questions, make inferences, and analyze what they read—thereby processing information, not merely memorizing it.

Writing strategies assist students as they complete the various writing expectations included in the *Core Knowledge Sequence*. These strategies and skills are taught at all grade levels, increasing students' confidence and skills as they move from grade level to grade level.

## A Framework to Grow Creativity

In the initial stages of instruction, students learn about structure and organization. Once they understand the need for structure in writing, they have the framework on which to build and expand their creativity. Because they have a sense of organization and understand the purpose for their writing—the reason they want to share a topic with readers—they are free to focus on content, word choice, sentence structures, and style.

Creativity flourishes when students have the skills and strategies necessary to help them tell a great story or make a strong point in an essay. Creativity, students learn, means taking raw information and making it their own— discovering topics and developing them into story/narrative or information/ expository text. They also learn that creativity means presenting information clearly and concisely so readers can understand, use, and appreciate it.

# A Program for All Students

*Step Up to Writing* can be used with students spanning a wide range of ability levels and learning styles. The strategies in *Step Up* can be easily adapted to meet the needs of students who are gifted, require special education supports, are at-risk, or for whom English is their second language. Typical students experience success, too. The multisensory strategies make it easy for all students to see the elements of sentences, paragraphs, and stories visually and therefore gain understanding and skills more readily.

In addition to hands-on, multisensory activities, *Step Up* provides a means to teach writing, reading comprehension, and listening and speaking skills with a step-by-step approach that enables all students to gain skills at their own pace. The strategy design makes it easier to differentiate and pace instruction individually.

## Gifted and Talented

Gifted students often have much to say and great word skills, but may have difficulty adequately expressing their thoughts because they do not have the organizational skills for their writing to reach its full potential. *Step Up to Writing* provides them the framework from which they can soar.

## Typical Students

Typical students are sometimes called the "forgotten middle." They benefit greatly from *Step Up to Writing*. Because they complete work regularly and receive average scores, these students sometimes do not receive the extra help they need to move to proficient and advanced levels. The structure, guidance for revision, and opportunities to practice skills contained in *Step Up* help these students reach their full potential.

## At-Risk and Special Education

Students who are at-risk or have learning differences often lack the organization skills, strategies for writing, reading comprehension skills, and the motivation and confidence needed in writing. *Step Up* uses multisensory strategies for students to learn how to organize their writing. The reading strategies tie reading and writing together so that students can benefit more from their content-area classes. As students are more successful and see their skills increase, they are more motivated and willing to write.

Students who are hearing impaired also benefit from the visual, kinesthetic strategies used in *Step Up to Writing*. The strategies help these students recognize and imitate the basic organizational patterns (information/expository and story/narrative) found in writing.

**Note:** Students who are color blind may have difficulty with the Traffic Light colors. If so, try substituting different colors or symbols that students can distinguish.

## A Way for Teachers to Meet District Goals, State Standards, and Grade-Level Expectations

*Step Up to Writing* can easily be aligned to curricular goals and to district or state standards. School district and state standards list **what** students should learn; *Step Up* strategies and Tools provide the **how**.

Each state has its own standards for student achievement in writing and reading. Although these expectations vary slightly from state to state, there are many similarities. The following expectations are common to many states and show how *Step Up to Writing* can be used to meet state (and district) standards. To ensure that your instruction meets the needs of your students, review the literacy standards and expectations for your state.

**Note:** Use the charts on the following two pages for discussion and for planning as you consider ways to meet your own district guidelines or state standards.

# District and State Expectations

Many of the standards for Middle and High School continue to emphasize critical reading skills, writing essays and compositions with appropriate text structure, and making oral presentations. Students use more sophisticated strategies as they analyze and evaluate text, to develop ideas and support them with evidence and examples. Writers refine their use of the writing process, emphasizing research-based discourse and practical writing applications.

**Some of the ways that *Step Up to Writing* supports the acquisition of reading and writing skills are as follows:**

| Grade 6–12 Expectations | Applicable *Step Up to Writing* Strategies |
|---|---|
| Continues to develop grade-level vocabulary, particularly in the content areas | Students master new vocabulary by:<br>• Breaking Down Definitions (Section 2)<br>• Meaningful Vocabulary Sentences (Section 2)<br>• Vocabulary and Concept Maps (Section 2)<br>• Vocabulary Study Guides (Section 2)<br>• Categories (Section 2)<br>• Personification of Abstract Nouns (Section 2)<br>• Unit- or Subject-Specific Word Lists (Section 2) |
| Strategically identifies and extends important ideas in text | Students identify important ideas and extend and respond to them through:<br>• What Were You Thinking? (Section 1)<br>• Quotation Responses (Section 1)<br>• Two Column Guided Response (Section 1) |
| Synthesizes ideas from several different sources | Students can collect ideas from different sources and synthesize them using:<br>• Three Column Notes (Section 1)<br>• Writing to Compare and Contrast (Section 9) |
| Makes inferences and analyzes text | Students infer and analyze text by collecting and organizing important information and using appropriate structures for communication:<br>• Three Column Notes (Section 1)<br>• Informal Outlines (Section 1) |
| Uses appropriate text structures for different genres | Students learn to recognize and use appropriate text structures in reading and writing by:<br>• Using Graphic Organizers (Section 1)<br>• Using Text Structures (Section 1)<br>• Defining Fiction, Nonfiction, Prose, Poetry, Explain, and Entertain (Section 4) |
| Summarizes important information from text | Students identify important ideas and concisely communicate this information through:<br>• Four-Step Summary Paragraphs (Section 1)<br>• Developing Study Guides (Section 1) |

| Grade 6–12 Expectations | Applicable *Step Up to Writing* Strategies |
|---|---|
| Asks and answers questions about text | Asking and answering questions are an important part of assessing student learning. Activities that support effective questions and responses include:<br>• Great Short Answers (Section 1)<br>• Responses to Essay Questions (Section 1)<br>• Levels of Questioning (Section 1) |
| Conducts research and collects information | Student strategies for collecting information during research include:<br>• Circle Once, Underline Twice (Section 1)<br>• One Idea per Paragraph Note Taking (Section 1)<br>• Research Note Cards (Section 1)<br>• Three- and Four-Column Notes (Section 1) |
| Independently uses all stages of the writing process | Effective writers use the writing process to produce writing that is purposeful and easily understood through:<br>• The Writing Process (Section 4)<br>• Color-Coding and the Five Elements of Expository Writing (Section 4) |
| Revises work using feedback, checklists, and scoring guides | Students improve their drafts using:<br>• Peer Review/Editing/Revision (Section 10)<br>• Checklists for Revision (Section 10)<br>• Expository Reports and Essays Scoring Guide (Section 10)<br>• Personal Essay Scoring Guide (Section 10) |
| Writes for specific purposes, including technical and career related documents | Students write for real world purposes in:<br>• Writing Letters (Section 9)<br>• Applying for a Job (Section 9)<br>• Technical Writing (Section 9) |
| Uses increasingly sophisticated strategies to create effective narratives, reports, and essays | Student writing reflects advanced knowledge of the strategies that support a "finished" text through:<br>• Leading with the Blues (Section 5)<br>• Defining Topic Sentences and Thesis Statements (Section 4)<br>• Obvious and Subtle Transitions (Section 5)<br>• Transitions in Narratives (Section 4)<br>• Planning For Changes/Growth in Characters (Section 6)<br>• Comparing Paragraph and Report Elaboration (Section 4)<br>• Conclusions Have a Purpose (Section 5) |
| Supports assertions with evidence and examples | Students support their statements and assertions with appropriate evidence and examples using:<br>• Supporting an Opinion with Facts (Section 9)<br>• Elaboration with Quotations and Citations (Section 5) |
| Applies standard structural elements to oral communication | Students use effective writing strategies to support clear oral communication through:<br>• Blocking Out a Speech (Section 8)<br>• Planning Longer Presentations (Section 8)<br>• Persuasive Speeches (Section 8) |

# Support for English Language Learners

English language learners have twice the challenge meeting grade-level standards. Not only do they have to master content knowledge, but they must also acquire the vocabulary and structure of English at the same time. Fortunately, students learning English learn to read and write in much the same way as English-only students. With good instruction that includes clear learning objectives, structured instructional routines, many opportunities to practice and apply new learning, and appropriate feedback on correct and incorrect responses, all students can achieve at high levels.

| Possible Areas of Need | How *Step Up* Helps |
|---|---|
| Developing Oral Language | • The structure of *Step Up* provides oral language support for English learners. Lessons begin with an emphasis on oral language and conceptual understanding before moving to direct instruction, guided practice, and application. Students can participate in grade-level lessons at their language level using informal organizers, sentence starters, and paragraph frames to scaffold the lessons' outcomes.<br><br>• Using text organizers, students can practice retelling stories and summarizing information orally, providing extended practice with language and opportunities for teachers feedback.<br><br>• The response starters (Section 1) and paragraph frames (Section 9) help teachers differentiate the level of support provided to students at varying levels of language proficiency. Strategies like these can develop both oral and written language.<br><br>• *Step Up* activities support highly interactive instruction, providing students many opportunities to verbalize their thoughts so they can understand age-appropriate material. |
| Development of Academic and Written Vocabulary | • *Step Up* clearly identifies and teaches the academic language of writing, such as the parts of an information/expository paragraph, essay, or report (Sections 4 and 5), parts of a story/narrative (Section 6), story grammar (Section 6), parts of speech (Section 3), and elements of a sentence (Section 3).<br><br>• Vocabulary is taught using a multisensory approach, including breaking down definitions, reading dictionary definitions, and creating vocabulary maps (Section 2).<br><br>• Students learn how to improve word choice and play with language in prewriting, planning, and revising strategies (Sections 3, 4, 5, and 10). |
| Reading Comprehension | • Writing IVF (Identify/Verb/Finish Thought) summary topic sentences and summary paragraphs (Section 1) is a good way for English learners to use information immediately after they learn it. Writing summaries provides a clear way to organize information so students can visualize and understand relationships between ideas. It is also an excellent informal assessment tool for checking comprehension.<br><br>• Teaching students to take two-column notes (Section 1) helps English learners understand and organize information/expository text, particularly in content areas.<br><br>• Response activities (Section 1) provide English learners with a structure for responding to text, and they support higher-level thinking skills.<br><br>• The active reading techniques (Section 1) can increase reading comprehension of both narrative and expository texts. |

| Possible Areas of Need | How *Step Up* Helps |
| --- | --- |
| Active Student Involvement | • Framed paragraphs (Section 9) and response starters (Section 1) help teachers scaffold student practice and are flexible enough to meet the different levels of language learners.<br>• Informal outlines, Accordion Paragraphs, and multiparagraph essays and reports (Sections 4 and 5) provide an active step-by-step approach to writing.<br>• Free response techniques (Section 1) support active reading and engagement with texts, whether story/narrative or information/expository. |
| Access to High-Quality, Grade-Level-Appropriate Curriculum | • Breaking tasks into smaller steps ensures that instruction remains challenging with high, but reasonable, expectations (Sections 3 through 6).<br>• The strategies in *Step Up* provide teachers with a format for facilitating English language development within content-area instruction (Section 1). Students can use two-column notes to identify main ideas in content-area text, learn important vocabulary, and develop question-and-answer relationships in the text. |
| Organizing and Relating Information | • *Step Up* provides visual representations to help English langugage learners organize their thoughts through:<br>  ▸ Informal outlines and quick sketches for planning (Sections 1 and 6);<br>  ▸ Practice guides when first learning to write sentences, paragraphs, reports, and essays (Sections 3, 4, and 5);<br>  ▸ Highlighting and marking text to improve reading comprehension (Section 1);<br>  ▸ Breaking down definitions and using graphic organizers to learn vocabulary words.<br>• The Traffic Light colors help students see structures, relationships, and important ideas that are a part of every information/expository writing assignment.<br>• Students learn to plan using an informal outline and to use information on the outline to write a paragraph, essay, or report.<br>• The Accordion Paragraph organizer allows students and teachers to review their writing word by word and sentence by sentence to check for meaning and to ensure the language and structure are appropriate for their language proficiency level. Students can also use the Accordion Paragraph format as a checkpoint for moving beyond revision at the word and sentence level to build an entire paragraph that makes sense.<br>• The quick sketch format (Parts of a Story, Section 6), using pictures rather than words, allows students to visually represent a story and allows an oral retelling or rehearsal of a story before having to write it. |

## Remember . . .

*Step Up to Writing's* multisensory strategies for supporting English learners endure across the grade levels. By using the common language of *Step Up to Writing*, students no longer have to master a different language of writing each year. By using the same structures and academic language year after year in all content areas, English learners are free to focus on practicing new language structures and content vocabulary during reading and writing instruction.

# Research Base

Writing is essential to academic success. Unfortunately, our children are failing in alarming numbers to master this important skill. In every state in the union, the majority of students do not write proficiently, based on the National Assessment of Educational Progress (NAEP) for 2002 (U.S. Department of Education, 2003). Instead, more than two-thirds of America's students show only partial mastery of the skills and knowledge needed for solid academic performance in writing. After analyzing numerous data sources, the authors of *Writing Next: Effective Strategies to Improve Writing of Adolescents in Middle and High Schools* stated that there is a "writing proficiency crisis."

However, a growing number of studies point to the elements of effective writing instruction. These elements, such as the ones identified in *Writing Next*, provide a framework for future study as well as a means to review current practices and instructional material. *Step Up to Writing* aligns with the fundamentals noted in current research. Following is a brief review of the research base for *Step Up to Writing*.

## Learning How to Write

Learning to write is a complicated process. Writing depends on several processes that operate together (Hayes and Flower 1980; Berninger 1996; Berninger and Swanson 1994 et al. 1995). Each of the critical steps in the writing process must be taught directly (Gersten and Baker 2001) and practiced repeatedly (Swanson, Hoskyn, and Lee 1999) if students are to write coherently and fluently.

*Step Up to Writing* provides a systematic approach that breaks writing skills into smaller pieces. Each piece is taught and practiced separately and then assembled and practiced together to meet the ultimate objective. For instance, color-coding is used to help students focus on one element, like writing a topic sentence, as well as to see the overall goal, such as writing an information/expository composition.

## Prewriting and Planning

Prewriting and planning includes generating ideas and organizing thoughts before writing. Many writers spend little time planning before they write; they plan as they write without thinking about content or organization (Burtis et al. 1983; Graham et al. 1991).

 *Step Up to Writing* teaches students how to organize their ideas before they write. Drawing on multisensory techniques, students visualize the organization by equating colors with different parts of a written piece. They use Traffic Light colors and folded paper to structure their main ideas and supporting information into cohesive, organized information/expository compositions. For writing narratives, students use quick sketches and quick notes as they plan for how to introduce the characters, setting, and plot. They also use quick sketches to determine the sequence of events as they plan for what will happen in the beginning, middle, and end. Additional organizational formats are provided for writing summaries and personal narratives. After students are taught each of these methods, they participate in guided exercises to practice their new organizational and planning skills collaboratively in small groups, with a partner, or individually and share their work for feedback.

## Putting Ideas into Words

Developing writers often have difficulty generating language to express their ideas, including selecting words that convey their intended message in a precise, interesting, and natural way. Others can express themselves orally, but lack knowledge of how to represent language in writing (Berninger et al., 1992). Many write in a disorganized manner, making their writing difficult to follow. Students need to be taught skills to create organized, well-constructed sentences and paragraphs that clearly state what they are trying to communicate.

*Step Up to Writing* assists students in translating their ideas into language and then written sentences. When using *Step Up*, teachers explain and model the elements and structures of writing. Students then practice both collaboratively with classmates and independently. *Step Up* explicitly teaches the conventions and elements of various writing genres, and how to use text structures to direct student writing. In addition to composition skills, students are taught sentence structures and how to vary them, and strategies that clarify and enrich linguistic expression, including the use of examples and word lists of lively verbs, interesting adjectives, and precise nouns. Students are taught several methods for composing topic and concluding sentences.

# Revising

Although revising is critical to the writing process (Graves 1983), many writers are unlikely to revise without strong encouragement and support. Developing writers often fail to recognize a need for revision, but if someone points out to them specific areas of text that would benefit from repair, they often can repair the text successfully (Beal 1993, 1996). Thus, low rate of revision is often due not to an inability to repair the text, but to a failure to detect that the text needs to be revised. Fortunately, the results from several intervention studies show that self-monitoring can be taught effectively and efficiently to children in the classroom, which results in improved revising activity.

With *Step Up to Writing,* students engage in revising activities that improve word choice, sentence structure, and sentence variety. *Step Up to Writing* provides writing models to show students what teachers want them to produce, along with examples of what not to write: vague, poorly organized writing. Students receive checklists and rubrics to evaluate their own work. They are not always expected to write a perfect draft the first time, but to revise and write multiple drafts whenever possible. At times, however, students are not given time to write multiple drafts and consider extensive revision. *Step Up* teaches students planning skills so they can create their best "first draft" as a way to save time and prepare for "real world" writing tasks. In content-area classes, for example, students often have limited time to write paragraphs and short essay responses. On class, school, district, and state assessments, students must be able to demonstrate their skills in a first-and-only draft. *Step Up* prepares students for this kind of writing while it also promotes and teaches revision.

In addition to these cognitive processes, motivational and social context processes influence the acquisition of writing skills. Research confirms that how students feel about writing impacts their response to writing intervention; furthermore, repeated writing practice prevents work-avoidance, and scaffolded instruction increases children's learning (Berninger et al. 1995). Through direct instructions, step-by-step guidelines, and detailed examples, coupled with guided, interactive, and independent writing practice, *Step Up to Writing* makes writing easier, faster, and more rewarding.

## Principles of Instruction

*Step Up to Writing* addresses the instructional variables—explicit and systematic instruction, collaborative learning, and scaffolded teaching of the writing process—that are associated with improved outcomes as identified in syntheses of research (Gersten and Baker 2001; Swanson, Hoskyn, and Lee 1999; Vaughn, Gersten, and Chard 2000; National Reading Panel 2000). Skills in *Step Up to Writing* are sequenced, beginning with instruction and use of examples, then eliciting frequent verbal responses from the students. Modeling, guided practice, extended interactive practice, and frequent feedback on student work ensure that students experience success in writing activities.

When using *Step Up to Writing*, students are provided numerous opportunities to collaborate with their peers by working in small groups or pairs as they learn new skills. This allows students to be actively involved in the learning, engage in problem-solving, and increase skills as they plan, write, revise, and edit their work. After working collaboratively with peers, students were able and willing to analyze their own work (Boscolo and Ascorti 2004).

## Writing for Content Learning

Because *Step Up to Writing* provides a common language for writing, it teaches skills that can be used across content areas. *Step Up* strategies connect reading and writing. Students are taught active reading and higher-order reasoning skills when they learn and see models of active reading, responses to literature, analysis, and note-taking strategies. Research shows that students' comprehension improves through direct explanation and modeling of strategies and relate what they read with background knowledge (Pressley and Wharton-McDonald 1997; Williams 1998). In *Step Up to Writing* students are taught to generate and answer questions that elicit both factual and inferential interpretations of text while they read. Teachers explicitly teach strategies for generating text summaries that logically support the answers to questions.

# Where Do I Begin?

"Where do I begin?" is a common question teachers new to *Step Up to Writing* ask. Because *Step Up* strategies cover so many writing tasks and the curriculum needs vary from classroom to classroom, it doesn't make sense for all teachers to start on page one and simply work their way through the book. Although this is the typical approach for most curricula, *Step Up to Writing* is different. It is a collection of strategies to choose from as you meet the needs of your students.

# Using Step Up to Writing *in Your Classroom*

*Step Up to Writing* instruction can be used throughout the school in every content area or in just one class or grade level.

## Preparing to Teach

Most teachers begin by asking themselves three questions. The answers to these questions will determine which strategies to use and how best to implement them in your classroom.

1. **What writing tasks do your students need to complete?**
   Begin by considering what types of writing and reading tasks your students need to perform to be successful. What are the state and district standards that your students need to meet? What kinds of writing skills do they need to have in order to be successful in all of their classes? What sort of tasks, such as note-taking and writing simple sentences, do they need to complete on a day-to-day basis? What sort of tasks will they be asked to complete for quizzes, tests, or other special assignments?

   > In teacher A's eighth-grade class, students are facing a big writing task this year: a five-page research paper. Even though students have written research papers before, they have never written one so long or detailed. Students will need to learn several new writing skills to help them complete this assignment. In addition, Mr. A requires his students to keep a writing notebook in which they take notes on class lectures and reading assignments. He also requires students to write a short paragraph each week summarizing what was learned that week.

**2. What are your students' abilities and needs?**

To answer this question, reflect on what you know about your students. Do they have trouble writing simple sentences and choosing good, descriptive words? Or are they writing sentences and paragraphs at grade-level but having trouble writing longer reports and essays? Do they have trouble in content-area classes because of poor note-taking and reading-comprehension skills?

> Most of Mr. A's students can complete basic writing tasks, but there are some low-performing students who struggle to write well-structured paragraphs and sentences. In addition, many students are turning in poor or incomplete notes. Finally, to complete their research papers, all of Mr. A's students need to practice every step of the writing process, with special attention to planning, editing, and revising. They also need to spend extra time reviewing some skills, such as how to create research note cards and cite the sources for their report.

**3. What *Step Up to Writing* strategies meet your students' needs and help them complete the writing tasks they face?**

To answer this question, compare your responses to the first two questions. By looking at what is expected of your students and comparing it to what they can actually do, you will be able to identify their needs. Then go through the *Step Up to Writing* Teacher's Guide and identify strategies that will help your students improve their writing skills and successfully complete the writing tasks you, your district, and your state expect of them. Once you have identified those strategies, you can think about where, when, and how you will incorporate them into your lesson plans.

> By comparing the needs of his students and the writing tasks they face, Mr. A realizes that he needs to focus on several key areas. First, he decides to review **5-3 Organizing and Writing, One Step at a Time** with all his students to help them improve their report writing. He will also review **3-6 Better Sentences** and **4-8 Accordion Paragraphs** with his struggling writers. He will go over **1-17 Easy Two-Column Notes** with his students to help them improve their daily notes. To help them write their summary paragraphs, he will review **1-31 Four-Step Summary Paragraphs**. And to prepare his students for their research papers, he will focus heavily on the strategies from Section 5, Accordion Essays and Reports, as well as **1-21 Research Note Cards**.

## Using Paper Folds

Many *Step Up to Writing* strategies direct teachers and students to use folded paper to help clarify a step or process. The folds divide paper into sections for organization. These folds are shown on regular notebook paper, but can be adapted to any type and size of paper. The illustrations here show an example of each type of fold.

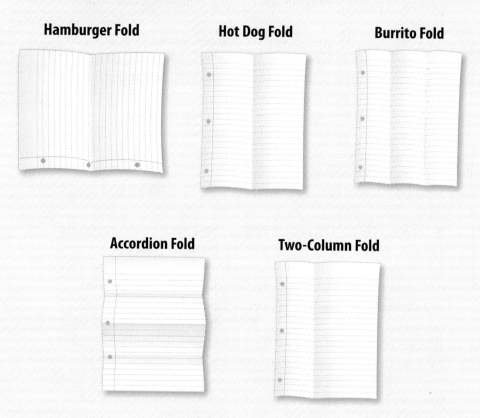

**Hamburger Fold**          **Hot Dog Fold**          **Burrito Fold**

**Accordion Fold**          **Two-Column Fold**

## Teaching

Once you have an idea of which strategies you will use, you are ready to implement them in your classroom. *Step Up to Writing* is designed to integrate with other programs.

1. Before you teach a new strategy, read it through a few times until you have a firm grasp on it. While you do so, pay special attention to the Before Class section found in most strategies. This section tells you the materials you need to prepare beforehand, as well as any other tasks you need to complete before you begin teaching.

2. When you actually introduce a strategy to your class, follow the guidelines in the During Class and Additional Ideas sections of the Teacher's Guide. *Step Up to Writing* strategies are not scripted, but they

include step-by-step directions for introducing, modeling, and practicing strategies with your students, as well as additional tips.

3. Students usually grasp a strategy faster if you use it in conjunction with material that is familiar to them. If you are introducing your students to informal outlines, for example, have them practice with content from a student magazine, science text, or social studies article.

4. It helps to follow the model–guided practice–independent practice approach with *Step Up to Writing* strategies. First, introduce students to strategies by modeling them on the board or an overhead transparency. Once you have provided adequate examples, guide your students as they try the strategy by working together as a class, or having students work together in pairs or in small groups. Finally, have students practice on their own. Monitor students' early practice by going around the room to support and assist as needed. Finally, when they have shown skill acquisition, have them practice the strategy independently, and continue to provide them with feedback.

5. Once your students are familiar with a strategy, instruct them to use it whenever they can. Most *Step Up* strategies can be used in multiple content areas, so encourage students to use the strategies they learn whenever they write, not simply when they are in your class or when you specifically tell them to do so.

6. Remember that all *Step Up to Writing* strategies are flexible. If some part of a strategy's instruction doesn't seem to be working for you or your students, adapt it to meet their needs. If you have an idea that you think might make a strategy more effective, fun, or comprehensible for your students, try it out. *Step Up* strategies are meant to help you; they are not set in stone.

## Assessing

Now that you've planned how you will use *Step Up to Writing* in your classroom and successfully taught several strategies, you have seen how effective it can be. However, *Step Up* is even more effective when you monitor your students' progress and adapt your instruction to meet their needs. There are several reasons to assess your students. First, assessment gives you a clearer picture of how your students are improving and what areas need additional instruction and practice. It also gives you concrete information about student performance that can be shared with parents, school administrators, and others. Finally, sharing assessment standards and results with your students lets them know the expectations for them, tells them what they need to do to become excellent writers, and motivates them as they see how much their writing has improved.

## Using *Step Up* Assessments

*Step Up to Writing* has two primary methods of assessment. The first method is the quick check. Quick checks are short lists of easy-to-understand criteria that break some common writing tasks down into four proficiency levels, from below basic through advanced. Quick checks can be used by you or by the students themselves to quickly and informally evaluate a piece of writing. The quick check involves students in assessment and helps them understand what needs to improve in their writing for it to be the best it can be. It is also a great tool for them to use when they move from their first draft to editing and revising.

The other method of assessment in *Step Up* is the scoring guide. Like quick checks, scoring guides provide criteria for evaluating a piece of writing as below basic, basic, proficient, or advanced. Unlike quick checks, scoring guides go into more depth. Scoring guides are useful because they are more thorough and they provide more detailed suggestions for improvement.

Section 10, Assessments and High Standards, has detailed instructions about how to use these two assessment methods. It also contains numerous examples of writing for all levels of assessment. Before you assess your students, it helps to share these examples with them, as well as the scoring guides you will use. This way, students will know what is expected of them, and will see what areas they need to work on to become proficient in all areas of writing.

## Evaluating Results

When you are evaluating assessment scores, look for both strengths and weaknesses in students' writing. Are they writing interesting, varied sentences but having trouble with basic grammar, punctuation, and spelling? Or perhaps they do not have significant problems with mechanics but do have trouble organizing their thoughts into coherent paragraphs or stories. This information allows you to fine-tune your approach to help all your students become accomplished, proficient writers.

- Don't be afraid to try a new strategy or a new approach to an old strategy if students don't seem to be improving in that area.

- If students show improvement but reveal an unexpected weakness in an area that hasn't been covered, expand your instruction to address these new concerns.

- If students' scores begin to slide in an area that had been improving, be sure to review strategies you have previously taught. Even students who seem to be familiar with a strategy will benefit from a review.

Above all, remember that even seemingly simple writing tasks can have complex parts and require a lot of explicit instruction, practice, and patience to master. With *Step Up to Writing*, all students can become proficient writers.

# Using Step Up Across Content Areas

Although some teachers and administrators associate writing with language arts or English classes, students need to write in all content areas, even mathematics and physical education classes. Using *Step Up to Writing* throughout the school will improve writing, test scores, and comprehension in all content areas, and will also help students become proficient writers more quickly. When students use *Step Up* strategies, terms, and approaches in all classes and grade levels, the concepts are constantly reinforced and students internalize them much more rapidly.

Writing across the content areas has been shown to produce significant improvement in students' writing abilities (van Allen 1991) and helps "students connect the dots in their knowledge" (The National Commission on Writing 2003). This is true because writing promotes learning and critical thinking in all contexts, helps students think through key concepts and ideas, gives students practice communicating using content-area vocabulary, and can be the thread that connects content areas and grade levels.

## What makes a good content-area writing assignment?

As noted by the Writing Across the Curriculum Clearinghouse (2007), "good writing assignments often take shape by thinking backwards. In effect, teachers ask themselves, 'What do I want to read at the end of this assignment?' By working from what they anticipate the final product to look like, teachers can give students detailed guidelines about both the writing task and the final written product…." Some key principles include:

- Tie the writing task to specific content-learning goals
- Alert students to the specific purpose and audience for the writing
- Make all elements of the task clear
- Include grading criteria on the assignment sheet (rubrics work well)
- Break down the task into manageable steps

## Must content-area teachers be experts in grammar and usage?

A common, valid concern that arises when implementing cross-content writing plans is a fear that content teachers must also teach writing conventions. This is not the case. Although writing conventions are important, the goal of writing across the curriculum is content learning. Some content-area teachers assign complex writing assignments such as essays or research reports, but most content-area writing activities are short, informal writing tasks meant to help students review, synthesize, and apply their knowledge. The goal is to give students practice with the conventions, formats, and vocabulary of a specific discipline. For example, students might write lab reports in a science class, art reviews for an art class, or news articles for a social studies class. Try doing the following:

- Partner with language arts teachers for joint writing assignments or general support.
- Consult language arts teachers to see what types of writing students are doing. If possible, use this information to build content-area writing assignments.

## Which *Step Up* strategies apply across content areas?

Many *Step Up to Writing* strategies can be infused into content-area classrooms to maximize instruction. Some examples are outlined in the following chart:

| Possible Areas of Need | How *Step Up* Helps* |
|---|---|
| Reading Comprehension | • **1-1** Free Responses helps students understand articles, textbooks, and other reading.<br>• **1-15** Circle Once, Underline Twice helps students identify key content and main ideas.<br>• Using **1-13** Text to Self, Text to Text, and Text to World, students interact with text for deeper comprehension. |
| Note-Taking and Study Guides | • **1-17** Easy Two-Column Notes helps students organize content from lectures, texts, films, and other resources.<br>• **1-21** Research Note Cards helps students collect and synthesize research information. |
| Answering Questions | • **1-36** Great Short Answers prompts students to give more complete, detailed answers to questions.<br>• **1-37** Responses to Essay Questions prepares students to respond to essay questions. |
| Vocabulary Strategies | • **2-3** Breaking Down Definitions helps students better understand unfamiliar words.<br>• **2-4** Meaningful Vocabulary Sentences gives students practice using vocabulary terms in their own writing. |
| Speaking | • **8-7** Informational Speeches and Oral Reports helps students create and deliver focused presentations.<br>• **8-16** Good Listening Skills gives students the skills they need to become better listeners. |
| Information/ Expository Writing Support | • Section 5 strategies help students compose clear, organized essays and reports.<br>• **4-22** Turning a Prompt into a Topic Sentence gives students an effective approach to writing topical essays.<br>• **1-31** Four-Step Summary Paragraphs gives students a method for summarizing what they learn. |

* These are just a few of the *Step Up* strategies that work well in content-area classes. For example, *Step Up* also offers specific activities for mathematics and science classes. Look for other strategies that will work with your class. Section 1, Writing to Improve Reading and Listening Comprehension; Section 2, Vocabulary; and Section 9, Specific Writing Assignments, are good places to start.

**Classroom Connection**

A few years ago, I transitioned from high school to middle school language arts teaching. I was extremely excited about the opportunity to be part of a more integrated team; my team included a science teacher, social studies teacher, mathematics teacher, and language arts teacher. I have always viewed reading and writing as the glue that holds content areas together, and my team members were enthusiastic about partnering for certain writing assignments that crossed the content areas.

One effective assignment I helped create was a joint project with the science teacher. He always had students write an essay to compare and contrast *protists* and *monerans*, but he was never fully satisfied with the results. He could see that students understood much of the content, but they were unable to organize their thoughts or communicate them logically. We decided this was the perfect opportunity to partner.

I worked with students on how to structure a compare/contrast essay, using *Step Up* strategies to explain the writing process, conventions, and appropriate transitions. The science teacher helped students generate and refine ideas and include ample and accurate support. When we assessed the final drafts, we each focused on specific aspects of the papers. The science teacher said that he had never had such good results and commented that this actually decreased his grading time because the papers were easy to read. I was satisfied that students produced great writing on a relevant topic that was of immediate academic importance.

—Jahnell Villeneuve, *Step Up to Writing* teacher; Longmont, Colorado

## Implementing *Step Up to Writing* Schoolwide

Implementing *Step Up to Writing* schoolwide helps teachers

- Teach and reinforce writing and literacy skills in all classes and grade levels by establishing a common language for talking about and teaching writing;
- Establish common high standards for assessing writing and other academic skills.

Planning for schoolwide implementation of *Step Up to Writing* follows the same planning process a teacher would use to implement *Step Up* in a single classroom (see pages T30 to T36). As a group, consider tasks you know your students must be able to complete along with their ability levels and needs. When you have a clear idea of your needs and goals, review the *Step Up* materials to see which strategies will be most helpful. If you still aren't sure where to begin, consider starting in Section 1. The strategies in Section 1 are easy to introduce and teach, and they focus on skills students need in all content areas, such as responding to texts, summarizing, and note taking. These skills improve comprehension, which in turn improves writing. These strategies can be taught in a short period of time using content that students are learning.

## Creating a Schoolwide Plan

Once you have identified a set of skills and strategies that you wish to teach and reinforce throughout the school year, and once teachers have learned the strategies, create a schoolwide plan to show how those strategies will be used in all content areas. Use the "Sample Schoolwide Plan for Summaries and Note Taking" as a snapshot of a schoolwide plan developed by one group. It shows their plan for teaching and using the *Step Up to Writing* strategies for summarizing and note taking.

### Some skill areas you might focus on in your plan include:

| | |
|---|---|
| Active Reading and Listening | Summarizing and Note Taking |
| Vocabulary Development | Sentence Mastery |
| Asking and Answering Questions | Paragraph Writing |
| Report and Essay Writing | Giving Speeches |
| Writing Stories | Writing to Persuade |
| Responding to Literature | |

## Schoolwide Plans Are Flexible

Remember that a schoolwide plan is flexible and changes over time. At first, the plan lists general commitments that teachers and grade-level (or subject-area) teams make to increase student skills. As teachers become familiar with the strategies, commitments should become specific—naming the times and subjects/topics where each strategy will be used. The plan should also grow in scope. Encourage teachers to experiment with new strategies and find new approaches that work with their students. Make sure everyone continues to follow the plan, though, so that all teachers are on the same page, reinforcing the same skills.

Another important part of schoolwide implementation is taking time to have teachers compare their experiences. The administrative team can use the schoolwide plan and assessment data to chart student progress, set goals, support classroom teachers in their efforts, and report results to the community.

### Classroom Connection

For schools that are looking to establish common writing language and corresponding, simple, consistent writing activities across all grade levels, the *Step Up to Writing* process is one of the best paths to choose. Many districts have correlated state/district standards with *Step Up to Writing* activities to ensure students that receive *Step Up to Writing* instruction have the best opportunities to master the writing skills they will need to be successful at their next level of education and pass high-stakes state/local tests. This process also provides teachers simple writing activities that they may use to differentiate instruction for individual students and small groups of students to fill skill gaps that these students may have in their writing abilities.          —Steve Hutchison, Principal; Winnemucca, Nevada

# Sample Schoolwide Plan for Summaries and Note Taking

| Grade | 6 | 7 | 8 | 9–12 |
|---|---|---|---|---|
| **Literature/ Language Arts/English** | • Summary paragraphs of short stories<br><br>• Two-column notes on grammar terms and examples | • Summary paragraphs of material in reading anthology book<br><br>• Two-column notes on expository readings | • Summary paragraphs of in class reading<br><br>• Two-column notes of story elements<br><br>• IVF summary topic sentence on selected reading assignments | • Summary paragraphs of novels, plays, poems studied<br><br>• Two-column notes on characters and their descriptions |
| **Science** | • Summaries of videos<br><br>• Summaries of science topics in the news<br><br>• Two-column study guides weekly | • Summaries of topics using unit vocabulary<br><br>• Two-column notes on reading assignments | • IVF topic sentence at end of class<br><br>• Two-column notes on each chapter with peer sharing and discussion to review before a test | • Summaries of science experiments<br><br>• Two-column notes on steps in lab activities and observations |
| **Math** | • Summary paragraph explaining solution to math problems<br><br>• Two- column notes of terms and definitions | • Summary paragraph explaining solution to math problems<br><br>• Two-column notes of processes and work done | • Summary paragraph explaining solution to algebra problems<br><br>• Two- and three-column notes of terms or processes with diagrams | • Summary paragraph explaining geometry theorems<br><br>• Two- and three-column notes on terms or processes with diagrams |
| **Social Studies** | • Summaries of news from weekly magazines and local papers<br><br>• Two-column notes of daily lessons and key topics | • Summaries of current events topics<br><br>• Two-column notes of teacher instruction | • Summaries of current events<br><br>• Two-column notes of teacher instruction<br><br>• Two-column study guides for branches of government | • Summaries of current events topics<br><br>• Two-column notes for interview questions and responses |
| **Special Enrichment/ Electives** | • IVF summaries of computer searches in technology class<br><br>• Two-column notes on reading assignments and teacher instruction | • Summary paragraph on elements to consider when doing an art project | • Summaries of a process used in healthful living or industrial arts | • Two-column notes on cooking, computer, vocational, or career-prep terms<br><br>• Two-column notes on rules of a sport |

Increases comprehension by prompting students to better attend to content so they can write a coherent summary.

Increases attention to the ideas and concepts learned during class projects.

Provides daily practice to help students become more proficient and organized note-takers.

Helps students organize important information and gives them useful study guides.

Allows students to demonstrate understanding and helps them think about recently learned content.

**Note:** Students will use many of these strategies across grade levels.

To save space, some strategies students have learned earlier have been omitted.

# Using Step Up to Writing Materials

## Teacher's Guide

**Objectives** let teachers know the main skills or concepts they will reinforce in each subsection.

**Strategy overview tables** give a snapshot of each strategy so teachers can quickly decide if a strategy will be helpful.

**Strategies** are organized by concept, so that strategies dealing with different aspects of a particular task or concept can all be found together.

**Posters** contain important information that students can use as an aid for many strategies.

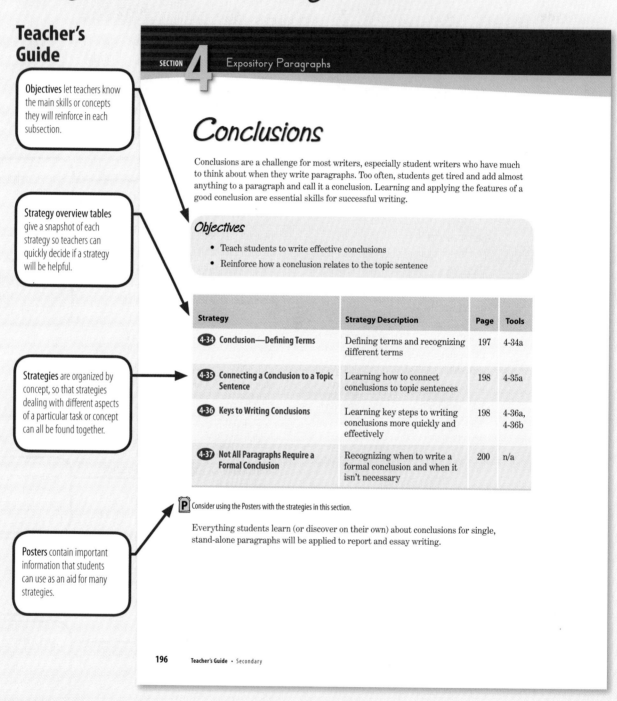

SECTION **4** — Expository Paragraphs

## Conclusions

Conclusions are a challenge for most writers, especially student writers who have much to think about when they write paragraphs. Too often, students get tired and add almost anything to a paragraph and call it a conclusion. Learning and applying the features of a good conclusion are essential skills for successful writing.

### Objectives

- Teach students to write effective conclusions
- Reinforce how a conclusion relates to the topic sentence

| Strategy | Strategy Description | Page | Tools |
|---|---|---|---|
| 4-34 Conclusion—Defining Terms | Defining terms and recognizing different terms | 197 | 4-34a |
| 4-35 Connecting a Conclusion to a Topic Sentence | Learning how to connect conclusions to topic sentences | 198 | 4-35a |
| 4-36 Keys to Writing Conclusions | Learning key steps to writing conclusions more quickly and effectively | 198 | 4-36a, 4-36b |
| 4-37 Not All Paragraphs Require a Formal Conclusion | Recognizing when to write a formal conclusion and when it isn't necessary | 200 | n/a |

**P** Consider using the Posters with the strategies in this section.

Everything students learn (or discover on their own) about conclusions for single, stand-alone paragraphs will be applied to report and essay writing.

## 4-34 Conclusion—Defining Terms

*Conclusion, closing statement,* and *clincher* all refer to a final statement, but they have slightly different meanings and are written in different tones. In this strategy, students review the terms and their meanings to consider different possibilities for conclusions.

**Prerequisite:** 4-17 Defining Topic Sentences and Thesis Statements

**Handy Pages**

> **Prerequisites** let teachers know whether a strategy builds on concepts first introduced elsewhere.

> **Handy Pages** contain important information that students can use as an aid for many strategies.

### Before Class

- Make an overhead transparency and student copies of *Bonus Tools 4-34a* and *4-34b*.
- Have available green highlighters and overhead markers.
- *Bonus Tool 4-34-I* provides additional examples.

> **Before Class** information tells teachers what they need to do to prepare to teach a strategy.

> **Bonus Tools,** found on the CD, provide additional examples, worksheets, and overheads.

**Conclusions—Terms and Meanings**

*Tool 4-34a*

**A Conclusion: The Final Important Statement**

*Tool 4-34b*

### During Class

1. Using *Tool 4-34a*, read and discuss the definition of a conclusion at the top of the page. Answer questions and provide examples as needed.

2. At the bottom of *Tool 4-34a*, point out the three terms used for the final statements in expository writing (conclusion, closing statement, and clincher). Explain that each term has a slightly different meaning, sends a different message, and is written in a different tone.

3. Display *Tool 4-34b* and read through the examples with your students. Have them highlight the three terms in the left column in green. Explain that green is used to remind them to go back to the topic sentence and focus again on the purpose of the paragraph. Green is used for conclusions, closing statements, and clinchers. The green ribbon on the package reminds students that a conclusion ties all of the ideas together.

4. Reinforce that the choice of which approach to use depends on the purpose and the audience for the paragraph.

5. Create topic sentences on a familiar topic. With your students, create a conclusion, a closing statement, and a clincher to fit the topic sentence. (See *Bonus Tool 4-34-I*.)

> **Teacher instructions** give teachers a step-by-step process for introducing and guiding practice of each strategy.

**Topic Sentence**
Shel Silverstein in *The Giving Tree* shows what it means to really love someone.
**Conclusion**
Read *The Giving Tree*. It will help you understand more about love.

> **Examples** illustrate concepts covered in *Step Up to Writing* strategies and give teachers a visual picture of the strategy.

## Using *Step Up to Writing* Tools

*Step Up to Writing* Tools provide

- Templates for learning and practicing strategies;

- Step-by-step instructions for organizing ideas;

- Information and strong, interesting examples for all kinds of writing;

- Hints and support for independent student writing, such as reference lists with definitions and examples for parts of speech, elements of fiction, transitions, leads, content-area writing assignments, writing conventions, and so on;

- Scoring guides that help students improve their work and final scores and help teachers assess student progress.

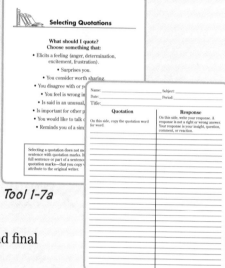

*Tool 1-7a*

*Tool 1-7b*

Use *Step Up to Writing* Tools regularly, both as directed by the Teacher's Guide and whenever you feel they might be helpful. Make sure students practice regularly with their tools to ensure they master writing tasks and are ready for the next level of instruction.

### CDs of Tools, Bonus Tools, and Prompts

Don't forget to use your CD of Tools and Bonus Tools and your Prompts CD! The Tools CD contains a copy of every *Step Up* Tool along with additional Tools called Bonus Tools. Bonus Tools are just like regular tools, but they are found only on the CD. They contain additional examples, worksheets, writing prompts, and more. They are not required to teach any strategy, but they provide lots of extra support if you need it. They also reproduce examples from the Teacher's Guide, giving you an easy way to share them with your students.

Many of the Tools on the CD of Tools and Bonus Tools are also customizable! These Tools are marked with a star in the menu of the CD. You can modify these Tools to create your own examples for your students. They are a great way to align *Step Up* instruction to content your students are learning and also provide a wider variety of examples to your students.

The Prompts CD provides numerous lists of writing prompts for a variety of topics and types of writing. Use it whenever you need ideas for writing assingments.

See the booklet that comes with the CD of Tools and Bonus Tools for technical details about how to use the CDs and customizable Tools with your computer.

## Using *Step Up to Writing* Handy Pages

*Step Up to Writing* Handy Pages are student booklets that are filled with 24 colorful pages of examples, lists, instructions, and support for writing and reading. They provide

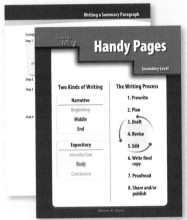

- A quick, student-friendly reference for major *Step Up* concepts, including information/expository and story/narrative writing as well as note taking and summarizing;

- A durable, three-hole-punched design so that students can store them in their writing notebooks and refer to them frequently during all stages of the writing process and in all content areas.

Use Handy Pages regularly to support and reinforce the skills writing students learn. When students are just learning a concept, make sure to incorporate Handy Pages into the direct, guided instruction students receive until you are certain students understand the concept well enough to practice with the Handy Pages independently.

Handy Pages also work well as a quick reference for student-teacher or parent-teacher conferences or during peer editing, in summer writing programs or workshops, and whenever a quick reference source for writing concepts is needed.

## Using *Step Up to Writing* Posters

*Step Up to Writing* Posters are a set of 16 large, colorful classroom posters that serve as a reminder and reference and support guided lessons. They provide

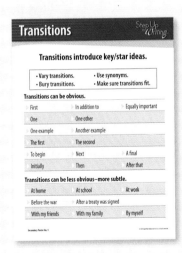

- Hints and examples for summarizing, note taking, and working with definitions;

- Help for writing sentences, information paragraphs, reports, essays, stories, and personal narratives;

- Reinforcement of the same concepts covered in the Handy Pages, Tools, and Teacher's Guide.

*Step Up* Posters can be used in several ways. Laminate them to use as a flip chart, or attach magnets to the back and display them on the board as part of a guided lesson. Display them in writing labs and media centers as well as classrooms to promote a common language and common high expectations throughout your school. Most importantly, display them in a way that meets your students' needs and helps them with concepts and lessons.

**Classroom Connection**

After a very intense morning of practicing topic sentence strategies, my students lined up to proceed to their next class. I was standing in the doorway as they left, and one little girl looked up at me and said, "Whew! You earned your paycheck today, Mrs. Lewis. I LOVE writing like this." She had this smile on her face that just lit my world.

That's what writing should be—a labor of love, but fun doing it.

—Bettye Lewis, Teacher; Sugar Land, Texas

*Above all,* remember that all *Step Up to Writing* strategies and materials are adaptable.

# Be creative!

Use them in any way that meets your and your students' needs.

# INTRODUCTION
## Writing to Improve Reading and Listening Comprehension

Good listening and reading are not only core academic skills; they are prerequisites for the development of good writing skills. Students need to appreciate the meaning of the written word and the power of communication before they begin to express themselves in writing. *Step Up to Writing* teaches strategies to improve reading comprehension not only to increase reading ability but also to improve writing skills. These skills provide the framework for success in all content areas.

However, recognizing and decoding words are not enough. Students must also be able to comprehend and think about what they read. Even students who are considered good readers can have difficulty obtaining useful information from classroom materials and lessons.

One of the main causes of poor reading comprehension is the lack of active involvement in the reading process. Many students have difficulty sustaining focus while reading and do not interact with the text because they do not know how. *Step Up to Writing* strategies increase students' reading and listening comprehension by teaching them to ask questions, make comments, and discover connections. Above all, active reading and listening builds students' thinking skills and empowers them to read and write about content areas with more confidence.

As students learn to read actively, they need numerous ways to note what they have read. *Step Up* teaches students to mark their text and take notes. Students also use graphic organizers to help them visualize relationships between ideas. Learning these relationships also helps students see organization patterns for information writing, such as sequencing and describing. As active readers, they gain authentic knowledge of language structure and conventions.

*Step Up* provides explicit instruction on the important skill of summary writing. When students can write a well-organized summary, it means they have mentally manipulated the information, understand it, and are likely to remember and use it later. When students can summarize, they are ready for higher-order thinking skills such as making inferences and analyzing what they read.

*Step Up* strategies in this section help guarantee students' success. Students are more successful when they can

- Read for comprehension;
- Note what they have read—marking important ideas and information in the text (with highlighting, underlining, or sticky notes) and taking notes;
- Write well-organized summary paragraphs and use what they have learned to develop higher-order thinking skills;
- Write great short answers and essays on quizzes and assessments.

## When Teaching These Strategies

- Provide direct instruction and incorporate your thinking (metacognition) into your model. When you demonstrate a strategy for your students, describe out loud how you determine what to do next.
- Remember to teach each skill before expecting students to use it independently. For instance, responding to the text and note taking are strategies that can be used to learn content-area information, but first students need to be shown how to respond to the text and take notes.
  - ▸ Begin with short passages until students are familiar with the skill.
  - ▸ Model the strategies often, provide numerous practice opportunities, and receive feedback before asking students to use a skill on their own.
- Offer students options for note taking, such as drawing pictures, in addition to traditional notes.

- Use Making Inferences and Analyzing the Text strategies **1-25**, **1-26**, and **1-27**) to move students to higher-level thinking skills.
- Use **1-24** Mapping and Webbing to address visual and kinesthetic learners' need to see the concrete relationship of ideas.

## Tips for Using These Strategies Across Content Areas

✓ Review these strategies as you use them to teach content material.

✓ When students have an assigned reading, require some form of student-generated written or graphic response at predetermined places in the text such as **1-4** Sticky Note Responses or **1-5** One-Word Responses.

✓ During class presentations, discussions, and videos, have students take **1-17** Easy Two-Column Notes. Consider providing them with the big ideas for the left column until they are able to generate their own.

✓ Have students write an IVF Topic Sentence from **1-30** Four-Step Summary Paragraphs as a "ticket out" at the end of class. The summary sentence can address what students have read, the day's lesson, or a discussion.

✓ Use **1-30** Four-Step Summary Paragraphs to reinforce core concepts. Have students write their summaries on index cards and use them to review information and quiz themselves and each other.

✓ Have contests with the **1-33** Money Summaries strategy.

✓ Create class webs and cognitive maps of content material on flip charts and use them for review. Keep these poster-sized webs displayed in the room and refer to them each time a concept is introduced and studied.

✓ Have students use the **1-38** Levels of Questioning strategy to write potential quiz and test questions. Many times students enjoy exchanging self-generated questions and quizzing each other.

# CONTENTS
## Writing to Improve Reading and Listening Comprehension

Choose those strategies that best meet the needs of your students.

# Responding to the Text

Responding to the Text strategies are quick, effective methods for keeping students active as they listen or read. Once learned, they can be used across content areas. Choose strategies that best support your students' needs.

## Objectives

- Teach students to be active readers and listeners
- Enable students to read quickly, remember more, and form questions as they read and listen
- Encourage class participation and discussion, and stimulate more detailed responses

| Strategy | Strategy Description | Page | Tools |
|---|---|---|---|
| **1-1 Free Responses** | Writing brief responses to text | 6 | 1-1a |
| **1-2 Response Starters** | Using writing prompts to encourage variety in responses | 7 | 1-2a |
| **1-3 Reading Notation Responses** | Writing responses in the margins of text | 8 | n/a |
| **1-4 Sticky Note Responses** | Writing responses on sticky notes | 8 | n/a |
| **1-5 One-Word Responses** | Writing single-word responses to text | 9 | n/a |
| **1-6 Agree/Disagree Responses** | Using a pair of specific terms for writing responses | 9 | n/a |
| **1-7 Quotation Responses** | Responding to selected quotations | 10 | 1-7a to 1-7c |

*(chart continues)*

| Strategy *(continued)* | Strategy Description | Page | Tools |
|---|---|---|---|
| **1-8** Framed Responses | Using paragraph frames to prompt writing | 11 | 1-8a |
| **1-9** Two-Column Guided Responses | Writing responses and supporting reasons | 13 | 1-9a |
| **1-10** Quick Sketch Responses | Responding to text by drawing | 14 | 1-10a, 1-10b |

**P** Consider using the Posters with the strategies in this section.

## **1-1** Free Responses

Free Responses (Santa 1988) are brief written responses to text that teach students to ask themselves questions as they listen and read. Use Free Responses to help your students focus their thinking and improve comprehension of reading selections.

The following directions for introducing Free Responses are general and can be applied with slight adaptations to all of the response strategies.

### Before Class

- Make an overhead transparency and student copies of *Tool 1-1a*.
- Select an article or story.
- Mark the spots where you will stop for demonstration and responses, and determine which sample questions you will use.
- Provide index cards or half sheets of paper for your students.

*Tool 1-1a*

### During Class

1. Introduce your students to Free Responses by explaining that asking questions as they read will help them focus on what they're reading and improve comprehension. Let them know that their responses to these questions should be fairly short—just one sentence or a couple of words or phrases.

2. Read *Tool 1-1a* with your students, discuss the questions, and give sample responses.
   - Tell them that free responses are made quickly and are used in silent reading or as directed by a teacher. Demonstrate how they will need to think and write quickly by giving quick responses to the sample questions.

- Tell your students that as you read you will stop several times to ask for responses. Encourage them to write appropriately brief responses.
- Let them know that they will practice a couple of times orally and then once they understand the process, they will practice writing their responses on index cards or half sheets of paper.

3. Explain to your students that they will start writing when you say, "Please respond," and stop when you resume reading, about one minute later. (Long breaks interrupt the flow of the reading.)

4. Read to your first marked place in the text, ask a question from *Tool 1-1a*, then give students an example of an appropriate answer. After giving several examples, continue to read, stopping to ask questions but calling on students to respond.

5. Once your students understand the process, have them begin to respond in writing on their own using index cards or paper. (Keep in mind that there is no right or wrong way to make responses. The questions on *Tool 1-1a* are a starting point.)

## Additional Ideas

- Use free responses in whole class read-aloud activities to promote good listening skills.
- Have your students give both written and oral responses.
- Have your students keep their copies of *Tool 1-1a* in their notebooks. Have them add more questions to the handout—ones you suggest and ones that they create.
- Have students share their free responses to stimulate class discussions.

## 1-2 Response Starters

Response Starters are sentence prompts that help students write more insightful responses and focus on certain kinds of responses.

Like **1-1 Free Responses**, Response Starters push students to think and to write more insightful responses. The words listed on *Tool 1-2a* will help your students write interesting responses using various sentence structures. You may want to make copies for your students to keep, use *Tool 1-2a* as a mini-poster in your classroom, or make bookmarks from *Tool 1-2a* for students to refer to during class read-aloud activities.

At times you may want to give your students only a few of the words on the list to use for responses. Do this to save time and to help your students learn how to use certain words or phrases.

**Response Starters**

| | |
|---|---|
| After | I'm surprised |
| Although | If |
| An important | In my opinion |
| As a result | In the beginning |
| As I read | Instead of |
| Because of | Just because |
| Before | Maybe |
| Despite | Perhaps |
| I agree | Since |
| I believe | The problem |
| I doubt | This reminds me |
| I guess | This topic |
| I question | Throughout |
| I suppose | Unless |
| I think | Whatever |
| I wonder | When |
| I'm certain | Whenever |
| I'm not sure | While |

*Tool 1-2a*

## 1-3 Reading Notation Responses

Reading Notation Responses are a variation for responses you can use when your students are able to write in the margins of a text or handout.

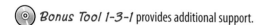 *Bonus Tool 1-3-1* provides additional support.

Reading Notation Responses are short, helpful responses made in the margins of a handout or text. When your students have the option to write directly on a handout, use Reading Notation Responses instead of **1-1 Free Responses**. This saves time, but more importantly, this gives your students a chance to practice a skill that will help them when they read independently and are free to write on the text. (Example is also on *Bonus Tool 1-3-1.*)

| Selected Text | Student's Notation |
|---|---|
| Generally, hockey players look for a stick that's light and balanced. But what's right for one player can be completely different for another. Players' sticks are as individual as their signatures. | *I am surprised. For fairness, it seems they should be all the same.* |

Until your students have mastered Reading Notation Responses, specify how often you expect them to make notations. For example, you may ask for notations at every other paragraph for short assignments and at every other page for long assignments.

## 1-4 Sticky Note Responses

Sticky Note Responses are short responses that students make on sticky notes. Use this version to add novelty to response activities, to help your students condense their responses, and to help them interact more with their texts.

Sticky Note Responses engage students by adding novelty to response activities and by making note-taking easy. Because sticky notes are generally small, students learn to condense responses in interesting and insightful ways.

Keep small sticky notes available. When your students may not write in a book, such as a school textbook, have them use sticky notes. Decide if you will ask for general responses or specific responses. For example, you may ask your students for responses to new vocabulary, to facts, or to opinions included in the text.

## During Class

- Tell your students that sometimes they can attach the sticky notes to the edges of pages of books they may not write in. At other times, they can use a corner of the note to point to a specific word or line.

- Teach your students to make good use of the sticky notes and the responses; for example, they can add them to more formal notes by putting the sticky notes on the left side of paper that has been folded into two columns. They can then use the space on the right for more information, comments, illustrations, and questions.

## 1-5 One-Word Responses

One-Word Responses help students focus on key elements of text. Students select important words from a text—strong vocabulary words and/or other words that remind them of what they have heard or read. Students use them to learn to think quickly.

One-Word Responses can be made in margins or on sticky notes. Try this strategy with a short text. Ask your students to write one word for each paragraph. Tell them to pick a word from the paragraph or to use a word that they think of as they read or listen.

Use the words to prompt discussion. Ask your students to summarize the story or article, relying on their lists of words. Have them share important facts using their One-Word Responses. Help them create one- or two-sentence summaries, using their words.

## 1-6 Agree/Disagree Responses

This strategy uses sets of words like agree/disagree to help students take a stand and state an opinion.

When your class reads news reports, columns, advertisements, or editorials, ask them to respond with their choice from a pair of words. Try these sets and create (or have your students create) other sets:

- agree/disagree
- important/unimportant
- like/dislike
- useful/not useful
- right/wrong
- fact/opinion

If possible, have them respond in the margins. Use sticky notes when they are not allowed to write on the text. Once your students have shared their choices and discussed the text, ask them to write complete sentences sharing their opinions.

## 1-7 Quotation Responses

Using this strategy, students select a quotation and then respond to it. Use it to help your students learn to select quotations and think more deeply about their meaning.

Quotation Responses are made on paper divided into two columns. On the left, students copy a quotation (a sentence or phrase) that interests them or that they question. In the right column, they explain why they selected the passage. This strategy requires students to read carefully. It also helps them learn how to select quotations.

### Before Class

- Create overhead transparencies and student copies of *Tools 1-7a, 1-7b,* and *1-7c.*
- Select a text to read with your students and mark quotations that you will use for demonstration.
- Copy the quotations onto the *Tool 1-7c* transparency and add your responses.

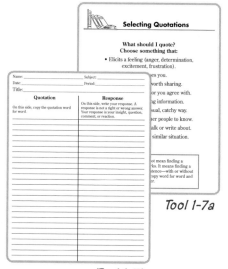

Tool 1-7a

Tool 1-7b

### During Class

1. Read through *Tool 1-7a* with your students and discuss the list of suggestions.

2. Using *1-7b,* share the quotations that you have selected, and explain why and how you made your choices. Share your responses to those quotations as part of the demonstration and class discussion.

3. Ask students to select other lines from the text that they can use for Quotation Responses. Write these quotations in the left column of *Tool 1-7b.* Together, add the responses to the right column.

4. Model this strategy several times. Give your students opportunities to share and to listen to their classmates' responses.

**Note:** Most students will need guidance as they begin selecting quotations. Remind them that quotations can be full sentences or phrases. Draw their attention to the message at the bottom of *Tool 1-7a*: *Selecting a quotation does not mean finding a sentence with quotation marks. It means finding a full sentence or part of a sentence—with or without quotation marks—that you copy word for word and attribute to the original writer.*

### Separating Facts from Opinions

1. Using *Tool 1-7c*, review the difference between a fact and an opinion.

2. Ask your students to select four quotations—two facts and two opinions—from a text they have read in class.

3. Give them time to read their quotations aloud before they write their responses on *Tool 1-7c*.

4. Together, discuss the fact quotations and the opinion quotations.

*Tool 1-7c*

## 1-8 Framed Responses

Framed Responses are short paragraphs created by teachers to check for comprehension and used by students to share insights and knowledge. They can be used across all content areas for different purposes.

### Before Class

- Create an overhead transparency and student copies of *Tool 1-8a*.

- Cut the student copies apart. Sort the three segments, and use the appropriate segment for a reading you have selected.

- Choose an article or story to use for modeling and practice.

 *Bonus Tool 1-8-1* provides additional support.

*Tool 1-8a*

### During Class

1. Read a story or article with your students, then complete the appropriate Framed Response as a group.

2. Point out the topic sentence and transitions, and remind students that they will fill in the blanks. Review your expectations about neatness, capitalization, spelling, and punctuation.

3. When there is time, have students edit, revise, and copy their responses on paper. Recopying gives students a chance to perfect writing and organization skills.

4. Continue to use this Tool throughout the year.

### Using a Framed Response as a Quiz

- Develop a Framed Response to use as a quick quiz.

- Prepare Framed Responses in advance and make copies to use with students, or write the Framed Response on the board. Have your students copy the frame, filling in the empty spaces as needed. (The following examples are also available on *Bonus Tool 1-8-1*.)

Title _____ "*The Instincts of Penguins*"

"*The Instincts of Penguins*" from *Wild Outside!* magazine gives a number of facts about the instinctive nature of penguins and how they are able to survive in one of the harshest environments. **One** amazing fact is that the eggs must be kept off the ground and out of the cold because they will crack instantly if exposed to the brutally cold temperatures. **Another** amazing fact is that the father will hold the egg on his feet for months, and during that time he will not eat. **A third** incredible fact about this animal is that after losing one-third of his body weight while incubating the egg, the male penguin will walk over 60 miles to get food. **The most interesting** fact is that scientists believe that the eggs are incubated during the harshest month of winter because the timing works out so that there are few predators around to harm the young penguins.

## Creating Your Own Framed Responses

1. Give the frame a title. Titles help students focus on the topic and task.

2. Start by writing a clear topic sentence. Use the topic sentence strategies found in Section 4 as models.

3. Add transitions to help with organization skills. Place them as you would expect to see them in a paragraph. Refer to the transition lists on *Tools 4-24a* and *4-25a*.

4. Leave enough space to let your students know that you want details, not just one-word responses, on the blank lines.

Title _____ A Poem

**As we read the poem** "*Fog*" **by** Carl Sandburg, **I noticed two examples of figurative language. First,** Sandburg uses personification when he turns fog into a cat. He says the fog "sits looking," and it rests on its "haunches." **I also** saw that the words "sits" and "silent" are an example of alliteration. When I read "sits looking . . . on silent haunches" the two sounds flowed together and made me think of a cat.

**Note:** For more information about using writing frames, see 9-9 Using Writing Frames.

## 1-9 Two-Column Guided Responses

Using the Two-Column Guided Responses strategy, students respond to prompts with details, facts, and examples based on readings. Then students share ideas, opinions, and the reasoning behind those responses.

### Before Class

- Make an overhead transparency and student copies of *Tool 1-9a*.

*Bonus Tool 1-9-1* provides additional support.

*Tool 1-9a*

### During Class

1. Model using stories, articles, and other class materials with *Tool 1-9a* to complete the responses.

2. Explain to your students that the goal of a Two-Column Guided Response is to encourage everyone to purposefully share opinions and insights. (Note that this does not require a two-column fold.) Let them know that you will look for details, facts, and examples, not just general statements.

3. Provide opening phrases for both sides. Have your students complete the sentences with their own thoughts and insights. (For this example, see *Bonus Tool 1-9-1*.)

**The information in this article would be useful for** *students who are looking for summer jobs or opportunities.*

**It could be used to** *make plans for this summer. Those who want to earn money have a list of companies in our neighborhood who need extra help in the summer. If someone just wants to volunteer, this article will help because it suggests ten organizations that always welcome extra help.*

## Additional Ideas

- Create your own Two-Column Guided Responses. Use half sheets of paper folded in half as bookmarks. The space inside the fold can be used for responses.
- Use these starter phrases or create your own, and encourage your students to offer ideas for responses.

| | |
|---|---|
| The article was fun to read because . . . | I learned that . . . |
| A good description in the story is . . . | This is a good description because . . . |
| One feeling shared in the story is . . . | This is an important feeling because . . . |
| The main character in the story . . . | He/she acts this way because . . . |
| I was surprised when . . . | I was surprised because . . . |
| The author makes an important point about . . . | To me this seemed important because . . . |
| One part of the story seemed . . . | I wondered about this because . . . |
| It was interesting to learn that . . . | This seemed unusual because . . . |

## 1-10 Quick Sketch Responses

Quick Sketch Responses are drawings that demonstrate comprehension. They are often used to illustrate the beginning, middle, and end of a story and show feelings, reactions, or insights. Instead of writing responses, students sketch pictures.

Quick Sketch Responses are often used with stories and narratives but can be used with expository material. Model this strategy several times as a listening activity before students use it while reading independently.

### Before Class

- Make overhead transparencies of *Tools 1-10a* or *1-10b* as appropriate or use half sheets of paper that students fold in thirds or fourths.
- Select a story or article to use for modeling and practice. Mark places where you will stop and ask for responses.

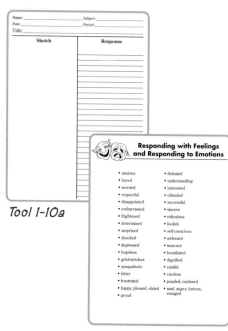

*Tool 1-10a*

*Tool 1-10b*

## During Class

- Introduce Quick Sketch Responses using *Tool 1-10a* or sheets of paper that students have folded in half lengthwise. Inform your students that instead of responding with words, they will be drawing a response—a quick sketch—each time you stop reading. Explain that they may draw anything that will help them remember a story or learn new information.

- Let your students know that the sketches are for their own use and are not meant to be detailed illustrations.

- Begin Quick Sketch Responses by reading the first segment of the selected story to the class. Stop as you would for a written response, and discuss what kinds of pictures would be appropriate. Explain that each time you stop they will have a minute or less to sketch. Remind them that not everyone will draw the same picture. Encourage your students to personalize their drawings.

- Have your students practice often. Later, ask them to add words, phrases, or complete sentences. Give students time to share and explain their responses.

- Incorporate sketches in all activities to help your students understand how much they can improve their memories.

## Additional Ideas

- Use Quick Sketch Responses with written responses.

- Use *Tool 1-10b* to note changing emotions at the beginning, middle, and end of stories.

- Use the left column of *Tool 1-10a* for random sketches. Add responses on the right.

- Ask your students to select an emotion from the list on *Tool 1-10b* and draw facial expressions in the left column of *Tool 1-10a*. The facial expressions might represent the feelings of a particular character in the text or story, or they could show a feeling the reader might have at this point in the text. Ask your students to explain their choices in the right column.

# Making Connections

Making Connections strategies help students find ways to express in writing the thoughts and ideas that come to mind as they read, listen, or observe.

## Objectives

- Teach methods that ensure active reading and listening
- Validate students' ideas, insights, and questions

| Strategy | Strategy Description | Page | Tools |
|---|---|---|---|
| **1-11** What Were You Thinking? | Connecting with text through drawing and/or quick notes | 16 | 1-11a, 1-11b |
| **1-12** Text to Self, Text to Text, and Text to World | Connecting to text at a variety of levels | 18 | 1-12a, 1-12b |

## 1-11 What Were You Thinking?

The What Were You Thinking? strategy encourages students to focus on the feelings and emotions they experience and to share insights as they read or listen to a narrative. They can use this strategy when you are reading all or part of a text to the class and with independent or whole-group reading assignments in all content areas.

### Before Class

- Make overhead transparencies and student copies of *Tools 1-11a* or *1-11b* as needed.
- Select a story or article to use for modeling and practice. Mark places where you will stop and ask for responses.

## During Class

*Tool 1-11a*

1. Use *Tool 1-11a* to introduce the idea of tracking your thinking while reading. Explain how important it is to be actively involved in the reading and listening process.

2. Explain that you will read segments of a story or article and when you stop, they are to write or draw their thoughts in the lightbulb on *Tool 1-11a*.

3. Tell them that the notes and pictures they add must relate to the text and that the goal is not to impress or influence others. The goal is to personalize their notes in a way that will help them remember more of what they hear.

4. Model by reading a selected text and stopping at key places to show the responses you created on an overhead transparency of *Tool 1-11a*. Have students sketch or make quick notes about the text on their copies of *Tool 1-11a*.

5. When your students have finished listening and making connections, ask them to share their notes and pictures in pairs or groups of three, where they can more easily explain their thoughts and sketches and listen to others.

## Using Writing Frames

*Tool 1-11b*

Students can also monitor their thinking by using *Tool 1-11b*.

1. Copy *Tool 1-11b*, cut along the dotted lines, and distribute to students.

2. To keep this activity quick and successful, allow students to cross out the starter terms and replace them with terms of their choice. This gives students independence and the opportunity to demonstrate comprehension.

3. Create similar handouts based on the subjects you teach and your goals for your students.

# 1-12 Text to Self, Text to Text, and Text to World

The Text to Self, Text to Text, and Text to World strategy teaches students how to move from random connections to specific, detailed connections. It can be used when your students read stories/narratives and expository text. You can use this strategy in all content areas with everyday reading assignments.

## Before Class

- Make overhead transparencies and student copies of *Tools 1-12a* and *1-12b*.

- Have your students keep their copies in their notebooks for future reference.

- Select a text for demonstration and practice.

  *Bonus Tool 1-12-1* provides additional support.

## During Class

1. Read and discuss *Tool 1-12a* with your class. Add words or phrases suggested by you and your students to the lists of examples on the right side of the page.

2. Select a text and model the first three types of connections. Tell your students to use the Text to Other connection when the connection they make does not easily fit one of the first three connections. (The following example is also on *Bonus Tool 1-12-1*.)

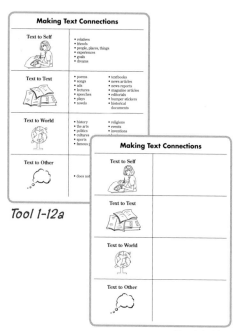

*Tool 1-12a*

*Tool 1-12b*

---

### "The Lion and the Mouse" by Aesop

**Text to Self**
Some girls like being short but not me. I have three very tall brothers. I've felt like a small mouse many times.

**Text to Text**
I just watched the movie about Stuart Little with my cousin. Stuart was definitely small but powerful.

**Text to World**
I wonder how much small countries help our country. I think we depend on some of them for products that we cannot produce in this country. I wonder if that makes them feel like the mouse in the fable.

**Text to Other**
Kindness conquers all. Everyone has something to offer.

---

# Marking the Text

Marking the Text strategies improve readers' focus and recall. Students can use pencils, pens, markers, and highlighters to mark key ideas and supporting details.

## Objectives

- Improve students' comprehension by teaching how to note main ideas and details
- Increase students' attention to text and memory of important information and details

| Strategy | Strategy Description | Page | Tools |
|---|---|---|---|
| **1-13** Highlighting and Underlining | Selecting important information to mark in text | 20 | 1-13a |
| **1-14** Mark Once | Marking one idea per paragraph in text | 21 | n/a |
| **1-15** Circle Once, Underline Twice | Selecting important information and supporting details | 21 | n/a |
| **1-16** Pick a Number | Limiting the information marked | 21 | n/a |

# 1-13 Highlighting and Underlining

The Highlighting and Underlining strategy gives students specific guidelines for marking a text. Use it to make note taking easier, to encourage careful reading, and to improve comprehension. Without direct instruction and modeling, most students will mark a text randomly, with little evidence of careful reading.

## Before Class

- Make an overhead transparency and student copies of *Tool 1-13a*.

- Ensure that your students have pens, pencils, or markers, as needed.

- Make an overhead transparency and student copies of articles or sections of text to use for modeling. Enlarge text if necessary.

*Tool 1-13a*

## During Class

1. Read and discuss *Tool 1-13a* with your class.

2. Using the transparency of the selected text, read aloud the first paragraph.

3. Reread the paragraph. Mark the text as you read. Ask your students to imitate your example.

4. Tell them that it is important to read a paragraph twice. When people mark text on the first reading, they tend to mark too much. They also have not taken time to reflect on what is really important.

5. Model this strategy with the next two or three paragraphs, while explaining other tips included on *Tool 1-13a*.

6. Once you have marked a few paragraphs, call on your students to read and work at the overhead. While one student reads, another marks the transparency. Have students suggest what to mark or not mark.

7. Model the Highlighting and Underlining strategy several times to help your students learn to identify important information. Consider making bookmarks from *Tool 1-42a* for students to keep.

8. Have your students mark the last few paragraphs independently. Monitor and provide additional modeling as needed. Review this skill regularly to keep students from lapsing back into bad habits, such as underlining everything.

**Note:** Sometimes combine underlining and highlighting, and occasionally have students underline with only pens, pencils, or markers, or use only highlighters. Remember, the goal is for students to identify big ideas.

## Additional Ideas

In most cases, students are not allowed to mark in textbooks. Use the following to model the highlighting and underlining strategy and to help your students master this academic skill.

| | | |
|---|---|---|
| newspapers | brochures | student school magazines |
| magazines | advertisements | students' own work |
| directions in workbooks | e-mail | photocopied material |
| old textbooks | articles from the Internet | junk mail/solicitations |

## 1-14 Mark Once

The Mark Once strategy helps students identify a paragraph's important ideas. Have your class use it on long articles.

To save time and to keep your students engaged, ask them to mark just one word or phrase in each paragraph. Keep the rules simple. Tell your students to mark any term that will help them remember the information.

## 1-15 Circle Once, Underline Twice

Try the Circle Once, Underline Twice strategy to add variety to other text-marking strategies.

In each paragraph of an article, have your students circle one important word or phrase. Have them underline two other terms that support/explain the circled text. As always, it is important to model the strategy. Let your students know that not everyone will circle and underline the same words.

## 1-16 Pick a Number

The Pick a Number strategy teaches students to limit their highlighting or underlining by identifying key words and phrases. Use this strategy to help your students limit the amount of information they mark.

Before your students read, pick (or have students pick) a number between 8 and 15. Students must mark only this number of words or phrases. They must, however, choose terms from the entire selected text, not just the first few paragraphs.

When your students have finished reading and marking the text, ask them to justify their choices or have them compare their choices with other students' choices. Occasionally ask your students to use their choices to create a quick one-sentence summary.

# Taking Notes

Taking Notes strategies are used in reading, listening, and viewing activities. Good note-takers jot down important information about a topic to learn, retain, and review the information.

## Objectives

- Improve students' listening, viewing, and reading skills
- Develop students' study skills and help them demonstrate comprehension

| Strategy | Strategy Description | Page | Tools |
|---|---|---|---|
| **1-17 Easy Two-Column Notes** | Taking and organizing notes in two columns | 23 | 1-17a to 1-17c |
| **1-18 One Idea per Paragraph Note Taking** | Taking notes using one idea per paragraph | 26 | 1-17b |
| **1-19 Using Two-Column Notes for Character Analysis** | Analyzing characters using two-column notes | 28 | 1-17b |
| **1-20 Three- and Four-Column Notes** | Expanding two-column notes to three or four columns | 29 | n/a |
| **1-21 Research Note Cards** | Using note cards to record research notes and references | 31 | 1-21a to 1-21d |
| **1-22 Developing Study Guides** | Making student-created study guides | 32 | 1-22a to 1-22d |
| **1-23 Three-Column Notes with Summaries** | Adding summaries, questions, and insights to three-column notes | 33 | 1-23a |
| **1-24 Mapping and Webbing** | Using diagrams to connect and organize facts | 34 | n/a |

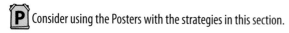 Consider using the Posters with the strategies in this section.

## 1-17 Easy Two-Column Notes

Easy Two-Column Notes help students organize their notes. Use them to introduce your students to note taking and help them practice their note-taking skills.

**Handy Pages**

### Before Class

- Make overhead transparencies and student copies of *Tools 1-17a*, *1-17b*, and *1-17c*. Students can use notebook paper in place of *Tools 1-17b* and *1-17c*.

- Select a text to use for modeling and student practice.

### During Class

1. Introduce Easy Two-Column Notes by reading and discussing *Tool 1-17a*.

2. Using *Tool 1-17b*, read the article about Gandhi and discuss how the sample two-column notes follow the rules: big ideas on the left and title and subtopics on the right, using words and phrases only. Stop to discuss rule 5 on *Tool 1-17a*, which says that each paragraph has a big idea. Use the **1-18 One Idea per Paragraph Note Taking** strategy to help students identify the big idea of each paragraph.

3. Using *Tool 1-17b*, point out that "Mohandas Gandhi" has four paragraphs. The sample notes have a word on the left for each paragraph; matching notes appear on the right. Students use the words on the left to help them study and remember the details on the right.

4. Begin to model by demonstrating how to prepare the paper for taking two-column notes. Using the transparency of *Tool 1-17b*, draw lines on the fold and on the top line of the page to form a letter T. Then write "Topic =" on the top line. Ask your students to do the same on their copies of *Tool 1-17b* or on notebook paper.

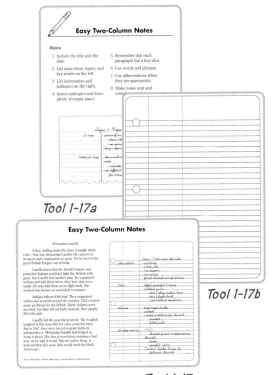

*Tool 1-17a*

*Tool 1-17b*

*Tool 1-17c*

5. Read the selected text to the class or have your students read individually or as a group.

6. Stop and take notes after students have read each paragraph a second time, following the process outlined on *Tool 1-17a*. Have your students do the same on their copies of *Tool 1-17b* or on notebook paper. Tell them that not everyone will choose the same big ideas.

7. Have your students practice using another segment of text. Walk around the room as they work, giving them feedback and support.

8. Have your students use two-column notes often. When they have short reading assignments, have them take notes one paragraph at a time. When they read textbooks and other long pieces, the bold headings from the text can be written on the left column.

**Note:** If you are using notebook paper, start by showing your students how to fold notebook paper for two-column note taking. Fold the left side of the page—the side with the holes—folding it over so its edge lies along the red margin line located on the back of the right side of the paper. You can see this red line through the paper. Crease the folded edge. When you open the page, the column on the left will be smaller than the column on the right.

## Additional Ideas

See 1-19 Using Two-Column Notes for Character Analysis for an in-depth look at another idea for using Easy Two-Column Notes.

Here are some other ways to use Easy Two-Column Notes.

| | | |
|---|---|---|
| **Stories** | Beginning, middle, end | Events, action, problem development & resolution |
| | Setting, plot, conflict | Description, quotations, page numbers, and other details |
| | Events, characters, setting | Descriptions |
| **Taking Field Trips and Nature Walks** | Observations | Facts |
| **Giving Directions** | Directions | Explanations |
| **Interviewing** | Create questions and answers; plan questions in advance | Jot notes as you listen to the answer |
| **Analyzing an Editorial** | Look for the position | State your opinion |
| **Viewing Films and Videos** | Teacher provides the big ideas | Students jot notes |
| **Listening to a Lecture** | Teachers provide big ideas for a lecture | Students listen for important "clue" words/phrases; they then jot notes, make sketches, and add comments |
| **Finding Quotations** | Quotation | Response, comments, significance, page number |
| **Solving Math Word Problems** | Steps described OR Actual work done | Actual work done OR Steps described |
| **Learning Vocabulary** | Term | Definition outlined |

(continued)

(continued)

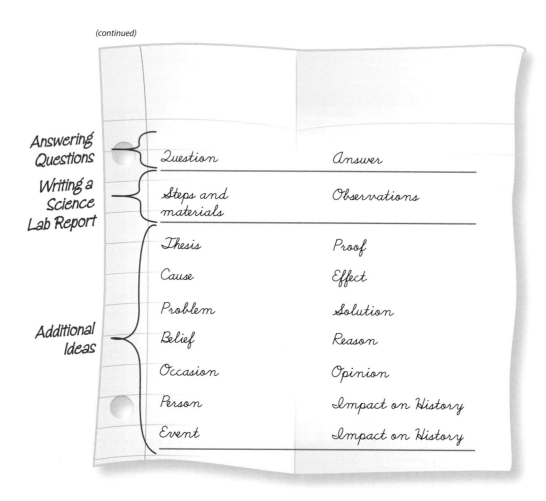

| | | |
|---|---|---|
| Answering Questions | Question | Answer |
| Writing a Science Lab Report | Steps and materials | Observations |
| | Thesis | Proof |
| | Cause | Effect |
| | Problem | Solution |
| Additional Ideas | Belief | Reason |
| | Occasion | Opinion |
| | Person | Impact on History |
| | Event | Impact on History |

 For a quick check and other support for assessment, see **10-12 Quick Check for Note Taking.**

## 1-18 One Idea per Paragraph Note Taking

**Handy Pages**

Students use the One Idea per Paragraph Note Taking strategy to learn basic note-taking skills and to become fast and accurate note-takers. Students learn to take notes one paragraph at a time using paper folded for two-column note taking.

**Prerequisite:** 1-17 Easy Two-Column Notes

## Before Class

- Select a short article or text (using required readings trains students to use this skill in their other classes).

- Make an overhead transparency of *Tool 1-17b.*

- *Bonus Tool 1-18-1* provides additional support.

## During Class

1. Read the first paragraph of a selected short article or segment of a text.

2. Display *Tool 1-17b*. With your students, list in the left column a "hanger" term for each paragraph, then draw a clothes hanger below the first term as a reminder. The hanger term is the big idea from the paragraph that reminds students of each paragraph's content. It can come directly from the text or be any term that reminds the student of the content. Students should read, work, and think quickly, choosing words that make sense to them. (See *Bonus Tool 1-18-1* for the example that follows.)

*Tool 1-17b*

3. In the right column, use dashes and dots, and indent as needed, to list details and subtopics that support or describe the corresponding hanger term.

4. Complete two or three paragraphs together as an interactive lesson, then have your students practice independently with other reading materials.

5. Remind students that when they take notes this way, they realize they must read the entire assignment. They also realize that note taking forces them to read more carefully and to notice facts and details.

### How are laws passed?

A law begins with a proposal called a bill. Most bills can start either in the House of Representatives or the Senate, but before a bill becomes a law, both branches of Congress must vote for it.

Then the President gets the bill. If he or she doesn't like it, the President can say no or veto it. (*Veto* comes from the Latin word for *forbid*.)

But the President's veto doesn't have to be the end of a bill. Congress can pass a bill over the President's veto if two-thirds of both the House and the Senate think the bill should be a law.

—Elizabeth Levy, *If You Were There When They Signed the Constitution*

Topic = How are laws passed?

| A bill 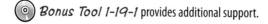 | - a proposal |
| | - leads to a law |
| | - starts in House or Senate |
| |    • both branches must agree |
| A veto | - president says no |
| |    • doesn't like bill |
| | - from Latin—to forbid |
| Still some hope | - Congress |
| |    • can vote against veto |
| |    • needs two-thirds support from members |

## 1-19 Using Two-Column Notes for Character Analysis

Expand two-column notes by using them to analyze characters from a story.

**Prerequisite:** 1-17 Easy Two-Column Notes

**Handy Pages**

*Bonus Tool 1-19-1* provides additional support.

Use a transparency of *Tool 1-17b* to model this strategy, using characters from a story your students are reading or using the following example. Explain to your students that in the left column, they will write the name of the character they are analyzing. In the right column, they will write down facts about that character. Beneath each fact, they should include examples from the story that show how the fact is true for that character. (Example is also on *Bonus Tool 1-19-1.*)

*Topic = The Tell-Tale Heart*

| Character | Description |
|---|---|
| Narrator | – madman<br>  • afraid of his master's eye<br><br>  • hearing voices<br>– murderer<br>  • kills the old man he works for<br>– guilty conscience<br>  • hears the old man's heart beating<br><br>  • admits his crime to the police |
| Old man | – afraid<br>  • wants to know who is shining a<br>    lantern on him |

## 1-20 Three- and Four-Column Notes

Three- and Four-Column Notes helps students expand their two-column notes. Using this strategy prompts your students to think more deeply about what they are reading.

**Prerequisite: 1-17 Easy Two-Column Notes**

Once your students have mastered the basics of taking **1-17 Easy Two-Column Notes**, explain to them that adding a third and fourth column for questions, comments, insights, or connections helps them think more deeply about their readings and take more in-depth notes.

1. Have each student divide a piece of notebook paper into three or four columns and pick categories for the third and fourth columns. Use ideas from the lists that follow or create your own.

2. Have your students take notes in the first two columns using the strategy outlined in **1-17 Easy Two-Column Notes**.

3. Fill in the remaining column or columns with questions, pictures, or comments appropriate to the headings chosen.

4. Encourage your students to create their own headings for specific assignments.

## Three-Column Notes

| Main Ideas | Subtopics | Questions, Comments, Insights, Connections |
|---|---|---|
| I know . . . | I want to learn . . . | I learned . . . |
| Questions | Explanation from the text | Class discussion |
| Opinion | Evidence | Conclusion |
| Questions | Answers | Details |
| Person | Accomplished | Impact on history |
| Event | Where/when | Why |
| Country | Culture | Government |
| Math term | Definition | Example |

## Four-Column Notes

| Title | Author | Major conflict | Theme |
|---|---|---|---|
| Title | Author | Setting | Summary of plot |
| Character | Reminds me of . . . | Explanation | Quotation from the text |
| Character | Description | Quotation from the text that tells about the character | My opinion |

 For a quick check and other support for assessment, see **10-12 Quick Check for Note Taking.**

# **1-21** Research Note Cards

The Research Note Cards strategy teaches students to note on index cards new information and information for reports. Once students have mastered **1-17 Easy Two-Column Notes**, introduce the Research Note Cards strategy. Teach this strategy well ahead of any assigned research projects.

**Handy Pages**

Use content materials, news articles, Web pages, and pamphlets for note-taking practice. Students typically enjoy taking notes on index cards, and they become skilled note-takers through practice. When it is time to do research, students will be prepared to take and use their notes effectively.

## Before Class

- Make overhead transparencies of *Tools 1-21a* through *1-21d*, as needed.
- Make student copies of *Tool 1-21d*. You may also want to make student copies of *Tool 1-21a* for students to use as a reference.
- Select and make student copies of a short article or segment of text to use for modeling and student practice.
- Fill out examples of note cards on *Tool 1-21d* based on the selected text to use when modeling.

 *Bonus Tools 1-21-1* and *1-21-2* provide additional support.

## During Class

1. Introduce your students to Research Note Cards by reviewing *Tool 1-21a* with them and showing the examples on *Tools 1-21b* and *1-21c*.
2. Read the selected text with your students. Show the note cards you made on *Tool 1-21d* as an example.
3. Work on note cards with your class and stop occasionally to have your students write note cards on their own. Keep each lesson short.
4. Have your students practice often, then have them work independently. Soon they will be ready to transfer use of this strategy to actual research assignments. For an example of using note cards to prepare an informal outline and a finished report, see *Bonus Tools 1-21-1* and *1-21-2*.

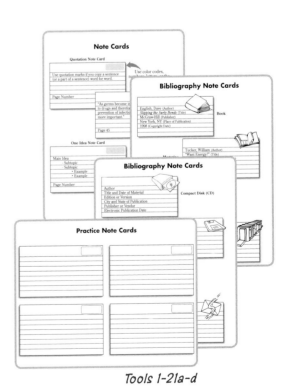

*Tools 1-21a-d*

## 1-22 Developing Study Guides

This strategy helps students learn to read for information and details by teaching them to make study guides.

Generally, students are expected to know how to get meaning from reading textbooks, but many students lack the experience to do so. Faced with history, science, and other content-area textbooks, students—even successful ones—frequently feel overwhelmed and unsure about how and what to read. Students must be taught how to read their textbooks.

Passively reading just to get to the end of each chapter is obviously not enough, nor is answering comprehension questions. Fortunately, textbook reading is a teachable skill. Creating study guides is an important part of it; students who do so can glean information and details from any text.

### Before Class

- Make overhead transparencies and student copies of *Tools 1-22a* through *1-22d* as needed.
- Select a chapter of a textbook used by your students.

### During Class

1. Using *Tool 1-22a*, introduce study guides to your students.

2. Try each suggestion on *Tools 1-22a* and *1-22b*. Pay special attention to the advice about starting at the end of the chapter.

3. In the beginning, you will want to do most of the work for your students. They will copy your examples. After a few group lessons, have students work more independently. Guide and support them as they progress.

4. Keep in mind that the goal is to give your students the confidence to read and use information from textbooks. To accomplish this goal, you must allow your students adequate time to learn and numerous opportunities for practice.

**Note:** For additional mapping ideas see 1-24 Mapping and Webbing.

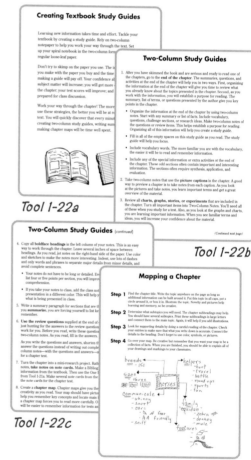

*Tool 1-22a*

*Tool 1-22b*

*Tool 1-22c*

*Tool 1-22d*

# (1-23) Three-Column Notes with Summaries

The Three-Column Notes with Summaries strategy prompts students to add summaries, comments, and questions to their three-column notes. Teach this strategy to help your students think more deeply about their notes.

**Prerequisites:** 1-17 Easy Two-Column Notes and 1-20 Three- and Four-Column Notes

Use *Tool 1-23a* when you want your students to add summaries and comments to their three-column notes.

After your students have taken notes on the top part of *Tool 1-23a*, ask them to write a three-part IVF (Identify the Item, Select a Verb, and Finish Your Thought) topic sentence to summarize those notes in the space at the bottom of the page. (See **1-30 Four-Step Summary Paragraphs** for more information about IVF topic sentences.)

*Tool 1-23a*

## 1-24 Mapping and Webbing

The Mapping and Webbing strategy uses lines and geometric shapes to organize notes. Webs and maps include words, quick sketches, and symbols. (See *Tool 1-22d* as an example.)

Share the following examples with your students to give them ideas for creating their own webs or maps. See **1-28 Using Graphic Organizers** for additional graphic organizers.

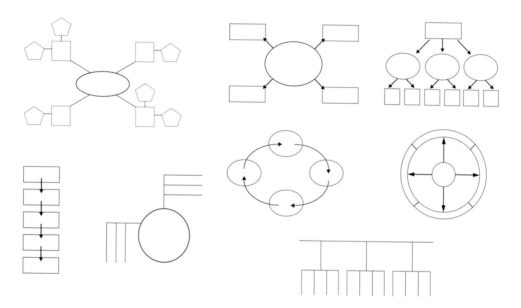

Use mapping and webbing after your students have mastered **1-17 Easy Two-Column Notes**. Try inserting small maps and webs into the right column. This is especially helpful when students need visual cues in history class and science class.

After students have taken notes, they can review the information by recasting it in webs or maps. Occasionally, have students take notes solely by webbing or mapping. Students who have practiced **1-17 Easy Two-Column Notes** will make maps and webs that better show major and minor details.

# Making Inferences and Analyzing the Text

Making inferences and analyzing a story or article are important skills. When students examine a text's ideas and information, they become more active readers and develop and demonstrate comprehension. An inference is a conclusion based on evidence and logic about a story's setting, conflict, or resolution, or about characters' actions and motives. A reader also makes inferences about the content of an expository text. When readers analyze, they make judgments, state opinions, and take positions.

## Objectives

- Improve students' organization of thoughts and information
- Improve students' comprehension
- Help students clarify their opinions
- Teach students to develop critical-thinking skills

| Strategy | Strategy Description | Page | Tools |
|---|---|---|---|
| **1-25** Making Inferences and Analyzing Text with Two-Column Notes | Organizing information and inferences using two-column notes | 36 | 36 |
| **1-26** Making Inferences and Analyzing Text with Informal Outlines | Organizing thoughts, information, and inferences using informal outlines | 36 | 1-26a |
| **1-27** Making Inferences and Analyzing Text with Topic Sentences | Organizing thoughts and inferences using topic sentences | 37 | n/a |

## 1-25 Making Inferences and Analyzing Text with Two-Column Notes

Students can use two-column notes to organize thoughts and information to support an inference or opinion. You can help your students use two-column guides to learn to look beyond basic facts, make inferences, and support opinions.

Use *Tools 1-25a* and *1-25b* to help your students make statements about what they believe as they read. Use the left and right columns to show your students how they can support and explain those statements.

*Tool 1-25a* presents questions that guide students to make inferences as they read. Other questions on the Tool encourage students to state an opinion.

*Tool 1-25b* shows on the left key terms that remind students about the important features of a poem.

*Tool 1-25a*

*Tool 1-25b*

## 1-26 Making Inferences and Analyzing Text with Informal Outlines

This strategy teaches students to use an informal outline to state and support inferences. With informal outlines, students learn to put their thoughts on paper and to support their opinions with details, facts, and/or quotations.

**Prerequisite:** 4-7 Planning with an Informal Outline

**Handy Pages**

Display *Tool 1-26a* and explain that informal outlines are made on two-column paper. Tell your students that when they make informal outlines, they add ideas and inferences that they make about the text on the left side of a two-column page. Remind them that when developing a fact outline and taking notes, they noted big ideas, but when writing informal outlines, they note key/star ideas. Key/star ideas are reasons, details, and facts that support a topic. They put stars next to the ideas on the left to show that they are key/star ideas. The key/star ideas show their thinking. On the right, have students add supporting facts and details. At the bottom, have them conclude by writing a word or phrase that sums up their thinking.

*Tool 1-26a*

# 1-27 Making Inferences and Analyzing Text with Topic Sentences

This strategy teaches students to use a topic sentence or a thesis statement to support an inference or an opinion. Use this strategy to help your students summarize and share their ideas about texts and to practice writing topic sentences.

**Handy Pages**

**Prerequisites:** 4-17 Defining Topic Sentences and Thesis Statements and 4-18 Topic Sentence Variety

Topic sentences in paragraphs, or thesis statements in essays, are one-sentence statements that often include the writer's position and reason for writing. Writing topic sentences or thesis statements about texts teaches students to make inferences and to analyze. During lessons, students may lack the time to write full paragraphs or reports, but can usually write a single topic sentence. Ask your students to write their statements on index cards or strips of paper as a "ticket out" at the end of class.

**"I'm Nobody! Who Are You?" by Emily Dickinson**

Although Emily Dickinson does not want a life of fame and public admiration, many of my friends and I would welcome the opportunity.

Like Emily Dickinson, I enjoy my simple life; however, I sometimes envy the "frogs."

# Recognizing Text Structures

The term *text structure* refers to one of six basic organization patterns found in expository/information text. These patterns are listed under **1-28 Using Graphic Organizers**.

## Objectives

- Increase students' understanding of relationships between main ideas and details
- Help students organize to aid note taking, writing, and comprehension

| Strategy | Strategy Description | Page | Tools |
|---|---|---|---|
| **1-28 Using Graphic Organizers** | Using graphic organizers to take notes | 38 | 1-28a to 1-28h |
| **1-29 Using Text Structures** | Using a variety of text structures for different kinds of writing | 39 | 1-28a to 1-28h |

## 1-28 Using Graphic Organizers

The Using Graphic Organizers strategy helps students organize their notes with graphic organizers. Teach this strategy to help your students improve comprehension and add variety to note taking.

### Before Class

- Using graphic organizers like those on *Tools 1-28a* to *1-28h* can help students read, remember, and organize information. Begin by determining which type of graphic organizer to use. Different texts or segments of text will lend themselves to different types. For example, graphic organizers can show the following:
  - ▸ sequencing
  - ▸ enumerating
  - ▸ describing
  - ▸ comparing or contrasting
  - ▸ cause and effect
  - ▸ problem and solution

- Make copies of the Tool that fits the reading assignment. Make a transparency of *Tool 1-29a* to help introduce the graphic organizers to your students.

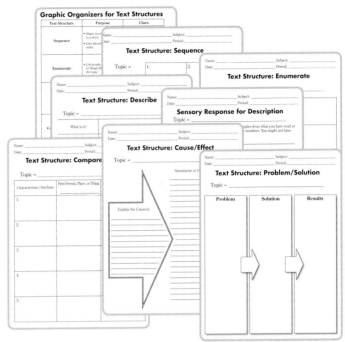

*Tools 1-28a through 1-28h*

## During Class

1. Introduce each graphic organizer, as needed.

2. Work with your students as they fill in information accurately. Add sketches and color to enhance the notes.

3. Once you have modeled the use of a Tool and your students have used it with you, assign and monitor use for independent assignments or group work.

It's good to remember that graphic organizers add variety to note taking, but more importantly, they improve comprehension.

**Note:** On *Tool 1-28c*, have students use obvious transitions (such as *first*, *second*, *third*) and subtle transitions (such as *good*, *very good*, *the best*) to help them organize their ideas.

## 1-29 Using Text Structures

This strategy teaches students to recognize various text structures and how they change depending on the writing tasks students face.

Use the graphic organizers from **1-28 Using Graphic Organizers** as prewriting aids when you want your students to write paragraphs or reports using one of the text structures. Section 9, "Specific Writing Assignments," covers various writing tasks that students face. These include examples and directions for each of the text structures presented on *Tools 1-28a* through *1-28h*.

**Note:** Text structures and their graphic organizers work well for short speeches and group discussion activities.

# Summarizing

A summary is a short restatement of the main points of articles, stories, films, or chapters in textbooks.

## Objectives

- Share ways to summarize the main ideas or key events from what has been read, listened to, or viewed in a clear, concise manner
- Help students develop and demonstrate comprehension abilities
- Teach ways to identify major and minor details
- Teach ways to remember details for assessment and writing assignments

| Strategy | Strategy Description | Page | Tools |
|---|---|---|---|
| **1-30** Four-Step Summary Paragraphs | Writing and organizing summary paragraphs | 41 | 1-30a to 1-30e |
| **1-31** Plot Line Summaries | Outlining a story's plot | 47 | 1-31a |
| **1-32** Summaries Without Words | Summarizing text with illustrations | 48 | n/a |
| **1-33** Money Summaries | Summarizing with a set number of words | 49 | 1-33a |
| **1-34** The 12-Word Trick | Summarizing with a list of 12 words | 50 | n/a |

P Consider using the Posters with the strategies in this section.

# 1-30 Four-Step Summary Paragraphs

This strategy teaches students an easy-to-follow method for writing a summary paragraph.

**Handy Pages**

The level of instruction on Four-Step Summary Paragraphs depends on the age and ability of your students, the amount of time available, and writing goals. You can introduce summary writing in one lesson, or you can give instruction in small segments over a number of days. Model the strategy many times and practice it with your students often, using reading assignments from all content areas.

## Before Class

- Make overhead transparencies and student copies of *Tools 1-30a* through *1-30e* as needed.
- Select a sample text, preferably a short piece that is easy to comprehend.

  *Bonus Tools 1-30-1* through *1-30-8* provide additional support.

**Note:** Students often confuse summarizing with retelling, writing a review, and giving book reports. The best way to help eliminate confusion is to share examples of each with your class. (Use *Bonus Tools 1-30-1* through *1-30-7* if a definition, description, and examples are needed.)

## During Class

- Inform your students that a good summary
  - ▸ Begins with a clear, direct topic sentence that identifies the text's main idea;
  - ▸ Contains key facts to support the topic sentence;
  - ▸ May use transitions but usually does not need them;
  - ▸ Keeps the same tone as the original piece;
  - ▸ Does not include the summary writer's opinion;
  - ▸ Does not need a formal conclusion.
- With the class read *Tool 1-30a*, "Adventure of a Country Doctor," as an example of a good summary paragraph.
  - ▸ Point out the IVF topic sentence that starts the paragraph.
  - ▸ Explain that all sentences in the body of the paragraph are facts—not opinions.
  - ▸ Notice that this paragraph does not have a formal conclusion. Conclusions almost always share opinions.

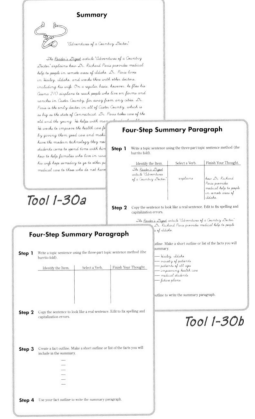

*Tool 1-30a*

*Tool 1-30b*

*Tool 1-30c*

- Tell your students that creating a good summary paragraph will be easy if they follow these four steps.

> *Step 1* **Write a three-part topic sentence using the burrito fold.**
>
> *Step 2* **Copy the complete topic sentence.**
>
> *Step 3* **Create a fact outline.**
>
> *Step 4* **Write a final summary paragraph using the fact outline.**

- Use *Tool 1-30b* to show your students what you will expect when they create their own plans for writing a summary paragraph. Review each step of the four-step process with them.

## *Step 1*
### Write a three-part IVF topic sentence using the "burrito fold."

- The three-part IVF (Identify the item, select a Verb, Finish your thought) topic sentence uses a burrito fold. This visual method helps students master writing topic sentences. (See **4-18 Topic Sentences Variety** for more information on IVF topic sentences.)

- Using *Tools 1-30a* and *1-30b*, show your students how the three-part IVF topic sentence was developed on *Tool 1-30b* and used in the paragraph on *Tool 1-30a*.

- Remind your students that writers often use the TED verbs (tells, explains, describes) when writing topic sentences for summaries. Using *Tool 1-30d*, show additional examples of good three-part IVF topic sentences.

- Have your students read the selected text with you or individually. With your class, develop a topic sentence using *Tool 1-30c*.

- If you have time, write additional topic sentences for the same text. Discuss with your students which is better and why. (They do not need to all share the same opinion.)

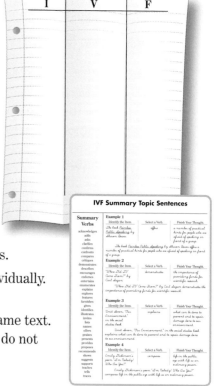

*Tool 1-30d*

- Remind your students that a three-part IVF topic sentence gives an overview without providing all of the details that will be in the rest of the paragraph.
- It is sometimes appropriate to include the title of the summarized item in the topic sentence. Provide students support in learning the rules for underlining and using quotation marks. (See *Bonus Tool 1-30-8* for an example.)

## Step 2
### Copy the complete topic sentence.
- Write the words from the burrito fold onto the board as a normal sentence, or use an overhead of *Tool 1-30b* to illustrate combining the sentence pieces into a complete topic sentence. Ask your students to copy the sentence pieces into complete sentences using their copies of *Tool 1-30c*. Tell them this sentence will be used to start their summaries.

**Note:** See *Bonus Tool 1-33-8* for an alternative Tool to use with Steps 1 and 2.

## Step 3
### Create a fact outline.
- Using *Tool 1-30c*, point out the area below the topic sentence and next to Step 3. Tell your students that they will use this area to create a fact outline. Explain that the fact outline will help them develop ideas for writing their summary paragraphs and that they will use the fact outline to list different thoughts, ideas, or details from the text they are summarizing. These words and phrases show the main events or the big ideas. Let them know that generally they will need four to seven dashes for a paragraph.
- Point out the dashes on the fact outline and explain that after each dash, they will use *just one*, *two*, or *three* words after each dash. They will use only words and phrases. Use the term JOTT to help your students with their fact outlines.

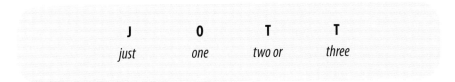

| **J** | **O** | **T** | **T** |
|-------|-------|-------|-------|
| *just* | *one* | *two or* | *three* |

- Model this concept for your students. Using the JOTT method will help them complete their fact outlines quickly by selecting only a few important words and phrases that will be useful as they write the summary. Remind your students that they will not be putting complete sentences on the fact outline.

- Using *Tool 1-30b*, review the fact outline for "Adventures of a Country Doctor." Discuss with your students how the fact outline served as a plan for writing the summary on *Tool 1-30a*.
- With your students, create a fact outline for the text you selected. Teaching your students to create fact outlines will take lots of modeling and guided practice. Practice this skill with the class often and in all content areas.

### Creating a Fact Outline for Story/Narrative Text

Have your students fill in the first dash with a word that reminds them of the beginning of the story. The last dash should be filled in with a word that reminds your students of the end of the story. The middle dashes are filled in with words that indicate the most important events.

**Step 2**   Copy the sentence so it looks like a real sentence. Edit; fix spelling and capitalization errors.

*The story "Don't Think Like a Slave" by Linda K. Shaw describes an important event in the life of Dr. Martin Luther King, Jr.*

**Step 3**   Create a fact outline. Make a short outline or list of the facts you will include in the summary.

— *speech contest*
— *second place*
— *heading home*
— *bus ride*
— *teacher's example*
— *father*
— *things would be different*

## Creating a Fact Outline for Information/Expository Text

Have your students fill in the dashes with main ideas in the order in which they were presented.

> **Step 2** Copy the sentence so it looks like a real sentence. Edit; fix spelling and capitalization errors.
>
> *The Reader's Digest article "Adventures of a Country Doctor" explains how Dr. Richard Paris provides medical help to people in remote areas of Idaho.*
>
> **Step 3** Create a fact outline. Make a short outline or list of the facts you will include in the summary.
>
> — *Hailey, Idaho*
> — *variety of patients*
> — *patients of all ages*
> — *improving health care*
> — *medical students*
> — *future plans*

## Step 4
## Write a final summary paragraph using the fact outline.

- Explain to your students that they will be using a fact outline to create a summary paragraph. Use the fact outlines you created from the text you selected for demonstration for your model. Before you have your students write the paragraph, have them go over the fact outline to see whether the facts are in the right order. Numbering each fact will help. Ask your students for help placing numbers by the facts to indicate the right order. Discuss the importance of keeping the facts in the right order.

• Model writing sentences based on the fact outline and show how one word or phrase can be turned into a complete sentence. Complete the first two or three sentences for your class. Ask for your students' help on the rest. Have them write a title for the summary paragraphs. (See *Bonus Tool 1-30-8*.) If they have trouble, share the following examples with them or use the example on *Tool 1-30e* to point out the link between the outline and the summary paragraph. (For additional examples of summaries, see *Bonus Tools 1-30-6* and *1-30-7*.)

*Tool 1-30e*

---

### Narrative Summary (Also on *Tool 1-30e*.)

*"Don't Think Like a Slave"*

The story "Don't Think Like a Slave" by Linda K. Shaw describes an important event in the life of Dr. Martin Luther King, Jr. As the story starts, fifteen-year-old Martin is competing in a speech contest. He and his teacher have traveled to the competition from their homes in Atlanta to Valdosta, Georgia. When Martin finishes his speech, he receives enthusiastic applause from the audience and a second-prize ribbon from the judges. Martin is happy and his teacher is proud. Later in the day they board a bus headed back to Atlanta. Martin and his teacher sit in the back of the bus and chat about Martin's success. Their conversation is interrupted by two white passengers who want a seat. Martin does not want to give up the seats but follows the example of his teacher who gives up her seat with a sense of pride and determination. As they stand, Martin remembers his father, Daddy King, and how he, like his teacher, was proud and determined. The example his teacher sets and the example he remembers from his father give Martin courage. As he stands, he remembers his father's words: "Nobody can make a slave out of you if you don't think like a slave." As the bus travels on to Atlanta, Martin thinks about these words and his father's message that someday things would be different.

---

**Expository Summary (Also on** *Tool 1-30a*)

*"Adventures of a Country Doctor"*

The *Reader's Digest* article "Adventures of a Country Doctor" explains how Dr. Richard Paris provides medical help to people in remote areas of Idaho. Dr. Paris lives in Hailey, Idaho, and works there with other doctors, including his wife. On a regular basis, however, he flies his Cessna 210 airplane to reach people who live on farms and ranches in Custer County, far away from any cities. Dr. Paris is the only doctor in all of Custer County, which is as big as the state of Connecticut. Dr. Paris takes care of the old and the young. He helps with many kinds of problems. He works to improve the health care for people in his area by giving them good care and making sure his clinics have the modern technology they need. Each year medical students come to spend time with him, so they can learn how to help families who live in rural areas. Dr. Paris and his wife hope some day to go to other parts of the world to give medical care to those who do not have doctors.

 For a scoring guide and other support for assessment, see 10-20 **Summary Writing Scoring Guide**.

## 1-31 Plot Line Summaries

Plot Line Summaries show the outline of a story's plot. Students can use them to learn or review terms used to write about stories, and to practice identifying the important events in a story or narrative.

### Before Class

- Make an overhead transparency and student copies of *Tool 1-31a*.
- Select a short story to use for modeling and student practice.

### During Class

1. Using *Tool 1-31a*, introduce or review the terms on the plot line. Use the following descriptions if your students are unfamiliar with these terms:

   - **Exposition**—The beginning of the story. Introduces the characters, setting, situation, and tone.
   - **Rising Action**—This is when you become aware of the problem. Things get exciting as tension increases.

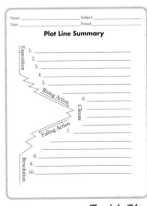

*Tool 1-31a*

- **Climax**—The most exciting part, when the conflict is most intense. Usually the turning point in the story.
- **Falling Action**—The problem is solved or worked out. Things start to go back to normal.
- **Resolution**—Presents the final outcome.

2. Together, fill in all ten lines. Start by filling in the first and last lines. This will remind students that the plot line must cover the entire story. It also makes it easier to complete the list.

Use Plot Line Summaries to have your students tell the story orally before they write the formal summary.

**Note:** If there isn't enough room for complete sentences, use phrases and clauses.

## 1-32 Summaries Without Words

In the Summaries Without Words strategy, students use large sheets of plain paper to draw pictures with markers and pencils. Students use these pictures later to give an oral summary.

1. Organize your students into small groups to summarize units in textbooks, short stories, novels, chapters in a novel, speeches, or articles.

2. Set a time limit and establish rules before your students begin. Everyone participates. Everyone draws.

3. Have each group member sketch or make symbols to illustrate key concepts. Students all work at the same time and on the same sheet of paper, drawing on different parts of the page. The goal is to create a page full of rough but meaningful sketches.

4. When groups have completed their Summaries Without Words, they explain their sketches to other students.

5. Take time to discuss with your students why and how they might want to use pictures to improve their memories and prepare for assessments. Explain that they can also use this strategy several days later to review for quizzes and tests.

The Summary Without Words strategy is an effective memory device. Anything goes! This strategy is not an art assignment; it is a chance for your students to show understanding through pictures.

**Note:** Review 1-24 Mapping and Webbing and remind students that their team may organize their sketches in a map or web.

## 1-33 Money Summaries

In Money Summaries, students "buy" words and use them to write summary sentences. This activity is fun and helps your students focus on themes and main ideas in articles and stories. It also teaches them to write concisely.

### Before Class

- Make an overhead transparency and student copies of *Tool 1-33a*.
- Decide which goal you will set for Money Summaries.

*Tool 1-33a*

### During Class

1. Tell your students that in Money Summaries, they will buy words that they will use to write a summary sentence. Each word will cost a dime, and they will have $2.00 available to buy words. Feel free to vary the amount of imaginary money used.

2. Tell them that the three articles *a, an,* and *the* are free.

3. Have students list the words they want to buy on a piece of notebook paper.

4. Once students have bought their words, have them use these words to write a sentence summarizing a story or article on *Tool 1-33a*. Remind students that they shouldn't try to use all the words they bought, only the words they need.

The goal of Money Summaries is to write either the shortest summary possible or to spend as much of the $2.00 as possible. In either case, the goal is to write a complete sentence and not a headline.

Here are some samples of Money Summaries for the Emily Dickinson poem "I'm Nobody! Who Are You?"

> *A poet prefers a quiet life.* (40 cents)
>
> *In her poem "I'm Nobody! Who are You?," Emily Dickinson reflects on the advantages of living a private rather than a public life.* ($2.00)

If time permits, ask your students to write a traditional summary paragraph. Compare the effect and purpose of each kind of summary.

> *"I'm Nobody! Who Are You?"*
> *Emily Dickinson's poem compares life in the public eye with a life as a nobody. She suggests that those in the public eye are like frogs who are on display all of the time. Life as a nobody, she reminds us, isn't all that easy either. Others want the quiet nobodies to speak up and be more public.*

## 1-34 The 12-Word Trick

The 12-Word Trick prompts students to pick 12 words related to a text to help them recall what they have learned.

1. After watching a film, reading an article, or enjoying a story, ask your students to pick 12 words from the text or from the content of the film.

2. After your students write their lists, ask them to share. Have three or four students write their lists on the board. Discuss the lists. Ask questions about words that are strong or important. Explain that the words that work best are ones that have special meaning for the list maker. Allow students to change words on their lists.

3. Next, have them sort the words on their lists into groups or categories. When a list—even a short one—is sorted into categories, it is easier to remember in the short and long term.

4. Have your students write and share a two- or three-sentence summary using the 12 words. Lead a discussion about how students might use this strategy on their own to remember information in other classes.

5. A few days or weeks later, ask your students to recall and write their lists again. You (and they) will be surprised about how many items they remember.

# Asking and Answering Questions

Asking and answering questions are important academic skills that students use to develop and demonstrate comprehension, explain any confusion, seek clarification, and share insights.

## Objectives

- Teach students how to ask good short questions and answer them accurately, orally or in writing
- Help students understand various levels of questioning
- Save students time and increase their confidence as they answer questions

| Strategy | Strategy Description | Page | Tools |
|---|---|---|---|
| **1-35** Great Short Answers | Recognizing and writing good one- to three-sentence answers | 52 | 1-35a to 1-35e |
| **1-36** Responses to Essay Questions | Writing clear, concise one-paragraph (or more) answers to prompts or questions | 54 | n/a |
| **1-37** Using the Two-Column Study Guide | Organizing and writing questions in a two-column study guide | 55 | n/a |
| **1-38** Levels of Questioning | Using different kinds of questions and answers | 56 | n/a |

P Consider using the Posters with the strategies in this section.

# 1-35 Great Short Answers

Students use this strategy to learn how to write great short answers. For class, district, or state assessments, students must be prepared to write good short answers that are one, two, or three sentences long. In class, teachers expect students to speak in complete sentences and to give complete answers.

To help students master the skill of writing short answers, many teachers like to start with the Tools that show the three faces (*Tools 1-35c* and *1-35d*). Even secondary students enjoy the three faces, which instantly demonstrate what's acceptable and what's not. Other teachers may choose to introduce their students to the concept by using *Tools 1-35a* and *1-35b*.

## Before Class

- Make overhead transparencies and student copies of *Tools 1-35a* through *1-35e*, as needed, or have available notebook paper.

- On *Tools 1-35d* and *1-35e*, create sample questions based on content that students are learning to use for modeling and student practice.

## During Class

1. Introduce Great Short Answers by reviewing *Tool 1-35a* and the examples on *Tools 1-35b* or *1-35d* with your students. Give them copies of *Tools 1-35a* as well as *1-35b* or *1-35d* to keep in their notebooks as reminders of what you expect for good short answers.

2. Model using examples you prepared on *Tools 1-35c* or *1-35e*.

3. Have your students practice as a whole class, in small groups, or in pairs with questions you have prepared. Have them use *Tool 1-35c* or *Tool 1-35e*, or have them fold notebook paper into a two-column fold.

*Tools 1-35a to 1-35e*

4. Guide your students as they practice the strategy independently. Have them practice all three levels several times.

5. Eventually, your students will be able to write at the acceptable (*Tool 1-35c*) or happy-face level (*Tool 1-35e*), especially if this level of answers is expected across content areas.

6. Some students can improve their knowledge of question words by writing questions. Use *Tool 1-35a* to review words that are used in questions. With your students, create questions for the right side of the page that will help students think about questions and how they are used. Write questions on the board to demonstrate.

> Question = *What are some similarities that all reptiles share?*
>
> ☹ *Look the same*
>
> 😐 *They look alike and have scales.*
>
> 😊 *Reptiles all share certain physical characteristics, including spinal columns, lungs, and scales.*

## Additional Ideas

The Great Short Answer strategy can also be used to teach students to write better sentences. For more information about sentence writing, see Section 3, Sentence Mastery.

1. Explain to your students that every time they write, they should try to make their sentences acceptable or happy-face sentences.

2. Give them a prompt or topic for their writing, and ask them to write several sentences in response. Try asking them to write a sentence for each level, or encourage them to aim to make all their sentences happy-face sentences.

3. Ask your students to share the sentences they wrote, and give them advice on how to improve sad-face or acceptable sentences to the happy-face level.

 For a quick check and other support for assessment, see 10-11 Quick Check for Short Answers.

## 1-36 Responses to Essay Questions

Teach this strategy to help students to write good answers to essay questions. As in **1-35 Great Short Answers**, students turn the essay question into the beginning of their answer by using topic sentences. (More in-depth information about topic sentences is presented in Section 4.)

**Handy Pages**

 *Bonus Tool 1-36-1* provides additional support.

### During Class

1. Tell your students to read the question carefully. If possible, they should selectively underline or highlight the key words in the question.

2. Have them turn the question into their topic sentence by using one of the topic sentence methods described in Section 4. Occasion/Position statements, Power (Number) Statements, and However Statements are easy to use.

3. Let them know that they should not change the words used in the question. They should keep the same words to let their readers know that they understand the question. Tell them that when they restate the question in a good topic sentence, they prove that they are in control, understand the question, and are ready to answer it.

4. Tell your students that they should use transitions in their answer. Transitions keep students moving in the right direction. They also help readers. (See *Tools 4-24a* and *4-25a* for more information about transitions. The following example is also on *Bonus Tool 1-36-1*.)

---

After the rise of Communism, why do you think traditional Chinese literature, drama, ballet, and opera were ignored?

*There are several reasons why traditional Chinese literature, drama, ballet, and opera were ignored after the rise of Communism in China in 1949.*

*First . . .*

*Next . . .*

*One other . . .*

Why did logging become a big business in the Northwest?

*Logging became a big business in the Northwest for three reasons.*

*First . . .*

*Another . . .*

*The last . . .*

---

## 1-37 Using the Two-Column Study Guide

Students use this strategy to organize and write questions in a two-column fold format. You can use it for many purposes, such as a class assignment, quiz, or study guide.

*Bonus Tool 1-37-1* provides additional support.

Ask your students to use paper divided into two columns. On the left side, have them write the question. On the right side, have them enter the answer. You will provide the question in some activities, such as quizzes or assignments. Students will provide the question in others, such as study guides.

Sometimes students will need to write out the entire question and answer. (The following examples are also on *Bonus Tool 1-37-1.*)

| Question | Answer |
|---|---|
| What are two ways that scientists use starlight as a tool? | Scientists use starlight to measure vast distances in space and to tell what a star is made of and how hot it is. |

At other times, your students can save time by turning the questions and answers into short fact outlines.

| Question | Answer |
|---|---|
| What are two ways that scientists use starlight as a tool? | - measure vast distances  • in space  - tell  • what a star is made of  • how hot a star is |

Using the Two-Column Study Guide helps your students with neatness, makes information easier to read, and saves you time as you grade papers.

## 1-38 Levels of Questioning

In this strategy, students create different types and levels of questions about what they have read. When students can name and describe different kinds of questions, they are often more prepared to answer questions independently during exams.

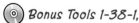 *Bonus Tools 1-38-1, 1-38-2,* and *1-38-3* provide additional support.

A wonderful way to develop and check for comprehension is to turn students into teachers and ask them to create questions from what they have read using direct thinking and/or application-questioning techniques. (The following examples are also on *Bonus Tool 1-38-1.*)

### Direct, Thinking, and Application Questions

#### Direct Questions

- Ask for specific information.
- Everyone will have the same answer to this type of question.
- Answers to these questions can be found in the book, article, or story.
- Students can literally put a finger on the words that answer the question.

#### Thinking Questions

- Require thinking and analyzing.
- Often call for opinion or insight.
- Push a student to make inferences, connections, judgments, and decisions.
- Answers depend on students' previous experience and knowledge, as well as the text and learning that has taken place.

#### Application Questions

- Assume that the student has read and comprehended the material, and is ready to use it in some way.

| | |
|---|---|
| **Direct Questions** | What is an apple? |
| **Thinking Questions** | What is the best kind of apple, and what is the best way to eat it? |
| **Application Questions** | What can parents and medical experts do to encourage children to eat more fruits, such as apples? |

## QAR Questions

In the Question, Answer, Relationship (QAR) method (Raphael 1982), questions about text are classified according to the way the student must relate to the text in order to answer the question. The relationships are *in the text*, *think and search*, *author and you*, and *on your own*. The examples in the following list, also on *Bonus Tool 1-38-2*, come from *Of Mice and Men* by John Steinbeck.)

### *Of Mice and Men* by John Steinbeck

| Question | Answer | Relationship |
|---|---|---|
| *In what state does the story take place?* | (The answer is in the text.) | In the text |
| *Name four ways that Lennie helped George.* | (The answer is found by putting parts of the text together.) | Think and search |
| *Do you think Lennie and George will ever be able to save enough money to buy their own land?* | (The answer comes from what you know and what the author says.) | Author and you |
| *What do you think Lennie should've done when he found George at the end of the story?* | (The answer is from your opinions and experiences.) | On your own |

## CROWD Questions

The CROWD strategy is one of the techniques suggested by *Starting Out Right: A Guide to Promoting Children's Reading Success* (Burns, Griffin, and Snow 1999). It provides suggestions to parents, child-care providers, and educators on how to help students become successful readers.

One suggestion is to use CROWD questions to make sure children have the opportunity to answer a variety of questions when they listen to adults read or speak. This strategy can be used to create questions for students of all ages and ability levels. It can be used in class and by family members and volunteers. (The example questions in the following list, also on *Bonus Tool 1-38-3*, are similar to those students might be asked in an Industrial Arts class.)

**C** Completion questions
*The number one safety rule for this class is_____.*

**R** Recall questions
*What safety equipment is needed to operate the table saw?*

**O** Open-ended questions
*How should a student who fails to follow safety rules be reprimanded?*

**W** "What" vocabulary questions
*What is an awl?*

**D** Distancing questions—making connections to real-life experiences
*Why do you think it is important to follow safety rules in and out of class?*

# Using and Creating Bookmarks

Bookmarks are tools that help readers. Bookmarks that promote comprehension are the most useful.

## Objectives

- Teach students to make and use bookmarks that help promote comprehension
- Teach students to make bookmarks that relate to strategies they have learned
- Teach students to make tools for review and test preparation in content-area classes

| Strategy | Strategy Description | Page | Tools |
|---|---|---|---|
| **1-39** **Three-Column Burrito Fold Bookmarks** | Creating bookmarks using topic sentences and supporting details | 60 | 1-39a, 1-39b |
| **1-40** **Sticky Note Bookmarks** | Using sticky notes as bookmarks to record summaries and facts | 61 | n/a |
| **1-41** **Two-Column Fold Bookmarks** | Creating two-column bookmarks for various topics | 61 | n/a |
| **1-42** **Cut-Apart Bookmarks** | Using hints and reminders to encourage active reading and to promote comprehension | 62 | 1-42a |

P Consider using the Posters with the strategies in this section.

## 1-39 Three-Column Burrito Fold Bookmarks

In this strategy, students learn to create three-column bookmarks using topic sentences and supporting details.

Three-Column Burrito Fold Bookmarks are made with half sheets of paper that require students to complete the three parts of the IVF topic sentence (Identify the item, select a Verb, and Finish your thought) plus a fact outline. (See **1-30 Four-Step Summary Paragraphs** for more information about writing burrito-fold topic sentences.)

### Before Class

Make overhead transparencies and student copies of *Tools 1-39a* and *1-39b*. Run these back-to-back, cut them apart, and give them to your students.

### During Class

1. Have your students fold their copies of *Tools 1-39a* and *1-39b* into bookmarks using a burrito fold. The inside of the bookmark should contain Identify the item, select a Verb, and Finish your thought (IVF) and fact outline.

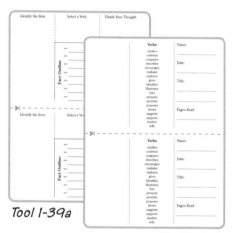

*Tool 1-39a*

*Tool 1-39b*

2. Point out the list of sample summary verbs that shows on the back of the folded bookmark.

3. Notice that when the bookmark is folded and filled with information, one section remains empty. Ask your students to do one of the following in this space:

   • Make an illustration.

   • Write a question about something they do not understand or a question that shows comprehension.

   • List words they do not know or words that show good word choice.

   • Copy a quotation worth sharing and discussing.

   • Create a timeline or sequence of events.

   • Make notes about a character, setting, plot, or conflict.

   • Make a prediction.

   • Make a connection to a previous chapter.

   • Identify several prepositional phrases, adjectives, action verbs, or other parts of speech that they are studying.

   • Ask a family member or peer to comment about their summary.

   • Make a connection to something learned in another subject or class.

   • Write a message to the author.

A second way to create the bookmark is to have your students do the work. Instead of receiving the bookmark as a handout, students fold half sheets of paper into thirds and write all the information that is included on *Tools 1-39a* and *1-39b*.

When students format and copy information onto the bookmarks, they are more engaged and more likely to internalize the steps for writing a summary.

## 1-40 Sticky Note Bookmarks

In this strategy, students use sticky notes as bookmarks to record summaries and facts.

Lined 3" × 5" sticky notes make good bookmarks. Students can place them at a chapter's end or where they have stopped reading. Using the **1-30 Four-Step Summary Paragraphs** strategy, students write on the bookmark a quick summary topic sentence with facts below it.

## 1-41 Two-Column Fold Bookmarks

Students use this strategy to create bookmarks in a two-column format.

**Handy Pages**

Bookmarks made with half sheets of paper folded into two columns are quick and easy to make. Label the columns on these bookmarks for a specific purpose or to reinforce concepts that you teach.

| Major Details | Minor Details |
|---|---|
| country | land formations |
| famous person | contribution |
| battle | details |
| invention | description |
| fact | importance |
| event | significance |
| character | description |
| quotation | response |
| theme | examples |
| figurative language | examples |
| questions | answers |

## 1-42 Cut-Apart Bookmarks

Cut-Apart Bookmarks allow students to practice short summaries and remind them to use reading comprehension strategies.

Copy *Tool 1-42a* on colored paper or on cardstock. Cut the bookmarks apart and share them with your students. The information on the bookmarks serves as a reminder to use reading comprehension strategies when they read independently.

Encourage your students to use the bookmarks as they read in all of their classes. An alternative is to have students design bookmarks of their own that demonstrate one or more of the comprehension strategies. They may design these with paper and markers or on a computer. Encourage them to share their bookmarks with other students, especially with students in lower grades.

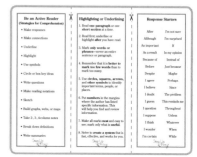

*Tool 1-42a*

*A* strong vocabulary is essential for success in both reading and writing. Learning new vocabulary is a natural process that can be enhanced through effective instruction and support. Success depends on practice that applies new words and integrates them in a meaningful fashion.

In class, students encounter academic vocabulary, content-specific words, and other unfamiliar terms they must master to fully understand the information they are expected to learn. A student's understanding of academic vocabulary is one of the strongest indicators of academic success.

In addition, writers with large vocabularies are free to express their ideas more clearly through the use of active verbs and precise nouns, adjectives, and adverbs. Such precise wording helps give a writer a unique voice and allows him or her to show what is happening, rather than simply telling the reader about it.

To master a new vocabulary term, students must not only learn its definition, but they must also apply the new word in a variety of ways. These applications include restating the definition in a student's own words, associating the term with synonyms and antonyms, using the word in a sentence that demonstrates understanding, and creating pictures or other connections to the new vocabulary.

The strategies in this section will help your students learn new vocabulary, demonstrate their understanding of new words, and apply new words in their writing assignments.

Success at mastering vocabulary comes when students can

- Identify the parts of a dictionary entry and understand the use of each;
- Develop methods for breaking down long definitions with pictures and brief phrases or synonyms that convey the word's meaning;
- Accurately pronounce words that are unfamiliar;
- Use new words in meaningful sentences or paragraphs, and understand the difference between using a new word as a meaningless substitute in a sentence and using it in a way that explains the word's meaning;
- Develop study guides, note cards, and concept maps to help them remember new words, especially for subject-specific vocabulary;
- Understand the different ways words can be used depending on their part of speech or the context of the sentence, as in the case of homonyms and homographs;
- Grasp abstract meanings through concrete strategies such as personification.

## When Teaching Vocabulary Strategies

- Preview each reading passage or presentation you give your students and select the words and terms they must know to understand the information or story.
- Provide the appropriate definitions for words that have more than one definition or part of speech.
- Pronounce new terms for your students, and make sure they understand pronunciation symbols so they can sound out words on their own. Remind or inform them that online dictionaries frequently include sound files containing the correct pronunciation.
- Have students create drawings or other nonlinguistic representations of each new vocabulary term to help them establish multiple associations to the word.
- Have students keep vocabulary notebooks or note cards they can use for reference and study.
- Review vocabulary frequently.

- Point out new definitions for previously learned words.
- Provide or create word lists for students to use in their reading, writing, and speaking. (See **2-14** Unit- or Subject-Specific Word Lists.)
- Use precise language and vocabulary terms as often as possible when speaking to your students.
- Recognize and reward students for using precise language and vocabulary terms themselves.

IDEA BANK

## Tips for Using These Strategies Across Content Areas

✓ Use **2-3** Breaking Down Definitions for all important terms.

✓ Use **2-3** Categories for content-specific words and terms.

✓ Sort new and previously learned vocabulary into categories.

✓ Have students use a modification of **2-3** Personification of Abstract Nouns to explore academic vocabulary terms.

✓ In art classes, ask students to create posters combining text and graphics to illustrate vocabulary words.

✓ Drama students can write monologues from the perspective of a vocabulary word or term, explaining its use and significance.

✓ In PE, have students create active, visual clues for their vocabulary terms.

✓ Play sorting games, matching games, charades, and so on with vocabulary terms.

✓ Every day, pick a new word of the day and mention it during class. Ask students to raise their hands when they hear the word. Consider giving a small prize or privilege to any student who can define the term when you call on her or him.

Choose the strategies that best meet the needs of your students.

# Mastering Vocabulary

The term *vocabulary* refers to words that are contained in a language as a whole. It means all of the words that students use or understand as they listen, read, write, and speak. Strategies presented in this section help students learn and use new words, as well as encourage students to do more with the words they already know.

## Objectives

- Help students expand their oral, reading, and writing vocabularies
- Help students read, comprehend, and use content-area vocabulary
- Help students improve study skills and pass tests
- Encourage students to make good word choices and experiment with words

| Strategy | Strategy Description | Page | Tools |
|---|---|---|---|
| **2-1 Vocabulary Teaching Tips** | Teaching tips for vocabulary strategies | 69 | n/a |
| **2-2 Reading Dictionary Definitions** | Recognizing the parts of a dictionary definition | 69 | 2-2a to 2-2c |
| **2-3 Breaking Down Definitions** | Breaking down definitions into useful chunks | 71 | 2-2a, 2-3a to 2-3c |
| **2-4 Pronunciation** | Pronouncing words correctly | 74 | n/a |
| **2-5 Meaningful Vocabulary Sentences** | Using vocabulary in a sentence | 75 | 2-5a, 2-5b |
| **2-6 Vocabulary Maps** | Using graphic organizers to learn and remember new vocabulary words | 77 | 2-6a, 2-6b |

*(chart continues)*

| Strategy (continued) | Strategy Description | Page | Tools |
|---|---|---|---|
| **2-7** Concept Maps | Using a map to analyze a term or concept and write a definition paragraph | 79 | 2-7a, 2-7b |
| **2-8** Vocabulary Study Guides | Using study guides for vocabulary tests | 81 | 2-8a to 2-8c |
| **2-9** Vocabulary Note Cards | Using note cards to learn and remember vocabulary words | 83 | 2-9a |
| **2-10** Categories | Grouping words into categories to help with memory and comprehension | 83 | n/a |
| **2-11** Personification of Abstract Nouns | Personifying abstract nouns to develop and demonstrate understanding | 85 | 2-11a to 2-11c |
| **2-12** Poetry Pieces | Writing poems using strong vocabulary words selected from a text | 87 | 2-12a |
| **2-13** Homonyms, Homophones, and Homographs | Learning about and demonstrating mastery of homonyms, homophones, homographs, and other difficult words | 88 | 2-13a to 2-13c |
| **2-14** Unit- or Subject-Specific Word Lists | Using content-area vocabulary lists to improve writing and speaking | 89 | n/a |

## 2-1 Vocabulary Teaching Tips

This strategy provides a number of tips for teaching vocabulary to students. Use it in conjunction with the other vocabulary strategies in this section.

Reading for information, especially from textbooks, requires the reader to know the meanings of content-area vocabulary in order to make sense of the text. When students need to master a set of words in order to read a selection, take time to teach the vocabulary explicitly in advance. Teaching your students new, difficult, and important vocabulary at the beginning of a unit will save time in the long run. If you give your students the definitions ahead of time, you can be confident that they will have complete and accurate definitions available when they study.

- Use an overhead projector and present terms one at a time. Have your students copy each word and its definition. Review the pronunciation of the word, make connections to other lessons and subjects, and define difficult words that are in the definition itself.

- When you want your students to use a strategy independently, start by having them work in pairs or in groups of three or four. Give each team a blank overhead transparency, an overhead marker, and two or three words. Have members of the group work together on their assigned words and share their ideas with the class. Add or correct information as needed.

- Expect your students to use the strategies you have taught them in all of their work.

- Always take time to model two or three words with each new lesson.

- Have your students save their work in folders or notebooks. Too often students see vocabulary as "just for the moment"—to enable them to pass a test. If you require vocabulary notebooks, they are more likely to remember the words and continue to use them.

## 2-2 Reading Dictionary Definitions

Using this strategy, students learn to read a dictionary entry and recognize the parts of a dictionary definition. It can be used with other vocabulary strategies included in this section.

When students are asked to define words using a dictionary or a glossary, they often simply copy what they find in the text without actually reading or making an effort to understand the definition. Definitions often use unfamiliar words and are in small print, making them hard to read. In addition, the extra information in each dictionary entry may be confusing, and sometimes more than one definition is included. These challenges can add to students' work and cause frustration.

## Before Class

- Make overhead transparencies of *Tools 2-2a*, *2-2b*, and *2-2c*.

- Make overhead transparencies of definitions from class dictionaries or textbooks.

## During Class

1. Using *Tool 2-2a*, read the definition of *electron microscope* and review the components of a definition with your class.

2. Point out and discuss the pronunciation keys and the rules for breaking words into syllables. (See **2-4 Pronunciation**.)

3. Remind your students about the parts of speech, and help them with abbreviations. (For more information see **3-13 Recognizing Parts of Speech**.)

4. Select words from the students' text that are unfamiliar, and practice pronouncing them using the pronunciation key and the syllable divisions.

5. Using *Tools 2-2b* and *2-2c*, read the definitions with your students and review each definition and other elements of the dictionary entry.

6. Notice the labels and explanations in the first column and the definitions in the second column.

7. Remind students that *synonyms* are words that mean the same or almost the same thing as the word being defined.

8. Explain that derivations, roots, prefixes, and suffixes can help people remember new words. They can also help with spelling and with figuring out meanings of unfamiliar words that contain familiar roots, prefixes, or suffixes.

9. Discuss problems that your students face when they must copy and then remember long definitions.

10. Brainstorm ways of attacking long definitions.

11. Tell your students that breaking down long definitions makes it easier to master words on their vocabulary lists. Model the **2-3 Breaking Down Definitions** strategy to teach this skill.

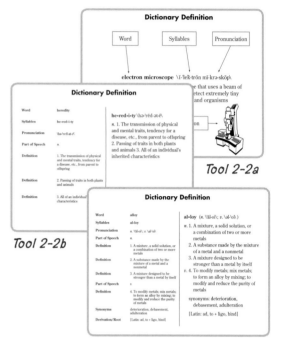

*Tool 2-2a*

*Tool 2-2b*

*Tool 2-2c*

## 2-3 Breaking Down Definitions

Students can use this strategy to break down definitions into useful chunks. When students break down a definition, they must read carefully, separate information, and make decisions.

**Handy Pages**

### Before Class

- Make overhead transparencies and student copies of *Tools 2-2a, 2-3a, 2-3b,* and *2-3c.*

- Select three or four definitions from a textbook glossary or class dictionary to use with your demonstration. Make transparencies or have your students use their books when you use these definitions as examples.

*Tool 2-3a*

### During Class

1. Preview the process of breaking down definitions.

    - Read all of the words and definitions on *Tool 2-3a* with your students.

    - Point out the organization of the definitions: The definitions are in an informal outline form, using dashes and indented bullets. (See **4-7 Planning with an Informal Outline.**)

    - Discuss why this format makes it easy to read the details in the definition.

2. Explain how to determine the category for definitions of nouns.

    - Tell your students that the word next to the dash in the center column will indicate the category to which the word belongs. (The category answers the question "What is it?") The category gives them the boldest and most important hint they need to remember a word.

    - Using *Tool 2-3a*, review the examples with your students and note the categories of each.

    - Have your students review additional definitions and determine the category for each. You may wish to write the following examples on the board and have your students start with these before moving on to words that they are using in other content areas.

        **pilgrimage,** n. A journey to a holy or sacred place; a journey through life

        **telescope, 1.** n. An instrument that can be used to see far-away objects such as stars and planets  —**2.** v. To slide something in or out in overlapping sections, as one would the sections of a small hand telescope

**3.** Break down a definition.

- Review the definition of *electron microscope* on *Tool 2-2a* with your students.

- Using *Tool 2-3b*, write *electron microscope* in the left column. Begin breaking down the definition by finding the category (answering the "What is it?" question). Write the category in the middle column next to a dash.

- Then add the rest of the information in the definition next to the bullets, using words and phrases.

- Have your students compare and discuss the difference between the definition of *electron microscope* on *Tool 2-2a* and the broken-down definition. Ask them why the broken-down definition might be more helpful and easier to study.

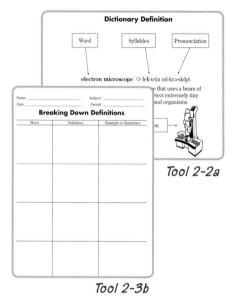

*Tool 2-2a*

*Tool 2-3b*

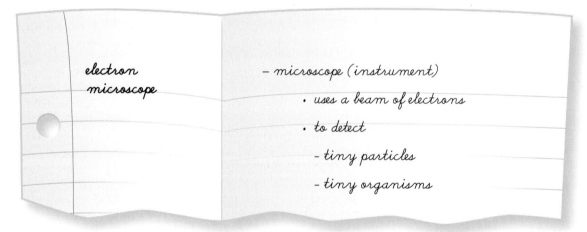

electron microscope

    – microscope (instrument)

        • uses a beam of electrons

        • to detect

          – tiny particles

          – tiny organisms

- Have your students review additional definitions and determine the category for each. If you used them as examples earlier you may wish to have your students complete breaking down the definitions of *pilgrimage* and *telescope*.

- Have them continue the process using words from their content-area classes.

**Note:** Words with more than one meaning will have more than one category.

*heredity*

- transmission of traits
  - physical
  - mental
- set of characteristics
  - inherited by an individual, plant or animal

**4.** Introduce verbs and adjectives.

- Verbs and adjectives do not have categories. Only nouns have categories. Definitions of verbs and adjectives use *synonyms*—words that mean the same or almost the same thing. Students often find definitions for verbs and adjectives easier to read and understand because they usually include two or more synonyms.

- Introduce breaking down the definitions of verbs and adjectives using *Tool 2-3c.*

- Have your students practice breaking down the definitions of verbs and adjectives by writing synonyms for verbs and adjectives that you have selected in the middle column on *Tool 2-3b.*

*Tool 2-3c*

**5.** Touch on the usefulness of illustrations and examples.

- Point out the pictures in the third column.

- Remind your students that sketches, illustrations, graphs, examples, and charts will help them remember words and their meanings.

- Discuss other options for using the third column, such as:

  | | |
  |---|---|
  | student's own definition | personal connection |
  | notes from class | teacher's comments |
  | definition in context (with page number) | sentence using the word |

**6.** Reread the broken-down definitions with your students and ask them to rephrase the definitions, putting them into their own words. Make plans for using the third column.

7. Continue to model breaking down additional words and have your students practice using content-area glossary terms and words from vocabulary lists that they must master.

**Note:** Most of the time students include only the term and its definition when they break down a definition. Adding the parts of speech and breaking the word into syllables are optional. How much you will want to include depends on time, the subject, your students, and your goals.

## 2-4 Pronunciation

This strategy presents a number of ways for students to learn the pronunciation of important words. When students can pronounce and spell a word, they are able to make the word a part of their working vocabulary. You can use these techniques together or separately.

### During Class

1. Start by reviewing pronunciation keys and words that are broken into syllables. Use a transparency of *Tool 2-2a* or of selected words from a textbook glossary or dictionary that your students use.

2. Select additional words from the students' text that are unfamiliar; practice pronouncing them using the pronunciation key and the syllables.

3. Break words into syllables for your students. Teach them to do the same.

4. Ask your students to echo words as you pronounce them. Together, read through a list of words two or three times until your students feel comfortable.

5. Consider making a recording of the vocabulary list for students who are absent or need to hear the words often.

### Additional Ideas

• Expect your students to use and correctly pronounce vocabulary words as they ask or answer questions.

• Give your students opportunities to work in pairs as they practice saying all of the words from a vocabulary list.

• Review new words frequently, asking your students to pronounce them the next day or a week after initial instruction.

# 2-5 Meaningful Vocabulary Sentences

Students can use the Meaningful Vocabulary Sentences strategy to gain a deeper understanding of their vocabulary words and how to use them correctly. It also helps students develop sentence-writing skills and sets a standard for good sentences.

Students will transfer the concept of writing meaningful vocabulary sentences to sentences that are not connected to learning new vocabulary. You will notice an improvement in the quality of their sentences in all writing assignments.

## Before Class

Make overhead transparencies and student copies of *2-5a* and *2-5b*.

## During Class

1. Define each kind of vocabulary sentence and discuss the differences.

   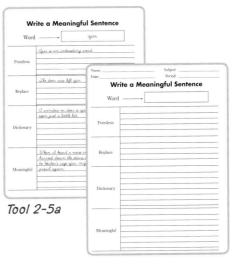

   *Tool 2-5a*

   *Tool 2-5b*

   • **Pointless sentence:** Does not demonstrate mastery of the word.

   • **Replace sentence:** Looks better than a pointless sentence but still does not demonstrate mastery or understanding of the word; often just adds more descriptors and prepositional phrases. In a replace sentence, a number of words could easily replace the vocabulary word.

   • **Dictionary sentence:** Turns a definition into a sentence. A student could write a good dictionary sentence and still not understand the new vocabulary term.

   • **Meaningful sentence:** Is filled with meaning and demonstrates mastery of the word; includes words and phrases that paint a picture for the reader.

2. Using *Tool 2-5a*, read the example and discuss the differences in the four kinds of vocabulary sentences for the word *ajar* with your class.

3. Ask your students if they have ever had difficulty writing sentences for new vocabulary words. Explain how you feel when you are trying to grade sentences that are well written but really do not demonstrate mastery of a word. Assure your students that they will all be able to write meaningful sentences.

4. Model writing the four kinds of sentences for one or two additional sets of sentences. You may want to use the words found on *Tools 2-2a, 2-2b, 2-2c, 2-3a*, or *2-3c*.

5. Have students practice with copies of *Tool 2-5b*, working individually or in pairs.

## Additional Ideas

Tell your students that they should apply what they have learned about meaningful vocabulary sentences to sentence writing in general. Instead of using a vocabulary word to write each sentence, they can try the following:

- Write a pointless and a meaningful sentence about the story that they just read.
- Describe the main character in a story by writing a pointless and a meaningful sentence.
- Write a meaningful sentence that describes the scene outside the classroom windows.
- Write a meaningful sentence to describe an event in their history textbook.
- Write a dictionary sentence to define or explain an unfamiliar term in a story.
- Write a meaningful sentence to describe the scene in a picture in a newspaper.

**Textbook Chapter on the Plague**

| | |
|---|---|
| **Pointless sentence** | I read about the plague. |
| **Replace sentence** | I read about the plague in my history book. |
| **Dictionary sentence** | A plague is a contagious disease that causes a disaster because it spreads quickly from one person to the next. |
| **Meaningful sentence** | Many plagues have occurred throughout history, but one of the worst was the Black Plague in medieval Europe, which wiped out nearly one-third of the population. |

### Meaningful Sentence Posters

1. Have your students work in pairs. Give each pair a piece of white legal-size paper, markers, rulers, and a word.

2. Have each pair create a mini-poster for the word they have been assigned. The posters should include a neat border (one that fits the meaning of the word, if possible), neat printing, straight lines, a list of the four types of sentences, and a sample for each type of sentence. The more specific your directions are regarding lettering, neatness, size of printing, and arrangement of information, the better their product will be.

3. Have each pair share their poster by reading all four samples. Celebrate your students' success. The poster activity establishes a common language about what you mean (and want) when you refer to good sentences.

4. Post your students' work around your classroom for several days.

# 2-6 Vocabulary Maps

The Vocabulary Maps strategy provides students with a visual way to learn and remember new vocabulary words. It will help your students see words in a new way and lets them show off by demonstrating all they know about particular words.

**Prerequisites:** 2-3 Breaking Down Definitions and 2-5 Meaningful Vocabulary Sentences

## Before Class

- Make an overhead transparency of *Tool 2-6a* and student copies of *Tool 2-6b*.

- *Bonus Tools 2-6-1* and *2-6-2* provide additional support.

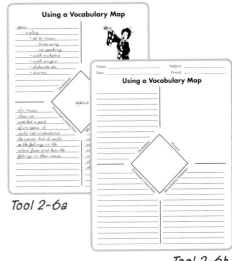

Tool 2-6a

Tool 2-6b

## During Class

1. Give students copies of *Tool 2-6b*. Using the overhead transparency of *Tool 2-6a*, read the vocabulary map for the word *opera* with the class. Discuss all four elements on the map.

2. Assure your students that the illustration is just a sketch—a drawing that will help them remember a word and its definition. If they wish, students can use pictures from magazines.

3. Tell your students that making a personal connection with a new word will help them learn and remember the word.

4. Point out that this format includes the **2-3 Breaking Down Definitions** and **2-5 Meaningful Vocabulary Sentences** strategies, which they have already learned.

5. Have your students complete *Tool 2-6b* using words they are learning.

6. Have your students save their Vocabulary Maps in folders or notebooks and prompt them to review them periodically. Too often students view vocabulary development as just for the moment—to enable them to pass a test. If you require vocabulary notebooks, your students are more likely to remember the words and continue to use them.

## Additional Ideas

Your students will enjoy looking for new ways to create Vocabulary Maps. Give them opportunities to experiment. Use the following examples or invent new approaches. (These examples are also found on *Bonus Tools 2-6-1* and *2-6-2*.)

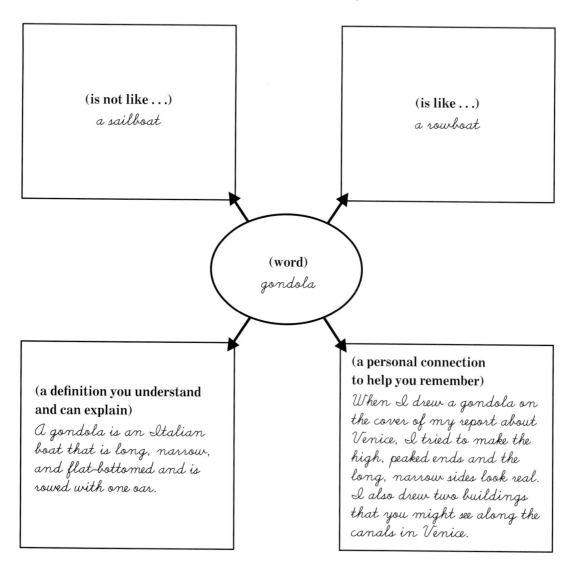

(is not like . . .)
*a sailboat*

(is like . . .)
*a rowboat*

(word)
*gondola*

**(a definition you understand and can explain)**
*A gondola is an Italian boat that is long, narrow, and flat-bottomed and is rowed with one oar.*

**(a personal connection to help you remember)**
*When I drew a gondola on the cover of my report about Venice, I tried to make the high, peaked ends and the long, narrow sides look real. I also drew two buildings that you might see along the canals in Venice.*

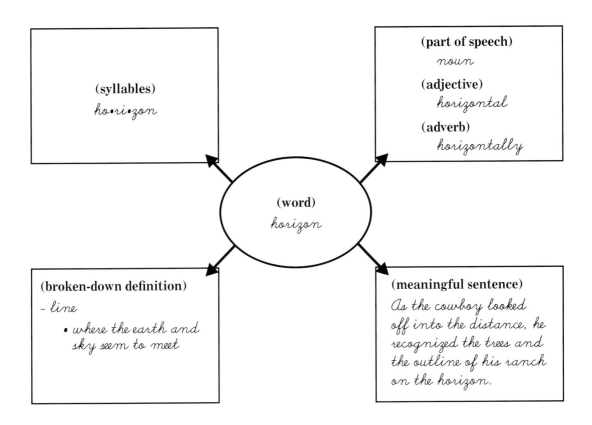

(syllables)

ho•ri•zon

(part of speech)

noun

(adjective)

horizontal

(adverb)

horizontally

(word)

horizon

(broken-down definition)

- line
  • where the earth and
    sky seem to meet

(meaningful sentence)

As the cowboy looked
off into the distance, he
recognized the trees and
the outline of his ranch
on the horizon.

## 2-7 Concept Maps

Students can use the Concept Maps strategy as a visual process for analyzing new terms and important concepts. Students will add details and examples to a Concept Map and then use that information to write a full definition in a paragraph format.

### Before Class

- Make overhead transparencies and student copies of *Tools 2-7a* and *2-7b*.

- Choose words to use for modeling and practice from content that your students are studying or have already learned.

*Bonus Tools 2-7-1* and *2-7-2* provide additional support.

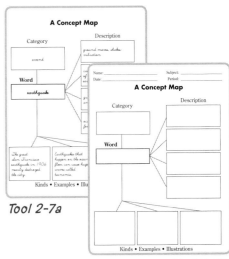

Tool 2-7a

Tool 2-7b

## During Class

1. With your students, review the concept map for the word *earthquake* on *Tool 2-7a*. Discuss each of the different sections with your students.

2. Model using one of the words you have chosen to fill in the "Term" box and the "Category" box on the left side of *Tool 2-7b*. Tell your students to ask themselves "What is it?" when they are searching for a word to use in the category box.

3. Together, fill in the "Description" boxes with words and phrases.

4. In the boxes at the bottom, add information that demonstrates understanding. Use examples or make illustrations. Students may write phrases or complete sentences.

5. Before asking your students to create concept maps on their own, have them work in pairs or groups of three. If possible, share and display the maps.

6. If time permits, have your students turn the information in the category and description boxes into a definition paragraph. Add a second paragraph to share the examples and illustrations. Definition paragraphs for Concept Maps are specific and stick to the facts. They give students the opportunity to show what they know about a term or concept. The following example, which also appears on *Bonus Tool 2-7-1*, and other examples from *Bonus Tool 2-7-2* show how students can use creative writing and personal experiences to describe a concept.

### Earthquake

An earthquake is an event caused by movements in the tectonic plates of the earth's crust. When this happens, the ground moves, shakes, and/or vibrates. Those in the earthquake zone can see and feel the ground move up and down or sideways. These quakes occur along geological formations called faults.

Some earthquakes are minor and are hardly felt at all, but the great San Francisco quake of 1906 nearly destroyed the city. When earthquakes happen on the ocean floor, they can cause huge waves called tsunamis. The tsunami on December 26, 2004, in the Indian Ocean killed nearly 300,000 people.

# 2-8 Vocabulary Study Guides

This strategy helps students study for vocabulary tests by prompting them to concentrate on words that they have not yet mastered. The goal is for students to create study guides of their own using the vocabulary strategies they have learned.

**Prerequisite:** 2-3 Breaking Down Definitions

## Before Class

- Make transparencies and student copies of *Tools 2-8a, 2-8b*, and *2-8c* as needed.
- Choose words that your students need to know to use for modeling and practice.

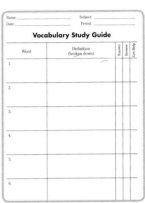

*Tool 2-8a*

## Introducing a Study Guide

1. Write one of the words you have chosen in the first column of *Tool 2-8a*.

2. Add the definition in the middle column. It is best for your students to write the definition in their own words, not just copy one out of the dictionary. Encourage students to break down the definition.

3. Explain to your students that they will use two columns to the right ("Known" and "Review") to self-evaluate how well they know their vocabulary words.

4. Explain that they should mark these columns to indicate which words they need to know and which they need to study. Point out that many students often spend time studying words they already know. Instead they should use their time on words they need to study.

5. Tell your students they will use the "Review" column to indicate words that need lots of review.

6. Explain that the third column, "Get Help," is meant to encourage them to ask for help if they have no idea what a word means or how to use it correctly.

7. Model with additional words and then have your students practice with words they are expected to know.

## Additional Ideas

- *Tool 2-8b* reminds students that it is not enough just to know the definition. In subjects like history, science, and art, it is important to move beyond definitions and give details about words' significance. Information students add to the third column explains why the word is important to learn.

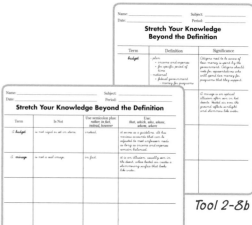

*Tool 2-8b*

*Tool 2-8c*

- *Tool 2-8c* helps students write compound sentences with conjunctive adverbs and semicolons that demonstrate students' mastery of the words. Review the examples on *Tool 2-8c* and point out how the first half of the compound contrasts with the second half. Explain how this demonstrates what a term is and what it is not. Have your students practice writing additional compound sentences in the space provided.

- Give or brainstorm with your students other headings that might be substituted or added to a study guide, such as:
  - ▶ Definition in Context
  - ▶ Prediction About the Meaning (jotted down as students read)
  - ▶ Page Number and Paragraph in Text (to help locate the word again)
  - ▶ Comments from a Class Discussion or Lecture
  - ▶ Part of Speech
  - ▶ Alternate Meaning
  - ▶ Synonym or Antonym
  - ▶ Personal Connection
  - ▶ Hint to Remember the Correct Spelling

  Have them collect their study guides in folders or in notebooks.

**Note:** The 2-3 Breaking Down Definitions, 2-6 Vocabulary Maps, and 2-7 Concept Maps strategies can also be used as study guides. The goal is for students to create study guides of their own using the vocabulary strategies they have learned.

## 2-9 Vocabulary Note Cards

In this strategy, students use note cards to learn and remember vocabulary words. Vocabulary note cards are great tools for studying because they are easy to use and can make information more visual.

### Before Class

- Make an overhead transparency of *Tool 2-9a.*
- Provide students with 3" × 5" cards so that they can make note cards for themselves.
- Choose words your students need to know for modeling and practice.

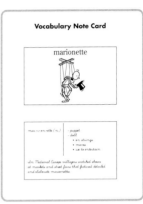

*Tool 2-9a*

### During Class

1. Begin by reviewing *Tool 2-9a* with your students and then continue modeling using one of your preselected words. Point out features on the front and the back of the card.

2. Have your students fill in their note cards as you model.

   - On the front of the vocabulary note card, have them neatly print the word in big letters.
   - Have them add a sketch that will help them remember the word's meaning.
   - On the back of the card, have them print the word, but this time divide it into syllables and identify the part of speech.
   - On the right side, have them break down the definition using the **2-3 Breaking Down Definitions** strategy.
   - At the bottom of the card, have your students add a sentence to show mastery of the word and to help them remember the word during a test.

3. After your students have become successful working as a class, have them work in pairs and individually.

## 2-10 Categories

Students use this strategy to group words into categories to help with memory and comprehension.

*Bonus Tool 2-10-1* provides additional support.

Whenever students categorize a new term and connect it with similar words and familiar concepts, they move closer to mastering it. The category puts the term into a space or mental folder they know and will remember. Once students connect with the category, they almost always remember more details from the definition.

- When your students receive a long list of words to study for a test, teach them to divide the words on the list into categories.

- Model a list of words that you want your students to remember, or use the following lists. Discuss the difference between List A and List B. (Also on *Bonus Tool 2-10-1*.) Which one would be easier to memorize? Which list is easier on the eyes? Which one makes more sense? How does sorting the words into categories make the list easier to read and remember?

| List A | List B |
|---|---|
| Niels Bohr | scientists |
| Chancellorsville | Niels Bohr |
| battles | Marie Curie |
| Gettysburg | Rene Descartes |
| Rene Descartes | battles |
| Shiloh | Chancellorsville |
| Marie Curie | Gettysburg |
| scientists | Shiloh |
| Manassas | Manassas |

- Teach your students to sort history terms into categories like *people, places, events, inventions, battles, documents,* and so on.

- Science terms can be sorted into *processes, formulas, discoveries, events, scientists, diseases, animals, plants, equipment,* and so on.

- In language arts class, your students can sort words into groups labeled *parts of speech, elements of a story,* and so on.

#  Personification of Abstract Nouns

Students personify abstract nouns to develop and demonstrate understanding and creativity.

Help your students develop and demonstrate mastery of abstract nouns by asking them to create sentences or short paragraphs that bring an abstract noun to life through personification.

## Before Class

- Make an overhead transparency of *Tool 2-11a* and copies of *Tools 2-11b* and *2-11c* for students to keep as a reference.

 *Bonus Tool 2-11-1* provides additional support.

## During Class

1. Explain to your students that abstract nouns are nouns that name intangible concepts, such as freedom, kindness, anxiety, and fear, and that when writers use *personification*, they give human attributes to these concepts.

2. With your class, read the example sentences on *Tool 2-11a*. Explain how the words are personified.

3. Read through the list of abstract nouns on *Tools 2-11b* and *2-11c*. Select two or three words. With help from your students, create your own personification sentences.

4. Give your students hints by asking questions about the selected abstract nouns.

*Tool 2-11a*

*Tool 2-11b*

*Tool 2-11c*

### Freedom

Where does Freedom live?

What are his or her goals for life?

What is his or her favorite color?

How does he or she spend weekends?

What are her or his hobbies?

Who are Freedom's best friends? His or her enemies?

5. When students first begin to write personifications, you may want to suggest that they first create a setting (a time and a place) and then use action verbs as they describe the abstract noun. Reinforce that sentences should paint a picture with meaningful details that demonstrate the concept being personified.

6. If your students struggle, try using a framed paragraph. (Also on *Bonus Tool 2-11-1*. For more information, see 1-8 Framed Responses.)

---

**Friendship**

Friendship _____ into the party wearing _____ _____. She went immediately to the hostess and _____.
Everyone was happy that Friendship could make it to the party because

_____. Friendship is _____ to everyone.
At work she _____. At home she _____ _____. She also _____ _____.

---

**Friendship**

Friendship *ran* into the party wearing *her favorite shirt, comfortable jeans, and bright red loafers.* She went immediately up to the hostess and *offered to help carry the picnic supplies outside.* Everyone was happy that Friendship could make it to the party because *she always has good stories to tell and listens as others describe their latest adventures.* Friendship is *sincere and kind* to everyone. At work she *encourages the college volunteers to try their best.* At home she *helps with homework assignments and gives advice about running for student council.* She also *makes sure that she has time each day to read and to take a two-mile walk.*

---

# 2-12 Poetry Pieces

Poetry Pieces prompt students to write poems using strong vocabulary words selected from a text.

One way to help your students apply new words they have learned to their writing is to use the Poetry Pieces strategy. (See **9-15 Poetry** for other poetry strategies.)

## Before Class

- Make an overhead transparency and student copies of *Tool 2-12a*.
- Select articles, historical documents, brochures, or a page from a novel your class is reading to use for demonstration and practice.

*Tool 2-12a*

## During Class

1. Have your students read an item that you have selected. As they read, have them highlight words and phrases that are interesting, unusual, unfamiliar, or just catchy.

2. Instruct them to cut out the words and place them on a white sheet of paper so they are easy to read. As they arrange and rearrange the words, they will create poems. (If students cannot cut the words out of their reading material, have them write the words on small pieces of paper.)

4. Use *Tool 2-12a* to demonstrate how to turn the words into poems. Students may use many or only a few of the words to create their poems. They can also add words of their own.

5. Give your students time and supplies so that they can display their work.

# 2-13 Homonyms, Homophones, and Homographs

Using this strategy, students learn about and demonstrate mastery of homonyms, homophones, and homographs.

## Before Class

Make overhead transparencies and student copies of *Tools 2-13a*, *2-13b*, and *2-13c* as needed.

## During Class

It is usually best to teach each of these types of words separately, starting with homonyms. Once your students understand and can use homonyms, introduce them to homophones and homographs as appropriate.

1. Use *Tool 2-13a* to introduce homonyms to your students. Use only the section of *Tool 2-13a* that you are explaining to them and cover up the sections you have not yet introduced.

2. Use *Tool 2-13b* to review examples of homonyms. Point out and discuss how the words are used differently in each sentence depending on their meaning. Write an additional word in the space provided and with your class write sentences that go with the different meanings of each word.

3. At the top of *Tool 2-13c* or on their own notebook paper, have your students write the type of word (homonyms, homophones, or homographs) you are having them practice. Using words you have chosen, have students write sentences on their copies of *Tool 2-13c*.

4. Make a list of words that you want to present and help students learn them throughout the school year.

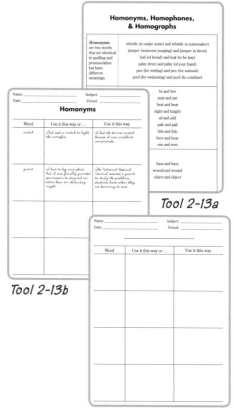

Tool 2-13a

Tool 2-13b

Tool 2-13c

## 2-14 Unit- or Subject-Specific Word Lists

In this strategy, students use content-area vocabulary lists to improve their writing and speaking.

When answering questions orally or in writing, students oftentimes forget new vocabulary. One way to help your students write and use content-area vocabulary in subjects like social studies, art, and science is to provide word lists as prompts. A list of words might be used for just a week as students study a specific unit or might be needed throughout the year as they study terms for a subject, such as geography.

### Before Class

Make an overhead transparency of a list of the words your students need to know for a particular subject or unit of study. Make copies for your students to keep in their notebooks.

### During Class

1. Display the overhead transparency frequently to review terms as you continue your unit. For example, a lesson on technology could include a word list like the one below.

**Technology**

| | | |
|---|---|---|
| Web page | control panel | browser |
| cell | capacity | cursor |
| operating system | word processing | search engine |
| PC | computer | format |
| electronic | HTML | disk |
| network | laser | scanner |
| media | tools | radar |
| URLs | transistor | hardware |
| solar | software | satellite |
| graphics | program | peripherals |
| patent | download | pixel |
| virus | byte | RAM |
| gigabyte | defragmenter | database application |
| backup file | configuration | cyberspace |

2. When you prepare a list of words, add a row of blank lines. As your students read, ask them to find other important words to add to the list.

3. Encourage your students to show off by using a set of words from the list to write a good short paragraph. Select (or have your students select) three or four words from the list to make up a set, and then have your students use all of the words from the set in a four- to six-sentence paragraph, showing off what they have learned.

## Additional Ideas

- With help from your students, divide the list into categories. (See the **2-10 Categories** strategy.)

- Using a transparency, show your students how to break the words into syllables.

- Ask your students to highlight the words they know. Explain that they know a word if they can use the word in a meaningful sentence. (See **2-5 Meaningful Vocabulary Sentences**.)

- Make copies of new words on cardstock. Have them posted in the room so that your students can refer to them during discussions and when they answer questions.

- Read the words aloud with the class to help develop fluency. Ask your students to read the lists to each other.

- Challenge your students to a two-minute conversation with a friend. The topic of the conversation is *technology*, and the goal is to stay on topic. Have them use their word lists to keep the conversation going.

- Put words on separate cards and ask students to arrange the words in alphabetical order.

- Have your students work in pairs. Each student in the pair selects two words from the list and explains to his or her classmate the word and its importance.

- Make a class set of pictures to represent each word. Find pictures for each word, using old magazines, daily newspapers, or clip art files. Use cardstock or construction paper. Ask your students to neatly display the picture on one side and the word on the other. When the pictures are complete, use them for review. Ask individual students for a sentence to match one of the pictures.

Sentence writing is the foundation for writing compositions of all types. Strong, vivid sentences provide an avenue for expressing the ideas, thoughts, and purpose of a composition. By establishing good sentence-writing skills, students will be more likely to succeed in school and in many occupations. *Step Up to Writing* provides students with a strong foundation that will enable them to write sentences that are not only well constructed and interesting, but ones that also communicate their ideas clearly and effectively.

Because we sometimes speak in single words, phrases, and incomplete sentences, some students assume it is acceptable to write this way, as well. As such, they require direct instruction to understand the structure of a complete sentence. In addition, we sometimes use different syntax—the pattern by which words, phrases, or clauses are put together to form sentences—when we speak than when we write. Because written syntax is often more complex than spoken syntax, students benefit from direct instruction and the chance to practice writing a variety of sentence types so their writing is fluent, without any jarring irregularities. Furthermore, it is important that students from all backgrounds master the global conventions of English so they can communicate with a wider audience.

Success with sentence mastery comes when students are introduced to

- The difference between fragments and sentences, and how to turn a fragment into a sentence, especially when they need to respond to a question or a prompt in a complete sentence;

- The types of sentence structures (simple, compound, interrogative, declarative, and so on), the need for variety in sentence length and structure, and opportunities to practice sentence writing;

- Good examples of clearly written sentences in others' writing;

- Parts of speech, sentence diagrams, and rules of grammar;

- Playing with language; experimenting with alliteration, comparison, or exaggeration; varying word choice and word placement, and so on;

- Writing for different audiences and purposes and the influence these have on the content, structure, and length of a sentence.

## When Teaching Sentence Writing

- Teach students who need help writing complete sentences the difference between a sentence and a fragment, and then give them adequate practice turning fragments into sentences. Also, provide students with the basic knowledge and skills they need to master English syntax, especially sentence diagramming.

- Have students combine shorter sentences into longer ones. This is a highly effective way to improve their writing. Remind students to read their sentences to themselves—silently or aloud—and ask if they make sense and are easy to follow.

- Once students are proficient at writing basic sentences and understand the components of a complete sentence, introduce strategies that will further develop their ability to write a variety of sentence types and structures.

- After students have developed initial sentence-writing skills, provide ongoing practice through daily activities such as warm-ups, tickets out, and lesson wrap-ups.

- Teach students the parts of speech as a way to help them improve word choice. Have students identify parts of speech using the labeling system presented in this section. You can also give students framed paragraphs in which the blanks require adjectives and adverbs. Then have students complete the framed paragraphs and share their results. Alternatively, substitute proper nouns for all pronouns in a paragraph, for instance, to illustrate how different (and silly) language would sound without certain parts of speech.

• Teach students to review their sentences during the revision process to develop precise, interesting word choice and to add additional descriptive details. Focus on varying the beginnings of sentences as a way to make their writing more interesting.

IDEA BANK

## Tips for Using These Strategies Across Content Areas

✓ Use content-specific terms and knowledge in a variety of sentence types, and have students do the same.

✓ Have students respond to questions in their textbooks in social studies, science, health, and so on, using a variety of sentence types and structures.

✓ Have students present **8-10** Persuasive Speeches on an issue in the content area or to evaluate a work of art, music, recipe, and so on.

✓ Consider using **1-35** Great Short Answers or **2-5** Meaningful Vocabulary Sentences to help students write about content they are studying using a specified sentence structure.

✓ Have English language learners use **3-2** Three- and Four-Part Sentences to help them master the conventions of English syntax, and use **3-4** Writing Rebus Sentences to help them practice both syntax and the appropriate use of vocabulary words.

Choose those strategies that best meet the needs of your students.

# Learning Sentence Writing

Some students need extra help mastering the basics of sentence writing. Others need encouragement to be more precise, accurate, or creative. The strategies in the first part of this section help students learn sentence writing by teaching them the difference between a sentence and a fragment and teaching them a variety of methods for writing effective sentences.

## Objectives

- Provide instruction, review, and practice to help students master sentence writing skills
- Give students visual and hands-on strategies to ensure success
- Empower students to vary sentence length and sentence structure

| Strategy | Strategy Description | Page | Tools |
|---|---|---|---|
| **3-1** Fragments and Sentences | Distinguishing fragments and complete sentences | 96 | 3-1a, 3-1b |
| **3-2** Three- and Four-Part Sentences | Visualizing sentences in small chunks that make up a complete thought | 97 | 3-2a, 3-2b |
| **3-3** Using Sentence Strips | Using a novel way to write sentences, and seeing a sentence as continuous text | 98 | 3-3a |
| **3-4** Writing Rebus Sentences | Writing sentences using pictures | 99 | 3-4a, 3-4b |
| **3-5** Sentences Using *Who, What, Where, When, Action,* and *How* | Using six terms to generate sentences and vary sentence lengths and structures | 100 | 3-5a to 3-5e |

[P] Consider using the Posters with the strategies in this section.

## 3-1 Fragments and Sentences

Using the Fragments and Sentences strategy, students distinguish between a fragment and a complete sentence or thought.

### Before Class

Make overhead transparencies and student copies of *Tools 3-1a* and *3-1b*.

### During Class

1. Explain that a sentence is a complete thought with a subject and verb, while a fragment is a phrase or group of words that are related but do not make a complete thought with a subject and a verb. Emphasize that fragments are almost always mistakes. Some writers use fragments for emphasis, to make a point, or to add variety to their writing, but the use of fragments should be a rare exception.

2. Display *Tool 3-1a*. Point out the differences between fragments and complete sentences. With students, arrange the fragments in different ways and create other complete sentences.

3. Using *Tool 3-1b*, turn additional fragments into sentences. For instance, discuss the word *because*. Create fragments using the word *because*, and then turn the fragments into complete sentences.

4. Give students additional fragments to list on the left side of the Tool, and have them write complete sentences on the right side. Alternatively, have students create their own fragments for the left column. They can then use their fragments or fragments created by another student to write complete sentences.

Tool 3-1a

Tool 3-1b

**Note:** Whenever possible, practice writing fragments and sentences using content-area materials.

# 3-2 Three- and Four-Part Sentences

With this strategy, students write a sentence in chunks on sections of folded paper so that they can better see the parts of a sentence. They then read all the chunks together to create a complete sentence.

**Handy Pages**

You can use the Three- and Four-Part Sentences strategy at any time, in any content area, to review concepts or to introduce new ideas.

## Before Class

- Make overhead transparencies of *Tools 3-2a* and *3-2b*.
- Make student copies and a teacher copy of *Tool 3-2b*, or have students use notebook paper.
- Have available red and green overhead markers and scissors.

## During Class

*Tool 3-2a*

1. Using *Tool 3-2a*, explain that each section represents a different part of a sentence.

   - The three-part sentence has:
     - ▸ A **who** section, telling who performed the action
     - ▸ An **action** section, telling what action was performed
     - ▸ A **what** section, telling who or what the action was done to

   - The four-part sentence has:
     - ▸ All of the same parts as a three-part sentence
     - ▸ A **when** section, telling when the action occurred

2. Point out that many of the folded sections contain phrases—a group of two or more related words.

| | | | |
|---|---|---|---|
| **when** | during the summer | **where** | on the dig site |
| **who** | the team of archaeologists | **what** | evidence of a settlement |

3. Cut a paper copy of *Tool 3-2b* in half along the dashed line. Different folds will be needed for three- and four-part sentences. Explain that the vertical dotted lines indicate where the paper will be folded. Demonstrate how to fold the paper with blank pieces of notebook paper. Have students do the same with their copies.

4. Then have students write *who, action, what,* for a three-part sentence in the column heads. When teaching four-part sentences, add a column for *when.*

5. Model writing sentences on *Tool 3-2b.* Start with a strong action verb—such as *developed, imitated,* or *secured*—and build a sentence around it. Demonstrate building a sentence around the verb by writing each chunk of the sentence separately and then putting the chunks together.

6. With your students, create other sentences using verbs like *inflated, escaped, conquered, bombarded, lounged, defended, salvaged, scampered, observed,* and *bothered.*

7. Use a green marker to emphasize the capital letter needed at the beginning of the sentence and a red marker to emphasize the punctuation needed at the end. Practice writing sentences often. Keep in mind that students who are either just learning to write or who have made a habit of writing incomplete or run-on sentences will need lots of practice.

*Tool 3-2b*

## Additional Ideas

• In a three-part sentence, place the action verb in the center section. In a four-part sentence, experiment with putting the verb in different positions. Experiment with different sentence configurations with your students.

• Once your students are familiar with the strategy, use content-area topics for writing. Ask your students to select strong action verbs from their textbooks to use for their sentences. Use pictures in textbooks to generate sentences.

## 3-3 Using Sentence Strips

Some students need to see how the segments of a three- or four-part sentence flow together to make one complete thought. Using this strategy promotes creativity and sets high standards for all sentence writing.

## Before Class

*Tool 3-3a*

• Make an overhead transparency and student copies of *Tool 3-3a.*

• Have available strips of paper approximately 4" × 36" (or commercial sentence strips), scissors, glue, and pictures from magazines or other sources (optional).

## During Class

Use long strips of paper—approximately 4" × 36"—and model the following process for students. Give students pictures, have them cut pictures from magazines, or use pictures on *Tool 3-3a*.

With two or three of the pictures, create a sentence that includes both the picture and the word to match the picture. Have students draft sentences on plain paper before they write them on the sentence strip. See 3-4 Writing Rebus Sentences for more ideas.

Display the strips around the room. Support your students when they have difficulty with spelling.

## 3-4  Writing Rebus Sentences

Using this strategy, students write sentences using a combination of words and images. This strategy helps beginning or struggling writers learn to write sentences by providing a visual, hands-on way to write. For more-skilled writers, the strategy provides a chance to be creative.

This can be a fun way to motivate students to write, and it will also reinforce neatness, attention to margins, and development of spelling and vocabulary skills.

### Before Class

- Make overhead transparencies of *Tools 3-3a* and *3-4a*.
- Make student copies of *Tool 3-4b* or use stickers.
- Have available a blank transparency, notebook paper, scissors, and glue.

### During Class

1. Display *Tool 3-3a* to introduce or review rebus sentences. Explain that these sentences will combine images and words.

2. Cut your transparency of *Tool 3-3a* apart. Choose one or more of the pictures and lay it on your blank transparency. With your students, make sentences using the pictures.

3. Give each student a copy of *Tool 3-3a*, scissors, and glue. (Stickers can be used instead of the Tool.) Have students cut the pictures on the Tool apart and select two or three to use for writing.

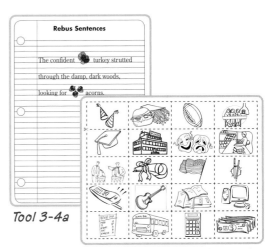

*Tool 3-4a*

*Tool 3-3a*

**4.** Ask students to create two rebus sentences on notebook paper, using the pictures followed by the words the pictures represent. Provide directions for what students should do when they do not know how to spell a word. Set high standards for neatness and use of margins. Require accurate spelling, punctuation, and capitalization. Give students time to share and display their work.

On the front porch of the [house icon] house, a friendly [dog icon] dog waited for the family to come home from the [park icon] park.

## 3-5 Sentences Using *Who, What, Where, When, Action,* and *How*

Students can use this strategy to write and rearrange sentences, identify the parts of a sentence, and expand sentences with descriptive words. Teach this strategy to help students eliminate sentence fragments and run-on sentences.

### Before Class

- Make overhead transparencies and student copies of *Tools 3-5a* through *3-5e*.
- Have available scissors.
- Optional: Have available red, pink, purple, orange, green, and yellow markers.

**Note:** This strategy builds on 3-2 Three- and Four-Part Sentences, and can be incorporated with 3-11 Sentence Variety.

### During Class

1. Using *Tool 3-5a*, explain that each part of the sentence can be labeled *Who, What, Where, When, Action,* or *How.*

2. Reviewing the examples on *Tool 3-5a*, illustrate how the same sentence can often be written in different ways by moving some sentence parts.

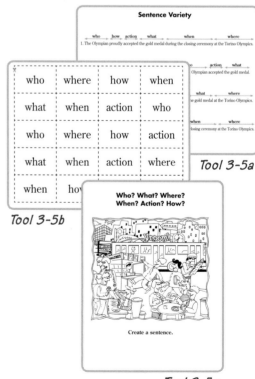

**Sentence Variety**

who    how    action    what         when         where
1. The Olympian proudly accepted the gold medal during the closing ceremony at the Torino Olympics.

| who | where | how | when |
|------|-------|--------|-------|
| what | when | action | who |
| who | where | how | action |
| what | when | action | where |
| when | ho... | | |

*Tool 3-5a*

*Tool 3-5b*

**Who? What? Where? When? Action? How?**

Create a sentence.

*Tool 3-5c*

3. Give your students copies of *Tool 3-5b* and scissors. Have students cut the words apart along the dashed line and use them at their desks. Consider having students highlight their pieces: red for Who , pink for What , purple for **Where** , orange for **When** , green for **Action** , and yellow for **How** .

4. Write several example sentences, and identify the sentence parts. Have students copy the sentences and then use their pieces of *Tool 3-5b* to identify each sentence part.

## Creating Sentences from Pictures

1. With your students, look at the picture on *Tool 3-5c*. You can also use pictures from content materials or magazines. Have students create sentences—or a story— describing the picture. Stress the use of strong action verbs, and expect sentences that show thinking and do more than state the obvious. Provide time to share.

2. Have your students use their pieces of *Tool 3-5b* to identify each part of their sentences.

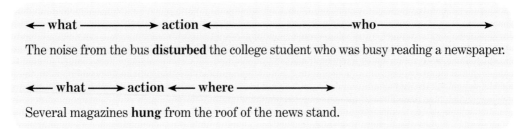

← what ———→ action ←————————who————————→

The noise from the bus **disturbed** the college student who was busy reading a newspaper.

←—— what ——→ action ←— where ——————→

Several magazines **hung** from the roof of the news stand.

## Creating Sentence Patterns

1. With your students, read the sample sentences on *Tool 3-5d*. Explain that one way to write creative sentences is to create a pattern and then write a sentence to fit that pattern. Point out that they can use some parts more than once in a sentence, as in the last example.

2. Using an overhead of *Tool 3-5e*, write words that show a sentence pattern—such as *Who, Action, What, When*—in the upper boxes in the first row. Then, write a sentence that matches that pattern in the boxes below. Remind students to use strong action verbs and lively descriptions.

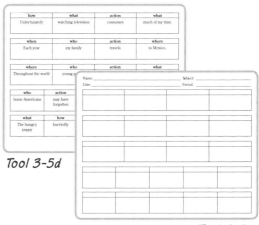

*Tool 3-5d*

*Tool 3-5e*

3. Have your students write patterns and sentences on their copies of *Tool 3-5e*. Remind them to start by selecting a strong action verb. Consider making a list of action verbs for or with your students before they start the assignment.

## Additional Ideas

- Have your students write sentences using content or vocabulary from history, science, math, or other subjects. Or, give them a theme or have them write about a color, a poem, a holiday, an assembly presentation, new school rules, the weather, or a world event.

- To help beginning or struggling writers with spelling, generate (on your own or with your students) a list of words to use in the sentences.

- Write words on index cards. Have students pull three to use in a sentence.

- Ask your students to find and copy sentences from newspapers that will fit the sentence sections on *Tool 3-5e*. Tell them to find and label the action verbs and the other parts in the sentences.

 For a quick check and other support for assessment, see **10-10 Quick Check for Sentences.**

# Practicing Sentence Writing

Students need practice to improve the quality of their writing. By using strategies that focus on various aspects of sentence writing and encouraging students to revise sentences until they are richly written and grammatically correct, *Step Up to Writing* gives all students numerous, guided opportunities to improve their writing.

## Objectives

- Help students revise sentences
- Teach and review different sentence types and structures
- Improve writing fluency and encourage creativity

| Strategy | Strategy Description | Page | Tools |
|---|---|---|---|
| **3-6** Better Sentences | Improving simple sentences with stronger action verbs and better descriptions | 104 | 3-6a |
| **3-7** Sentence Structures | Recognizing and using four different sentence structures: simple, compound, complex, and compound/complex | 105 | 3-7a, 3-7b |
| **3-8** Kinds of Sentences | Recognizing and using the four kinds of sentences: declarative, imperative, exclamatory, and interrogative | 106 | 3-8a |
| **3-9** Kinds of Sentences Combined with Sentence Structures | Writing different kinds of sentences and sentence structures | 107 | 3-9a, 3-9b |
| **3-10** Topic Sentences and Thesis Statements | Writing a variety of topic sentences and thesis statements using different sentence structures | 108 | n/a |

*(chart continues)*

| Strategy *(continued)* | Strategy Description | Page | Tools |
|---|---|---|---|
| **3-11** Sentence Variety | Writing several sentences for the same assignment, prompt, or topic, using different sentence structures | 108 | 3-11a, 3-11b |
| **3-12** Ticket Out | Writing interesting, error-free sentences | 116 | 3-12a, 3-12b |

P Consider using the Posters with the strategies in this section.

## 3-6 Better Sentences

Using this strategy, students improve simple sentences when they use better descriptions and stronger action verbs. It sets a high standard for sentences that your students write.

**Prerequisite: 3-2 Three- and Four-Part Sentences**

**Handy Pages**

### Before Class

- Make an overhead transparency of *Tool 3-6a*.

- Have available blank overhead transparencies, glue, and magazines and newspapers with lots of pictures. Cut out some of the pictures.

- Optional: Have available a thesaurus and 1½" × 2" sticky notes for each student.

### During Class

1. Display *Tool 3-6a*. Point out the fold lines and model folding a piece of notebook paper into sections.

2. Discuss the three rows. Point out the picture in the top row and explain that the sentence will describe something in the picture. Examine the difference between the two sentences, pointing out the vivid descriptors in the "better" sentence.

3. Display some of the pictures you selected. Using the blank transparencies, write several "first try" sentences with students.

4. Discuss the "first try" sentences. Ask for suggestions on making them "better" sentences. Write the "better" sentences below the "first try" sentences.

*Tool 3-6a*

5. Have your students search for pictures in the magazines and newspapers. Consider giving them a small sticky note and telling them to find pictures of a similar size. That way the pictures will be small enough to fit easily on their paper. Have them glue each picture onto notebook paper that they have folded.

6. Ask them to write a "first try" sentence or two for each picture in the middle row of their paper and then make those sentences into "better" sentences with strong action verbs and vivid descriptions.

7. Provide opportunities for them to share their "first try" and "better" sentences with the class.

## Additional Ideas

- Use the **1-35 Great Short Answers** strategy to get students to write better sentences. This strategy teaches students to use detailed complete sentences to answer questions, but it can also be used to write better sentences in general.

- The **2-5 Meaningful Vocabulary Sentences** strategy pushes students to demonstrate how well they understand and can use new words. Students can also use this strategy to write more meaningful, descriptive sentences. Use it to set high standards for the writing you expect from all your students.

- Use a variation on the **1-33 Money Summaries** strategy by providing a topic for students to write sentences about, rather than providing a text for them to summarize.

 For a quick check and other support for assessment, see **10-10 Quick Check for Sentences**.

# 3-7 Sentence Structures

Using this strategy, students learn or review how to recognize and use the four possible sentence structures—simple, compound, complex, and compound/complex—in all types of writing.

## Before Class

- Make overhead transparencies of *Tools 3-7a* and *3-7b*. Make additional transparencies of *Tool 3-7b*.

- Make student copies of *Tool 3-7b*.

- Have available overhead markers.

## During Class

1. Display *Tool 3-7a*. Read and discuss the four sentence structures with your students. Answer student questions and provide additional examples if needed.

2. Display *Tool 3-7b*. Read the example of all four sentences about the moon.

3. Select a topic or theme with your students, and as a group create sentences for each sentence structure and write them on the lines provided on *Tool 3-7b*.

4. Using the same or another topic, have your students develop additional sentences for all four sentence structures. This is a great activity for students to do in pairs or small groups. Give one transparency of *Tool 3-7b* and an overhead marker to each group. Have them write their sentences on the transparency so that it is easy for them to share with their classmates.

5. Discuss the different sentence structures and ask how they might vary the sentence types they write for other assignments. Provide numerous opportunities for them to practice independently.

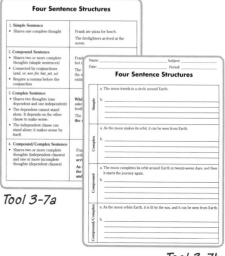

*Tool 3-7a*

*Tool 3-7b*

 For a quick check and other support for assessment, see **10-10 Quick Check for Sentences.**

## 3-8  Kinds of Sentences

Using this strategy, students learn and review the four kinds of sentences: declarative, imperative, exclamatory, and interrogative.

### Before Class

- Make multiple overhead transparencies and student copies of *Tool 3-8a*.

- Have available overhead markers.

### During Class

1. Display *Tool 3-8a*. Review or introduce the four kinds of sentences and read the example sentences with your students:

   - **Declarative:** A *declarative* sentence makes a statement.
   - **Imperative:** An *imperative* sentence gives a command.
   - **Exclamatory:** An *exclamatory* sentence shows emotion.
   - **Interrogative:** An *interrogative* sentence asks a question.

*Tool 3-8a*

2. Select a topic or theme with your students. With input from your class, create sentences for each kind of sentence on the Tool. Provide additional models if necessary. Discuss the purpose, structure, and end punctuation of each kind of sentence.

3. Allow students to work in pairs or in small groups to write additional sets of sentences on a transparency of *Tool 3-8a*. Have each group share with the class. Once they have understood how to write each kind of sentence, have them continue to practice independently.

For a quick check and other support for assessment, see 10-10 Quick Check for Sentences.

## 3-9 Kinds of Sentences Combined with Sentence Structures

Using this strategy, students reinforce knowledge of and practice writing different kinds of sentences and sentence structures.

**Prerequisites:** 3-7 Sentence Structures and 3-8 Kinds of Sentences

### Before Class

Make overhead transparencies and student copies of *Tools 3-9a* and *3-9b*.

### During Class

1. Display *Tool 3-9a* and review the different kinds of sentences and sentence structures. Have students keep their copies in their folders for future reference.

2. Using *Tool 3-9b*, develop sentences with your class on a topic they have studied or are familiar with. Once students are able, have them work independently. Provide support and feedback as appropriate.

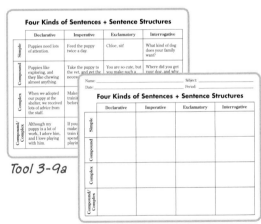

Tool 3-9a

Tool 3-9b

# 3-10 Topic Sentences and Thesis Statements

Have students use 4-17 Defining Topic Sentences and Thesis Statements and 4-18 Topic Sentence Variety to learn about these important parts of composition. Topic sentences and thesis statements have a special purpose—to introduce the topic.

**Handy Pages**

As students learn about the purpose and variety of topic sentences, they practice a variety of sentence structures. All topic sentence methods can be used as a starting point for writing general sentences in all subject areas.

# 3-11 Sentence Variety

Using this strategy teaches students how to write sentences using different sentence structures and teaches students to put their thoughts on paper. The same sentence structures can be used for general and topic sentences. See 4-17 Defining Topic Sentences and Thesis Statements and 4-18 Topic Sentence Variety for more information about topic sentences.

**Handy Pages**

These practical and easy-to-imitate sentence types can be used in all subjects. This strategy is especially helpful if students are expected to use multiple sentence structures and when instruction is visual, direct, and explicit. The following methods are presented in no particular order, but Action Verb Sentences and Where or When Plus What's Happening Sentences are easy to teach and learn. Both reinforce the importance and power of action verbs.

## Before Class

- Make overhead transparencies and student copies of *Tools 3-11a* and *3-11b*.

- Write example sentences on the transparency of *Tool 3-11b* based on a topic you have chosen.

- *Bonus Tools 3-11-1* through *3-11-4* provide additional support.

## During Class

1. Display *Tool 3-11a*. Read the sentence types in the left column, and explain that these terms help writers remember certain types of sentences.

2. Explain that each sentence type uses a different sentence structure or arrangement of sentence parts and can be used across content areas.

*Tool 3-11a*

*Tool 3-11b*

3. Read each example in the right column, and point out that the examples share a single topic—government. Share the additional example sentences you wrote on *Tool 3-11b*.

4. Using *Tool 3-11b*, model each type of sentence with input from your class. Refer to *Tool 3-11a* and provide additional models as needed. Depending on the needs of your students, you can have them practice each type of sentence as you explain it (one at a time) or after you have introduced all types.

5. Have students write in pairs or small groups and share with the class. Provide additional opportunities for students to practice independently.

To help students write sentences for stories and narratives, see Section 6, Story and Narrative Writing.

### Action Verb Sentences

These sentences are declarative statements with strong action verbs. Use the **3-2 Three- or Four-Part Sentences** strategy to model this sentence type. (These examples are also on *Bonus Tool 3-11-1.*)

| Clay's gas station | **offers** | the best service. |
| They | **love** | the new flavored cereals. |

### Where or When Plus What's Happening Sentences

These sentences start with words that indicate where or when an action takes place, took place, or will take place. Use the hot dog fold paper to model this type of sentence. (The following examples are also on *Bonus Tool 3-11-1.*)

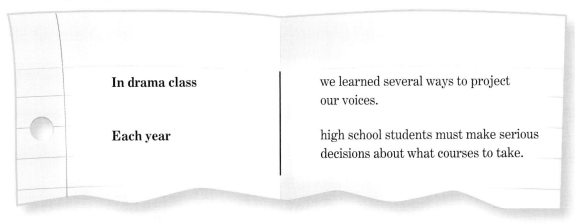

| **In drama class** | we learned several ways to project our voices. |
| **Each year** | high school students must make serious decisions about what courses to take. |

## Power (Number) Statements

These sentences include number words or phrases to organize information and help the reader anticipate key ideas in the text (Sparks 1996). (The following examples are also on *Bonus Tool 3-11-1.*)

**Three** cities have serious pollution problems.

The new recruits learned **four** important procedures.

## And, But, So, and Or Sentences

Sentences of this type are compound sentences with coordinating conjunctions (*and, but, so, or, yet*). Use the hot dog fold to model this type of sentence. (The following examples are also on *Bonus Tool 3-11-1.*)

Some people find it difficult to program a DVD player,

**but** most will succeed if they just remember to follow these guidelines.

My grandmother likes to help others,

**so** she volunteers at the hospital and my school.

## Side-by-Side Sentences

Use two simple sentences—one for the occasion (the reason for writing) and one for the position (what the writer plans to prove or explain)—to create Side-By-Side Sentences. This technique is especially powerful if the goal is to emphasize the position. Use the hot dog fold to model this type of sentence. (The following examples are also on *Bonus Tool 3-11-1*.)

| | |
|---|---|
| A little stress may be good. | Too much is dangerous. |
| Young children belong in car seats. | The child's car seat belongs in the back of the car, not in the front. |

## However Statements

These sentences use conjunctive adverbs—such as *however, in fact, instead, therefore, meanwhile, as a result,* and *next*—to write compound sentences and organize thoughts. They are called However Statements because *however* is the most common conjunctive adverb. Conjunctive adverbs are preceded by a semicolon—not a comma—because they are not true conjunctions and followed by a comma. Use the hot dog fold to model this type of sentence. (The following examples are also on *Bonus Tool 3-11-2*.)

| | |
|---|---|
| The new rules for the school cafeteria seemed unfair to the students; | **however**, the rules have made the cafeteria a better place to eat lunch. |
| Many students arrive late to class each day; | **therefore**, the faculty has created a plan to reward those who arrive on time and encourage others to do the same. |

## Semicolon Sentences

These sentences are compound sentences where two main ideas, as complete thoughts, are connected by a semicolon. Use the hot dog fold to model Semicolon Sentences. (The following examples are also on *Bonus Tool 3-11-2*.)

| | |
|---|---|
| The football team deserves the state championship; | the players and the coach are talented and dedicated. |
| Buying a new car is exciting; | it's also stressful. |

## Rhetorical Questions

In these sentences the writer asks a rhetorical question to get the reader's attention. The question is followed by a statement that addresses the question and states the main idea. Use the hot dog fold to model Rhetorical Questions. (The following examples are also on *Bonus Tool 3-11-2*.)

| | |
|---|---|
| What is your school doing to improve test scores? | Our school has purchased an exciting new literacy program. |
| How are community centers meeting the needs of teenagers? | In our city, they offer places to gather, help with homework, and provide scholarships for summer camp. |

## Occasion/Position Statements

These complex sentences begin with a dependent clause stating the occasion (reason for writing) and end with an independent clause stating the position (what the writer plans to prove or explain). Occasion/Position Statements start with words or phrases called *subordinate conjunctions,* such as:

| | | |
|---|---|---|
| after | even if | until |
| although | even though | though |
| as | if | when |
| as if | in order that | whenever |
| as long as | in order to | where |
| because | since | wherever |
| before | so that | whether |
| even | unless | while |

Use the two-column fold to model this sentence type. (The list of subordinate conjunctions, along with the following examples, are also on *Bonus Tool 3-11-3.*)

| If students use chemicals in a science experiment, | it is important that they learn the proper way to dispose of them. |
|---|---|
| Even though bike helmets may seem uncomfortable or unfashionable, | all cyclists should wear them. |

## A Few Good Prepositions

Like the subordinate conjunctions listed under Occasion/Position Statements, prepositions help students create good sentences. A complete list of prepositions is included on *Tool 3-131.* (The following examples are also on *Bonus Tool 3-11-3.*)

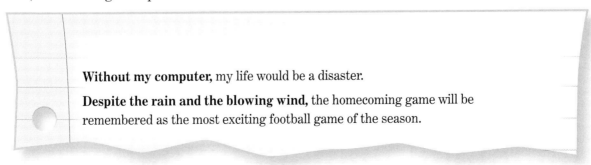

**Without my computer,** my life would be a disaster.

**Despite the rain and the blowing wind,** the homecoming game will be remembered as the most exciting football game of the season.

## To Plus Verb Sentences

An infinitive—a verb preceded by the word *to*—is used to start these sentences. Some examples of infinitives are *to succeed, to accomplish, to finish, to win,* and *to teach.* Sentences with infinitives are clear and direct. (The following examples are also on *Bonus Tool 3-11-3.*)

> **To win** at chess, players need to master three skills.
>
> **To impress** her guests at our New Year's dinner, my aunt created the most incredible culinary surprises.

## Two Nouns and Two Commas

This type of sentence uses an appositive, which sets off a noun or a noun phrase with commas. An appositive does not have a verb; it is simply a noun followed by a description that tells more about the noun. (The following examples are also on *Bonus Tool 3-11-4.*)

> Deckers, **a small town nestled in the Colorado Rockies,** is a fishing haven for many serious anglers.
>
> The medulla, **an important part of the brain,** controls our breathing.

## Compare/Contrast Statements

These sentences are statements about how two people, places, things, or ideas are alike or different. Students can make almost any sentence into a compare/contrast sentence by including one (or sometimes two) of the words from the following list of compare/contrast words:

| | | | |
|---|---|---|---|
| alike | differences | similar | resemble |
| different | the same | similarities | opposite |
| differ | in common | vary | |

To practice, create several sentences with your students. Ask them to underline or highlight the compare/contrast words in each sentence. Look for more words to add to the list of compare/contrast words. Collect sample sentences from newspapers and magazines. (The list of compare/contrast words, along with following examples, are also on *Bonus Tool 3-11-4*.)

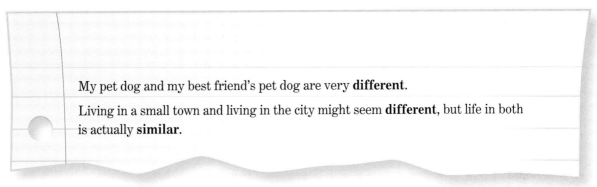

My pet dog and my best friend's pet dog are very **different**.

Living in a small town and living in the city might seem **different**, but life in both is actually **similar**.

## Quotations in Sentences

The quotation is often the position, or what the writer plans to prove or explain. The quotation gives an idea about what will be explained or proved in the paragraph to follow. (The following examples are also on *Bonus Tool 3-11-4*.)

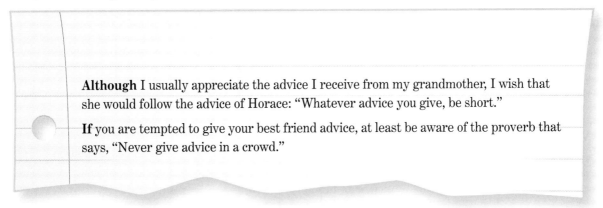

**Although** I usually appreciate the advice I receive from my grandmother, I wish that she would follow the advice of Horace: "Whatever advice you give, be short."

**If** you are tempted to give your best friend advice, at least be aware of the proverb that says, "Never give advice in a crowd."

Model using this strategy several times, and create several sentences using quotations before you ask students to work on their own.

 For a quick check and other support for assessment, see **10-10 Quick Check for Sentences**.

## 3-12 Ticket Out

Using the Ticket Out strategy, students write interesting, error-free sentences on a ticket they hand you as they leave class or begin a preferred activity. If used regularly, it gives your students extra practice and helps you assess their sentence-writing skills.

Make sentence writing a high priority in your class. When students write sentences using content area or news topics, they can practice writing sentences and you can check for comprehension.

### Before Class

Make student copies of *Tools 3-12a* and *3-12b* and cut them apart.

### During Class

1. On *Tool 3-12a*, have students write complete Ticket Out practice sentences. Set clear expectations for content, structure, grammar, and mechanics.

2. Collect students' tickets during class or as students are leaving. Circle errors on each ticket.

3. Staple a new ticket on top of the old ticket. Return the tickets at the beginning of the next class. Give students who had errors time to try again. Have all students revise and expand their sentences, even if the sentences do not contain any errors.

4. When your students are ready, have them write their revised sentences on a strip from *Tool 3-12b*. You can collect these sentences, display them in class, or ask students to keep them in their notebooks.

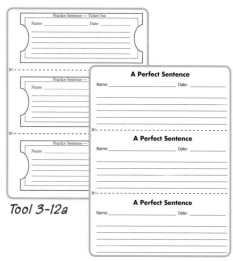

*Tool 3-12a*

*Tool 3-12b*

# Mastering Sentence Writing

As students learn to write with greater ease, they are increasingly able to develop individual voices and experiment with more creative, focused sentences. These strategies help students break down the components of a sentence, practice writing more creative sentences, and consider their purpose and audience while writing.

## Objectives

- Help students master sentence writing and teach them to write for a specific purpose or audience
- Improve sentence writing fluency and encourage creativity

| Strategy | Strategy Description | Page | Tools |
|---|---|---|---|
| **3-13** Recognizing Parts of Speech | Identifying and writing sentences that focus on one or two parts of speech | 118 | 3-13a to 3-13j |
| **3-14** Learning Parts of a Sentence with Diagrams | Using diagrams to label and identify parts of a sentence and visualize sentence organization | 122 | 3-14a to 3-14c |
| **3-15** Playing with Language | Experimenting with words and phrasing | 124 | n/a |
| **3-16** Adding Quotations | Writing sentences that include quotations | 127 | n/a |
| **3-17** Analyzing Sentences in Context | Identifying sentence types and structures in stories, news items, and class materials | 128 | n/a |

*(chart continues)*

| Strategy *(continued)* | Strategy Description | Page | Tools |
|---|---|---|---|
| **3-18** Writing Headlines and Sentences | Writing sentences from headlines and headlines from sentences to learn good word choices | 129 | n/a |
| **3-19** Purpose and Audience Considerations | Considering sentence types and lengths appropriate for different writing tasks and audiences | 130 | 3-19a, 3-19b |

**P** Consider using the Posters with the strategies in this section.

## **3-13** Recognizing Parts of Speech

Using this strategy, students learn or review the parts of speech and write sentences focusing on each part of speech.

When students master sentence writing, they are able to teach and encourage others to write sentences. To teach others, students must also be able to define and explain the terms for the words that make up a sentence.

Check your state's standards and make sure that you cover all required parts of speech.

### Before Class

- Make overhead transparencies and student copies of *Tools 3-13a* through *3-13j*.
- Have available highlighters.

 *Bonus Tool 3-13-1* provides additional support.

**Note:** You will want to give students an overview for all parts of speech but then spend time stressing each part of speech. Students learn parts of speech best when they can practice over time, ask and answer questions, and participate in guided lessons.

| Parts of Speech | |
|---|---|
| Noun | The **balloon** floated into the **air**. |
| Article | I blew up **the** balloon and tied it to a string. |
| Adjective | **Large red, white,** and **blue** balloons filled the room. |
| Verb | The balloons **popped** and **made** a loud noise. |
| Adverb | **Yesterday** I was **so** excited about the party that I paced the room **impatiently**. |
| Conjunction | The clown gave the child **and** his mother two yellow balloons. |
| Interjection | **Oh, no!** The balloons are all deflated! |
| Preposition | **In** the morning, the children hung balloons everywhere **around** the room. |
| Pronoun | **She** helped **him** give **everyone** in the room a balloon. |
| Participle | **Filled** with excitement, the twins wrapped gifts and prepared to go to the party. |
| Infinitive | The twins tried very hard **to win** the game of musical chairs. |
| Gerund | **Eating** cake and ice cream was the best part of the celebration. |

*Tools 3-13a*

## During Class

1. Display *Tool 3-13a* and review the terms in the left column. Ask students to echo your pronunciation.

2. Ask your students to use their background knowledge to define the terms and to discuss how the symbols at the top of the page might be used and how they might fit the parts of speech.

3. Remind students that the terms on *Tool 3-13a* name the parts of speech we use to write sentences; they do not name the parts of a sentence.

4. Read through the example sentences in the right column. Note that the examples for each part of speech are in bold. Using *Tool 3-13b*, provide additional examples for your students, as needed.

5. Review *Tools 3-13c* through *3-13j* with your students. Take your time reviewing each part of speech.

   • Point out the symbols, abbreviations, definitions, and categories for each part of speech. Read the examples with your students, noting the symbols used to identify each part of speech.

   • Ask your students to highlight the parts of speech, definitions, and titles for each of the categories on each tool.

6. Model and review the use of each part of speech often.

7. Provide many practice opportunities for your students.

   • Have your students focus on a specific part of speech and write sentences using that part of speech.

   • Have your students write sentences and label the parts of speech with appropriate symbols.

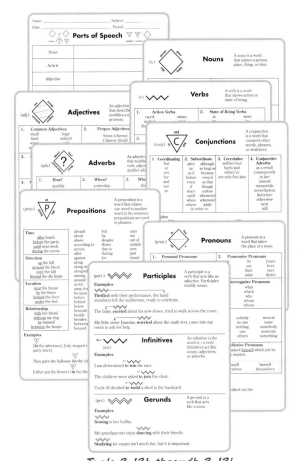

*Tools 3-13b through 3-13j*

**Note:** *Tools 3-13c* through *3-13j* contain lots of information to give students a full picture when they review or are introduced to each part of speech. The Tools can be used in many ways with other sentence-writing lessons.

### Symbols for the Parts of Speech

Have students add the symbol for each part of speech to their copies of *Tools 3-13a* and *3-13b* next to the words in the left column. (The following information on the parts of speech is also available on *Bonus Tool 3-13-1.*)

1. **Noun**

   Use the four-sided diamond to remind you that nouns name people, places, things, and ideas.

2. **Article**

   Use a checkmark to remind you to check for three simple words: a, an, the. These words—called articles—introduce nouns.

3. **Verb**

   Use the letter V—three Vs in a row—to remind you that verbs show action.

4. **Adjective**

   Use the decorated diamond to remind you that adjectives describe (decorate and modify) nouns and pronouns.

5. **Adverb**

   Use the diamond with a question mark in the middle to remind you that adverbs answer four important questions: Where? When? How? To What Extent?

6. **Conjunction**

   Use the half diamond with a C in the middle to remind you of conjunctions. Conjunctions connect words, phrases, clauses, or sentences. Use the C to remind you of conjunction and connect.

7. **Interjection**

   Use the half diamond with the letter I in the middle to remind you of interjections. Interjections are words that show strong emotion or feelings. Interjections are followed by "!"—an exclamation point.

8. **Pronoun**

   Use the four-sided diamond with a line in the middle to remind you that a pronoun replaces a noun; pronouns refer to specific people, places, things, and ideas.

9. **Preposition**

   Use the half diamond with a P in the middle to remind you of prepositions. Prepositions are always a part of a phrase. Use the P to remind you of preposition and phrase.

10. **Participle**

    Use a combination of the decorated diamond (adjective) and the three Vs (verb) to remind you of participles. Participles are verbs that function as adjectives. A participle gives more information about a noun. (Sitting at his desk, John wondered about the future.)

11. **Infinitive**

    Use the word to plus the three Vs (verb) to remind you of infinitives. An infinitive can stand alone (to win) or it can be part of a phrase (to win the game on Tuesday).

12. **Gerund**

    Use a combination of the diamond (noun) and the three Vs (verb) to remind you of gerunds. Gerunds are verbs that function as nouns. A gerund can stand alone (Singing is fun.) or it can be part of a phrase (Singing with my friends in chorus is fun.)

**Note:** A prepositional phrase always begins with the proposition and ends with a noun or pronoun. Generally, when prepositions aren't a part of a phrase, they become adverbs.

| preposition | adverb |
| --- | --- |
| I walked **down** the street. | I fell **down**. |

**Note:** Participles can stand alone, or they can be part of a phrase.

I understood the **hidden meaning** in his poem.

**Hidden behind the bushes,** the rabbit was difficult to spot.

**Note:** Infinitives can stand alone, or they can be part of a phrase.

I decided **to try**.

My aunt wanted me **to test her new recipe**.

**Note:** Gerunds often end in *-ing*. Gerunds can stand alone, or they can be part of a phrase.

**Walking** is good exercise.

The children like **playing in the yard**.

## Additional Ideas

- Have your students write short paragraphs describing or defining each part of speech. Use the **2-7 Concept Maps** strategy to make the task easier and more visual. Consider having students work in pairs or small groups. Give each group time to share their work.

- Using *Tool 3-13b*, have students write their own set of sentences all on the same theme, as on *Tool 3-13a*.

- Have your students memorize the parts of speech listed on *Tool 3-13a* and be able to write an example.

- Use *Tool 3-13b* to have your students record the definitions and abbreviations for each part of speech. (Definitions are provided at the tops of *Tools 3-13c* through *3-13j*.)

- Place your students in pairs or small groups. Have each pair or group teach one of the parts of speech. Let them use an overhead projector to make instruction more visual.

# 3-14 Learning Parts of a Sentence with Diagrams

Using this strategy helps students visualize how a sentence is organized and identify the parts of a sentence by diagramming.

**Prerequisite:** 3-13 Recognizing Parts of Speech

## Before Class

Make overhead transparencies and student copies of *Tools 3-13l, 3-14a, 3-14b,* and *3-14c.*

## During Class

Explain to your class that to master sentence writing, they also need to be able to recognize the basic parts of a sentence. Diagramming is a powerful visual tool that will help them learn and remember the parts of a sentence.

Inform them that sentences of all structures and lengths can be diagrammed. When they diagram, they place words on specific lines to show how each word is used in the sentence.

### Diagramming Prepositional Phrases

A good way to introduce diagrams is by teaching students to diagram prepositional phrases. Prepositional phrases usually account for a large portion of many sentences, so dealing with the prepositions first eliminates a lot of the words and makes it easier to find the subject and the predicate.

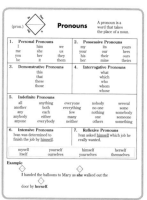

*Tool 3-13l*

1. Explain to your students that they will first learn how to diagram prepositional phrases.

2. Display *Tool 3-13l* and remind students that prepositional phrases always start with a preposition and end with a noun or pronoun.

3. Display *Tool 3-14a.* Read the first example sentence with your students and help them identify the prepositional phrases.

4. Read the examples and discuss how each prepositional phrase is represented in the diagram. Point out that words in the diagram are organized by their part of speech.

   - Prepositions go on the top-left slanted line.
   - The object of the preposition (noun and pronoun) goes on the horizontal line.
   - Any articles or adjectives go on slanted lines below the object.

*Tool 3-14a*

*Tool 3-14b*

*Tool 3-14c*

## Diagramming Subject and Predicate

1. Explain that bracketing a sentence's prepositional phrases, then diagramming them before the other parts of the sentence, makes it easier to identify the subject and predicate, since prepositional phrases never contain the subject (the doer) or the predicate (the doing word). Remind students that the subject and verb are the two major parts of every sentence. Emphasize the need for subject/verb agreement (a singular noun takes a singular verb, and a plural noun takes a plural verb)

2. Display *Tool 3-14b* and read the first example. Ask students to put the prepositional phrases in brackets and then identify the subject and predicate.

3. Discuss how the simple subject and simple predicate are organized in the diagram.

   - The subject (soldiers) and predicate (guarded) appear on a horizontal line that is divided by a vertical line. The subject is on the left, and the predicate is on the right.

   - If the verb has a direct object, it is written to the right and separated from the verb by a smaller vertical line. Explain that a direct object is a noun or pronoun that receives the action of the verb.

4. Read and discuss the remaining example with your students.

## Diagramming Complete Sentences

1. Display *Tool 3-14c*. Read and discuss the first example with students. Explain that the diagrams from *Tools 3-14a* and *3-14b* have been combined here to show a completely diagrammed sentence. Point out that the articles and modifiers have also been diagrammed.

2. Explain and point out on *Tool 3-14c* that in sentence diagrams:

   - Prepositional phrases are placed below the subject/predicate line.

   - If a prepositional phrase tells about the subject, it is placed below the subject line.

   - If a prepositional phrase modifies the predicate (verb), it is placed below that part of the line.

   - If a word has any other modifiers (adjectives or articles for nouns, adverbs for verbs, adjectives, or other adverbs), they appear below it on slanted lines.

   - Conjunctions, such as *and, but,* and *or,* have special treatment. In a compound subject or predicate, each half of the compound is written on a parallel line, joined by a triangle with the conjunction. (See *Tool 3-14c.*)

## Additional Ideas

- Have your students practice diagramming sentences you provide and sentences they select from stories or textbooks. Guide students as they diagram new or unusual elements in their sentences, such as predicate adjectives, compound predicates, and indirect objects.

- Periodically review diagramming and the parts of speech. Remind your students that dealing with prepositional phrases first will help them isolate the subject and predicate.

## 3-15 Playing with Language

Using this strategy, students write about a topic using playful language and various kinds of sentences. It encourages students to have fun while writing and to increase their creativity in writing. You may wish to introduce 3-13 Recognizing Parts of Speech to your students before teaching this strategy in order to familiarize them with some of the parts of speech used in this strategy, like gerunds.

## Before Class

- Select a sentence type or language component—such as comparisons, alliteration, or exaggeration—you want to have your students practice. Use the list provided in this strategy, or think of new types of sentences.

- Choose a topic such as a favorite book or game, and have ready one or more examples.

  *Bonus Tools 3-15-1* and *3-15-2* provide additional support.

**Note:** It is best to have students practice only one type of sentence at first. Once they are comfortable writing sentences of this type, gradually introduce them to others.

## During Class

1. Discuss the sentence type and provide an example. Point out the features of the sentence type.

2. Write your topic on the board or transparency and provide an additional example if appropriate. Ask your students to write one or more sentences about the topic using the specified sentence type.

3. Ask volunteers to share their sentences with the class. Have students explain how their sentences meet the characteristics of the sentence type.

**Types of Sentences (Also on** *Bonus Tools 3-15-1* **and** *3-15-2*)

**Comparison:** A sentence or more comparing two items to identify how they are similar or different.

> When Mom carried in my new brother, I thought that she was carrying a funny-looking soccer ball. For just an instant, his round head **reminded me** of my favorite game.

**Phrases and fragments:** A phrase or clause that is written like a sentence but is incomplete. They are often used intentionally to convey emotions like frustration, fear, or excitement. If you have students practice writing fragments, make sure they understand that it is very rarely acceptable to use fragments. Fragments are used for emphasis to get a point across, or to set a mood or tone.

> **In the morning, in the afternoon, at night.** It seemed like he would never stop crying.

**Clause:** A group of words with a subject and predicate that is part of a larger sentence. It can be used to add details and description to a simple sentence.

> The gooey mixture **that my mother made and put into his baby dish** didn't look too appealing to me.

**Compound verb:** A simple predicate with two or more verbs showing different actions or conditions.

> My new baby brother **squirmed** and **giggled** as my dad tried to fasten the diaper.

**Gerund:** A verb that ends in *-ing* and is used as a noun.

> **Crying** was all he did.

**Alliteration:** The repetition of the initial consonant sounds in two or more neighboring words or syllables.

> My **b**aby **b**rother needs **b**ottles, **b**ibs, **b**lankets, and his **b**inky.

**Exaggeration:** The intentional enlargement of a description beyond the truth. This is often a comical way to describe a situation.

> My baby brother drooled so much that I followed him around with a **mop and bucket**.

**Collective noun:** A noun that refers to a group of people, animals, or things.

> My baseball **team**, my history **class**, and my **group** of best friends were really tired of hearing me complain about the new baby.

**Compound sentence:** Two complete sentences joined by a conjunction or some kind of punctuation.

> I covered my ears with my hands, **but** I could still hear him crying.

**Questions:** A type of sentence used to ask for information.

> What would you do if a small, bald creature took over your life?

**Adverbs:** Words that modify verbs, adjectives, and other adverbs.

> I walked **quietly** into his room.

**Definition:** A statement explaining the meaning of a word or phrase.

> My aunt from England pushed the pram, **a baby carriage**, through the park.

## Additional Ideas

- Ask your students to experiment with writing sentences that feature compound verbs, gerunds, collective nouns, compound sentences, questions, definitions, and other types of language.
- Encourage them to write playful sentences for other assignments, as appropriate.

# (3-16) Adding Quotations

Using this strategy, students learn to include a quotation in a sentence.

Learning how to include a quotation in a sentence takes time and practice. The Adding Quotations strategy helps students learn and master this skill. It gives students opportunities to practice long before they are asked to include a quotation in a paragraph or a report. For more information about using quotations see 5-17 Elaborating with Quotations and Citations and 5-24 Writing Documented Essays and Reports.

## Before Class

- Have available magazines and newspapers.
- *Bonus Tool 3-16-1* provides the following example.

## During Class

1. Introduce words and phrases that writers use before a quotation in a sentence. (The following example is also on *Bonus Tool 3-16-1.* For additional examples see *Bonus Tool 5-17-1*)

> **According to the superintendent**, what has impressed him the most so far this year is "the unwavering support for education from the parents in this great district."
>
> **One of the governor's strongest supporters, Ahmad Williams of Greenfield,** told the assembly that "all districts should begin the school year by Labor Day—and no later."
>
> **The mayor said,** "A stoplight really should go up at that intersection; there have been far too many accidents there."

2. Brainstorm other words or phrases that could be used to introduce a quotation.
3. Have students use magazines and newspapers to find examples of sentences with quotations. Discuss the ways the writers of these sentences introduced their quotations.
4. Ask your students to create their own sentences, imitating the examples they find. Provide quotations, have students select quotations from a story or article, or have them make up quotations.

## 3-17 Analyzing Sentences in Context

Using this strategy, students practice identifying sentence parts and how they are written. This strategy provides an opportunity to rewrite sentences using different sentence structures.

**Prerequisites:** 3-5 Sentences Using *Who, What, Where, When, Action,* and *How*, 3-7 Sentence Structures, **and** 3-8 Kinds of Sentences

### Before Class

Have available magazines, newspapers, and/or content-related material.

### During Class

1. Give your students magazines and/or newspapers. Ask them to find six to ten sentences that they can use to demonstrate their knowledge of sentences.

2. In pairs or small groups, have them describe their sentences to each other by doing one or more of the following:

    - Identifying the verbs.
    - Explaining the kind of sentence that they are sharing (declarative, imperative, exclamatory, or interrogative).
    - Describing the sentence structure (simple, compound, complex, or compound/complex).
    - Dividing the sentence into a *Who, What, Where, When, Action, How* grid.
    - Pointing out good word choices and examples of descriptive language.

3. After your students have finished describing their sentences, have them rewrite their sentences using different sentence structures.

# 3-18 Writing Headlines and Sentences

Using this strategy, students write sentences from headlines and vice versa to learn to make good word choices.

By writing sentences from headlines, students learn how to write various types of sentences that convey the same information. If you wish, you can also have your students write concise, informative headlines from sentences, which helps them learn to pick out the most important information in sentences.

## Before Class

Have available magazines and newspapers. Select headlines and topic sentences to use as examples.

## During Class

1. Using one of the headlines and topic sentences you have gathered, discuss the difference between them. Demonstrate with input from your students how to create a complete sentence from a headline. Provide as many examples as needed.

2. Have your students, working in groups or independently, use magazines and newspapers to pick out a couple of headlines and then create sentences based on those headlines. If students have the article, they may use it to add details to the sentence. If they do not have the article to refer to, have them make up the details. Alternatively, provide topic sentences and ask students to write headlines from them.

3. Ask your students to share their sentences or headlines with the class.

**Headlines** (From *USA Today*, Monday, March 6, 2006)

The Southwest Suffers Historic Drought

Legislator to Announce Political Plans

Tenacious Termites Survive Katrina Flooding

**Sentences**

A drought in several states in the Southwest has caused problems for plants and animals, as well as for people living in major cities such as Phoenix.

Representative Bill Thomas will announce his political plans today at a conference in his hometown.

Despite the massive flooding caused by Hurricane Katrina, huge colonies of termites have survived.

## 3-19 Purpose and Audience Considerations

Using this strategy, students consider sentence types and lengths appropriate for different writing tasks and audiences. It introduces students to various factors—such as content, structure, and sentence length—that must be considered when writing.

### Before Class

Make overhead transparencies and student copies of *Tools 3-19a* and *3-19b*.

### During Class

1. Explain to your students that the sentences they write will be different depending on their audience and purpose for writing and that these considerations will affect their decisions about sentence length and what words and ideas to include.

2. Introduce the issue of sentence length. Display *Tool 3-19a* and read the John F. Kennedy quotation, which is actually a single sentence, with students.

3. Compare President Kennedy's words with the advice from Eeyore about being considerate. Ask your students why they might want to use short sentences in some types of writing and long sentences in others.

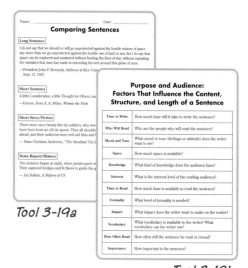

*Tool 3-19a*

*Tool 3-19b*

4. Have students compare the lines from a short story with the lines from a news story and ask them how the purpose and audience for each type of writing is different. Discuss how the sentences in each type of writing are different.

5. Display *Tool 3-19b* and explain to students that they should consider these questions every time they write. Discuss the questions and how the answers to them affect the kinds of sentences they write. Emphasize that good writers use many different sentence types when they write. Have them save *Tool 3-19b* in their writing notebooks.

### Additional Ideas

• Have your students collect sentences from brochures, letters, notes, science textbooks, poems, news articles, editorials, directions in cookbooks, and so on. Have them write each sentence on a large index card. Display all of the cards and guide a discussion about what your students have found and what they see on the board. Together, make a list explaining the differences in the sentences.

• Ask your class to choose from several different kinds of writing, such as a letter to the editor from the local newspaper, a report for a science class, or a short story for a fiction-writing contest. Have students discuss how each is unique and what kinds of sentences they might use to complete each task. Have them describe the audience for each kind of writing and how having a different audience affects their writing.

# SECTION 4 INTRODUCTION
## Expository Paragraphs

The ability to write expository compositions is necessary for all students, and there is a high correlation between students' success and their use of specific writing strategies. Using a clear writing process, such as the one described in this section, helps all students become proficient writers.

The traditional writing process moves students directly from prewriting to drafting, but *Step Up to Writing* adds a crucial intermediate step—planning. By separating prewriting from planning, students can focus on organizing their ideas before they write their first drafts. As a result, they are able to write compositions that are better organized and more focused.

Revise — Draft — Edit

The ability to write coherent, well-developed essays and reports begins by learning the skills to write expository paragraphs. *Step Up to Writing*'s step-by-step method helps teachers develop their students' paragraph-writing skills through direct, explicit instruction. Students learn to write paragraphs by carefully examining and practicing each step of the process and the skills required to complete it.

Success with expository paragraphs comes when students are introduced to

- The two kinds of writing—expository and story/narrative—to prevent confusion about the required components in their writing and provide a framework for understanding;

- The writing process, from generating ideas through polishing a final draft;

- Adequate models and practice opportunities when learning to:
  - ▸ Prewrite (such as reading, brainstorming, and discussing);
  - ▸ Plan (using an informal outline);
  - ▸ Develop clear topic sentences for a variety of purposes;
  - ▸ Choose strong key/star ideas (reasons, details, and facts) to support the topic;
  - ▸ Use a variety of effective transitions to guide the reader through the presentation of key/star ideas;
  - ▸ Develop explanations, examples, evidence, and elaboration (the E's) that support the key/star ideas;
  - ▸ Write strong conclusions that refer back to the topic.

## When Teaching Expository Paragraphs

- When you begin teaching expository paragraphs, focus on specific skills such as creating informal outlines. It is not necessary for students to write a complete paragraph every time they practice. Developing well-written paragraphs takes practice and does not occur after just a few lessons.

- Writing is a complex process, made up of many skills that must be taught in isolation. Students learn to write only when given ample opportunities to practice. Remind students that authors repeat the process of thinking, writing, revising, and editing many times before readers see the finished product.

- When you begin to teach the writing process, repeat instruction on prewriting, planning, and drafting until students understand the process of creating the first draft before moving to other stages. Stress that paragraph writing is just one of many writing forms students will need to know to successfully communicate their ideas.

- Use content students have studied or are studying to help them generalize and apply their new writing skills across content areas. Many writing assignments already connect content reading with writing.

- Scaffold writing instruction. Until students can create informal outlines on their own, for example, model them often and provide explicit direction.

- It is sometimes appropriate to prewrite parts of your students' paragraphs for them. For example, you might provide the topic and conclusion sentences if the objective is to have students develop the key/star ideas or the elaboration. This helps students fine-tune specific elements of a paragraph without getting distracted writing the entire paragraph.

- Struggling writers typically master the enumeration, or list, paragraph first. This paragraph requires a simple list of facts or details to support the controlling idea in the topic sentence. Also, early writing skills are developed by speaking, so allow students who need it time to talk about their writing and rehearse their ideas before putting them on paper.

- Give students opportunities for peer review, editing, and collaboration. Explain that in the workplace expository writing often occurs as part of a team, so learning to write collaboratively while they are in school will be a valuable skill for their futures.

- Students from diverse backgrounds have different patterns of speech that feel natural to them. Find out what these are, and help students master the global conventions of English while preserving their own voices.

*IDEA BANK*

## Tips for Using These Strategies Across Content Areas

✓ Have students write informal outlines (**4-7** Planning with an Informal Outline) about specific topics they have just studied in social studies or science as a way to cement what was covered in that day's instruction.

✓ Have students use obvious transitions to write a paragraph that explains a specific math problem, a science experiment, or the relationship between primary and complementary colors in art, for example.

✓ Have students generate topic sentences (**4-18** Topic Sentence Variety) to explain what they think about stories they have read. If you choose, have students expand these sentences into paragraphs.

✓ Have students color-code handouts in science, social studies, and so on with the Traffic Light colors (**4-6** Color-Coding and the Five Elements of Expository Writing) to help them identify main ideas (key/star ideas) and details (elaboration).

✓ Have students work in small groups and develop informal outlines on chart paper that relate to the most important ideas in a chapter or unit of study. Give students the key/star ideas or have them determine what they are. Have each group present their informal outline. Discuss their examples and together create a new informal outline that combines the ideas generated during the discussion. Then have students use the informal outline as a study guide for a test.

✓ In art or music, have students write about the pieces or artists that they are studying. Use topic sentence strategies that push students to share an opinion and support their position with evidence and examples.

✓ In subjects like industrial arts, home economics, or art, create a framed paragraph and have students describe and evaluate projects they have completed.

Choose those strategies that best meet the needs of your students.

# Two Kinds of Writing

The phrase "two kinds of writing" refers to the two basic types of writing that students will be asked to produce—expository and narrative writing. Too often, students at all levels confuse expository and narrative writing. They ask for help editing their "story" when they are actually writing an informational report; or, they try to add an exciting ending when they should write a conclusion. They are not clear about the purpose of each kind of writing.

The strategies dealing with the two kinds of writing offer clear, practical instruction and examples. When students understand the distinction between expository and narrative writing, they can successfully plan for and make good decisions about their own writing.

## Objectives

- Teach students to recognize and analyze the two patterns for writing
- Help students increase productivity and save time when they write

| Strategy | Strategy Description | Page | Tools |
|---|---|---|---|
| **4-1** Introducing Two Kinds of Writing | Learning the proper terms for the organizational patterns and common traits of expository and narrative writing | 136 | 4-1a to 4-1c |
| **4-2** Comparing Two Kinds of Writing | Comparing the differences between expository and narrative writing | 139 | 4-2a, 4-2b |
| **4-3** Prompts for Two Kinds of Writing | Recognizing writing prompts and making decisions about what kind of writing is needed | 142 | 4-3a |
| **4-4** Defining *Fiction, Nonfiction, Prose, Poetry, Explain*, and *Entertain* | Defining terms used to describe different types of writing and purposes for writing | 142 | n/a |

P Consider using the Posters with the strategies in this section.

## 4-1 Introducing Two Kinds of Writing

One good way to support students' understanding of writing is by using and encouraging them to use the proper terms for the two kinds of writing and to provide visual representations for those terms. Students use this strategy to learn to recognize the different patterns of organization and the common traits of both types of writing.

**Handy Pages**

**Note:** Detailed instructions for multiparagraph expository report and essay writing are presented in Section 5, and instructions for narrative writing are presented in Section 6.

### Before Class

- Make overhead transparencies and student copies of *Tools 4-1a, 4-1b,* and *4-1c.*
- Have available green, yellow, red, purple, and lilac highlighters and overhead markers.

 *Bonus Tool 4-1-1* provides additional support.

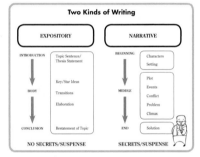

*Tool 4-1a*

### During Class

1. Using *Tool 4-1a,* discuss the two kinds of writing with your students. Talk about important terms and the different organizational patterns used for each.

   Explain that:

   - Expository writing has an introduction, body, and conclusion.
   - Narrative writing has a beginning, middle, and end.

2. Ask students to circle the words *introduction, body,* and *conclusion* in the Expository column and *beginning, middle,* and *end* in the Narrative column.

3. Explain that the terms used to describe the organizational pattern for each kind of writing might seem very similar, but they are actually different. Review any terms students do not know or understand. (If needed, a definition and comparison of terms is available on *Bonus Tool 4-1-1.*)

4. Point out the "Secrets/Suspense" and "No Secrets/Suspense" phrases at the bottom of *Tool 4-1a.* Explain that the introduction of an expository paragraph basically does not have any secrets; the writer wants the reader to know what will be presented, proved, or explained in the text. On the other hand, the beginning of a narrative is filled with secrets and suspense; the writer wants readers to keep reading to find out what will happen next.

## Planning with Informal Outlines and Quick Sketches

1. Use *Tool 4-1b* to explain that when developing a writing plan, students will use:

   - Informal outlines for expository writing
   - Quick sketches for narrative writing

2. Explain how to use an informal outline to plan expository writing. Students will write their planned introductions next to the "T," their proposed key/star ideas next to the stars, their elaboration next to the dashes and dots, and their planned conclusions next to the "C." See also **4-7 Planning with an Informal Outline**.

*Tool 4-1b*

3. Explain how to use a quick sketch to plan a narrative. Point out that the beginning, middle, and end are noted on the quick sketch. Their sketches in the boxes on the left side of the quick sketch will help them develop and remember the different parts of the narrative. On the lines on the right, they will add words and phrases that will aid them in writing.

4. Reinforce that informal outlines and quick notes are just that—created informally and quickly, using only words and phrases. These tools are flexible and have few rules. Writers can add, delete, or rearrange items on either the informal outline or quick sketch.

5. With your class, compare the informal outline (expository) with the quick sketch (narrative). Discuss their similarities and differences. Point out that expository writing is organized by key/star ideas (the big ideas) and narrative writing is generally organized by the sequence of events or the quick sketch.


## Introducing Color-Coding

Explain to your students that color will help them visualize the organizational pattern of both kinds of writing. The color-coding systems will also help them identify each part and help them plan. They will use different colors for each kind of writing to keep them focused on the type of writing they are doing.

As you describe each color-coding system, highlight the transparency of *Tool 4-1b* and have your students mark their copies.

### Informal Outlines for Expository Writing

- Have students add Traffic Light color-coding to the informal outline to help make the introduction, conclusion, and body of the topic obvious. (See **4-6 Color-Coding and the Five Elements of Expository Writing**.) Direct them to highlight as follows:
  - ▸ Green —Topic
  - ▸ Yellow —Key/star ideas
  - ▸ Red —Elaboration (dots and dashes)
  - ▸ Green —Conclusion

### Quick Sketch for Narrative Writing

- Have students color-code the narrative quick sketch using lilac and purple on *Tool 4-1b*. This will help them visualize the *beginning, middle, end* organizational pattern. Creating a quick sketch and adding quick notes to each sketch is a great way to plan. Direct students to highlight as follows:
  - ▸ Lilac—Box that contains the B for beginning
  - ▸ Purple—Boxes that contain the two M's and the E for middle and end

Using green, yellow, and red (the colors of a traffic light) will help students see and remember the parts of an expository paragraph or report. For narratives, the lilac and purple show the growing intensity of a story plot. Using two different color sets helps students see that the two kinds of writing are different—they have different patterns of organization.

### Common Traits

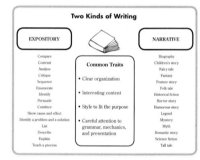

*Tool 4-1c*

1. Review *Tool 4-1c* with your class and point out the middle section and the common traits of expository writing and narrative writing. Both types of writing:
   - ▸ Demand clear organization;
   - ▸ Need to be interesting and engaging to readers;
   - ▸ Need to follow the writing styles and organizational patterns for that kind of writing;
   - ▸ Require good grammar and mechanics and must be presented in a way that pleases the reader.

2. Discuss the words listed under the categories of expository writing and narrative writing.

3. To reinforce recognition of the two types of writing, ask students to identify the different types of writing assignments they have done in their classes. Write them on the board in two columns under the headings *Expository Writing* and *Narrative Writing*.

**Comparing Two Kinds of Writing**

This strategy helps students see the differences between the two kinds of writing by comparing text samples.

**Prerequisite:** 4-1 Introducing Two Kinds of Writing

**Handy Pages**

## Before Class

- Make overhead transparencies and student copies of *Tools 4-2a* and *4-2b*.
- Collect other examples of expository paragraphs and narratives in which the same topic is discussed.

## During Class

### Different Approaches to the Same Topic

Display and read *Tool 4-2a* with your class. Explain that these two pieces of writing cover the same general topic (dolphins), but one is an expository paragraph and the other is a narrative.

Point out the following differences between the two pieces. By marking the transparency as you review, the differences between the two will be more explicit for your students.

*Tool 4-2a*

1. **The beginning and the introduction differ.**
   - "Dolphins," an expository paragraph, starts with a clear topic sentence. The reader is not confused about the topic of the paragraph.
   - "Shadow" is part of a narrative. The first few lines set the scene and the tone, but the reader will have to read the entire story to really understand its purpose. A story is filled with secrets to keep the reader wondering and reading on.

2. **The organizational patterns differ.**
   - Expository writing has an introduction, body, and conclusion.
   - A narrative has a beginning, middle, and end.

### 3. The lengths of paragraphs differ.

- Generally, paragraphs in expository writing are longer than one sentence. The lengths of expository paragraphs are more uniform than those of narrative paragraphs.

- In narratives, paragraphs may be only one sentence long. This is especially true when there is dialogue. The variation in paragraph length gives a narrative action, rhythm, and movement.

### 4. The transitions differ.

- Display *Tool 4-2b* and explain to your students that transitions are powerful tools. They support the organization of both kinds of writing. Knowing how and when to use them is important. (See **4-24 Transition Sets** for more information about using transitions when writing an expository paragraph.)

*Tool 4-2b*

- In expository writing, transitions:
  - ▸ Introduce the key/star ideas;
  - ▸ Are words that show organization ("One," "Another," "A third") or words that are repeated or emphasized for organization.

- In narrative writing, transitions:
  - ▸ Often begin paragraphs and might be part of a phrase, so they are easy to spot ("An hour later," "When we finished," "For a long time");
  - ▸ Usually have to do with time ("At dinner time," "On Wednesday").

- With your students, read each passage aloud and pick out and color-code the transitions on *Tool 4-2a*.
  - ▸ Transitions in expository writing introduce the key/star ideas that support the topic sentence. In "Dolphins," a transition is used each time another fact is presented.

    First of all . . .

    Like other mammals, dolphins also . . .

    Finally . . .

  - ▸ In a narrative, transitions help the reader move from one event to the next. In "Shadow," the events are connected by transitions that show the passage of time.

    Before I learned to walk . . .

    When I was older . . .

    One of those mornings . . .

    Each morning . . .

    On my lunch break . . .

### Noting the Different Features of the Two Kinds of Writing

- Collect with your students different examples of expository and narrative writing that cover the same topic. Have students look for features that make the writing different.
- Point out the *beginning-middle-end* pattern of a narrative and the *introduction-body-conclusion* pattern used for expository writing. Ask discussion questions like the following:
  - ▸ How are the expository paragraphs different from the paragraphs in the narrative?
  - ▸ How is the topic sentence in the expository piece different from the beginning of the narrative?
  - ▸ How is the conclusion in the expository piece different from the ending of the narrative?
  - ▸ What are the transitions in the expository piece? How do the transitions help organize the piece?
  - ▸ What is the difference between the purpose of the expository paragraph and the purpose of the narrative?

## Additional Ideas

- Create displays or bulletin boards dedicated to each type of writing.
  - ▸ Post examples of each kind of writing and label them expository or narrative.
  - ▸ Color-code the writing samples.
- Create a class/family project. Ask students (with help from family members) to collect one-page samples of each kind of writing by looking at magazines, newspapers, mail, and so on. Display these items, separating the two kinds of writing.
- Ask students to identify the kind of writing in their reading for other classes or when you read something in class. Ask them to support their opinions with reasons and examples. Have them report about the writing they find in other classes.
- Ask students to find two books in the school's media center on the same topic: one that is expository writing and one that is narrative. Have them write a comparison of the two books or share their observations in small groups.

## 4-3 Prompts for Two Kinds of Writing

This strategy helps students learn to recognize and respond to prompts for expository and narrative writing.

**Prerequisite:** 4-1 Introducing Two Kinds of Writing

**Handy Pages**

### Before Class

Make an overhead transparency and student copies of *Tool 4-3a*.

### During Class

1. Display *Tool 4-3a*. If necessary, define the term *prompts* for the class. Explain that in writing, a prompt gives directions for an assignment or a test item. It can be as simple as a general idea, or it can tell writers exactly what they are expected to do.

2. Point out that the prompts on *Tool 4-3a* contain specific words to tell students what they should write, such as an expository report or a narrative.

3. Have students read each of the prompts, marking the word that describes how to approach the prompt. Explain that when the prompt asks them to write a paragraph, report, or essay, they are being asked to use an expository format.

4. Talk about which prompts require an introduction, body, and conclusion, and which prompts require a beginning, middle, and end.

5. With your class, create additional prompts and write them on the board. Circle the words that describe how to approach the prompt.

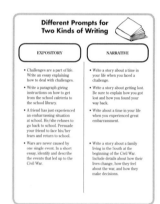

*Tool 4-3a*

**Note:** Prompts that do not include the words *story, report, essay, paragraph,* and so on can confuse students, who may misinterpret the prompt. To prevent confusion, a prompt should always name the specific writing task to be completed: *report, paragraph, story,* and so on.

## 4-4 Defining *Fiction, Nonfiction, Prose, Poetry, Explain,* and *Entertain*

This strategy answers students' questions about terms often used to describe expository and narrative writing.

 *Bonus Tools 4-4-1* and *4-4-2* provide additional examples.

### Fiction and Nonfiction

The terms *fiction* and *nonfiction* show how literature is grouped. They do not refer to the organizational pattern used within each piece of writing.

- Nonfiction is writing about real people, places, and things. It often has content that follows the *introduction-body-conclusion* pattern. But students will also find nonfiction books about people (biographies) and animals that are told as stories, with a *beginning-middle-end* pattern.
- Fiction is narrative writing and tends to follow the *beginning-middle-end* pattern.

## Prose and Poetry

It is important for students to know the terms *prose* and *poetry*. Recognizing the two formats is usually not a problem because they look so different in print. Explain that prose is writing with sentences and paragraphs, and poetry is writing with words and phrases (and sometimes sentences) that often have rhyme and rhythm. Poems often try to stimulate emotions and images apart from the literal meaning of the words. If your students would benefit from an example, use *Bonus Tool 4-4-1*. For additional information about Poetry and Prose, see *Tool 9-15b*.

## Writing to Explain and Writing to Entertain

Tell students that both writing to explain and writing to entertain are valuable and important, but different.

- When students write to explain, they must stick to the facts and present them in a logical order. They must write clearly and use details to make sure that the readers have all of the information necessary to understand the topic. This type of writing is almost always nonfiction.
- Writing to entertain can be fiction or nonfiction, and expository or narrative. Often those who write poems, stories, and plays use their imaginations, make up details and descriptions, and do not always stick to the facts. Their objective is to entertain, not inform. However, there are writers who use an entertaining style to inform.

When people write to entertain, they sometimes break the rules of grammar and mechanics to make a point—to add a certain feel to their writing. But those who write to explain are careful. They follow the rules and make every effort to be clear and concise in their writing.

## Mixing the Two Kinds of Writing

Writers combine expository and narrative writing when they create personal narratives. (For more information about personal narratives, see Section 7.) In addition, writers sometimes include expository paragraphs in a short story or novel. These expository paragraphs include information that the reader might find interesting or need to know to fully understand the setting, conflict, or characters. If your students would benefit from an example, see *Bonus Tool 4-4-2*.

# The Writing Process and Organization

Understanding the writing process and organization are key skills that writers need in order to present ideas, facts, and opinions in a clear, logical manner. They aid the writer in presenting ideas and aid the reader in comprehension. Expository writing includes stand-alone paragraphs as well as reports, essays, research papers, and letters. As students learn to write expository paragraphs using the writing process, they develop the skills needed to write longer reports and other multiparagraph expository pieces.

## Objectives

- Enable students to recognize the steps in the writing process
- Teach students the key elements of expository writing
- Provide students with practice in informal outlines of various lengths

| Strategy | Strategy Description | Page | Tools |
|---|---|---|---|
| 4-5 The Writing Process | Defining and introducing each step in the writing process | 146 | 4-5a to 4-5c |
| 4-6 Color-Coding and the Five Elements of Expository Writing | Introducing the five elements of expository writing and the Traffic Light colors | 148 | 4-6a, 4-6b |
| 4-7 Planning with an Informal Outline | Using an informal outline to plan expository writing | 150 | 4-5c, 4-7a |
| 4-8 Accordion Paragraphs | Writing short and long expository paragraphs | 153 | 4-8a |
| 4-9 Determining Key/Star Ideas with the Thinking Game | Practicing creating categories of information to use when planning to write | 156 | 4-9a |

*(chart continues)*

| Strategy (continued) | Strategy Description | Page | Tools |
|---|---|---|---|
| **4-10** The Organization Game | Sorting sets of words and phrases into categories, and creating informal outlines | 158 | 4-10a to 4-10c |
| **4-11** Informal Outlines of Various Lengths | Learning to tailor informal outlines and paragraph writing to the number of ideas needed to write about a topic | 160 | 4-9a, 4-11a to 4-11d |
| **4-12** Planning Guides for Organizing an Accordion Paragraph | Using planning guides to write Accordion Paragraphs | 161 | 4-12a |
| **4-13** Practice Guides for Writing Accordion Paragraphs | Creating clear, organized paragraphs using practice guides | 162 | 4-13a, 4-13b |
| **4-14** Organization with Framed Paragraphs | Filling in a skeletal frame of a paragraph to practice writing the basic components of a paragraph | 163 | n/a |
| **4-15** Accordion Races | Organizing sentences into paragraphs using a game format | 163 | 4-15a, 4-15b |
| **4-16** Writing in First, Second, and Third Person | Learning to write from different points of view | 164 | 4-16a to 4-16c |

P Consider using the Posters with the strategies in this section.

## 4-5 **The Writing Process**

This strategy defines and introduces each step in the writing process.

**Handy Pages**

Traditionally, teachers have taught that prewriting leads directly to drafting. Adding the planning stage can help students give form to their writing before the drafting stage, saving time and decreasing frustration.

### Before Class

- Make overhead transparencies and student copies of *Tools 4-5a, 4-5b,* and *4-5c.*
-  *Bonus Tool 4-5-1* provides additional support.

### During Class

1. Display *Tool 4-5a* and quickly read each of the steps. Explain that the writing process names the steps that writers take as they move from general ideas to finished, well-written pieces. The steps can be used for all kinds of writing—long or short and narrative or expository.

2. Point out the circular arrow in the middle of the Tool. Explain that writing is a process and that good writers often write and rewrite the same paragraph until they are satisfied with what they have written. Encourage your students to review their writing and learn ways they can improve what they have written, versus trying to finish as quickly as possible.

3. Using *Tool 4-5b,* explain and discuss each of the steps in more detail.

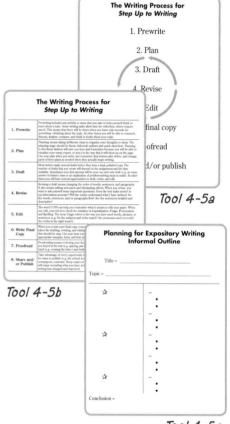

*Tool 4-5a*

*Tool 4-5b*

*Tool 4-5c*

*Step 1*

**Prewriting** includes the different activities that help a person think about, learn about, and narrow a topic, such as taking a field trip, watching a film, reading, brainstorming, and making a cognitive map of possible ideas. There are many possible prewriting activities. With your students, list ways they can learn more about their topic before they write. (For more information about prewriting, see *Bonus Tool 4-5-1.*)

## Step 2

**Planning** is how writers organize their thoughts and ideas so that what they write will make sense to readers. Planning gives form to good intentions. Display *Tool 4-5c* to show that an informal outline is used to plan for expository writing. Discuss why planning before writing is so important. (See **4-7 Planning with an Informal Outline** for additional information.)

## Step 3

**Drafting** means using the plan to make a draft (not final) copy. Reinforce that sometimes there isn't time to do multiple drafts, but when students are completing important assignments, it is worth their time to do more than one draft.

## Step 4

**Revising** means changing words, sentences, and paragraphs to make them better. It might also mean adding new parts and taking away parts that aren't needed or don't make sense.

## Step 5

**Editing** includes fixing mistakes in writing. See **10-7 Editing with CUPS** for additional information. Have your students check for common conventions such as:

C = capitalization

U = usage

P = punctuation

S = spelling

## Step 6

**Writing the Final Copy** means using their best handwriting or word processing skills to make a neat copy.

## Step 7

**Proofreading** means checking over the paper one last time to catch small mistakes before turning in the work. Remind students that even if they used a computer, they need to proofread their work.

## Step 8

**Sharing and/or Publishing** includes all the ways students might let others enjoy their writing.

4. Clear up misunderstandings that students have about any of the steps. Ask students to repeat and/or explain various steps. Encourage students to refer to their copies of *Tools 4-5a, 4-5b,* and *4-5c* as they write.

For scoring guides and other support for assessment, see Section 10.

## 4-6 Color-Coding and the Five Elements of Expository Writing

This strategy introduces students to the Traffic Light colors and elements used in all forms of expository writing.

**Handy Pages**

### Before Class

- Make overhead transparencies and student copies of *Tools 4-6a* and *4-6b*. Encourage students to keep their copies of *Tool 4-6a* in their writing notebooks for reference.

- Have available green, yellow, and red highlighters and overhead markers.

### During Class

1. Explain that the term *expository writing* means *writing to give someone information*. Tell students that expository writing includes single paragraphs and multiparagraph essays and reports.

**Elements of Expository Writing**

**Organization is the key.**
Use the colors of a traffic light and informal outlines to plan a paragraph, essay, or report.

**Topic sentences are the heart.**
Use green to remember that topic sentences tell your reader what you are going to prove or explain. In essays the topic sentence is called a thesis statement.

**Transitions are the glue for the key/star ideas.**
Use yellow to remind yourself to slow down and make smooth, yet clear transitions when a new key/star idea is introduced.

**Examples, evidence, and explanation are the meat.**
Use red to remind yourself to stop and explain. Explanation, evidence, and examples will push you to elaborate your key/star ideas.

**Conclusions tie it all together.**
Use green again! This will remind you to go back to your topic. A good conclusion reminds your reader about the purpose of your paragraph or essay.

*Tool 4-6a*

2. Point out that we use the Traffic Light colors to help us see the different parts of expository paragraphs, essays, and reports. Explain the Traffic Light colors as follows:

- Green on a traffic light means go. Topic sentences and thesis statements are colored green because they show what the writer is *going* to prove or explain.

- Yellow on a traffic light means slow down. The sentences that support the topic are colored yellow to remind writers to *slow down* and provide support for the thesis statement.

- Red on a traffic light means stop. Sentences used to elaborate and add examples or explanations are colored red to remind the writer to *stop*, explain, and add evidence.

- Green for the conclusion reminds students to *go back* and remind the reader of the topic.

3. Using *Tool 4-6a*, introduce the five elements of expository writing. Color-code using the Traffic Light colors as follows and have students do the same on their copies. Reinforce that all forms of expository writing should include all five of the elements. Provide an opportunity for students to ask questions.

**Organization is the Key**

- Explain to your students the importance of making plans before they write. Tell them that Traffic Light colors and informal outlines are the keys to organizing their writing. They are visual strategies that will help them organize their ideas and make it easier to write.

### Topic sentences and thesis statements are the Heart

- Tell your students that in an expository paragraph the topic sentence or thesis statement is colored green; it is also the heart of the paragraph. The color green is a reminder that in a topic sentence or thesis statement, writers should tell readers what they are going to prove or explain.

### Transitions are the Glue for the key/star ideas

- Explain that in expository writing, the topic sentence is supported by reasons, details, or facts that prove or explain the topic. These key/star ideas are introduced by transitions and are colored yellow to remind students to *slow down* and support their topic sentences. Transitions are like glue; they keep all of the pieces together.

### Elaboration, Examples, Evidence, and Explanation are the Meat

- The meat of a paragraph contains elaboration, examples, evidence, and explanation to support each key/star idea. Red from the Traffic Light reminds students to *stop* and explain. These examples are the meat of the paragraph. There are many words that begin with the letter *e* that can help students remember to elaborate. These words—the E's—are also called the Reds.

### Conclusions tie it all together with a Ribbon

- The green ribbon on the package reminds students to tie all of their ideas together and give their readers something to think about in the conclusion. Green reminds students to *go back* to the topic sentence and make a strong, meaningful connection with it—not just copy it.

4. Use *Tool 4-6b* to reinforce and review color coding and the different parts of a paragraph. Tell students that the colors of a traffic light can help them remember the parts of expository writing. Color-code the paragraph at the bottom of *Tool 4-6b* with your students as follows and give them the opportunity to ask questions.

*Tool 4-6b*

   ▸ Green—First and last sentence (Introduction and Conclusion)
   ▸ Yellow—Sentences beginning "First," "Next," and "Finally" (Key/Star Ideas)
   ▸ Red—All other sentences (Elaboration and Explanation, or the E's)

**Note:** When students color-code paragraphs with the Traffic light colors, the entire key/star idea sentence is colored yellow even when that sentence contains a bit of explanation or elaboration (the E's). Discuss with your students how key/star ideas and the E's can be used together to make more interesting sentences. Remind them that both simple and elaborate key/star idea sentences are appropriate depending on their purpose and audience.

key/star idea       elaboration

*The first day, we visited the museum where Babe Ruth's bats and gloves are displayed.*

## 4-7 Planning with an Informal Outline

Teach this strategy to help students learn to plan a topic quickly and to visualize the parts of their paragraphs before they begin writing.

**Handy Pages**

### Before Class

- Make an overhead transparency and student copies of *Tool 4-5c* and *Tool 4-7a*.
- Have available notebook paper, green, yellow, and red highlighters and overhead markers.

### During Class

1. Display *Tool 4-5c* to introduce the parts of an informal outline. Explain to your students that informal outlines used for planning lead to independence and success with expository writing. They will help students think about a topic and make a plan for writing. Planning is the key to writing success.

2. Let them know that informal outlines are made by quickly jotting down words and phrases that show the main ideas (next to the stars) and the supporting information (by the dashes and dots) that will be used to prove or explain the topic.

3. Use the informal outline on the left side of *Tool 4-7a* to give a visual of what an informal outline will look like on notebook paper. Explain that they will be using the same format on their regular notebook paper. Have your students use notebook paper to make their own models as you demonstrate. Refer to the outline on the Tool as needed.

   - Have students fold notebook paper into a two-column fold and draw a line at the top and along the fold—a T. (See "Folds" in the Introduction.)
   - Write "Title=" at the top and say that this is where they will write their draft title. This will help them focus on what they want to write about.
   - Write "Topic=" below the title and explain that this is where they will write their topic and/or a draft of the topic sentence. This will later be used to write the introduction.

*Tool 4-5c*

*Tool 4-7a*

- Add stars to the left column for the key/star ideas. Explain that key/star ideas are the big ideas (reasons, facts, or details) that support the topic, and when it comes to key/star ideas, two are as good as three and as good as four. In other words, there is no preset number of sentences in a paragraph.

- Tell students that it is always best to select the key/star ideas first and then go back to add the dashes for elaboration. Explain that the example on *Tool 4-7a* uses only two key/star ideas, but paragraphs (and later, reports) can have two, three, or more.

- Add dashes and dots to the right of the fold line for the words and phrases that show the E's (evidence, examples, and explanation). Dashes are used to elaborate on the key/star ideas. The dots provide even more elaboration, evidence, examples, and explanations that are specific, convincing, interesting, and engaging. The dots support the words after the dash.

- Have students add transitions that they might want to use, and put them in parentheses under the key/star ideas. Remind them that, if needed, they can change the transitions when they write their first draft.

- Write "Conclusion=" at the bottom. Tell students that when they develop their informal outlines, they can write draft conclusions here. This could be a full sentence or just a word or phrase as a reminder of their thinking about how to conclude in an interesting and meaningful way.

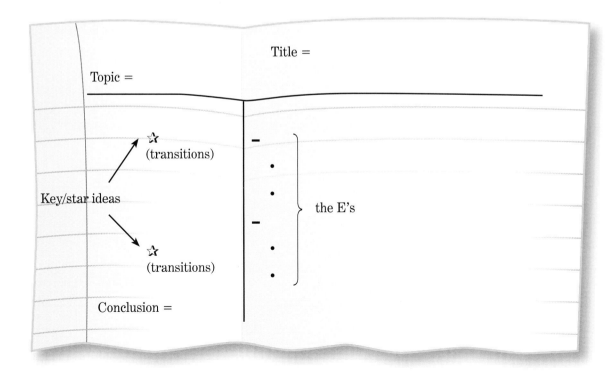

4. After modeling the structure of an informal outline, explain that the success of a paragraph will depend on the clarity of the topic sentence and key/star ideas and the quality of the E's in the body of the paragraph. Note also that the key/star ideas are always added before the E's (evidence, examples, and explanation). Explain that these elements give students the big picture and help them see their entire plan in advance.

5. If needed, clarify for students the difference between an informal outline and the format used for two-column note taking (**1-17 Easy Two-Column Notes**) and fact outlines (**1-30 Four-Step Summary Paragraphs**). The "star" symbol is not used in note taking and fact outlines.

**Note:** Informal outlines can be created using a number of different symbols to show the relationship of ideas. For instance, 1s or ■ could be used instead of stars, and 2s, 3s, and ▲ could be used instead of dashes and dots. Roman numerals (I, II, III) and decimals (1.2, 1.2.1, 1.2.2) are used to note major and minor details on formal outlines .

### Color-Coding the Informal Outline and Paragraph

1. Read through the informal outline and finished paragraph on *Tool 4-7a* with your class. As a group activity, color-code the outline using the Traffic Light colors.

   - Color "Topic:" green at the top of the page. Explain that when the topic turns into a topic sentence (also green ), it serves as part of the introduction to the paragraph.
   - Color the key/star ideas yellow .
   - Color the dashes and dots red to indicate the elaboration and explanation.
   - Color "Conclusion =" green at the bottom of the page.

2. Have students color-code the paragraph on their own. When they have finished, model the correct color coding on the transparency and have students check their work. The color coding should be as follows:

- Green—First and last sentences (topic sentence and conclusion)
- Yellow—The three sentences with the transitions and the key/star ideas:
  ▸ First, the book tells many exciting tales of how ordinary people have changed their lives by finding a bottle on the beach with a message tucked neatly inside and a cork stuck on the top.
  ▸ The book also tells of many other uses for bottle messages.
  ▸ In addition, *The Twelve Million Dollar Note* tells how the ocean currents were charted by the use of bottle messages.
- Red—all other sentences (elaboration, examples, and evidence).

3. Review the informal outline and paragraph again with your students. Discuss the organization and color coding. Ask them to explain how the informal outline would make writing the paragraph easier.

## 4-8 Accordion Paragraphs

This strategy helps students determine the best length for a clear and effective paragraph.

**Prerequisite:** 4-7 Planning with an Informal Outline

**Handy Pages**

### Before Class

- Make an overhead transparency and student copies of *Tool 4-8a*.
- Have available notebook paper and green, yellow, and red highlighters and overhead markers.

⊙ *Bonus Tools 4-8-1 and 4-8-2 provide additional examples.*

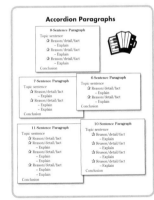

*Tool 4-8a*

## During Class

- Display *Tool 4-8a* and explain to your students that expository paragraphs may be short or long. Use the image of an accordion to help them remember this concept. Explain that, like an accordion, a paragraph can be stretched to become longer.

- Reinforce that the length of a paragraph depends on the topic, purpose, and audience. Discuss how the length of a paragraph depends on the number of key/star ideas and the number of E's (explanation, examples, and elaboration) for each key/ star idea.

- Print in large letters each step for the *Step Up* Writing Process (*Tool 4-5a*) on separate pieces of cardstock. Add magnetic tape to the back of each card. During writers' workshop display the cards to help students use their time effectively.

### Avoiding Five-Sentence Paragraphs

- Tell students that the five-sentence paragraph is sometimes too short to include enough details to make the paragraph interesting. Encourage them to write paragraphs that include numerous E's. Remind them that the E's are the "meat" of the paragraph. (If you make five-sentence paragraphs the standard, your students will put more emphasis on length than on content. The length of a paragraph should be based on the purpose and not any preconceived notion of length.)

- Share the following example (also on *Bonus Tool 4-8-1*) to demonstrate how weak a five-sentence paragraph can be.

Title = Basketball

Topic = enjoying basketball

☆ coach and players

☆ game

☆ cheering

Conclusion = like the game

Basketball

I like basketball for three reasons. First, I like the coach and all of the players. Next, I like the game and the action in the game. Finally, I enjoy the cheering from the crowd. I definitely like this game.

After sharing the example, work together with the class to improve the paragraph by adding additional E's (examples and elaboration). The following example (also on *Bonus Tool 4-8-2*) is one way to expand the paragraph. Note that the E's are added with dashes on the informal outline and are colored red. (See **4-31 Paragraph Elaboration—the E's/the Reds** for more information.)

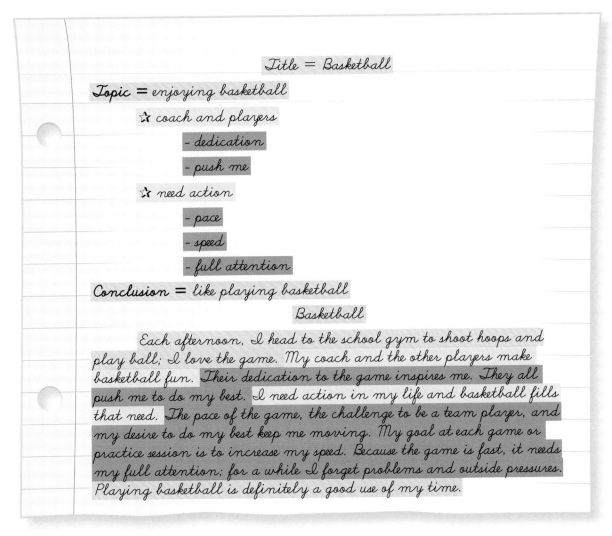

Title = Basketball

Topic = enjoying basketball

☆ coach and players
- dedication
- push me

☆ need action
- pace
- speed
- full attention

Conclusion = like playing basketball

**Basketball**

Each afternoon, I head to the school gym to shoot hoops and play ball; I love the game. My coach and the other players make basketball fun. Their dedication to the game inspires me. They all push me to do my best. I need action in my life and basketball fills that need. The pace of the game, the challenge to be a team player, and my desire to do my best keep me moving. My goal at each game or practice session is to increase my speed. Because the game is fast, it needs my full attention; for a while I forget problems and outside pressures. Playing basketball is definitely a good use of my time.

For assessment and scoring support, see **10-15 Expository Paragraphs Scoring Guide**.

## 4-9 Determining Key/Star Ideas with the Thinking Game

One problem that writers sometimes have is deciding which big ideas they want to write about. This strategy will help students practice thinking about their topics before creating their informal outlines.

**Handy Pages**

**Prerequisite:** 4-7 Planning with an Informal Outline

### Before Class

Make an overhead transparency of *Tool 4-9a*.

 *Bonus Tool 4-9-1* provides an additional example.

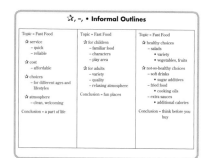

*Tool 4-9a*

### During Class

#### Thinking in Categories

1. Explain to your students that before they begin writing, they will first need to figure out what to write about. Even when they have a topic and are given a prompt, they may have difficulty coming up with key/star ideas to write about. By practicing accordion thinking in the thinking game, they will be able to do it quickly and without frustration.

2. Review the concept of key/star ideas with your students. Explain that in expository writing, the topic sentence is supported by key/star ideas (reasons, details, and facts) that prove or explain the topic and are introduced by transitions. Display *Tool 4-9a* and point out the key/star ideas on the informal outlines. Sentences with key/star ideas (and transitions) are colored yellow to remind them to slow down and support their topic sentences. Key/star ideas can be:

| | | |
|---|---|---|
| problems | events | issues |
| people | places | features |
| qualities | feelings | kinds |
| traits | types | characteristics |

3. Display *Tool 4-9a* to illustrate how there are different key/star ideas they could use to write about the topic "fast food." Read the example informal outlines with your class and then discuss the different key/star ideas.

4. Review the different symbols used in informal outlines. Stars represent key/star ideas, dashes elaborate on those big ideas, and dots provide examples or evidence that support an elaboration.

5. Emphasize the importance of thinking in categories. Point out that the dashes and dots give support to the category of the key/star idea.

6. Remind students that informal outlines can have one or more key/star ideas, depending on the topic and purpose.

### Playing the Thinking Game

1. Explain that the Thinking Game is easy. You will give students a topic and they will give you as many sets of key/star ideas as they can think of, or you will give them a specific number and they will give you that many ideas. Keep the game oral to save time, or have them write their ideas. Either way will give students a chance to share and learn from each other. Just say:

   "The topic is _____ and I need  (number)  key/star ideas."

2. If time permits and students are ready, list on the board key/star ideas that go together and ask students for the dashes and dots to elaborate on them.

3. Model, encourage, and give suggestions as needed to make the activity a success for all students. Use the following examples if they need help getting started. (These and additional examples are on *Bonus Tool 4-9-1.*)

   Topic = *Fast Food Restaurants*
   ☆ part-time jobs
   ☆ full-time jobs
   ☆ careers

   Topic = *Fast Food Restaurants*
   ☆ breakfast
   ☆ lunch
   ☆ dinner
   ☆ snacks

4. Have students continue to practice individually or in small groups with topics they have studied or are familiar with, such as music, sports, space travel, and so on.

## Additional Ideas

• This is a good activity to use as a review of content-area material. For instance, at the end of a math class, have students give three key/star ideas to show that they understand percentages.

- Have students develop informal outlines and color-code them. If there is time and they are ready, have them write paragraphs based on their informal outlines.

## 4-10 The Organization Game

The Organization Game teaches students to think in categories and to sort information.

### Before Class

- Make enough copies of *Tools 4-10a, 4-10b*, and *4-10c* so that each group of students will have a copy of each Tool (cardstock works best).

- Cut each Tool into pieces as indicated and store the pieces from each Tool in separate zip-shut plastic bags.

*Tool 4-10a*

*Tool 4-10b*

### During Class

1. Explain that the object of this game is to divide a collection of words into categories. Tell your students that they should first find the overall topic(s) for the other words and phrases.

2. For each topic there are a number of categories. These are like the key/star ideas in an informal outline. For each key/star idea, there are a number of E's (examples or explanations) that tell about that key/star idea. (See 4-7 Planning with an Informal Outline.)

3. Model the sorting process using a topic of your own on an overhead or use blocks to which you have added magnetized tape from *Tool 4-10a* or *Tool 4-10b* or an example you have developed. (Make the blocks large enough so that all your students can see them.) Demonstrate how you would sort the blocks. Use a topic that students are familiar with, such as musical instruments or different sports.

4. Divide your class into small groups or pairs, and give each group one of the zip-shut bags you prepared before class from *Tool 4-10a* or *Tool 4-10b*. Tell them that there is more than one category in each bag, and have them sort and organize the pieces. Remind them that this is the way to organize their thoughts and then put them on informal outlines—with a topic followed by key/star ideas and then elaboration. Do not give your students the topic or key/star ideas unless they get stuck.

*Tool 4-10a*

Topic = states

&#9734; East Coast states

&#9734; West Coast states

Topic = sports

&#9734; winter sports

&#9734; summer sports

Topic = school resources

&#9734; the library

&#9734; the computer lab

*Tool 4-10b*

Topic = education

&#9734; things to do at school

&#9734; things to learn at school

5. Have students share their work. Point out that when they are developing an informal outline, they sometimes will come up with more ideas than they can write about. To write a successful paper, they should use enough key/star ideas to prove their point, but not so many that their writing is confusing or uninteresting. It is not necessary or appropriate to share everything they know about the topic.

6. Keep in mind that content topics work best for this game. The process pushes students to think about what they have learned.

7. Provide additional opportunities for practice using a copy of *Tool 4-10c* that you have filled in.

## Additional Ideas

- Provide copies of the blank grid on *Tool 4-10c* for students who are ready to make their own organization game. After they have completed filling in all the boxes, have them turn in a key with the game pieces noting the topic, key/star ideas, and the E's.

- Use *Tool 4-10c* to write key/star ideas and examples from a topic recently discussed in class as another version of The Organization Game for students to sort and organize.

- Create a "live" organization game using small cards. Write words or phrases that can be used to form several key/star ideas and E's about class content. Give each student one of the cards and have them hold their card up where the other students can see it. Then ask them to organize themselves in line like an informal outline, using the words or phrases on their cards.

*Tool 4-10c*

## (4-11) Informal Outlines of Various Lengths

Writers sometimes may think that every paragraph should have a set number of key/star ideas. Teach this strategy to help students learn to write informal outlines of different lengths, as appropriate for their topic.

**Prerequisite:** 4-7 Planning with an Informal Outline

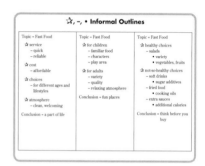

**Handy Pages**

### Before Class

Make transparencies and student copies of *Tools 4-9a* and *4-11a* through *4-11d*.

### During Class

1. Display *Tool 4-9a* and point out that the three informal outlines each have a different number of key/star ideas (details), dashes (explanations), and dots (examples).

2. Reinforce that the number of key/star ideas, dashes, and dots depends on the assignment, topic, and amount of time available to write.

3. With your students, create informal outlines of different lengths on a chosen topic using *Tools 4-11a, 4-11b,* and *4-11c*.

4. Have your students continue developing a number of informal outlines of different lengths on the same topic (working individually or in small groups). Then have them share their outlines. Finally, lead a discussion on why sometimes you need fewer key/star ideas and E's than other times.

*Tool 4-9a*

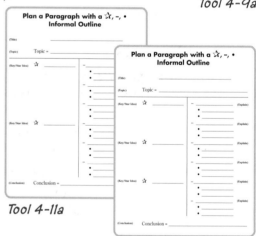

*Tool 4-11a*

*Tool 4-11b*

### Informal Outlines for Essays and Reports

Using *Tool 4-11d*, explain that essay and report writing are important for students at all grade levels. While students are developing paragraph-writing skills, be sure to keep in mind that they will be learning to stretch their skills to essay and report writing. Use **5-22 Moving from a Paragraph to an Essay or Report** to introduce the concept of stretching ideas into a report or essay instead of stacking Accordion Paragraphs.

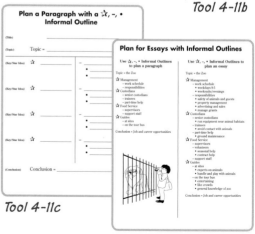

*Tool 4-11c*

*Tool 4-11d*

## Additional Ideas

Often, there is not enough time in class to take every informal outline and turn it into a complete paragraph. Sometimes just making the informal outline is enough. The thinking that goes into creating the outline is what is important.

## 4-12 Planning Guides for Organizing an Accordion Paragraph

Students need to learn to plan before writing in order to develop and improve their organizational skills. Planning Guides serve the same function as informal outlines. Use the one that best supports the needs of your students.

**Prerequisites:** 4-6 Color-Coding and the Five Elements of Expository Writing **and** 4-7 Planning with an Informal Outline

### Before Class

- Make an overhead transparency and student copies of *Tool 4-12a*.
- *Bonus Tools 4-12-1* and *4-12-2* provide additional support.

*Tool 4-12a*

### During Class

1. Display *Tool 4-12a*, and review the guide with your students. Point out the small words to the side of each box and review the meaning of the Traffic Light colors as you highlight the transparency and your students highlight their copies. Discuss how this guide is related to an informal outline.

2. Model using *Tool 4-12a* with a topic your students have covered in class. As you write on the transparency, have students fill in their copies. Remind them that they should use only words and phrases for their key/star ideas and the E's.

3. Provide numerous models and practice opportunities on additional topics. For a planning guide for paragraphs with three or four key/star ideas see *Bonus Tools 4-12-1* or *4-12-2*.

4. Emphasize that the number of key/star ideas that they generate depends on their topic and purpose and is not determined by the planning tool they use.

5. Once students are skilled at planning, model or remind them how to go from planning to writing. Consider initially using 4-13 Practice Guides for Writing Accordion Paragraphs.

## 4-13 Practice Guides for Writing Accordion Paragraphs

Using a paragraph practice guide will help students see the organization of a paragraph, sentence by sentence. Use this strategy to give your students initial practice in writing Accordion Paragraphs.

**Prerequisites:** 4-6 Color-Coding and the Five Elements of Expository Writing **and** 4-7 Planning with an Informal Outline

### Before Class

- Make overhead transparencies and student copies of *Tools 4-13a* and *4-13b*.

 *Bonus Tools 4-13-1* through *4-13-4* provide additional support.

### During Class

- Display *Tools 4-13a* and *4-13b*. Explain to your students that this guide will help them expand their informal outlines from words and phrases into sentences and help them organize.

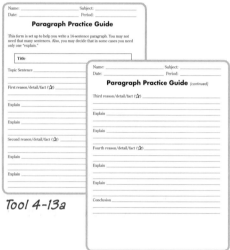

*Tool 4-13a*

*Tool 4-13b*

- Tell them that the format of the guide is flexible. They may not need all fourteen sentences. For instance, they may have only two or three key/star ideas. Space is provided on this guide for four key/star ideas. Parts that are not used should be crossed out. Reinforce that the "accordion" name of this strategy is to suggest flexibility for writing less or more, depending on the points they want to make. (If students need more than fourteen sentences, they can expand the guide using extra sheets of notebook paper.)

- In most cases, students will edit and revise the draft that is on their practice guide and create a formal copy. But keep in mind that the quantity of rehearsal/practice opportunities is important. When students complete the practice guide, they complete several steps in the writing process. Often it is appropriate—and good— for students to just complete the practice guide.

- Consider making several overhead transparency copies of *Tools 4-13a* and *4-13b*. Let students work in pairs. Give them overhead markers to use when they write a paragraph. Give each pair time to share their work at the overhead projector. (See *Bonus Tools 4-13-1* through *4-13-4* for an alternative practice guide format.)

## Additional Ideas

- To help students who are just learning to write paragraphs, add a topic sentence and/or key/star ideas before making student copies.

- Practice Guides for Writing Accordion Paragraphs can be used throughout the year for quizzes, responses, and essay questions with time limits, or when you want to reinforce the importance of organization.

## 4-14 Organization with Framed Paragraphs

Use 9-9 Using Writing Frames to support skill development and give students early success in paragraph, essay, and report writing. This strategy is a visual means of helping students quickly see the parts of a paper and recognize the organization of essays and reports.

Writing frames provide support as students develop their skills. A paragraph frame includes part of a paragraph and spaces for students to fill in missing information. For instance, a paragraph frame could contain a title, a strong topic sentence, and obvious transitions. Students then fill in the key/star ideas and examples that support the topic sentence as they organize their own thoughts and words into formal paragraphs.

## 4-15 Accordion Races

Use Accordion Races as a fun way to help students recognize and analyze the organization of expository paragraphs.

**Prerequisite:** 4-23 Definition and Function of Transitions

### Before Class

- Make several copies of *Tools 4-15a* and *4-15b*, cut the strips apart, then clip the pieces from each Tool together or put them into separate envelopes. Make as many sets as needed for the class to work in small groups or pairs.

 *Bonus Tools 4-15-1* and *4-15-2* provide additional support.

### During Class

1. This strategy works well as a friendly race between teams. Break the class into small groups or pairs and give each group the sentences from *Tool 4-15a*.

*Tool 4-15a*

*Tool 4-15b*

2. Tell your students that the goal is to see which group can arrange the sentences into a meaningful paragraph the quickest. Remind them that they must read the sentences and make decisions about how the sentences should be arranged.

3. Have them race against each other and congratulate the winner. Then give each team the sentences from *Tool 4-15b* and have another race. (For additional examples, see *Bonus Tools 4-15-1* and *4-15-2*.) At the end of the races, discuss the activity using these questions and questions of your own:

   - Were the topic sentences easy to find? Why?
   - Did the paragraphs have lead sentences as background for the topic sentences? Were these sentences helpful? Why?
   - How quickly could your group find the key/star ideas? Why?
   - What were the transitions in each paragraph? Did the transitions in the sentences help with organization or reading? Why? How?
   - Did this activity take careful reading? Why?
   - Could the sentences for either paragraph be arranged differently and still make sense?

## Additional Ideas

Use Accordion Races with content that students are learning. When students work with content material, they learn the content and improve their writing at the same time.

## 4-16 Writing in First, Second, and Third Person

Accordion paragraphs, reports, and essays can be written in first, second, or third person. Use this strategy to introduce writing from a different point of view.

## Before Class

- Make overhead transparencies and student copies of *Tools 4-16a, 4-16b*, and *4-16c*.
 *Bonus Tools 4-16-1* and *4-16-2* provide additional examples.

## During Class

1. Using *Tool 4-16a*, inform or remind your students that first, second, and third person are terms used to describe different points of view, then review the descriptions and pronouns for each. Emphasize that these three approaches can and are used in all types of writing; the choice always depends on the purpose and the audience.

2. Display *Tool 4-16b* and show that you cannot tell if a paragraph is going to be written in first, second, or third person from the informal outline. Then show *Tool 4-16c* to illustrate that the difference is in how the ideas from the informal outline are used. On the transparency, circle the pronouns to show the point of view of each paragraph. (See *Bonus Tool 4-16-1* for an additional sample of paragraphs written from each point of view on the same general topic.)

3. Have your students write about the same topic three times—in first person, second person, and third person. Use direct instruction as well as guided lessons to help students master this skill. Select a topic familiar to everyone in class, such as multiplication in math, rivers in geography, and fossils in science, or use one of the prompts from the *Bonus Tool CD*. Have them use *Bonus Tool 4-16-2* or notebook paper for planning.

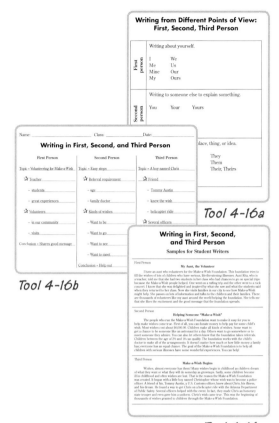

*Tool 4-16a*

*Tool 4-16b*

*Tool 4-16c*

## Additional Ideas

When students read, stop to ask if the text is in first person, second person, or third person. Start a class collection of examples that demonstrate each point of view.

# Topic Sentences, Thesis Statements, and Leads

A strong, clear topic sentence or thesis statement is the heart of expository writing. The structure of each topic sentence or thesis statement serves a slightly different purpose. As students learn these strategies, they will also be learning about parts of speech, sentence structures, grammar, and punctuation, and therefore will improve their overall writing skills.

**Note:** Review Section 3, Sentence Mastery, for examples and explanations of various sentence structures that can be used for instruction along with materials in this section.

## Objectives

- Improve understanding of the function of topic sentences and thesis statements
- Enable students to write and recognize strong topic sentences and thesis statements
- Help students learn to write an engaging lead

| Strategy | Strategy Description | Page | Tools |
|---|---|---|---|
| **4-17** Defining Topic Sentences and Thesis Statements | Defining and describing the purpose of topic sentences and thesis statements | 167 | 4-17a |
| **4-18** Topic Sentence Variety | Learning key features of topic sentences and how to write them | 168 | 4-18a to 4-18n |
| **4-19** Getting Caught in the *Things* Trap | Replacing the word *things* with other words to improve the quality of a topic sentence | 179 | 4-19a |
| **4-20** Mastering Topic Sentences | Improving topic sentence writing skills, and recognizing topic sentences in various texts | 180 | n/a |

*(chart continues)*

| Strategy *(continued)* | Strategy Description | Page | Tools |
|---|---|---|---|
| **4-21** Turning a Prompt into a Topic Sentence | Reading prompts carefully and critically, and turning prompts into topic sentences | 181 | 4-21a |
| **4-22** Adding a Lead—the Blues—to a Paragraph | Adding leads and background information that either educates or entertains the reader before the topic sentence | 182 | 4-22a |

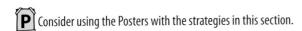 Consider using the Posters with the strategies in this section.

## **4-17** Defining Topic Sentences and Thesis Statements

Teach this strategy to introduce and/or review the concept of topic sentences and thesis statements.

**Handy Pages**

### Before Class

Make an overhead transparency and student copies of *Tool 4-17a*.

### During Class

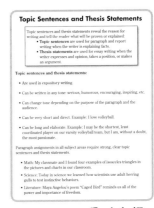

- Using *Tool 4-17a*, introduce or review the terms *thesis statement* and *topic sentence*. Read through the definition and examples. Explain that in a stand-alone expository paragraph, the thesis statement or topic sentence tells what the paragraph is about. The green heart is a reminder that the topic sentence is the heart of the paragraph.

- Tell students that a thesis statement is similar to a topic sentence, but it is not the same.
  - *Topic sentences* are used for report and paragraph writing when the writer is explaining facts.
  - *Thesis statements* are used for essay writing when the writer expresses an opinion, takes a position, or makes an argument.

*Tool 4-17a*

Because topic sentences and thesis statements have similar functions, *Step Up to Writing* uses *topic sentence* to mean both terms. Use the term appropriate for your class.

- Ask students to highlight or underline these key phrases in the definition: "showing the main idea(s)" and "noting what will be proven or explained."

- Have students look for the reason for writing and what will be proven or explained in each sample sentence at the bottom of *Tool 4-17a*.

| | What is the reason for writing? | What will be proved or explained? |
|---|---|---|
| Math | *learned about triangles* | *examples of isosceles triangles* |
| Science | *read about adult herring gulls* | *how scientists used them for a test* |
| Literature | *read poem* | *message about freedom* |

- Encourage students to look for these two features—the reason for writing and what will be proved or explained—in other examples.

 For a quick check and other support for assessment, see **10-10 Quick Check for Sentences.**

## 4-18 Topic Sentence Variety

There are a variety of methods for writing topic sentences. Use them to help students learn how to write effective thesis statements with ease.

**Handy Pages**

Not all of these methods should be taught at the same time, and each might take a period of time for students to master. The following methods are presented in no particular order, but Action Verb Topic Sentences and Where or When Plus What's Happening Topic Sentences are easy to teach and learn. Both reinforce the importance and power of action verbs.

### Before Class

- Make overhead transparencies and student copies of *Tools 4-18a* through *4-18n*.

- Write several topic sentences to use as examples for each strategy.

 *Bonus Tool 4-18-1* provides additional support.

# During Class

- Explain and model each method. Remind your students that a good topic sentence leads to key/star ideas. Explain that a good topic sentence can be "proven or explained" and provides a framework for creating an informal outline as a plan for the paragraph.

- Use the following steps with each of the topic sentence structures. Provide the added hints noted with the explanation of each type of topic sentence.

> **Step 1** Using the designated Tool, read the information in the definition box and discuss how the example sentences follow the pattern.
>
> **Step 2** Write examples of the type of topic sentence being studied on a blank transparency, using sentences you provide or that you create with your class. Have students copy the examples on their paper. Model as many sentences as necessary.
>
> **Step 3** Have your students work in pairs or individually to write their own topic sentences on topics you have provided.
>
> **Step 4** As students develop skills, have them revise and edit their topic sentences. Expect their best efforts; expect accuracy and creativity; and demonstrate and expect quality.

- The quality of rehearsal time is important. Practice topic sentences even when there is not time to write out a formal paragraph or report.

## Action Verb Topic Sentences

- Use *Tool 4-18a* and follow the four steps provided at the beginning of this strategy. Model folding a piece of notebook paper using a burrito fold (paper folded lengthwise into three columns) and have students fold their papers likewise.

- As you discuss Action Verb Topic Sentences, provide the following hints:
  ▸ Action Verb Topic Sentences are declarative statements.
  ▸ To write an Action Verb Topic Sentence, first write down the verb.
  ▸ Finish by adding details in the first and third columns.

*Tool 4-18a*

Men and women who serve in the military | face | unusual challenges every day.

## IVF Topic Sentences

The IVF (Identify the Item, Select a Verb, and Finish Your Thought) topic sentence is a form of the Action Verb Topic Sentence. They both stress strong verbs that send a clear message about the purpose of the topic sentence and both incorporate the burrito fold for instruction. IVF topic sentences differ only in the fact that specific verbs are used. The verbs fit a specific kind of writing and a specific prompt (eg. analyzing a graph, explaining a science lab experiment, or writing about a theme in literature.) Students writing IVF topic sentences often use the TED verbs (tell, describe, explain). For more information about IVF topic sentences, see **1-30 Four-Step Summary Paragraphs, 9-5 Responding to Literature, 9-12 Writing in Math, and 9-13 Writing Reports on Science Experiments.**

Action Verb Topic Sentences are not limited to any list of verbs; however, teachers and students may want to create a list of strong action verbs. This list will help students generate ideas, and it may help them with spelling.

## Where or When Plus What's Happening? Topic Sentences

- Use *Tool 4-18b* and follow the four steps provided at the beginning of this strategy. Model folding a piece of notebook paper using a hot dog fold (paper folded in half lengthwise) and have students fold their papers likewise.

- As you discuss Where or When Plus What's Happening? Topic Sentences, provide the following hints:
  - ▸ Begin with either a phrase or a clause.
  - ▸ Begin with an adverb (yesterday, today, Wednesday).
  - ▸ Use a strong action verb.
  - ▸ Use good sentence variety.

*Tool 4-18b*

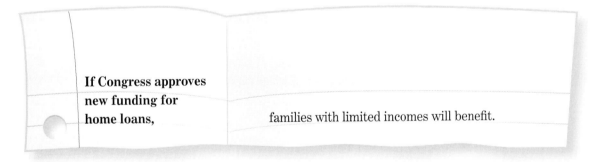

| At last week's state competition, | our jazz band impressed the judges with two inspiring pieces. |

## Occasion/Position Topic Sentences

- Use *Tool 4-18c* and follow the four steps provided at the beginning of this strategy. Model folding a piece of notebook paper using a two-column fold and have students fold their papers likewise.

- Explain that Occasion/Position Topic Sentences:
    - Have two clauses—dependent and independent (complex sentences);
    - Have a comma separating the dependent from the independent clause;
    - Have the dependent clause first, followed by the independent clause;
    - Begin with adverbial clauses using subordinating conjunctions.

*Tool 4-18c*

| If Congress approves new funding for home loans, | families with limited incomes will benefit. |

After your students have learned several ways to write topic sentences and can recognize topic sentences in what they read, help them find the occasion and the position in all topic sentences. This will push your students to read closely and help them learn to analyze topic sentences. For examples, see *Bonus Tool 4-18-1.*

### And, But, Or, and So Topic Sentences

- Use *Tool 4-18d* and follow the four steps provided earlier in this strategy. Model folding a piece of notebook paper using a hot dog fold and have students fold their papers likewise.

- As you discuss And, But, Or, and So Topic Sentences, provide the following hints:
  - ▸ Notice the two clauses—both clauses are independent (creating a compound sentence)—on each side of the fold.
  - ▸ The clauses are connected by conjunctions.
  - ▸ There is a comma after the first independent clause and before the conjunction. (Remind students that conjunctions do not *always* need commas, only when two independent clauses are being connected.)
  - ▸ The two clauses are part of one thought.

*Tool 4-18d*

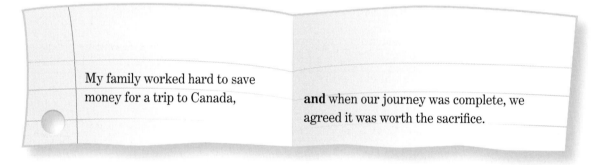

My family worked hard to save money for a trip to Canada,

**and** when our journey was complete, we agreed it was worth the sacrifice.

### Power (Number) Topic Sentences

- Use *Tool 4-18e* and follow the four steps provided at the beginning of this strategy. (There is no paper fold for this type of topic sentence.)

- As you discuss Power (Number) Topic Sentences, provide the following hints:
  - ▸ Any sentence structure (simple, compound, or complex) can be used.
  - ▸ Use number words for emphasis and organization.

*Tool 4-18e*

▸ Avoid using phrases like "there are," "these are," and "here are." Instead, use words that tell *who, what, when,* or *where:*

> **Who**—*My brother taught me several strategies to help me win at chess.*
>
> **What**—*Two rules for playing Monopoly are really hard to understand.*
>
> **When**—*Every weekend, my grandfather plays dominoes at two different places near our house.*
>
> **Where**—*In our class, we have many good games to play when we finish our work.*

▸ Avoid using phrases like "for these reasons," or "for several reasons." These phrases are often overused or used as a crutch.

▸ Power (Number) Topic Sentences should be used in moderation because they are not appropriate for all assignments.

### A Few Good Prepositions Topic Sentences

- Use *Tool 4-18f* and follow the four steps provided earlier in this strategy. (There is no paper fold for this type of topic sentence.)

- As you discuss A Few Good Prepositions Topic Sentences, provide the following hints:
  ▸ Any sentence structure (simple, compound, complex) can be used.
  ▸ Use different prepositional phrases to provide variety.

- Have students experiment using prepositions. Ask them to create a topic sentence using prepositions like the following:
  ▸ Throughout—Throughout the world, Throughout the room, Throughout history
  ▸ Without—Without my computer, Without my friends, Without a high school diploma

- Add hard-to-spell prepositions to spelling lists. Prepositions are common vocabulary words but are sometimes challenging to spell.

*Tool 4-18f*

**During this summer break** I spent time volunteering at the animal shelter, learning how to care for pets of all kinds.

## Compare or Contrast Topic Sentences

- Use *Tool 4-18g* and follow the four steps provided earlier in this strategy. (There is no paper fold that is part of this type of topic sentence.)

- As you discuss Compare or Contrast Topic Sentences, provide the following hints:
  - ▸ Use with any sentence structure (simple, compound, complex, compound-complex).
  - ▸ Any of the other topic sentence types can be used.
  - ▸ Use a compare/contrast word or phrase.

*Tool 4-18g*

Our media specialist purchased two **similar** sets of encyclopedias.
During this year's school play the audience enjoyed three **different** types of costumes worn by the lead characters.

**Note:** Use compare or contrast topic sentences with the materials in 9-3 Writing to Compare or Contrast.

## A Rhetorical Question Plus a Statement Topic Sentences

- Use *Tool 4-18h* and follow the four steps provided earlier in this strategy. Model folding a piece of notebook paper using a hot dog fold and have students fold their papers likewise.

- As you discuss A Rhetorical Question Plus a Statement Topic Sentences, provide the following hints:
  - ▸ Write two sentences—a question and a regular sentence. The regular sentence can have any structure (simple, compound, or complex).

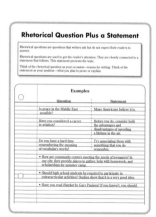

*Tool 4-18h*

- Use them to provide variety.
- Use them sparingly; they are good for certain topics but not appropriate for all writing assignments.
- Encourage your students to read their sentences out loud to be sure they make sense.
- It is good to be clever and creative, but sentences should also be clear.

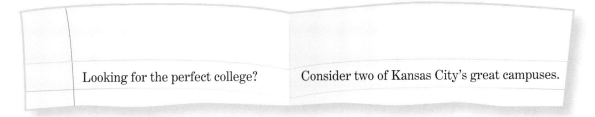

| Looking for the perfect college? | Consider two of Kansas City's great campuses. |

## However Topic Sentences

Tool 4-181

- Use *Tool 4-181* and follow the four steps provided earlier in this strategy. Model folding a piece of notebook paper using a hot dog fold and have students fold their papers likewise.
- As you discuss However Topic Sentences, provide the following hints:
  - Notice the two clauses—both clauses are independent (creating a compound sentence)—on each side of the fold.
  - The clauses are connected by conjunctive adverbs.
  - Use a semicolon between the first independent clause and the conjunctive adverb. Put a comma after the conjunctive adverb.
  - The two clauses must be connected logically; they must make sense.

| Maintaining a healthy diet is important; | however, for many Americans eating right is a challenge. |

## Semicolon and Side by Side Topic Sentences

- Use *Tool 4-18j* and follow the four steps provided earlier in this strategy. Model folding a piece of notebook paper using a hot dog fold and have students fold their papers likewise.

- As you discuss Semicolon and Side by Side Topic Sentences, provide the following hints:
  - ▶ Notice the two clauses—both are independent (creating a compound sentence)
  - ▶ The clauses can be connected by a semicolon or written as two simple sentences.
  - ▶ The two clauses must be connected logically; they must make sense.

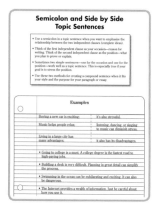

*Tool 4-18j*

| My sister just left for college; | I have already taken over her living space! |
| I am learning to drive. | I am also learning to be patient with other drivers. |

## Infinitives in Topic Sentences

- Use *Tool 4-18k* and follow the four steps provided earlier in this strategy.

- Remind students that an infinitive is the word "to" plus a verb. As you discuss Infinitives in Topic Sentences, provide the following hints:
  - ▶ Use them for giving directions or instructions.
  - ▶ Use them for assignments that share a process or a set of instructions.
  - ▶ Experiment with verbs.
  - ▶ Use them in technical and business writing.
  - ▶ Read the topic sentence aloud to be sure it makes sense.

*Tool 4-18k*

| To protest the Tea Act passed by Parliament in 1773, | Bostonians staged a memorable tea party. |

## Two Nouns and Two Commas Topic Sentences

- Use *Tool 4-18l* and follow the four steps provided earlier in this strategy. (There is no paper fold for this type of topic sentence.)

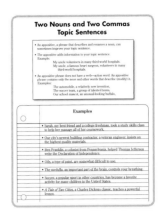

*Tool 4-18l*

- As you discuss Two Nouns and Two Commas Topic Sentences, provide the following hints:
  ▸ Use them to give extra information.
  ▸ Use them for variety and to enhance and improve a topic sentence.
  ▸ Commas separate the apposition—a word or phrase that describes and renames the noun—from the rest of the sentence.
  ▸ Appositions are phrases, not clauses, and do not have verbs.
  ▸ Make sure that the appositive phrase matches the noun that it describes.

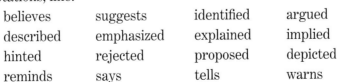

My uncle, **a rancher and a business owner,** juggles many responsibilities.

## Using a Quotation in Topic Sentences

- Use *Tool 4-18m* and follow the four steps provided earlier in this strategy. (There is no paper fold for this type of topic sentence.)

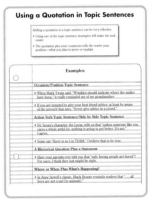

*Tool 4-18m*

- As you discuss Using a Quotation in Topic Sentences, provide the following hints:
  ▸ Use quotations from books of quotations.
  ▸ Use lines of poetry.
  ▸ Quote from news articles.
  ▸ Practice using quotations with a number of different topic sentence strategies.
  ▸ Learn to use words and phrases that work well with quotations, like:

| | | | |
|---|---|---|---|
| believes | suggests | identified | argued |
| described | emphasized | explained | implied |
| hinted | rejected | proposed | depicted |
| reminds | says | tells | warns |

When Caleb White, the architect for the new county library, said, "The entryway will invite both the young and the old into a wonderland of books and technology," everyone was impressed.

## Lists in Topic Sentences

- Use *Tool 4-18n* and follow the four steps provided earlier in this strategy. (There is no paper fold for this type of topic sentence.)
- As you discuss Lists in Topic Sentences, provide the following hints:
    ▸ Use them sparingly—only for specific purposes and audiences.
    ▸ Make lists with words, phrases, or clauses, but make sure they are parallel (constructed the same way).
    ▸ Read the sentence aloud to be sure it makes sense.
    ▸ Be careful using lists in single-paragraph assignments; lists may have too much information or be too long.

*Tool 4-18n*

In the mid-1800s, many Americans traveled to California to discover gold, but they often found serious hardships, unsanitary living conditions, and unfriendly competition.

## Additional Ideas

Consider making a packet of all the topic sentence strategies (*Tools 4-18a* through *4-18n*) and have students keep them in their writing notebooks for reference throughout the year. Also include information from "IVF" topic sentences from **1-30 Four-Step Summary Paragraphs, 9-5 Responding to Literature, 9-12 Writing in Math,** and **9-13 Writing Reports on Science Experiments.**

 For a quick check and other support for assessment, see **10-10 Quick Check for Sentences.**

# Getting Caught in the *Things* Trap

When students write topic sentences, they sometimes use the word *things* too much. Replacing the word *things* with other words can improve the quality of a topic sentence. Use this strategy to help students expand their vocabulary and write stronger topic sentences.

**Handy Pages**

## Before Class

- Make an overhead transparency and student copies of *4-19a*.

- Develop a list of ten simple topic sentences that use the word *things*. Prepare a double-spaced list of these sentences on a page and make student copies.

## During Class

1. Display the topic sentences that you created. Read them together and discuss the difficulty in knowing exactly what the writer meant and how the sentences could be stronger if the word *things* were replaced with a more descriptive word.

| Don't Get Caught in the *Things* Trap | | |
|---|---|---|
| abilities | facts | projects |
| actions | features | promises |
| advances | feelings | qualities |
| advantages | frustrations | reasons |
| adventures | ideas | remedies |
| agreements | impressions | resources |
| attributes | improvements | responses |
| behaviors | incidents | rules |
| benefits | items | sections |
| characteristics | matters | situations |
| choices | movements | skills |
| concerns | occasions | successes |
| conflicts | occurrences | surprises |
| contributions | parts | talents |
| corrections | performances | themes |
| details | periods | thoughts |
| difficulties | places | troubles |
| effects | points | types |
| events | powers | weaknesses |
| experiences | problems | variations |

*Tool 4-19a*

> **Weak:** As I read about Ben Franklin, I learned many *things* about his life.
> **Better:** As I read about Ben Franklin, I learned that his life was filled with *challenges*.
>
> **Weak:** The article we read told three *things* about the White House.
> **Better:** The article we read in social studies class described three *features* of the White House.

2. Using *Tool 4-19a*, discuss other words that can be used in place of the word *things*. Have your students suggest additional replacement words and add them to the Tool.

3. With your class, replace the word *things* in the topic sentences that you created. As you rewrite the sentence, make sure the changes do not change the meaning.

4. Remind your students to use words other than *things* in their writing, and when they do use the word, have them replace it with a more descriptive term.

 For a quick check and other support for assessment, see **10-10 Quick Check for Sentences.**

## 4-20 Mastering Topic Sentences

One of the goals for teaching a variety of topic sentence strategies is to encourage students to add their own voice, style, and flair when they write. Use these strategies to help students recognize and develop topic sentences quickly and effectively.

**Handy Pages**

**Prerequisite:** 4-18 Topic Sentence Variety

Students benefit from many opportunities to practice writing topic sentences. Repeated practice helps students perfect their skills. The following activities are quick ways to incorporate topic sentences into daily practice:

- Give students time to work in small groups. Using content studied in class, challenge each group to write as many topic sentences as it can. Limit the writing time to two or three minutes. Take time to share.

- Using slips of recycled paper or tickets from **3-12 Ticket Out**, have students write topic sentences on content shared during class. Have students hand them in as they leave class. Start the next day's class by sharing several of the better ones.

- When it is time to write, ask for three or four topic sentences, using a different strategy from **4-18 Topic Sentence Variety** for each sentence. Then have students select the one that will work best for their readers.

> When people shoplift even very small items, they may not realize the effect they have on all other shoppers.
>
> Shoplifting can become an addiction.
>
> Some young people shoplift just for fun or to prove something to their friends; unfortunately, when they are caught, their foolishness is still considered a crime.

### Finding Topic Sentences in Magazines and Newspapers

This is a fun, hands-on activity in which students practice identifying different types of topic sentences and see creative examples.

- Collect magazines or ask students to bring in school-appropriate magazines that can be cut and destroyed. News and professional magazines work best.

- Break students into small groups. Give each group magazines, newspapers, markers, scissors, glue, and one half of a poster board or large pieces of construction paper.

- Explain that they are to find topic sentences in the magazines and newspapers, cut them out, and glue them to their poster boards. Advertisements, as well as the beginnings of articles, are often good places to start. Encourage them to look for a variety of topic sentences.

- Practice in a whole-group guided lesson and then give students time to fill their pages with topic sentences. Have them add borders and decorate the pages so they are ready for display.

- Take time to share and discuss the sentences your students have found.

### Using Topic Sentence Frames

Using Topic Sentence Frames for various lessons and activities can be a good way to give students early success. The frames can be used with other activities, including when students view videos or films. See **9-9 Using Writing Frames** for more information.

 For a quick check and other support for assessment, see **10-10 Quick Check for Sentences**.

## 4-21 Turning a Prompt into a Topic Sentence

Prompts are an important aspect of many types of academic assessments. Use this strategy to teach students how to turn a prompt into a topic sentence.

**Handy Pages**

### Before Class

Make an overhead transparency of *Tool 4-21a*.

### During Class

Define *prompt* for the class. Explain that a prompt gives direction to an assignment or a test. It is a question or direction that *prompts* students to respond in writing. It can be as simple as a general idea, or more specifically tell the writers what they are expected to do.

*Tool 4-21a*

- Display *Tool 4-21a*. Read and discuss the three steps for using a prompt to write a topic sentence with your students.

- Have your students practice noting the verb. Pay close attention to the verb that gives the strongest directions for writing (*describe, tell, explain, convince,* or *persuade*). Explain that this verb will help them focus their thinking.

- Next, have them look for the key words, such as number words and any other specific directions that are part of the prompt. Tell them to watch for words like *one* or *single*. These words ask them to describe a single event or time that something happened.

- Using *Tool 4-21a*, discuss how circling and underlining parts of the prompt can be helpful.

- Provide your students with additional examples by taking one of the following prompts and turning it into one or more topic sentences. Then have students write topic sentences of their own from the remaining prompts.

> Write a paragraph that explains what happens during a fire drill in your school.
>
> Look carefully at your shoes. In a paragraph, describe your shoes for someone who can't see them.
>
> Write a paragraph convincing others they should read your favorite book.

 For a quick check and other support for assessment, see **10-10 Quick Check for Sentences.**

## 4-22 Adding a Lead—the Blues—to a Paragraph

Leads are sentences that introduce a topic sentence. They function as attention-getters for writing. Use this strategy to introduce leads to students after they have practiced topic sentences.

When students are not clear about their topics and have not formulated a clear, concise topic sentence, they may be unsure about how to start and about what they want to prove or explain. Teach and have students practice writing leads only after they have learned about and understand the need for and importance of topic sentences. (For more information about writing leads, see **5-8 Leading with the Blues.**)

### Before Class

*Tool 4-22a*

- Make an overhead transparency and student copies of *Tool 4-22a*.

- Make copies of leads from textbooks and magazine articles.

- Have available blue, green, and yellow highlighters and overhead markers.

- *Tools 5-8b* and *5-8c* provide additional support.

### During Class

1. Explain to your students that when they use the Traffic Light colors, the color blue signals a lead in a paragraph, essay, or report.

2. Tell them that the lead introduces a topic sentence and is used to get a reader's attention by:

   - Entertaining the reader with an interesting idea or clever thought;

- Educating the reader by providing important information that helps him or her understand the topic sentence.

3. Display *Tool 4-22a* and point out the lead and topic sentence in the first example, "Strong, Healthy Bodies." (The details and conclusion have been omitted.) Discuss how the lead is an invitation for the reader to continue reading.

4. Color the first two sentences blue (the lead), the third and fourth sentences green (the topic sentences), and the next four sentence starters yellow (the key/star ideas). With your students, review and color-code the next two examples. Continue to discuss the use of leads.

5. Share examples of leads you have collected from textbooks and magazine articles and highlight them in blue. Point out that leads are sometimes several sentences long and sometimes just one sentence. The length of the lead depends on the purpose and the audience for the writing. Explain that there are different types of leads.

- Humor related to the topic
- A quotation hinting at the topic
- Lines from poetry connected to the theme or topic
- A question to be answered in the paragraph
- Important facts
- A bold, startling statement
- A connection to the news, T.V., history, movies, or literature
- Clever statement(s) or a short story to get the reader's attention or clarify the topic

6. Share the following tips with students as they look for leads in their samples:

- Paragraphs (reports and essays) do not always have or need a lead.
- Leads should be used only when they make sense and fit the purpose of the writing; clear, concise writing is the goal of any paragraph, essay, or report.
- If students write long leads during a timed writing assessment, they may eat up time and confuse the person grading the paper, who is looking for a response to the prompt.

## Additional Ideas

- Point out the leads as you read with your class and have students analyze their function.
- Review examples of leads as a whole class or with students in small groups and discuss what types of leads are used.

# Transitions for Key/Star Ideas

Transitions are an important aid for organization and help both the writer and the reader. Students learn about transitions by imitating what they read and by following directions that they receive in guided and interactive writing lessons.

## Objectives

- Teach students to write effective transitions
- Improve students' knowledge of the variety of transitions they can use

| Strategy | Strategy Description | Page | Tools |
|---|---|---|---|
| **4-23** Definition and Function of Transitions | Learning the function of transitions and how they help organize writing | 185 | 4-23a, 4-23b |
| **4-24** Transition Sets | Developing transition sets | 186 | 4-24a |
| **4-25** Transitions for Different Purposes | Recognizing different types of transition sets | 187 | 4-25a |
| **4-26** Using Transitions Effectively | Using transitions effectively | 188 | 4-26a |
| **4-27** Obvious and Subtle Transitions | Exploring how to use obvious and subtle transitions | 189 | 4-27a |
| **4-28** Using a Variety of Transitions | Learning ways to use more sophisticated transitions | 190 | 4-28a |
| **4-29** Transitions in Reports and Essays | Visualizing how transitions function in multiparagraph essays or reports | 190 | 4-29a |
| **4-30** Transitions in Narratives | Learning the differences between the transitions used in narratives and expository writing | 191 | 4-30a |

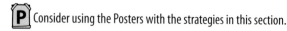 **P** Consider using the Posters with the strategies in this section.

# 4-23 Definition and Function of Transitions

Transitions are words and phrases that writers use when they move from one key/star idea to another in their writing. Students can use this strategy to learn or review the definition of transitions for expository paragraphs.

**Prerequisite:** 4-6 Color-Coding and the Five Elements of Expository Writing

**Handy Pages**

## Before Class

Make transparencies and student copies as needed of *Tools 4-23a* and *4-23b*.

## During Class

1. Display *Tool 4-23a*. Read and discuss the definition in the top box with your class. Have students mark important words as they read.

2. Point out the first box in the second row. Explain that yellow is used for the transition sentences when students use the Traffic Light colors. The yellow reminds them to slow down and present key/star ideas to support their topic sentences. Transitions are considered the glue that holds the ideas together in a paragraph, essay, or report. The yellow bottle of glue is a reminder of the importance of transitions for organization.

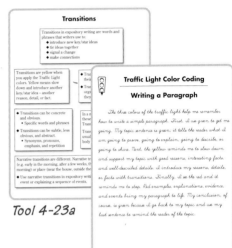

**Tool 4-23a**

**Tool 4-23b**

3. Read and discuss the box on the right of the second row. Reinforce that good transitions help both the writer and the reader. Use *Tool 4-23b* or other example paragraphs such as those on *Tool 4-2a* (Dolphins) or *Bonus Tool 4-8-2* to show and model transitions. Color the transitions yellow and discuss how they support the organization of the paragraph. Then color the rest of the paragraph using the Traffic Light colors. Provide additional models as needed. (Use only paragraphs containing obvious transitions until your students have been introduced to subtle transitions. See 4-27 Obvious and Subtle Transitions.)

4. Review the rest of *Tool 4-23a*. The information in these last three boxes is meant to introduce concepts that will be taught in greater depth in later strategies or sections (Section 5 Essays and Reports, Section 6 Narrative Writing).

**Transition Sets**

Students can use this strategy to use transitions in sets and to understand the variety and flexibility of transitions.

**Prerequisite:** 4-23 Definition and Function of Transitions

**Handy Pages**

## Before Class

Make an overhead transparency and student copies of *Tool 4-24a*. Encourage students to keep a copy of it in their writing notebooks for reference.

## During Class

- Display *Tool 4-24a* and explain how transitions are often used together in sets. Point out that some words are used in more than one set. Remind your students that the function of transitions is to help organize writing.

- Let your students know you will be expecting them to use a variety of transitions and not just the same ones, like *first, second,* and *third,* over and over. This may also be a good time to point out that on state assessments, one of the things that graders look for is the use of a variety of good transitions.

- Have your students make their own transition sets, modeled after those on *Tool 4-24a*. Have students divide a page of notebook paper into four columns and six rows, using *Tool 4-24a* for an example. Then have them work in pairs or small groups and give them three to four minutes to fill in as many of the boxes as possible. Have students share their transitions with the class and fill in any boxes left empty on their own grids.

- Remind students that these transition sets are just examples and words from the sets can be mixed to create new sets.

## Additional Ideas

- Have students work in pairs and choose one of the transition sets from *Tool 4-24a* to use in a short paragraph. Have students use their imaginations as they create topic sentences and gather content to fit the transition sets they picked.

**Transition Sets**

| | | | |
|---|---|---|---|
| One / Another / Finally | First / Next / At last | First of all, / The second / A third | First / Second / Third |
| One / Also / Another / Finally | Start by / Next / Then / Finally | Initially / Then / After / Later | In the spring / In the summer / In the fall / In the winter |
| My first choice / My second choice | First of all / More importantly | A good / An even better / The best | One important / Equally important |
| During the week / On the weekend | With my friends / With my family / On my own | I first heard / I also heard | One / Another |
| One example / Another example / A third example | In the beginning / As / By the time / Then | One good choice / Another choice / The best choice | Early each morning / Throughout the day / In the evening |
| To begin / After that / Then / Next / Finally | One example / A better example / The best example | One difference / A second difference / The most obvious difference | Before winter break / During winter break / After winter break |

*Tool 4-24a*

**Transitions for Different Purposes**

Using this strategy, students practice choosing transition sets for different writing tasks.

**Prerequisite:** 4-23 Definition and Function of Transitions

**Handy Pages**

## Before Class

- Make an overhead transparency and student copies of *Tool 4-25a*. Encourage students to keep copies in their writing notebooks for reference.

- Collect advertisements, junk mail, newspaper clippings, and magazine articles.

- Have available yellow highlighters.

## During Class

- Display *Tool 4-25a* and read through the lists with your students. Explain how and when writers might use certain transitions for different purposes.

- Using the advertisements, junk mail, newspaper clippings, and magazine articles you have collected, show how transitions are used for different reasons. Highlight the transitions to make them easy for your students to see.

- A good activity for small groups or pairs is to have students bring in additional examples and add them to the collection. Have them find transitions and be prepared to discuss their use with the class.

## Additional Ideas

- Use 1-29 Using Text Structures to have students prewrite and/or plan for a short paragraph. Ask students to complete each paragraph—paying special attention to the way they use transitions—each for a different purpose.

- Use Tools with paragraph samples from Section 9 in whole-group guided lessons and discussions about transitions for different purposes.

- Point out the different ways that transitions are used in the Samples for Student Writers in the Section 10 Tools.

*Tool 4-25a*

# 4-26 Using Transitions Effectively

Mastering transitions takes time and practice. Students need guidance and opportunities to discuss the use of transitions in text that they read. Students can use this strategy to experiment with transitions.

**Prerequisite:** 4-23 Definition and Function of Transitions

**Handy Pages**

## Before Class

- Make an overhead transparency and student copies of *Tool 4-26a*.
   *Bonus Tool 4-26-1* provides additional support.

## During Class

- Display *Tool 4-26a* and read the first row with your class. Explain that is it important for them to vary their transitions. Transitions like *first, second,* and *third* are the right choice for some kinds of paragraphs, but not all. Remind them that they should not become dependent on any set of transitions.

- Review the second row with your students. Explain that transitions do not always need to be the first word in the sentence; they can also be buried. When a transition is buried, it is placed somewhere other than at the beginning of the sentence. Point out that in the better example, the transition *also* is the buried transition.

- Review the third row and discuss the use of the common transitions *first* and *first of all*. Point out that these words can sometimes be dropped from a paragraph. Use the following activity to help students make better decisions about using *first* and *first of all*.
  - ▸ Have your students write a draft paragraph using *first* or *first of all* as the transitions (or use *Bonus Tool 4-26-1*). Have students read their paragraphs to their peers and decide if *first* or *first of all* is needed. Have them look for ways to drop the word or phrase in the final copy. For example, when a second key/star idea is introduced, students can use transitions like *also, another,* and *next*. This lets readers know that a new key/star idea is being introduced.

- Also tell your students that they should not write "First is" or "Second is." Demonstrate the problem by sharing the following examples. Create additional sets of right and wrong examples with suggestions from the class.

> **Wrong:** *First* is pizza.
> **Right:** *First,* we picked our favorite pizza.
> Our *first* choice for lunch is pizza.

### Using Transitions Effectively

| | |
|---|---|
| **Vary Transitions** | • Don't fall into the *first, second, third* trap. These three words are ideal for some paragraphs and essays, but they do not work all of the time.<br>• Experiment with different transition sets.<br>• Look for and add new words and phrases to the transition lists. |
| **Bury Transitions** | • Sometimes a transition works best as the first word(s) in the sentence, but often the sentence will sound better if the transition is buried.<br>**Okay** <u>Second,</u> the pioneers were unprepared to deal with the harsh winters.<br>**Better** The pioneers who settled in Nebraska were <u>also</u> unprepared for the harsh winters.<br>• Burying the transition does not always improve the sentence. Read sentences aloud to hear what sounds best. |
| **First and First of all,** | • Sometimes a sentence (and the entire paragraph) sounds better if "First" or "First of all" is dropped. Because the first supporting sentence is so close to the thesis statement, it may not need an obvious transition like "First" and "First of all."<br>• Use "First" or "First of all" in the draft to help with organization, but drop the word in the final copy |

*Tool 4-26a*

**Obvious and Subtle Transitions**

Use this strategy to review obvious and subtle terms used for sorting transitions.

**Prerequisite:** 4-23 Definition and Function of Transitions and 4-6 Color-Coding and the Five Elements of Expository Writing

**Handy Pages**

## Before Class

- Make an overhead transparency and student copies of *Tool 4-27a*.
 *Bonus Tools 4-27-1* and *4-27-2* provide additional examples.

*Tool 4-27a*

## During Class

1. Explain to your students that transitions take on many different forms. One way to sort them is to use two sets of terms: obvious and subtle. Using *Tool 4-27a*, review the attributes of obvious and subtle transitions at the top of the page.

   **Obvious/Direct/Concrete**

   - Easily recognized: *first, second, third*
   - Stand out in the text: *first of all, also, in addition, finally*
   - Can be added to a list: *one, another, next*
   - Often used as the first word in a transition sentence, but can be buried in the text

   **Subtle/Abstract/Not so obvious**

   - Vary in each written piece
   - Help with organization and comprehension but do not always stand out
   - Cannot be put into a list; there are too many possibilities
   - Create by using synonyms, repetition, phrases, pronouns, and emphasis

2. Point out the obvious and subtle transitions in each paragraph. Remind your students that the purpose of transitions is to help with organization. Have students compare the paragraphs and discuss how transitions are used to help organization in each. Have them color-code the paragraphs using the Traffic Light colors.

3. Display paragraphs on an overhead and ask for volunteers to come to the overhead, circle transitions, and explain their choices. Use paragraphs that you have created or those found on various *Step Up to Writing* Tools. Provide your students with additional practice in identifying transitions and color-coding using the Traffic Light colors. Continue to discuss the function of transitions. Use examples of your own or *Bonus Tools 4-27-1* and *4-27-2*.

4. Let students know that writers frequently mix obvious and subtle transitions in a paragraph or report. They are, however, always careful to make sure that the transitions will help the reader with comprehension.

5. Post examples of paragraphs with obvious and subtle transitions for students to read and use for reference.

## 4-28 Using a Variety of Transitions

This strategy helps students develop a larger variety of and more sophisticated transitions.

**Prerequisite:** 4-23 Definition and Function of Transitions

**Handy Pages**

### Before Class

Make an overhead transparency and student copies of *Tool 4-28a*.

### During Class

1. Display *Tool 4-28a* and read through the examples with your students. As you read, discuss the various transitions used and how well they worked. Explain that these examples are condensed to make a point and to quickly review variety in the use of transitions. These are not examples of well-developed paragraphs. In good writing, there is better elaboration—the E's.

2. Choose a general topic and have students work in pairs to write paragraphs, imitating several of the methods presented on *Tool 4-28a*.

3. Afterward, lead a discussion on what they learned from the exercise. Then post the completed paragraphs around the class for all to enjoy.

*Tool 4-28a*

## 4-29 Transitions in Reports and Essays

Using this strategy, students learn the differences in the way that transitions are used in single versus multiparagraph essays and reports. Use 5-9 Transition Topic Sentences to teach your students how to use transitions in multiparagraph expository writing.

**Prerequisite:** 4-23 Definition and Function of Transitions

**Handy Pages**

### Before Class

Make an overhead transparency and copies for students of *Tool 4-29a*.

## During Class

1. Display *Tool 4-29a* and inform your students that there are some differences in the way that transitions are used in single versus multiparagraph essays and reports.

- In a single, stand-alone paragraph, transitions are woven throughout the paragraph as key/star ideas are presented.

- In an essay (or other written pieces like letters, reports, and research papers), transitions are used in the sentences that start body paragraphs. These are called *transition topic sentences*.

2. Using *Tool 4-29a*, point out the use of transitions in the paragraph and in the multiparagraph essay. Color-code the paragraph and the essay using the Traffic Light colors. Explain that in the example on the Tool, each body paragraph starts with a yellow transition topic sentence; all the other sentences in the body paragraphs are elaboration and are highlighted in red.

*Tool 4-29a*

## (4-30) Transitions in Narratives

Using this strategy, students learn that the transitions used in narrative writing are generally different from those used in expository writing. Narrative transitions are described and explained in Section 6.

**Handy Pages**

Use *Tool 4-30a* to illustrate narrative transitions and expository transitions. Point out that transitions in the narrative are designed to take you through the story, while expository transitions are meant to organize the information that is being presented. In short, narrative transitions almost always indicate time and/or location. Expository transitions point out key/star ideas used to support or explain a topic.

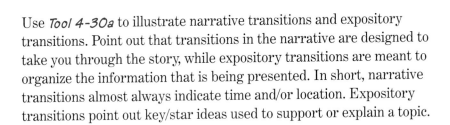

*Tool 4-30a*

# Paragraph Elaboration

The quantity and quality of elaboration is an important component in all forms of expository writing but unfortunately this is the part that many students fail to include. In *Step Up to Writing*, the terms *the E's* and *the Reds* are used to help students remember to stop and elaborate to support the key/star ideas.

## Objectives

- Teach students to create detailed, interesting paragraphs
- Help students decide when more detail in a paragraph is necessary

| Strategy | Strategy Description | Page | Tools |
|---|---|---|---|
| **4-31** Paragraph Elaboration— the E's/the Reds | Color-coding paragraph elaboration and summarizing the ways to elaborate key/star ideas | 193 | 4-31a |
| **4-32** Learning More About Elaboration | Recognizing different types of elaboration | 194 | 4-32a, 4-32b |
| **4-33** Comparing Paragraph and Report Elaboration | Revising and improving elaboration; expanding paragraphs into reports through elaboration | 195 | 4-33a, 4-33b |

 Consider using the Posters with the strategies in this section.

# 4-31 Paragraph Elaboration—the E's/the Reds

This section defines and examines the function of elaboration—"the E's," also called "the Reds."
This strategy helps students learn the many ways they can elaborate on their key/star ideas.

**Prerequisites:** 4-6 Color-Coding and the Five Elements of Expository Writing and
4-7 Planning with an Informal Outline

**Handy Pages**

## Before Class

Make an overhead transparency of *Tool 4-31a*.

## During Class

1. Display *Tool 4-31a* and read and discuss the importance of using elaboration—the E's—when students write. Explain that even if they have engaging topic sentences, good transitions, and supporting key/star ideas, their paragraphs will not be as interesting or insightful if they do not add examples and evidence. Without it they will not be rated proficient or advanced on local or state assessments. Emphasize that the function of elaboration is to support the key/star ideas.

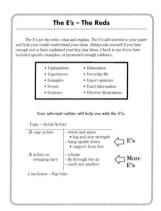

*Tool 4-31a*

2. Point out the rectangle in the center of the Tool. Discuss and define each term and point out why elaboration and examples are called the E's. Explain that the term *the E's* should remind them to add specific information needed to bring their writing to life. The E's are an important and major part of every paragraph.

3. Explain that in the Traffic Light color-coding system, the E's are red. The color red is meant to remind students to stop and explain their key/star ideas. It also reminds them that the reds are the meat of the paragraph.

4. Have your students focus on the informal outline at the bottom of the Tool. Explain that the informal outline is the best way for them to plan for and add elaboration to their paragraphs. Point out how the words and phrases in the right column of the outline give explanations and examples about the key/star ideas.

5. Color the words by the dashes and dots in red. Challenge students familiar with Traffic Light color-coding to suggest what phrases in the informal outline should be colored green (topic and conclusion) and yellow (key/star ideas).

## 4-32 Learning More About Elaboration

This strategy helps students use the E's to elaborate a key/star idea.

**Handy Pages**

### Before Class

- Make overhead transparencies and student copies of *Tools 4-32a* and *4-32b*. Encourage students to keep copies in their writing notebooks for reference.

- Have available magazines, books, student textbooks, and other materials.

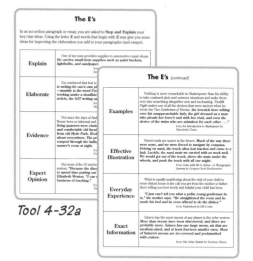

*Tool 4-32a*

*Tool 4-32b*

### During Class

1. Using *Tools 4-32a* and *4-32b*, read through each example, explaining each as needed and giving students time to ask questions.

2. Put students in small groups and assign E words from the first columns of *Tools 4-32a* and *4-32b* to each group.

3. Have students fold notebook paper using the two-column fold. Ask them to write their E words in the left column, as on *Tools 4-32a* and *4-32b*.

4. Have students find examples of effective E's in magazines, books, and /or their social studies and science textbooks. Have them write the examples in the right column. Provide them time to share and discuss with the rest of the class.

5. When your students read expository text as part of class work, take time for them to point out elaboration—examples, evidence, and expert opinion—that they find.

### Additional Ideas

Use colored strips of paper to make learning about elaboration more visual and tactile. Cut 1" strips from standard copy paper to match Traffic Light colors. Have students write topic sentences and conclusions on the green strips and key/star ideas on the yellow strips. Then use the red strips for elaboration. Have students arrange the strips in the correct order on their desks. Have them experiment with the quantity and the content of the reds—the E's. Model this activity at the board using colored strips with magnetic tape attached on the back. Large colored strips cut from poster board also make great visual aids. Laminate the strips and then use markers to write on them.

Topic Sentence
Key/Star Idea
Explain
Key/Star Idea
Explain
Explain
Conclusion

# 4-33 Comparing Paragraph and Report Elaboration

Using this strategy, students compare elaboration in a paragraph to elaboration in a report or essay.

**Prerequisite:** 4-6 Color-Coding and the Five Elements of Expository Writing

**Handy Pages**

## Before Class

- Make overhead transparencies and student copies of *Tools 4-33a* and *4-33b*.

- Have available green, red, and yellow highlighters and overhead markers.

## During Class

1. Display and read "The Best at the Circus" from *Tool 4-33a* as your students follow along on their copies. Ask them to highlight the E's in red. Color coding will help them focus their attention (the E sentences are in bold print).

2. Have students read the paragraph a second time, and then discuss the quality and quantity of the elaboration with them. Ask questions like the following:

   - Do the sentences make sense?
   - Is there variety in the structures and in the way they start?
   - Is the content too general? Is it specific?
   - Does the elaboration connect with the topic?
   - What would you add or eliminate? What would you revise?
   - If you wanted to lengthen the paragraph into a short report or an essay, what would you add?

4. Color-code the rest of the paragraph using the Traffic Light colors.

5. Using *Tool 4-33b*, read and discuss the essay just as you did the paragraph. Have your students color-code the E's in red. (The E sentences are in bold print.) Color-code the rest of the paragraph using the Traffic Light colors.

6. Ask your students to lay *Tools 4-33a* and *4-33b* side by side so they can compare the two writing samples.

7. Discuss the differences between the two examples. Point out that the multiparagraph essay has more elaboration. Explain that when it is time to write essays and reports, they will use all of the same strategies they use to write paragraphs. For additional information on using elaboration in essays and reports, see 5-15 Increasing Elaboration in Essays and Reports.

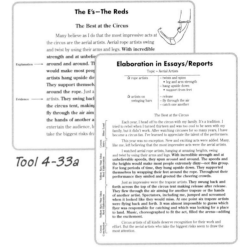

*Tool 4-33a*

*Tool 4-33b*

# Conclusions

Conclusions are a challenge for most writers, especially student writers who have much to think about when they write paragraphs. Too often, students get tired and add almost anything to a paragraph and call it a conclusion. Learning and applying the features of a good conclusion are essential skills for successful writing.

## Objectives

- Teach students to write effective conclusions
- Reinforce how a conclusion relates to the topic sentence

| Strategy | Strategy Description | Page | Tools |
|---|---|---|---|
| **4-34** Conclusion—Defining Terms | Defining terms and recognizing different terms | 197 | 4-34a |
| **4-35** Connecting a Conclusion to a Topic Sentence | Learning how to connect conclusions to topic sentences | 198 | 4-35a |
| **4-36** Keys to Writing Conclusions | Learning key steps to writing conclusions more quickly and effectively | 198 | 4-36a, 4-36b |
| **4-37** Not All Paragraphs Require a Formal Conclusion | Recognizing when to write a formal conclusion and when it isn't necessary | 200 | n/a |

P Consider using the Posters with the strategies in this section.

Everything students learn (or discover on their own) about conclusions for single, stand-alone paragraphs will be applied to report and essay writing.

# 4-34 Conclusion—Defining Terms

*Conclusion, closing statement,* and *clincher* all refer to a final statement, but they have slightly different meanings and are written in different tones. In this strategy, students review the terms and their meanings to consider different possibilities for conclusions.

**Handy Pages**

**Prerequisite:** 4-17 Defining Topic Sentences and Thesis Statements

## Before Class

- Make an overhead transparency and student copies of *Bonus Tools 4-34a* and *4-34b*.

- Have available green highlighters and overhead markers.

 *Bonus Tool 4-34-1* provides additional examples.

## During Class

1. Using *Tool 4-34a*, read and discuss the definition of a conclusion at the top of the page. Answer questions and provide examples as needed.

2. At the bottom of *Tool 4-34a*, point out the three terms used for the final statements in expository writing (conclusion, closing statement, and clincher). Explain that each term has a slightly different meaning, sends a different message, and is written in a different tone.

3. Display *Tool 4-34b* and read through the examples with your students. Have them highlight the three terms in the left column in green. Explain that green is used to remind them to go back to the topic sentence and focus again on the purpose of the paragraph. Green is used for conclusions, closing statements, and clinchers. The green ribbon on the package reminds students that a conclusion ties all of the ideas together.

4. Reinforce that the choice of which approach to use depends on the purpose and the audience for the paragraph.

5. Create topic sentences on a familiar topic. With your students, create a conclusion, a closing statement, and a clincher to fit the topic sentence. (See *Bonus Tool 4-34-1*.)

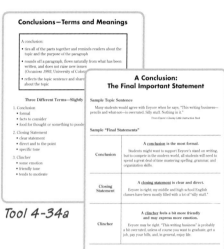

*Tool 4-34a*

*Tool 4-34b*

## 4-35 Connecting a Conclusion to a Topic Sentence

Good conclusions always connect with the topic sentence in some way. Students can use this strategy to connect a conclusion with a topic sentence.

**Prerequisite:** 4-17 Defining Topic Sentences and Thesis Statements

**Handy Pages**

### Before Class

Make an overhead transparency and student copies of *Tool 4-35a*.

### During Class

1. Read the paragraphs on *Tool 4-35a* to the class. Discuss the connections between the topic sentence and the conclusion in both paragraphs. Remind students that you want to find the same kinds of connections when you read their paragraphs.

2. Collect good conclusions throughout the year from editorials, articles, and advertisements. Use paragraphs found on other Tools in this section, also. Take time to discuss these examples.

3. When students "hit a home run" with a conclusion, ask permission and then share the conclusion with the class. Students learn a great deal from their peers.

*Tool 4-35a*

## 4-36 Keys to Writing Conclusions

This strategy helps students write conclusions more easily, quickly, and successfully.

**Prerequisite:** 4-17 Defining Topic Sentences and Thesis Statements

**Handy Pages**

### Before Class

- Make a transparency and student copies of *Tools 4-36a* and *4-36b*.
- Collect drafts of student paragraphs.

 *Bonus Tool 4-36-1* provides additional examples.

*Tool 4-36a*

## During Class

- Using *Tool 4-36a*, read and discuss the keys to writing a conclusion with your students.

- Explain that it can be effective to remind the reader of the topic in a way that is new but does not introduce a different topic. The following is an example of a conclusion that has restated the topic:

**Topic Sentence**
Shel Silverstein in *The Giving Tree* shows what it means to really love someone.

**Conclusion**
Read *The Giving Tree*. It will help you understand more about love.

- Tell students to use synonyms to replace words from the topic sentence or to add new action verbs that reinforce the topic and reuse one two of the key words.

**Topic Sentence**
Before you decide to let water run from the faucet while you brush your teeth, think about the serious problems caused by water shortages.

**Conclusion**
The problems caused by water shortages should encourage everyone to try to conserve water whenever possible.

- Point out the fourth row on *Tool 4-36a* and encourage your students to try using common concluding words and/or phrases. Make it clear that these words are not required. Explain that conclusion words and phrases can be used to start a conclusion or they can be buried in the sentence.

- Tell them to avoid phrases such as: "As I have said," "As I proved," and "As you can see." These phrases can easily become overused and can be a crutch that prevents students from writing interesting and effective conclusions.

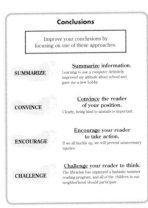

*Tool 4-36b*

## Have a Purpose for Your Conclusion

Explain that a conclusion must have a purpose. Display *Tool 4-36b* and explain each example. Show students how each example serves a different purpose. Have students write a set of conclusions based on each method (summarize, convince, encourage, and challenge). See *Bonus Tool 4-36-1* for additional examples.

## 4-37 Not All Paragraphs Require a Formal Conclusion

Using this strategy, students learn that not all expository paragraphs, essays, or reports require a formal conclusion.

**Handy Pages**

Explain to your students that conclusions are an important part of many assessments and assignments but they are not appropriate for all. Help them understand that writing is always flexible—that writers create expository text for various reasons and for many different audiences.

Inform them that for formal writing assignments and assessments, conclusions are generally required. This is especially true for high-stakes local and state assessments. Tell students that as they read and examine their own writing assignments carefully, they will discover that:

- Essay answers (often written as paragraphs) do not need conclusions.
- If a paragraph (or report) comes to a natural close after a final key/star idea has been presented, a conclusion probably won't be needed. (Formal assessments are an exception.)
- Short reports and articles in magazines often do not have a formal conclusion.
- Business letters seldom have formal conclusions; they often end with a statement, a promise, or a plan.
    - ▸ I look forward to hearing from you.
    - ▸ I would appreciate any information you can provide.
- Report or essay writers may not include a conclusion for a specific reason to make a point with the readers.

Take on a class challenge. Look for expository text that doesn't have a formal conclusion. Analyze the piece, and make guesses about why the writer did not add a formal conclusion.

# SECTION 5 INTRODUCTION
## Speeches

$S$tudents who have mastered organizing and writing Accordion Paragraphs are ready to begin writing multiparagraph essays and reports. The organizational supports provided in *Step Up* (Traffic Light colors, informal outlines, and so on) enable even developing writers to move from stand-alone paragraphs to well-structured multiparagraph essays and reports.

Both essays and reports are referred to as compositions, and they share a common introduction-body-conclusion structure. However, they differ in purpose: essays share the writer's opinion, give a personal insight, or attempt to persuade, whereas reports share information without making the writer's personal point of view the reason for writing.

*Step Up to Writing* guides students through a step-by-step process for writing multiparagraph compositions. This process shows students how to write more effective introduction and conclusion paragraphs. Students also learn to stretch a single paragraph into an essay or report by adding more elaboration and explanation. These skills are what students need for successful compositions.

Success with writing Accordion Essays and Reports comes when students are introduced to the following:

- The elements of an essay or report—introduction, body, and conclusion
- Concrete prewriting and planning processes, such as blocking out and informal outlining

- The importance of using appropriate transitions to organize an essay or report and to guide the reader through the information that the writer wants to communicate

- Increasing elaboration as a means to stretch the amount of information in an essay or report

- Using leads as useful attention grabbers in introductions

- Understanding the need for effective conclusions

# When Teaching Accordion Essays and Reports

- Remember that writing consists of many subskills that must be taught and practiced in isolation before students can write an entire composition. When they practice, it isn't necessary for students to complete a composition. Focus on the individual skills, combining them only when students are ready. Often, planning and writing part of a composition is as important as writing a complete composition.

- Stress to students that, although essays and reports are usually the most frequent types of writing assignments they will encounter in school, these writing formats are not the *only* ones they will need to know to be successful at communicating their ideas. (See Section 6, Narrative Writing; Section 7, Personal Narratives; and Section 9, Special Writing Assignments for information on additional writing formats.)

- Incorporate content students have studied or are studying as they learn writing skills. This will help them apply their writing skills when needed in other content areas.

- When possible, encourage students to collaborate on their compositions. They will gain "real world" skills since information/expository writing (such as a report) often occurs collaboratively.

- Have students block out their essays and reports in words or phrases (see **5-5** Blocking Out Essays and Reports). Blocking out—using blocks that contain the ideas to be covered in writing—assists visual and kinesthetic learners by giving them a visual map of the entire essay or report.

- Use the writing frames (**9-9** Using Writing Frames) and guides (**4-12** Planning Guides for Organizing an Accordion Paragraph) provided in the Tools to help students write parts of their compositions.

- Writing good leads, or the Blues (**5-8** Leading with the Blues), can be delayed until students have mastered the other components of an essay or report.

- Use the strategies for transitions (such as **4-27** Obvious and Subtle Transitions and **5-12** Burying Transitions) during revision.
- The continuous use of the Traffic Light colors for paragraph writing makes the transition to multiparagraph essays and reports easier because students will see how to take their key/star ideas (yellow) from one paragraph, add more elaboration (red), and develop several stand-alone paragraphs.

IDEA BANK

## Tips for Using These Strategies Across Content Areas

✓ Have students color-code multiparagraph essays and reports in all subjects to reinforce the introduction-body-conclusion structure.

✓ Have students block out handouts and other texts in all content areas to better grasp their organizational structure.

✓ Have students write and color-code two-sentence introductions (**5-4** Creating Two-Sentence Introductions), and then block out and create informal outlines (**5-6** Informal Outlines for Essays and Reports) for information gathered from lectures, books, or films.

✓ Use varying combinations of two-sentence introductions, blocking out, informal outlines, and writing conclusions.

✓ Have students write essays and reports in science, social studies, health, and elective classes using the step-by-step strategy (**5-2** Writing Essays and Reports Step by Step) and framed essays and reports (**5-21** Using Framed Essays and Reports to Promote Success).

✓ Have students write research reports about famous people from all disciplines.

✓ Have students analyze multiparagraph handouts in all content areas to differentiate between essays (with opinions) and reports (with mostly facts).

✓ Have students experiment with writing topic sentences about the same general topic. Help them see that topic sentences control the focus of information, while thesis statements express the writer's opinion. This activity also challenges students to move from concrete information to abstract opinion.

✓ Provide reports about issues in social studies and science to students and ask them to write essays expressing their opinions of each report.

✓ Have students write reports about a process used in an elective such as fine art, consumer economics, or industrial arts. Then have them write a brief essay about the value of the process or how to improve the process or product.

Choose those strategies that best meet the needs of your students.

Make sure your students can write good Accordion Paragraphs before introducing them to Accordion Essays and Reports.

# Writing Accordion Essays and Reports

These strategies offer an approach to learning the essential parts of multiparagraph essays and reports and how to organize them. Students have more success with writing when they understand the function of all writing elements and how to arrange them.

## Objectives

- Teach students the basic parts of essays and reports
- Teach students how to organize the basic parts of essays and reports

| Strategy | Strategy Description | Page | Tools |
|---|---|---|---|
| **5-1** Elements of Accordion Essays and Reports | Identifying and labeling the elements of essays and reports to improve writing, planning, and assessing | 206 | 5-1a, 5-1b |
| **5-2** Writing Essays and Reports Step by Step | Understanding and using a twelve-step process for essay and report writing | 209 | 5-2a |
| **5-3** Organizing and Writing, One Step at a Time | Using framed handouts or half sheets of paper to organize the basic parts of essays and reports | 212 | 5-2a, 5-3a to 5-3c |

## 5-1 Elements of Accordion Essays and Reports

Using this strategy, students learn the basic elements of essays and reports and how to use them when planning their own essays and reports.

### Before Class

- Make overhead transparencies and student copies of *Tools 5-1a* and *5-1b*.
- Have available red, yellow, green, and blue highlighters and overhead markers.

 *Bonus Tool 5-1-1* provides additional support and examples.

**Note:** The Traffic Light colors and the heart, key, glue, meat, and tied ribbon icons are also discussed in Section 4.

### During Class

1. Introduce or review the term *Accordion Essays and Reports*. Explain that the name comes from the fact that an essay or report can be short or stretched to a greater length, just like an accordion.

**Note:** Students who have learned Accordion Paragraphs sometimes think an Accordion Essay or Report is several stacked Accordion Paragraphs instead of one essay or report stretched to greater length and depth. If your students struggle with this concept, use **5-22 Moving from a Paragraph to an Essay or Report** and **5-23 Stretch, Don't Stack Practice** to help students see the difference.

2. Explain to your class that although the terms *essay* and *report* are sometimes used interchangeably, they are actually different. (Also on *Bonus Tool 5-1-1*.)

| Essay: A composition that | Report: A composition that |
|---|---|
| • Describes the writer's personal views | • Presents facts about a subject, like a short research paper |
| • Addresses one specific subject | • Helps readers learn about and understand a subject |
| • Informs readers: | • Writers may draw some conclusions, but the primary purpose is to inform readers and help them learn. |
| ▸ What the writer believes about that subject | |
| ▸ Why the writer believes it | |
| • **Example:** Explain why you think students should eat more fresh fruits and vegetables. | • **Example:** Write a report listing and describing the health benefits of eating fresh fruits and vegetables. |

3. Using *Tool 5-1a*, introduce the five elements of essays and reports to your students. Let them know that the Traffic Light colors and the heart, key, glue, meat, and tied ribbon icons they learned in Section 4 also apply to essay and report writing. Make connections to Accordion Paragraphs and give students time to ask questions.

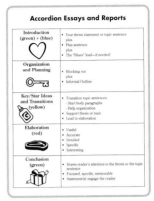

*Tool 5-1a*

## Heart

- Tell your students that in a report, the introductory paragraph is green; it is also the *heart* of the paper. Explain that in this section they will learn to:

  - ▸ Write an introduction by combining a topic statement with a plan sentence that hints at how they will prove or explain the topic. (See the topic sentence strategies in Section 4 and **5-4 Creating Two-Sentence Introductions** for more information about topic sentences.)
  - ▸ Add a lead (the Blues) to the introduction if it is needed. (See **5-8 Leading with the Blues** for more information about leads.)

**Note:** Since the strategies in this section can be used for both report and essay writing, we have consistently used the term *topic sentence*. In some instances, the term *thesis statement* may be more appropriate, especially when expressing opinions or beliefs in an essay. Use whichever term is appropriate for your students.

## Key

- Review with your students that an important key to success is to first make a plan before writing essays and reports. Remind students that they will use two visual strategies to organize ideas.
  - ▸ **Blocking out**—Planning by drawing rectangles in a sequence and filling in the key/star idea for each paragraph needed in the report.
  - ▸ **Informal outlining**—Writing words or phrases indicating the key/star ideas and examples, explanation, and elaboration students will use.

## Glue

- Discuss with your students the importance of transitions in writing essays and reports. Explain that in multiparagraph essays and reports, the transitions are part of transition topic sentences. Tell them that transition topic sentences
  - ▸ Present the key/star ideas for each section (some key/star ideas may use more than one paragraph);
  - ▸ Support and link the paragraphs to the introductory paragraph;
  - ▸ Are colored yellow as a reminder to slow down and support the topic;
  - ▸ Are like *glue*; they bond all of the pieces.

**Meat**

- Inform your students that the *meat* of the paper contains examples, evidence, and elaboration to support each key/star idea.
  - ▸ Using an informal outline will help them make good judgments about the quality and the quantity of elaboration they will need.
  - ▸ Red from the Traffic Light should remind them to stop and explain.

**Ribbon**

- Tell students that the *ribbon* on the package is to remind them to tie their ideas together and give their readers something to think about in the conclusion.
  - ▸ The green reminds them to go back to the introduction and make a strong, meaningful connection. Never just copy it.

## Finding the Elements

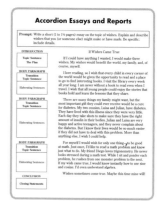

*Tool 5-1b*

1. Use *Tool 5-1b*, "If Wishes Came True," with your class to demonstrate how organization supports the writing of quality essays and reports.

2. Color the transparency with the Traffic Light colors as you review each element and have your students color their copies. Explain that

   - The introduction and conclusion paragraphs are green;

   - The three transition topic sentences are yellow; they contain the key/star ideas and support the topic;

   - All other sentences are red; they contain the elaboration that explains and supports the key/star ideas.

3. Discuss the strengths and weaknesses of the essay using questions like the following:

   - What is the thesis of the essay (what the writer believes and why)?

   - Is there a connection between the introduction and the conclusion?

   - Are the transition topic sentences smooth and easy to follow? Do they help with organization? How could they be improved?

   - Does the elaboration—the examples and explanation—fit the key/star ideas? Is it interesting? Does it make sense?

   - Ask your students to evaluate the essay. Have them decide if they think it was excellent, okay, or poor and tell them to give reasons for their answers.

**Note:** Even though the essay on *Tool 5-1b* has five paragraphs, do not encourage your students to always write five-paragraph essays and reports. Different topics support different numbers of key/star ideas and paragraphs, so students should not be allowed to think that they always need to write a certain number of paragraphs to write an essay or report. Like accordions, their reports and essays can be stretched to many different lengths.

## Additional Ideas

- Have your students color the icons on their copies of *Tool 5-1a* and keep them as a reference.
- Have students work in small groups to discuss and add Traffic Light color-coding to text from informational handouts, magazines, or newspapers.

## 5-2 Writing Essays and Reports Step by Step

Students can use this multistep strategy to see at a glance all that they will need to write essays and reports.

When students learn to break the writing process down step by step, they learn a manageable way to write essays and reports. They also learn how essays and reports are organized.

### Before Class

Make an overhead transparency and student copies of *Tool 5-2a*.

### During Class

Read *Tool 5-2a* with your students to introduce the steps for writing an essay or report. Explain that this step-by-step method can help make writing easier and more organized.

Use the following information to describe these steps:

*Tool 5-2a*

### Step 1
**Write a draft title.**

- Give your paper a title right away, even if it is only a temporary title.

### Step 2
**Refine the topic and write a draft of your topic sentence or thesis statement.**

- Decide what the assignment is asking you to do or what you want to do with the topic—persuade, compare, contrast, define, prove, inform, describe, and so on.
- At this initial step you may want to brainstorm (or use some other prewriting activity) to consider many possible ideas before choosing those you will use in your paper.
- Write a draft of your thesis statement. It is the controlling sentence that lets the reader know exactly what the paper will prove or explain.

**Note:** At this point, encourage students to narrow their focus and not include everything from their brainstorming session.

## Step 3
### Write a plan sentence using your key/star ideas in the draft introductory paragraph.

- In an introductory paragraph, the plan sentence tells the reader what to expect. It provides structure for the paper and presents the key/star ideas. Together with the topic sentence or thesis statement, it creates a short, clear introduction for the essay or report. (See **5-4 Creating Two-Sentence Introductions** for more information about plan sentences.)

- After you have written your draft and are ready to revise and edit, you may want to change and improve the introduction.

**Note:** At times students may add a lead to their introductions. See **5-8 Leading with the Blues.**

## Step 4
### Block out what you want to cover in each paragraph.

- Blocking out helps you develop a general plan for the report or essay. (See **5-5 Blocking Out Essays and Reports.**)

- To block out, draw a rectangle to illustrate each paragraph that will be a part of your essay or report. You will need a block for the introduction, for the conclusion, and for each key/star idea that will support the topic. (If you have a lot of elaboration with many examples, you will need more blocks with each key/star idea. See **5-13 Using Transition Topic Sentences in Longer Essays and Reports** and examples in *Tools 5-5a, 5-5b,* and *5-5c.*)

## Step 5
### Create an informal outline based on your plan and how you have blocked out the paper.

- The informal outline helps you to see if you have enough information to support your main ideas. (See **5-7 Using an Informal Outline Practice Guide.**)

## Step 6
### Choose transitions that might introduce your key/star ideas. Add these to the informal outline.

- Choose transitions you think will help express your ideas and add them to the informal outline. You can always change transitions later, but setting them in the outline will help you remember these important tools for writing essays and reports. (See **5-9 Transition Topic Sentences.**)

## Step 7
### Jot down ideas for your conclusion.

- The draft of your conclusion does not need to be perfect. It can be just a quick list of things you think you might include in this paragraph.
- Planning the conclusion before writing the first draft helps you think about all the elements that should go into the conclusion. It's also easier to write the first draft of a conclusion if you've already planned what you would like to say. (See **5-18 Writing Successful Conclusions**.)

## Step 8
### Write the first draft.

- Using your informal outline, write your first draft. This is your first try at the paper. You should write it quickly without worrying about making it perfect.
- Skip lines as you write. This will give you space to revise (make changes) and edit (find and fix errors).

## Step 9
### Revise your first draft to improve content, sentence structure, vocabulary, and organization.

- It is always important to reread your paper and look for ways to improve the content, sentence structure, vocabulary, and organization. Apply what you know, use grammar books and other resources, and ask for help regarding the rules of grammar.
- Look at the big message. Does your paper say what you wanted it to say?

## Step 10
### Edit your paper. Repeat steps 8, 9, and 10 as needed.

- Check for mistakes in capitalization, usage, punctuation, and spelling (see **10-7 Editing with CUPS**). Look at the little details, and fix any mistakes. These mistakes might include
  - Using *the* instead of *that;*
  - Missed periods;
  - Using *you* instead of *your;*
  - Adding extra spaces or not enough space between words;
  - Leaving words out or in the wrong place.

## Step 11
### Create a final copy of your essay or report.

- Create a final copy that shows you have done your best.

## Step 12

### Proofread and prepare to share!

- Proofread your final copy once more to make sure you didn't miss any careless errors. If you did, go back to Step 10. Otherwise, you are ready to share your work!

## 5-3 Organizing and Writing, One Step at a Time

Students can use this strategy to quickly learn the steps for writing an Accordion Essay or Report. It gives them a chance to see and experience the process and helps them visualize how to tackle more sophisticated writing assignments.
**Prerequisite:** 5-2 Writing Essays and Reports Step by Step

## Before Class

- Make overhead transparencies of *Tools 5-2a, 5-3a, 5-3b*, and *5-3c*.

- Make student copies of *Tools 5-2a* and *5-3c*. Make student copies of *Tools 5-3a* and *5-3b* on colored paper as directed on the Tools.

- Optional: Use half sheets of notebook paper instead of student copies of *Tools 5-3a* and *5-3b*. Each student will need two or more sheets of paper.

- Have available red, yellow, green, and blue highlighters and overhead markers.

## During Class

1. Tell your students that this activity can help them identify the steps used in essay and report writing. They will use these cards to plan a report or essay, one paragraph at a time.

2. Review *Tool 5-2a* with your students and ask them to check and make sure you are following all of the steps.

3. Have students cut their copies of *Tools 5-3a* and *5-3b* in half, or have them use four half sheets of paper instead of the Tools.

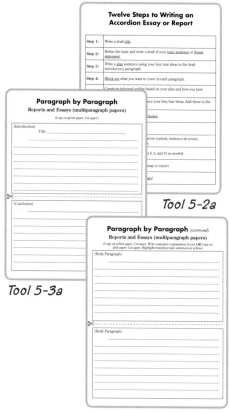

Tool 5-2a

Tool 5-3a

Tool 5-3b

## Top of *Tool 5-3a* (or First Half Sheet)

On the top half of *Tool 5-3a*, have students follow the first four steps of writing an Accordion Essay or Report.

- As you model on the overhead, have students copy on their paper the example that follows. Explain to students that this activity and example are intentionally simple in order to model using all of the steps.
- Remind them that the essential pieces of an introductory paragraph are the topic sentence or thesis statement and the plan sentence. Point out the two key/star ideas in the plan sentence.
- Remind your students that blocking out provides a visual structure of paragraph organization and that each block represents a different paragraph for the report.

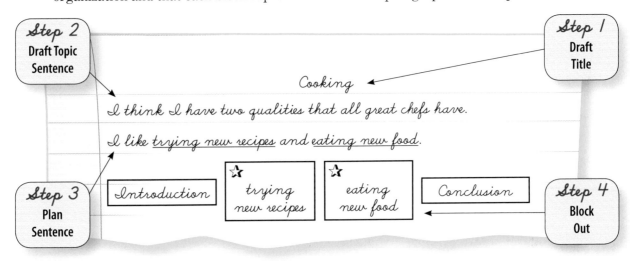

## Top and Bottom of *Tool 5-3b* (or Second and Third Half Sheets)

On the next two cards, have students complete and label Steps 5 and 6. Remind them that they will use the informal outline to write their first draft and that it should include lots of description and explanation. Explain that each card will become a new paragraph.

1. Show students how they will use information they blocked out to create their informal outline, by modeling the following example.
2. Add a star and the words *trying new recipes* on one card, and a star and the words *eating new food* on the other. Explain that these are the key/star ideas that support the thesis statement: I love to cook.
3. Add dashes beneath each key/star idea. Fill in the dashes with elaboration for each key/star idea.

4. Add dots below each dash. Tell students that the dot level in the informal outline is important because this is where they will include specific examples and detailed explanations. Fill in dots with student suggestions or use words from the example provided.

5. In the parentheses beneath each key/star idea, add an appropriate transition.

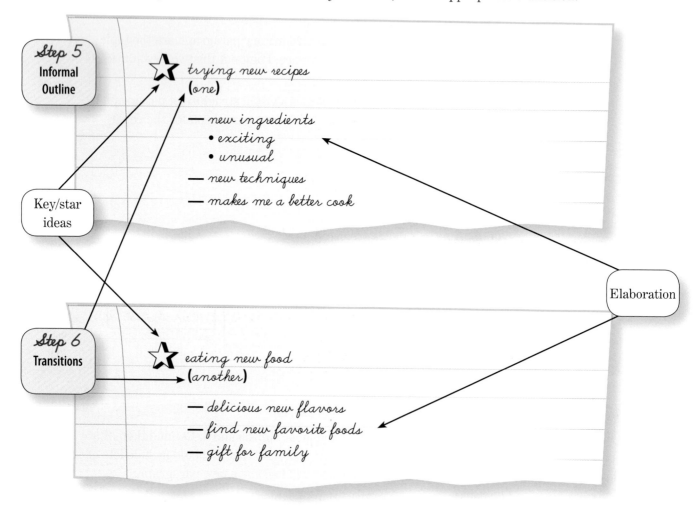

## Bottom of *Tool 5-3a* (or Fourth Half Sheet)

On the last card, students plan the conclusion. Make some quick notes about the sorts of information to include in the conclusion. The conclusion should relate back to the introduction in some way. (See 5-18 **Writing Successful Conclusions** for more information about conclusions.)

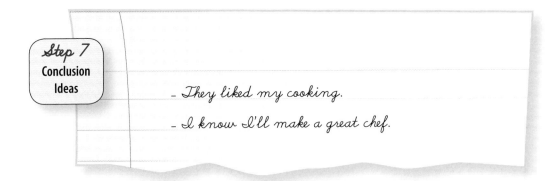

Step 7
Conclusion Ideas

‐ *They liked my cooking.*

‐ *I know I'll make a great chef.*

## Providing Adequate Models and Opportunities for Practice

Model using *Tools 5-3a* and *5-3b* several times before students begin to practice or use them independently. Have your students imitate your work using their copies as you demonstrate. When students use the paragraph-by-paragraph cards the first time, they will need lots of help and guidance. Later, they will be able to use the cards on their own.

## Creating a Draft From the Paragraph-by-Paragraph Cards

*Step 8*
### Write the first draft.

- In a whole-group lesson, use the informal outline for the "Cooking" report to help students complete the remaining steps from *Tool 5-2a*.

- Have students write a "Cooking" essay of their own using the informal outline they have created as well as their own experiences and creativity.

- After they have finished writing, use *Tool 5-3c* to show them an example essay. Color the sentences on your overhead with the Traffic Light colors as shown on the following example and have students color in the sentences in their copies. This will help them visualize the parts of the essay.
  - ▸ Title and first and last paragraphs (introduction and conclusion)—green
  - ▸ First sentence of the second and third paragraphs (key/star ideas)—yellow
  - ▸ All other sentences (elaboration)—red

- Have students color-code the sentences on their essays.

**Cooking**

I have known since I was little that I want to become a professional chef. I think I have two qualities that all great chefs have. I like to try new recipes, and I love to eat the new dishes I cook.

The challenge of preparing new kinds of food is one of my big motivations. I like trying new ingredients and tasting how their flavors combine. For example, I recently made pasta using fresh tomatoes and basil. It was so delicious! I also enjoy learning new cooking techniques. Last month, I learned how to stir-fry vegetables in a wok. These explorations help me become a better cook.

Eating the new meals I prepare is the best part about cooking. It is like a reward for all the hard work I put into preparing a dish. I get to see how everything turned out and sample all the delicious new flavors. I've discovered new favorite foods, like butternut squash, by cooking them. I love it when friends and family really enjoy something I've prepared.

To celebrate my mother's birthday last week, I made her favorite dish—chiles rellenos. It was a lot of work, but I learned how to deep-fry the chiles and prepare the spicy sauce for them. Everyone devoured them! They liked them so much that I know I'll make a great chef.

*Tool 5-3c*

**Step 8**
First Draft

Cooking

I have known since I was little that I want to become a professional chef. I think I have two qualities that all great chefs have. I like to try new recipes, and I love to eat the new dishes I cook.

The challenge of preparing new kinds of food is one of my big motivations. I like trying new ingredients and tasting how their flavors combine. For example, I recently made pasta with fresh tomatoes and basil. It was so delicious! I also enjoy learning new cooking techniques. Last month, I learned how to stir-fry vegetables in a wok. These explorations help me become a better cook.

Eating the new meals I prepare is the best part about cooking. It is like a reward for all the hard work I put into preparing a dish. I get to see how everything turned out and sample all the delicious new flavors. I've discovered new favorite foods, like butternut squash, by cooking them. I love it when friends and family really enjoy something I've prepared.

To celebrate my mother's birthday last week, I made her favorite dish—chiles rellenos. It was a lot of work, but I learned how to deep-fry the chiles and prepare the spicy sauce for them. Everyone devoured them! They liked them so much that I know I'll make a great chef.

## Revising and Sharing

- Using *Tool 5-2a*, discuss with your class Steps 9 through 12.

- As a group, review the "Cooking" essays the students wrote and make recommendations for how they can be improved.

- Have students revise and edit their own essays. Challenge your students to meet or exceed the level of writing in the sample essay. Provide them support as needed.

- Have students proofread their final copies and post them in the room or find another way to show off their good work.

# Planning Essays and Reports

Students need many opportunities and different kinds of lessons to master introductory paragraphs, blocking out, and informal outlining. These strategies give students frequent opportunities to experience success by approaching learning from different angles.

## Objectives

- Teach students different types of introductions and help them understand the function of the thesis statement and the plan sentence
- Teach students a visual method for planning and organizing essays and reports

| Strategy | Strategy Description | Page | Tools |
|---|---|---|---|
| **5-4** Creating Two-Sentence Introductions | Learning and describing the parts of an introduction; learning how to write a two-sentence introduction | 218 | n/a |
| **5-5** Blocking Out Essays and Reports | Practicing blocking out an essay or report | 222 | 5-5a to 5-5d |
| **5-6** Informal Outlines for Essays and Reports | Reviewing informal outlines | 225 | n/a |
| **5-7** Using an Informal Outline Practice Guide | Using a template to build an informal outline | 225 | 5-7a, 5-7b |
| **5-8** Leading with the Blues | Adding leads to essays and reports to make them more inviting and interesting | 227 | 5-8a, 5-8b |

## 5-4 Creating Two-Sentence Introductions

Writing an introductory paragraph presents a challenge for many student writers. Using this strategy, your students master this skill by creating simple two-sentence introductions.

**Prerequisite:** 5-2 Writing Essays and Reports Step by Step

### Before Class

- Create several two-sentence introduction frames, using stated and implied plan sentences on a variety of topics and content-area subjects.

- Create several example plan sentences on one topic to share with your students.

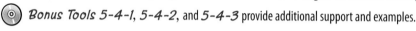 *Bonus Tools 5-4-1, 5-4-2,* and *5-4-3* provide additional support and examples.

### During Class

#### Introducing and Modeling the Introductory Paragraph

1. Explain that sometimes a short introduction is best. The length of an introduction plus its lead depends on the topic, the amount of time available to write, and the audience for the essay or report.

2. Tell your students that they can create a good introduction simply by using two important sentences: the topic sentence and the plan sentence.

3. Select a topic you have talked about in class, and tell your students you are going to write an introduction for a report or essay about this topic.

4. Tell them that the first thing to do is write a topic sentence or thesis statement. Remind them that there are many different types (see **4-18 Topic Sentence Variety**). Then write a topic sentence or thesis statement on the board or a blank overhead transparency.

5. Tell them that the next thing to do is write a plan sentence. The plan sentence tells the reader the big ideas the writer is going to write about by giving a glimpse of the key/star ideas in the report or essay.

6. Tell your students that the plan sentence can either be stated, or, as they become more advanced, it may be subtle or implied.

   - A stated plan lists each key/star idea that will be addressed in the essay or report.

- An implied or subtle plan doesn't state the key/star ideas but provides a clue to what the key/star ideas will be. It lays a framework for discussion or elaboration on the topic. When the plan is implied, the sentence often includes a number word. The number words tell (or hint at) the number of key/star ideas there will be in support of the topic. Implied plans might also be written with words like these (also on *Bonus Tool 5-4-1*):

| | | |
|---|---|---|
| tips | hints | reasons |
| suggestions | ideas | warnings |
| signs | recommendations | instructions |
| directions | steps | plans |
| challenges | problems | topics |
| styles | methods | strategies |

The underlined words in the following examples illustrate how the key/star ideas become part of plan sentences (also on *Bonus Tool 5-4-2*).

### Stated Plan

> *Sacrifices*
>
> Throughout the Civil War, women in both the North and the South made incredible sacrifices. They <u>raised children alone</u>, <u>managed farms</u>, <u>faced their enemies</u>, and <u>gave up cherished family heirlooms</u>.

### Implied or Subtle Plan

> *Sacrifices*
>
> Throughout the Civil War, women in both the North and the South made many sacrifices. <u>Many of these incredible sacrifices</u> went unnoticed.

7. Finish the introduction by writing a plan sentence after your topic sentence or thesis statement. Continue to model writing two-sentence introductions for your students until they are ready to write their own. Stress that subtle and implied plans are not necessarily better than stated plans. Guide students to use the method that works best for their purpose and audience.

## Practicing Two-Sentence Introductions

1. After you have introduced the process for writing two-sentence introductions, have your students practice writing their own two-sentence introductions.

   - Have students select their own topics based on things they have learned in class, or give them simple, straightforward topics to write about.

   - If students have difficulty writing two-sentence introductions, have them work in pairs or small groups to come up with sentences together.

2. Give your students many opportunities to practice writing introductions. Consider having them write a number of introductions without the additional work of creating full essays or reports. Students will learn to write introductions quickly and proficiently if they have many opportunities for practice.

## Framed Introduction Paragraphs

One way to introduce your students to writing two-sentence introductions is to have them fill in paragraph frames like the following examples (also on *Bonus Tool 5-4-3*). See **9-9 Using Writing Frames** for more information.

1. Create frames for a variety of topics and subjects, such as for a book report or topics students are studying. Frames can help them focus on just the topic sentence, thesis statement, the plan sentence, or both. Frames focusing on the plan sentence should use both stated and implied plans.

2. Once your students are comfortable filling in these frames, they can transition to writing their own two-sentence introductions.

> ### Similarities
> As I read _____ by _____, I realized that _____, the main character, and I have a lot in common. We both _____, _____, and _____.

> ### Dramatic Changes
> After reading the chapter on the Industrial Revolution for history class, I realized that the world has changed dramatically since the 19th century. Its effects on society were enormous and created problems in _____ and _____.

## Additional Ideas

- After students have written an introduction on a subject they are currently studying, have them add an informal outline and a conclusion using the practice guide on *Tools 5-7a* and *5-7b*. Take time for them to share. If time permits, ask students to write out the essay or report.

- Have your students write a number of introductory paragraphs on the same topic using the same key/star ideas. Encourage them to use both stated and implied plans.

- Have students revise an existing introductory paragraph, changing the plan from stated to implied.

- Use framed introductory paragraphs when students watch a movie in class. This will give them extra practice in writing introduction paragraphs and also increase their attention to the main ideas of the movie.

**Fascinating Animal**

After watching the movie *The Bear* in biology class, I realized that bears are fascinating animals. This creature is amazing because of its _____, _____, and _____.

## 5-5 Blocking Out Essays and Reports

This strategy teaches students to plan before they begin writing, helping them organize their thoughts and select the key/star ideas they will use as they write.

**Prerequisite:** 5-4 Creating Two-Sentence Introductions

## Before Class

- Make overhead transparencies and student copies of *Tools 5-5a* through *5-5d*.

- *Bonus Tool 5-5-1* provides additional examples.

## During Class

1. Explain to your students that their plan sentences can help them to block out their essays and reports before they create informal outlines and before they write their first drafts. Blocking out creates a visual plan of the paper.

2. Display and read *Tool 5-5a* with your students. Show them that the two introductory paragraphs at the bottom of the page both have two sentences.

   - The first sentence is the thesis statement. It tells the reader what will be proved or explained.

   - The second sentence lays out or hints at a plan for how the author will prove or explain the thesis statement.

3. Point out the boxes below each paragraph. Explain that each box represents a paragraph, and the word or phrase in it represents the key/star idea of the paragraph. Notice that the blocks stay the same, but the introduction either states or implies the plan.

4. Remind your students that these simple introductions include all the basic information needed to plan an entire essay or report.

5. Use the following as additional examples of how to block out essays and reports. The first example shows a stated planned sentence, the second illustrates an implied planned sentence, and the third a subtle plan sentence. (Example also on *Bonus Tool 5-5-1*.)

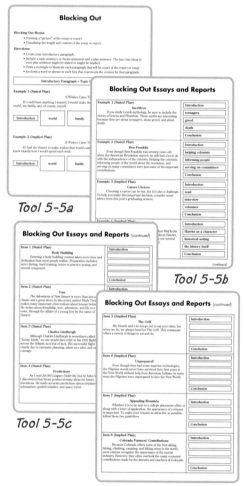

Tool 5-5a

Tool 5-5b

Tool 5-5c

Tool 5-5d

### Sacrifices

Throughout the Civil War, women in both the North and the South made incredible sacrifices. They raised children alone, managed farms, faced their enemies, and gave up cherished family heirlooms.

| Introduction | raising children | managing farms | facing enemies | giving up heirlooms | Conclusion |

---

### Sacrifices

Throughout the Civil War, women in both the North and the South made many sacrifices. Often these incredible sacrifices went unnoticed.

| Introduction | raising children | managing farms | facing enemies | giving up heirlooms | Conclusion |

---

### Sacrifices

Throughout the Civil War, women in both the North and the South made incredible sacrifices. Their efforts marked a turning point in the traditional roles of women in the United States.

| Introduction | raising children | managing farms | facing enemies | giving up heirlooms | Conclusion |

## Practicing Blocking Out

1. With your students, carefully read the introductions on *Tool 5-5b*. Point out that each example has only two sentences. Explain that keeping the introduction short makes it easier to focus on the purpose for the essay or report. The two-sentence introductory paragraph can be used for writing in all classes.

2. Have your students identify the topic sentence and the plan sentence in each example. If the plan is stated, have them underline the key/star ideas. If there is an implied plan, have them underline the clue(s) to the key/star ideas.

3. With your students, fill in the empty blocks with the key/star ideas from the plan sentences on *Tools 5-5b, 5-5c,* and *5-5d*. If the key/star ideas are not listed, ask students to look at the clues in the plan sentence to come up with their own key/star ideas that fit the topic. Remind them that each block represents a paragraph in the completed essay or report. Point out that blocks can be drawn either horizontally or vertically.

**Key/Star Ideas for *Tools 5-5c* and *5-5d***

| Item 1 | Item 2 | Item 3 | Item 4 |
|---|---|---|---|
| dieting | friendship | planning | airplanes |
| training | love | talent | submarines |
| practice posing | adventure | courage | guided missiles |
| mental composure | small town life | | space travel |

**Key/Star Ideas for *Tool 5-5d***

| Item 5 | Item 6 | Item 7 | Item 8 |
|---|---|---|---|
| food | weather | content | farmers |
| games | lack of food | appearance | ranchers |
| friends | wrong crops | | |
| | hunting/fishing | | |

4. Tell students that after they block out, they will make informal outlines. Each key/star idea on the informal outline will match one of the blocks on the plan.

## 5-6 Informal Outlines for Essays and Reports

Review 4-7 Planning with an Informal Outline to prepare your students to write informal outlines.

Review the informal outline as a quick way to organize thoughts for essays or reports. Informal outlines can be of any length. They provide a visual structure for an essay or report.

- Students begin informal outlines with the topic and/or thesis statement and the key/star ideas, which provide the basic frame for the outline.
- Then students should add the elaboration—the dots and dashes. These provide the explanations, examples, and evidence that will complete the body paragraphs. (See 5-14 Reviewing Elaboration for more information about the dots and dashes.)

## 5-7 Using an Informal Outline Practice Guide

Students use this strategy to visualize the organization of a report or essay. Informal outlines make it easier for students to learn about and practice essay and report writing. Use this strategy to practice creating informal outlines.

**Prerequisite:** 4-7 Planning with an Informal Outline

When students write about content that they are studying, they learn the content while improving their writing and reading skills. In several guided lessons, provide sentences for the introduction, then help students add the rest of the outline. Then move on to assignments that call for more student independence.

### Before Class

- Make transparencies and student copies of *Tools 5-7a* and *5-7b*.
- Have available red, yellow, and green overhead markers and highlighters.

### During Class

1. Display *Tools 5-7a* and *5-7b* and remind students that good essay and report writing always starts with planning. Explain that one of the best ways to plan is by developing an informal outline, and that using a practice guide as shown on these Tools is a great way to learn how to create their own informal outlines.

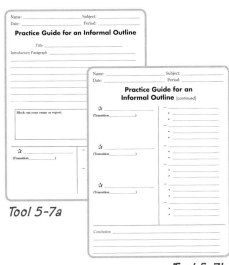

*Tool 5-7a*

*Tool 5-7b*

2. Review and discuss the parts of the practice guide on *Tool 5-7a*: the title, the introductory paragraph, blocking out, key/star ideas, transitions, dashes with dots, and the conclusion.

3. Highlight the labels for each part of the practice guide with the Traffic Light colors—green for title, introduction, and conclusion; yellow for transitions and key/star ideas; red for elaboration (dots and dashes). Have students color-code their copies.

4. Using *Tools 5-7a* and *5-7b*, develop an informal outline with your students on a topic from one of your students' recent content-area classes or a topic that is familiar to everyone in your class. Tell them they can use as many or as few of the key/star idea spaces as needed to fit the topic and the task.

5. Read through the informal outline a second time and discuss the contents using the following questions:

   - Is the introduction clear?
   - What is the thesis statement? What is the plan sentence?
   - How clear are the key/star ideas?
   - How does blocking out help?
   - Are there enough dashes and dots? Are they clear? Do they make sense?
   - Does the conclusion fit the introduction? How?

6. Start with several guided lessons and when students are ready, have them work independently. Tell your students they can use *Tools 5-7a* and *5-7b* in all subjects.

## Additional Ideas

- Provide your students with an introductory paragraph and ask them to complete the rest of the practice guide on *Tools 5-7a* and *5-7b*.

- Give students blank copies of *Tools 5-7a* and *5-7b* to take home the day before an essay exam so they can plan. Allow them to use their practice guides during the test.

- Make several transparencies of *Tools 5-7a* and *5-7b*. Let students work in pairs to complete the informal outline on the transparency using overhead markers. Have students display their outlines and explain the content.

- Have relay races. Divide your students into small groups and have them race each other to complete a practice guide with *Tools 5-7a* and *5-7b*. Provide the introduction and have your students pass the guide around their group, filling in all of the spaces. Have them share their responses. Award not only the quickest, but more importantly, the most thorough responses.

**Leading with the Blues**

Students can use this strategy to add leads to introductions.
**Prerequisite:** 5-4 Creating Two-Sentence Introductions

Since basic two-sentence introductions start with just the topic sentence and the plan sentence, students almost always have a strong sense of purpose for their writing. This sense of purpose helps them when they are ready to add a lead.

The lead of an essay or report is extra information added to the introduction to make it clearer or more interesting. This information can educate or entertain the reader. The two-sentence introduction can be used for many writing assignments. The need for a lead and the length of the lead will depend on the report's purpose and audience.

## Before Class

- Make overhead transparencies and student copies of *Tools 5-8a, 5-8b*, and *5-8c*.
- Have available blue and green markers and highlighters.

 *Bonus Tool 5-8-1* provides additional examples.

## During Class

1. Explain the purpose of a lead to your students by telling them that leads can be used to educate or entertain the reader. The purpose is to make the introduction clearer or more interesting. Leads can be one sentence or several sentences.

2. Display *Tool 5-8a* and point out that this Tool uses the term *the Blues* to refer to the lead. In the color-coding system, the lead is colored blue. The lead is also called the *hook*, the *attention getter*, or the *grabber*.

3. In each example, contrast the shorter introduction to the introduction with the lead.

*Tool 5-8a*

4. Discuss the examples using the following questions:
   - What does the lead provide that might help the reader?
   - Does the lead make sense?
   - Does the lead encourage the reader to continue reading and find out more?
   - Does the lead fit with the thesis statement and the plan sentence?
   - How would you change the lead?
   - How does the graphic "Jazz It Up" on *Tool 5-8a* remind you to use a lead?
   - How would you describe the lead in a report to another student?

5. If any students are confused about whether and when they should add leads, explain that the two-sentence introduction can be used just as it is for many writing assignments. The need for a lead and its length will depend on the purpose and the audience for the report.

## Writing Leads

1. Remind your students of the purpose of the lead. Explain that adding a lead is like decorating the topic. The extra information in the lead can give readers the background they need to understand a complicated topic. It can also be used to excite readers and encourage them to keep reading.

*Tool 5-8b*

*Tool 5-8c*

2. Display *Tools 5-8b* and *5-8c* and tell your students that there are several ways to write a lead—to add the Blues to their introductions. Review the examples of different ways of writing a lead. Color the transparency and have students color the lead blue and the topic and plan sentences green to help them visualize how the lead functions. (For additional examples, see *Bonus Tool 5-8-1.*)

3. Be sure your class understands that sometimes a short introduction is the best choice. Even one-sentence introductions work. The length of an introduction plus its lead depends on the topic, the amount of time available to write, and the audience for the essay or report. Push students to revise their introductions several times, focusing on word choice, style, voice, and sentence structure.

4. Give students many opportunities to practice writing introductions—with and without leads. Do this even when students will not be completing the essay or report. If students practice this skill only when there is time to write an essay or report, they will not have enough opportunities to practice.

## Additional Ideas

1. Reading and analyzing leads that others write is a powerful way to help students improve their skills at adding leads to introductions. Look for examples of leads for students to use as models.

2. Encourage students to look for leads and start a collection of the leads they find. Looking for leads as they read closely will also help them find the topic sentences or thesis statements in articles and reports and will help students improve their reading comprehension.

3. Make transparencies and student copies of the best examples. Read and color-code the examples with your class to help them visualize how the Blues function.

# Using Transitions in Essays and Reports

Transitions are key elements in an essay or report. They introduce the key/star ideas that prove or explain the thesis statement. They are the glue that holds the report together. With explicit directions and instructions, specific examples, and opportunities to practice, all students will build the confidence and skills needed to use transitions effectively.

## Objectives

- Teach students the function of transitions
- Improve use of transitions to make writing flow smoothly
- Empower students to choose from a variety of transitions

| Strategy | Strategy Description | Page | Tools |
|---|---|---|---|
| **5-9** Transition Topic Sentences | Learning and understanding transitions in transition topic sentences | 230 | 5-9a |
| **5-10** Using Obvious and Subtle Transitions | Experimenting with and improving the use of transitions | 231 | 5-10a to 5-10c |
| **5-11** Using *First*, *Second*, and *Third* as Transitions | Learning to use a variety of transitions beyond *first*, *second*, and *third* | 233 | 5-11a, 5-11b |
| **5-12** Burying Transitions | Burying transitions in sentences to add more variety | 235 | n/a |
| **5-13** Using Transition Topic Sentences in Longer Essays and Reports | Organizing long reports with lots of information | 235 | 5-1b, 5-13a, 5-13b |

## 5-9 Transition Topic Sentences

Students can use this strategy to learn or review transition topic sentences.

Transition topic sentences are the first sentences in the key body paragraphs of an essay or report. They introduce the supporting details that prove or explain the topic sentence or thesis statement. The number of transition topic sentences depends on the plan (stated or implied) in the introductory paragraph. When students can write effective transition topic sentences, the different pieces of their essays and reports will flow together into a coherent whole.

### Before Class

- Make an overhead transparency and student copies of *Tool 5-9a*.
- Have available red, green, and yellow markers and highlighters.

### During Class

1. Using *Tool 5-9a*, read the descriptions of transition topic sentences and discuss them with your students, taking time to clear up any terms students don't understand.

2. Point out the diagram on *Tool 5-9a*. Explain that this diagram shows how a short essay or report is structured. The color labels on the left show how each part of the report should be colored using the Traffic Light colors.

3. Have students add the Traffic Light colors to their copies of the diagram.

   - Start with yellow. Explain that the yellow sentences start the body paragraphs and that these sentences present the key/star ideas to support the topic. Yellow is meant to remind students to slow down and present support for their topic with reasons, details, or facts.

   - Next, add red to each body paragraph. The red will remind students that transition topic sentences are followed by examples and elaboration.

   - Finally, add green for the introduction and the conclusion.

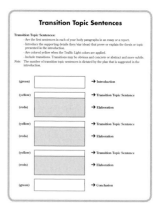

*Tool 5-9a*

## Additional Ideas

- Make an enlarged version of each of the paragraphs on *Tool 5-9a* by using colored construction paper, cardstock, or poster board.
  - ▸ Add magnetic tape to the back side of each card so that they can be displayed on the board. Laminate the pages. Use overhead markers to write on them.
  - ▸ Ask five students to hold these large cards and organize themselves in the order the paragraphs would appear in a report.
- Use colored index cards, half sheets of paper, or sticky notes in green, yellow, and red (pink) as manipulatives. Have students arrange the parts of the report at their desks.

## 5-10 Using Obvious and Subtle Transitions

Using this strategy, students skillfully employ transitions in multiparagraph essays and reports.

Over time and with guidance and practice, students will learn to choose transitions that fit their purpose for writing and their audience. This strategy might be best used with students who already understand the basics of writing essays and reports.

## Before Class

- Make transparencies and student copies of *Tools 5-10a, 5-10b,* and *5-10c.*
- Have available yellow highlighters and overhead markers.

## During Class

1. Introduce the concept of obvious and subtle transitions.
2. Explain that obvious transitions are words and phrases that students will recognize because they are transitions that they hear and use frequently. Present the following examples of obvious transitions:

> One, Another, A third, The fourth
>
> First, Second, Third
>
> At first, Then, Later, After that

3. Explain that subtle transitions are words and phrases that aren't as obvious. They function as transitions in different ways, usually by being similar to words in the topic. Present the following examples of subtle transitions:

> Synonyms (the little dog, the excited puppy, the racing beagle)
>
> Related words (the catcher, the pitcher, the batter)
>
> Words on the same topic (a comet, the telescope, some astronauts)

4. Display *Tool 5-10a* and read Example 1 to the class. In this report, the writer used the obvious transitions ("One," "A second," and "Third") to help the reader learn about some difficult issues teenagers face on a daily basis. Have students highlight the transition topic sentences in yellow.

5. Do the same with Example 2 and point out the use of the obvious transitions ("To begin" and "also").

6. Introduce the subtle transitions on *Tools 5-10b* and *5-10c*. Note that in these examples, the transitions are less obvious. Point out the transitions and highlight the transition topic sentences in yellow.

7. Compare the yellow sentences—the transition topic sentences—on both *Tools 5-10a* and *5-10b*. Help students see that both methods help organize ideas, and make them easy to read and understand.

## Additional Ideas

- Challenge students to bring in samples of transitions. Encourage them to look for examples of transitions in newspapers, magazines, and online texts.

- Collect transitions that students bring in. List them on chart paper and ask students to add to the list whenever they find or think of a new transition. Display the list to use for reference in writing assignments. Include both new transitions and ideas for subtle transitions on the list.

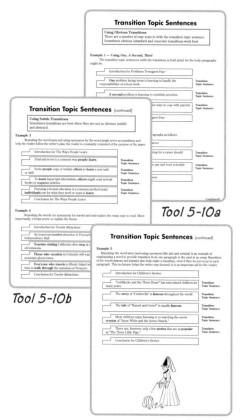

*Tool 5-10a*

*Tool 5-10b*

*Tool 5-10c*

- Write the transition words and phrases on half sheets of yellow construction paper. Laminate the cards and add magnetic tape to their backs. Use them as a border for the front board. Move them around when it is time to write a report. Create several sets to inspire students to "vary" their transitions.

- Use the sets on *Tools 5-10a*, *5-10b*, and *5-10c* for creating informal outlines and then writing reports or essays.

## 5-11 Using *First*, *Second*, and *Third* as Transitions

Using this strategy, students limit their use of *First*, *Second*, and *Third* to times when they are appropriate and fit the purpose of the essay or report. See Section 4 for additional information on transitions.

### Before Class

- Make overhead transparencies and student copies of *Tools 5-11a* and *5-11b*.

- Have available red, green, and yellow highlighters and overhead markers.

- *Bonus Tool 5-11-1* provides additional examples and support.

### During Class

1. Explain to your students that it is important to vary transitions whenever possible. This means using more than just *First*, *Second*, and *Third*.

2. Using *Tool 5-10a*, show how to use obvious transitions like *First*, *Second*, and *Finally* to make a point. Mark the transition words on the overhead and have students mark their copies in yellow. With your students, color-code the rest of the essay.

3. Discuss using transitions like *First*, *Second*, *Third*, and *First of all* with your students.

   - Explain to your students that it is okay to use *First*, *Second*, and *Third*, especially to help organize their first drafts. Tell them that these are powerful transitions, but that they do not fit all reports and are easy to overuse. A good question to ask about such transitions is: "Does it fit the purpose and the audience, or are there any better options?" Encourage students to branch out in the final copy and replace these words with transitions that are not so obvious.

4. Using *Tool 5-11b*, show the example of how to use subtle transitions. Highlight the words on the overhead and have students color-code their copies using the Traffic Light colors.

Tool 5-11a

Tool 5-11b

5. Use the following example to demonstrate how students can replace *First* with a less-obvious transition (also on *Bonus Tool 5-11-1*):

> **Obvious transition:** <u>*First,*</u> *I gave my hamsters some food.*
>
> **Subtle transition:** <u>*After I put the hamsters in their cage,*</u> *I gave them some food.*
>
> **Obvious transition:** <u>*Next,*</u> *I locked the cage because the pet store owner said they like to climb out.*
>
> **Subtle transition:** <u>*Before I left for school,*</u> *I locked the cage because the pet store owner said they like to climb out.*

6. Have your students write a number of transition topic sentences using obvious transitions and replacing them with subtle transitions.

7. Encourage your students to read their reports out loud. Explain that this practice helps them hear what does and does not sound good. Encourage them to try different transitions or to eliminate the transition in order to experiment with different options.

## Story Transitions Versus Essay and Report Transitions

Remind students that there are differences between the types of transitions used in narratives and those used in reports.

- Narrative transitions show time and place (*in the morning, later, when, as, after*). (See **6-15 Function and Variety of Narrative Transitions.**)

- Essay and report transitions list and present key/star ideas (*one, another, next, finally*). (See **4-23 Definition and Function of Transitions.**)

## 5-12 Burying Transitions

Using this strategy, students add more variety to their writing by burying transitions in sentences.

*Bonus Tool 5-12-1* provides additional examples and support.

Explain that the transition does not need to be the first word in the sentence. Sometimes, but not always, it helps to bury the transition. Ask students what it means to bury something and have them guess what it might mean to bury a transition. Demonstrate and discuss buried transitions with the following examples (also on *Bonus Tool 5-12-1*).

**Transition starts sentence:** *First,* my family decided to visit the zoo.

**Buried transition:** Going to the zoo was the *first* big event of my summer.

**Transition starts sentence:** *First,* we read the directions.

**Buried transition:** We knew it would be tricky to assemble the model, so *first* we read the directions carefully.

Have your students practice writing sentences both ways. Have them write the transition first in the sentence and then buried in the sentence. Tell them to check that burying the transition does not change the meaning of the sentence. Remind them to consider improving their choices of transitions when they are revising their essays and reports.

## 5-13 Using Transition Topic Sentences in Longer Essays and Reports

Students can use this strategy to organize essays and reports that have a great deal of elaboration.

### Before Class

Make overhead transparencies and student copies of *Tools 5-1b, 5-13a,* and *5-13b.*

### During Class

1. Using *Tool 5-1b,* point out that in "If Wishes Came True," each transition topic sentence and its elaboration is contained in a *single* body paragraph.

2. Read *Tools 5-13a* and *5-13b* with your class, and mark the transitions. The three transition topic sentences are:

- *First of all,* an ideal Anglo-Saxon warrior needed to possess confidence and courage.

- Beowulf was *also* admired for his generosity.

- *Last,* epic heroes like Beowulf were respected for their strength.

3. Point out that unlike *Tool 5-1c*, each transition topic sentence paragraph in "What Makes an Epic Hero?" is followed by one extra paragraph of elaboration.

4. Using *Tools 5-13a* and *5-13b*, discuss the use of elaboration and remind students that there are only three transition topic sentences in this report but lots of elaboration. Explain that elaboration in reports is not always contained in a single body paragraph. Sometimes there are several paragraphs for each key/star idea.

5. Tell students that when they have lots of elaboration, it makes sense to break it into smaller paragraphs. The breaks should come at logical places. All of the elaboration paragraphs should continue to support the key/star idea in the transition topic sentence. (If Traffic Light colors are applied, these extra paragraphs are red. Only the transition topic sentences, which hold the key/star ideas, are yellow.)

6. Explain to students that when they block out reports and essays that have more than one paragraph of elaboration for each key/star idea, they should still draw one block for each paragraph. For paragraphs that don't have key/star ideas, they can write "elaboration for _____" in the box, where the blank is the key/star idea they are elaborating on. They can also use a word or phrase to remind them what elaboration to include in that paragraph.

7. Review the transition topic sentences and elaboration in "What Makes an Epic Hero?" taking time to discuss the report using the questions in **5-1 Elements of Accordion Essays and Reports.**

*Tool 5-1b*

*Tool 5-13a*

*Tool 5-13b*

# Using Elaboration in Essays and Reports

Elaboration is all the details a writer brings to an essay or report to support a thesis statement. An easy way to visualize elaboration is with a list of E words: examples, evidence, explanation, events, expert opinion, effective illustrations, experiences, everyday occurrences, exact information, and so on. See Section 4 for more on elaboration.

## Objectives

- Learn how to use elaboration effectively
- Develop plans for using elaboration

| Strategy | Strategy Description | Page | Tools |
|---|---|---|---|
| **5-14 Reviewing Elaboration** | Reviewing the use of elaboration and how it functions in multiparagraph writing | 238 | 5-14a |
| **5-15 Increasing Elaboration in Essays and Reports** | Learning to recognize when to be more specific in a report or essay | 238 | 5-15a, 5-15b |
| **5-16 Using Informal Outlines to Improve Elaboration** | Using Informal Outlines to plan the use of elaboration | 239 | 5-16a, 5-16b |
| **5-17 Elaborating with Quotations and Citations** | Using quotations to add elaboration and support to essays and reports | 241 | 5-13a, 5-13b |

## 5-14 Reviewing Elaboration

This strategy helps students better use elaboration by having them analyze elaboration in existing essays and reports. Specific examples will support their learning and help them remember how elaboration functions.

### Before Class

- Make an overhead transparency and student copies of *Tool 5-14a*.
- Have available red and yellow highlighters and overhead markers.

### During Class

1. Explain that elaboration refers to the examples, evidence, explanation, events, expert opinion, effective illustrations, experiences, everyday occurrences, exact information, and so on (the E's) that support the thesis statement. If necessary, make a list of the E's on the board, and define any unfamiliar terms (see **4-31 Paragraph Elaboration–the E's/the Reds**).

2. Read *Tool 5-14a* with your students. Identify the transition topic sentences and elaboration. Mark the transparency and have your students mark their copies with the Traffic Light colors. Remind them that transition topic sentences are colored yellow and elaboration sentences—the E's—are red. Red reminds students to stop and explain. Mark *Tool 5-14a* as follows:

   - Green—(Neither the introduction nor the conclusion are shown on the excerpt.)
   - Yellow—First sentence in each body paragraph
   - Red—All other sentences

3. Have your students identify the elaboration in other reports or essays they find in magazines or newspapers.

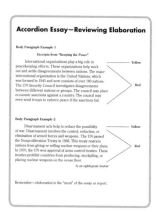

*Tool 5-14a*

## 5-15 Increasing Elaboration in Essays and Reports

Students benefit from seeing what is expected of them. They can use this strategy to compare two examples—one that does not have enough elaboration and one that does—so they will be better able to write papers using the appropriate amount and quality of elaboration.

### Before Class

- Make overhead transparencies and student copies of *Tools 5-15a* and *5-15b*.
- Have available red, yellow, green, and blue overhead markers.

## During Class

1. Display *Tool 5-15a* and read through the vague book report with your class. Tell students that vague is the opposite of specific. As you read, ask your class to point out filler sentences. Tell them the vague book report has little value because it is not informative.

2. After you have finished reading the vague book report, display *Tool 5-15b* and read through the report on *Leah's Pony*.

3. Add the Traffic Light colors to both reports to help your students compare the Reds—the elaboration— in the reports.

4. As the class compares the two reports, ask the following questions:

   • How are the transition topic sentences different?

   • How many facts or details are included in each body paragraph?

   • How specific are the examples and explanations?

   • Which report is more informative? Why?

   • Which report is more interesting? Why?

   • How are the introductions and the conclusions different?

5. Have your students review additional reports or essays and look for ways to add elaboration. Give them time to rewrite and reinforce the concept that revising and rewriting is a normal and important step in being a successful writer.

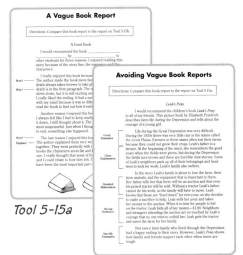

*Tool 5-15a*

*Tool 5-15b*

## 5-16 Using Informal Outlines to Improve Elaboration

Students can use this strategy to prepare to write an essay or report and to improve elaboration in their informal outlines. See Section 4 for more on informal outlines.

## Before Class

• Make overhead transparencies of *Tools 5-16a* and *5-16b* and student copies of *Tool 5-16b*.

• Have available notebook paper and red, yellow, green, and blue highlighters and overhead markers.

## During Class

1. Explain to your students that informal outlines can help them decide what elaboration they will use in order to have a quality essay or report. Tell them that they should use the time before the first draft—during outline preparation—to make sure they have what they need to write a detailed and interesting essay or report.

2. Let them know that making an informal outline should not be time consuming. Discuss with them the routine they should follow for writing.

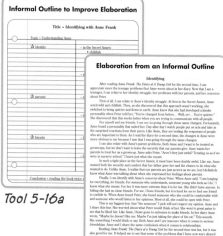

**Tool 5-16a**

**Tool 5-16b**

- Have students start with the topic sentence and key/star ideas. These provide the outline's basic frame.

- Then they should add the elaboration—dashes and dots (the E's). They provide the explanations, examples, and evidence that will complete the body paragraphs. Remind students that the dashes support the key/star ideas, and the dots support the dashes. The more dots and dashes they use, the more elaboration they will have.

3. Using the transparency of *Tool 5-16a*, share the informal outline about Anne Frank's diary. Ask your students to fold a sheet of notebook paper using a two-column fold. Explain to your students that they will use this sheet to create informal outlines.

4. Ask them to copy the informal outline from *Tool 5-16a* as you explain and describe the parts of the outlines. This practice will set the standard for good informal outlines and help students see what it takes to write a good essay or report.

5. Have your students color code their outlines with the Traffic Light colors—green for the introduction and conclusion, yellow for key/star ideas, red for elaboration (dots and dashes).

6. Display *Tool 5-16b* and review the essay made from the informal outline. With your students, compare the outline to the finished essay and as you mark the transparency, have students mark their copies with the Traffic Light colors as follows:

- First and last paragraphs green (introduction and conclusion)
- First sentence in paragraphs 2, 4, and 6 yellow (key/star ideas)
- All other sentences red (elaboration)

7. Discuss and analyze the essay and its informal outline, using the following questions:

- How did the outline help with the elaboration?
- How many paragraphs are in the report? How do they match the outline?
- Are the paragraphs clear and interesting? Why? Explain.
- Did the examples and explanations support the thesis statement?

- Did the elaboration follow the plan?
- How would you change and/or improve the elaboration?

8. Rehearse informal outlining frequently. In the beginning, you will need to do much of the work, but as students progress, they will be able to do the work independently. With adequate modeling and guided practice, they will be able to complete good informal outlines on their own.

## Additional Ideas

- Post large sample informal outlines around the room for students to use as models.
- Make an outline with everything filled in but the elaboration, and either pass out copies or place it on the board when you do activities like the following with your class:
  - ▶ When you read information articles with your class, ask students to offer suggestions for the dashes.
  - ▶ When your students watch a video in class, ask them to listen and watch carefully for information to use in the outline when the video is over.
  - ▶ When you review content material prior to a quiz or test, give students time to fill in the missing elaboration with a partner. Have them share with the class to help everyone study for the exam.

## 5-17 Elaborating with Quotations and Citations

One common way to support a topic is by including quotations from a reliable source. Using this strategy, students include quotations in their reports and essays.

*Bonus Tool 5-17-1* provides additional support.

In essays and reports, students often want to use quotations to support their topic and make their explanations more specific. To help your students select quotations, review **1-7 Quotation Responses**. To insert quotations into text, review **3-16 Adding Quotations**. See **5-24 Writing Documented Essays and Reports** for an example of using quotations and citations. Find and discuss the use of quotations in *5-13a* and *5-13b*.

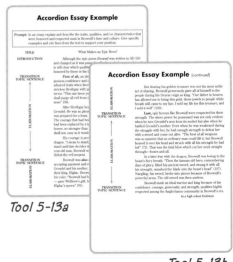

*Tool 5-13a*

*Tool 5-13b*

# Writing Conclusions for Essays and Reports

Conclusions—also called *closing statements* or *clinchers*—need special attention. These strategies help students develop the skills they need to write strong conclusions.

## Objectives

- Improve understanding of the function of the conclusion
- Learn different approaches to writing conclusions and improving their quality

| Strategy | Strategy Description | Page | Tools |
|---|---|---|---|
| **5-18 Writing Successful Conclusions** | Reviewing the function of a conclusion and learning different ways to write it | 243 | 5-18a to 5-18d |
| **5-19 Conclusions Have a Purpose** | Reviewing the different goals of a conclusion and writing conclusions for different purposes | 245 | 5-19a |
| **5-20 Practicing and Improving Conclusions** | Practicing varied strategies to improve conclusions | 245 | 5-18a to 5-18d |

# 5-18 Writing Successful Conclusions

Students can use this strategy to review the function of a conclusion and to learn concrete ways to write outstanding conclusions. See Section 4 for more information about conclusions.

Conclusions need special attention. Because the introduction, transitions, key/star ideas, and elaboration take much of their energy, students may neglect their conclusions and hope this goes unnoticed. This is unfortunate, because the difference between a great essay or report and merely a good one is often an effective conclusion.

## Before Class

Make overhead transparencies and student copies of *Tools 5-18a* through *5-18d*.

## During Class

Using *Tools 5-18a* through *5-18d*, read and discuss each tip and example one at a time. Answer any questions students might have about any of the tips.

- **Remember the basics:** Read the list and emphasize that these are the basic rules for the conclusion. Illustrate these rules with the example on *Tool 5-18a*.

- **Use conclusion words:** Show students how certain words or phrases can be used to help them summarize their key/star ideas and remind readers of their topic. Point out how embedding the conclusion word in the middle of the sentence makes the conclusion more effective. Stress to students, however, that the conclusion words are one of several options for writing a conclusion and aren't needed in all conclusions.

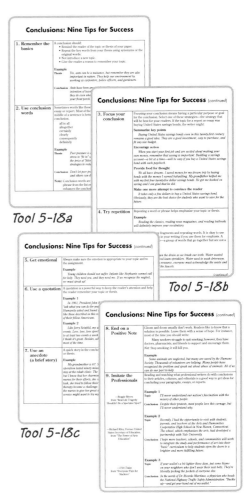

*Tool 5-18a*

*Tool 5-18b*

*Tool 5-18c*

*Tool 5-18d*

- **Focus your conclusion:** Review the four strategies for focusing the conclusion: summarize key points, encourage action, provide food for thought, and make one more attempt to convince the reader.

- **Try repetition:** Show your students how repeating a word or phrase in the conclusion helps emphasize the topic.

- **Get emotional:** Show students how emotion can be used in certain circumstances, such as in a persuasive essay, to reinforce the topic.

- **Use a quotation:** Tell your students that quotations can be a powerful way to keep the reader's attention and help the reader remember the topic.

- **Use an anecdote (a brief story):** Show your students how using a quick story in the conclusion can drive home the point of the topic. Tell students they can also try introducing an anecdote in the introduction and then finishing it in the conclusion.

- **End on a positive note:** Even when students are trying to convince someone of the existence of a problem, they should end by presenting solutions and hope for a resolution of the problem. Readers don't respond well to gloomy endings, even if they agree with the topic.

- **Imitate the professionals:** Ask your students to read and collect articles from newspapers and magazines and examine their conclusions to learn new tips and techniques. Have them imitate in their own writing interesting conclusions they find.

### Create a Booklet of Tips

- Make extra copies of *Tools 5-18a* through *5-18d* to create a booklet of tips for each student, or have them keep copies in their writing notebooks.

- Add two or more lined pages to the booklet. Students can use the lined paper to add more ideas and examples for conclusions as they come up.

- Ask students to keep the booklets in their writing folders for use throughout the year. Have them use the booklets frequently as they write their own essays and reports.

**Note:** Students need to see and hear many samples of conclusions (and introductions) to help them develop confidence and style. Provide time for students to share and discuss conclusions.

## 5-19 Conclusions Have a Purpose

Conclusions can do much more than summarize. Using this strategy, students explore the variety of purposes for conclusions and increase the variety and effectiveness of their conclusions.

### Before Class

Make an overhead transparency and student copies of *Tool 5-19a*.

### During Class

1. Explain to students that writers usually have one or more purposes in mind when they write a conclusion. The purpose might be to summarize, encourage, convince, or challenge.

2. Use *Tool 5-19a* to demonstrate how to write conclusions with such goals for both single paragraphs and multiparagraph essays and reports.

3. Share with your class conclusions in articles you have collected or use *Tools 5-1b, 5-11a, 5-11b, 5-13a, 5-13b,* and *5-15a*. Read the conclusions and discuss the purpose of each example.

4. First as a group and then individually, have students write different conclusions for the same topic, each with a different purpose. Provide them with topics that will allow them to write conclusions that summarize, encourage, convince, and challenge.

*Tool 5-19a*

## 5-20 Practicing and Improving Conclusions

Students achieve greater success with their essays and reports when they practice writing the different parts of the paper and try different writing strategies. Using this strategy, students practice and improve their conclusions.
**Prerequisite:** 5-18 Writing Successful Conclusions

### Before Class

Make student copies of *Tools 5-18a* through *5-18d*.

## During Class

Choose activities from this list to help students practice and improve their conclusions:

1. Reread and critique the conclusions you collected for 5-19 Conclusions Have a Purpose for extra practice evaluating and revising conclusions. Rewrite these conclusions using the tips from *Tools 5-18a* through *5-18d*.

2. Instead of writing a full essay or report, have your students write only their informal outlines but with the introduction and conclusion as paragraphs. Provide adequate models and guided practice until students can do this independently. Guide students as they add the key/star ideas and the dots and dashes for elaboration.

3. Use the color green to help students think about the connection between the introduction (topic sentence or thesis statement) and conclusion. The green will help students remember to go back to their topic and/or thesis in the introduction.

4. Have students exchange papers and write revised conclusions for each other.

5. Have students work in pairs or small groups. Tell each group to write several introduction/conclusion sets on index cards. Have groups exchange their sets and compare their introductions and conclusions.

6. With each read-aloud, remind students about the differences between narrative writing and essay and report writing. Remind them of the terms: *beginning, middle,* and *end* for narrative writing and *introduction (topic sentence or thesis statement), body paragraphs,* and *conclusion* for essay and report writing. Ask students to write paragraphs comparing narrative endings with conclusions for reports or essays. (See Section 4 and Section 6.)

*Tool 5-18a*

*Tool 5-18b*

*Tool 5-18c*

*Tool 5-18d*

# Practicing Essay and Report Writing

After being taught how to write essays and reports, it is very important for students to have ample opportunities to practice writing. This practice should include support until students are able to write independently.

## Objectives

- Practice writing essays and reports with varying amounts of support
- Write essays and reports with confidence and increasing levels of success

| Strategy | Strategy Description | Page | Tools |
|---|---|---|---|
| **5-21 Using Framed Essays and Reports to Promote Success** | Using a framed structure to help understand the organization of essays and reports | 248 | n/a |
| **5-22 Moving from a Paragraph to an Essay or Report** | Using elaboration to stretch from a single stand-alone paragraph to an essay or report on the same topic | 248 | 5-22a to 5-22c |
| **5-23 Stretch, Don't Stack Practice** | Avoiding stacking paragraphs and instead stretching ideas into a multiparagraph essay or report | 250 | 5-23a, 5-23b |
| **5-24 Writing Documented Essays and Reports** | Documenting sources when writing essays, reports, and research papers | 251 | 5-24a |

## 5-21 Using Framed Essays and Reports to Promote Success

Have students use 9-9 Using Writing Frames to support skill development and experience early success in essay and report writing. This strategy is a means of helping students quickly see the parts of a paper and recognize the organization of essays and reports.

Framed essays and reports work well with learners of all ages, but they are especially helpful for beginning writers. Frames that provide the introduction and the first few words of transition sentences give students an opportunity to experience success.

## 5-22 Moving from a Paragraph to an Essay or Report

Students who use this strategy avoid stacking paragraphs and instead stretch their ideas into several smoothly flowing paragraphs filled with examples and elaboration.

There is more to writing an essay or report than writing a series of separate paragraphs or just dividing paragraphs into smaller pieces. "Stretch, Don't Stack" is an especially important message to give students who have learned to write Accordion Paragraphs. They may be tempted to stack several unrelated paragraphs together to create a report. Encourage students instead to stretch their ideas to make interesting, connected paragraphs.

### Before Class
- Make overhead transparencies and student copies of *Tools 5-22a, 5-22b*, and *5-22c*.
- Have available red, yellow, green, and blue highlighters and overhead markers.

### During Class

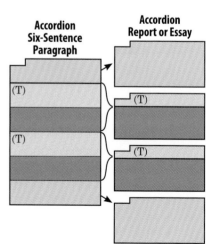

**Accordion Six-Sentence Paragraph**

**Accordion Report or Essay**

1. Help students understand the difference between Accordion Paragraphs and Accordion Essays or Reports by defining the terms as follows:

   **Accordion Paragraphs**
   - ▶ Have their own thesis statements or topic sentences, supporting sentences, elaboration, and conclusion.
   - ▶ Stand alone and make sense by themselves.

   **Accordion Essays or Reports**
   - ▶ Have a thesis statement or a topic sentence and a plan sentence as part of the introductory paragraph. The plan sentence gives a preview of the main concepts (key/star ideas) presented in the paper.

- Have several body paragraphs filled with elaboration. These paragraphs do not stand alone.
- Have body paragraphs without formal conclusions, but the essay or report generally has a concluding paragraph.

## Accordion Paragraph

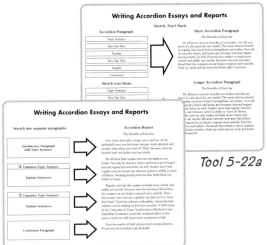

1. Read the two paragraphs on *Tool 5-22a* with your students. Have them compare these paragraphs with the set of strips on the left side of the page. Lead a class discussion comparing these paragraphs.

2. Highlight on the transparency and have students color their copies using the Traffic Light colors on both the strips on the left and the corresponding paragraphs. Point out that the Reds explain the topic and give examples of it.

3. Point out that there are more red sentences in the second paragraph on *Tool 5-22a*. Explain that the added elaboration in the second paragraph is good but that it does not give enough elaboration for it to be broken into paragraphs.

*Tool 5-22a*

*Tool 5-22b*

## Accordion Essays and Reports

1. Using *Tool 5-22b*, review the report with your students. Mark the transparency and have students color their copies using the Traffic Light colors on both the report and the strips to the left.

   - The introductory paragraph and the conclusion are green.
   - The transition topic sentences at the beginning of the second and third paragraphs are yellow.
   - The remaining sentences and the explain sentence strips are red.

   The colors help them see that the message in the Accordion Paragraphs and the Accordion Report is the same, but the amount and organization of elaboration varies.

2. Display and compare the paragraphs on *Tool 5-22a* and the report on *Tool 5-22b*. Have your students focus on the similarities between the topic sentences and the supporting key/star ideas in both the report and the paragraphs. Point out the large difference in the amount of elaboration in the body paragraphs of the essay.

3. Explain that because there is a lot of elaboration in the report, the text has been split. Each body paragraph in the report now starts with a sentence that states the key/star idea for that paragraph. These transition topic sentences are not topic sentences for the whole report, but only for that paragraph.

4. Using *Tool 5-22c*, practice color-coding paragraphs that stretch into an Accordion Report. Highlight as follows:

Short and Longer Accordion Paragraphs (*Tool 5-22c*)

- Green—First and last sentences
- Yellow—Sentences beginning in First, Next, You will need to, and Finally
- Red—All other sentences

Accordion Report

- Blue—First two sentences
- Green—Third and fourth sentences in first paragraph and all of last paragraph
- Yellow—First sentence in paragraphs 2, 3, 4, and 5
- Red—All other sentences

For more information about leads, see **5-8 Leading with the Blues**.

*Tool 5-22c*

## Additional Ideas

Make this activity visual and kinesthetic by making large colored strips from construction paper. Make several strips in all colors of the Traffic Light. Add magnetic tape to the back of the strips. As students color the small strips on *Tools 5-22a* and *5-22b*, arrange these large colored strips on the board.

## **5-23** Stretch, Don't Stack Practice

This strategy reinforces the importance of elaborating key/star ideas with examples and gives practice in stretching a paragraph into an essay or report. "Stretch, Don't Stack" activities will help students as they learn about and work to master essay and report writing.

## Before Class

- Make overhead transparencies and student copies of *Tools 5-23a* and *5-23b*.
- Have available green, yellow, and red highlighters and overhead markers.

## During Class

1. Remind your students of the slogan "Stretch, Don't Stack" when they need to write multiparagraph essays and reports. Display *Tool 5-23a* and have students color-code the strips as indicated. As they color, remind them of the meaning behind each color and lead a discussion about how you can stretch a paragraph into a report or essay.

2. Display *Tool 5-23b* and color-code the strips on the transparency as indicated. Have students color their copies. Discuss how paragraphs of different lengths and Accordion Essays or Reports can all be on the same topic. Discuss differences between each.

3. As a group, create informal outlines for a paragraph and for a report using a topic that you have covered in class. Model the outlines on a blank transparency, the board, or chart paper, and have students copy.

4. Color-code the outline—the title, topic sentence, and conclusion are green; the key/star ideas are yellow; and the elaboration is red.

5. Together with your class, write a paragraph and a report on chart paper from this outline. Discuss how a paragraph and a report are alike and how they are different. Hang them up as an example of how to stretch ideas. (See *Tools 4-33a* and *4-33b* "Let's Go to the Circus Again" for an additional example of "Stretching from a Paragraph to a Report.")

6. Have your students create additional informal outlines, paragraphs, and reports independently.

*Tool 5-23a*

*Tool 5-23b*

## 5-24 Writing Documented Essays and Reports

When students include facts and figures in their writing, they need to document their sources so their information can be verified. Students use this strategy to write research papers.

### Before Class

Make an overhead transparency of *Tool 5-24a*.

Review and consider teaching 1-21 Research Note Cards and 3-16 Adding Quotations prior to teaching this strategy.

**Note:** There are a number of styles for writing citations. The one used in this example is MLA. Change the examples if needed to reflect the style your students should use in their writing.

1. Explain to your students that documented reports (such as term papers and scholarly reports) are like regular reports except the sources for the facts used to support and elaborate on the key/star ideas are included. This helps anyone who reads the report know where that information came from.

2. Discuss plagiarism with your students and remind them to cite the source whenever they quote or paraphrase someone else's work.

3. To help your students understand how to write documented reports, display *Tool 5-24a*. Point out the phrase in parentheses at the end of the lead (Simmons 2004).

4. Explain that this is a method of documentation that includes the last name of the author who is the source of the quote or information cited, the date the article was published, and the page number the quote is found on, if necessary. Anyone who wants to look up the original source can look at the works-cited section at the end of the report to see where they can find the article.

*Tool 5-24a*

5. Tell students that if the name of the author appears in the sentence being documented, as in the second paragraph, it is acceptable to put only the date in parentheses—(2005).

6. Explain that the works-cited section contains the same information students put on their bibliography note cards in **1-21 Research Note Cards**, and although they are slightly different, the works-cited section may also be called a *reference list* or *bibliography*.

7. Explain that there are many ways to add quotes and citations, but students

   - Should always use quotation marks when using a quote;

   - Should not use quotation marks when summarizing or paraphrasing another person's words. They should, however, state the source of material they use in their writing.

8. Have students write new documented reports. Guide them through the report-writing process outlined in **5-2 Writing Essays and Reports Step by Step**, reminding them to record their sources on bibliography note cards, document their sources in their reports, and include the information for their sources in works-cited sections at the ends of their reports.

## Additional Ideas

- Have your students practice adding documentation to their reports by taking reports they have already written, finding and recording source information for the facts in their reports, and including documentation for the facts they used.

- Have students gather examples of citations from newspapers and magazines and encourage them to look for the use of citations in some of their textbooks.

# SECTION 6 INTRODUCTION
## Story and Narrative Writing

*N*arrative writing has always been an important part of schools' writing curricula and is often tested on local, state, and national writing assessments.

It is part of a well-balanced literacy program. Effective instruction in narrative writing encourages students to develop their understanding of narrative structure and to enhance their creativity. Narrative writing is also the foundation for autobiographies, personal stories, and biographies.

Additionally, through the process of writing narratives, students develop familiarity with academic terminology used in literary analysis, such as *plot*, *theme*, and *characterization*. Learning the terminology of narrative writing and gaining experience analyzing plot development helps students not only write better narratives but also better analyze the narratives they read.

*Step Up to Writing* provides students with the strategies they need to successfully move through the narrative-writing process. Students learn to develop characters, provide vivid descriptions, and include sensory imagery. Students also have the opportunity to continue to improve their sentence-writing skills (Section 3). As a result, they learn to express themselves with a personal style and voice.

Success with narrative writing occurs when students are introduced to the following:

- The terms used to describe a narrative and its structure
- Prewriting with a story map
- Planning with quick sketches (nonverbal organizational cues) and quick notes (brief words and phrases)
- Ideas for starting a narrative, especially when they "have no ideas"
- Ways to develop their characters and settings, concentrating on showing, not telling
- Understanding the purpose and definition of narrative transitions
- Understanding when and how to use dialogue effectively
- Options for the end of a narrative
- Tips for revising, editing, and proofreading

# When Teaching Narrative Writing

- Remember writing is a complex skill made up of many subskills. The subskills must be taught and practiced in isolation. Demonstration, guided lessons, and opportunities to practice both with peers and individually are equally important.
- Do not expect students to write complete narratives until they have multiple experiences prewriting, planning, and creating beginnings and ends.
- Teach the strategies that further develop characters, setting, and plot only after students understand how to plan and write a narrative.
- Use 6-23 Ten Tips for Revising as a guide. Target only one or two of the tips for each revision.
- Keep portfolios of students' narratives. Have students revisit and revise earlier drafts as their skills improve. Allow students to choose the narrative to revise.

## Tips for Using These Strategies Across Content Areas

✓ Writing narratives in all content areas helps students both broaden and deepen their knowledge and understanding of the subject matter.

✓ Have students research a key person in the content area and write a biographical narrative.

✓ In social studies, have students use a specific era or event as the setting of a narrative, or write a narrative set in the childhood of a historical figure.

✓ Use a specific science concept being studied, such as evaporation, metamorphosis, or the water cycle, as the main character for students' narratives.

✓ Use issues in the given content area, such as global warming, expanding technology, or water shortages as the main problem or conflict for a narrative.

✓ Have students rewrite first-person narratives in social science class from a different point of view.

✓ Have students in language arts class write the same incident in a play or novel from the perspective of two or three characters.

✓ In art or music, students can write narratives based on a specific song.

✓ Have students in art class write and illustrate a children's book.

# Story and Narrative Writing

Choose those strategies that best meet the needs of your students.

# Understanding Story Structure and Terms

When students become familiar with the structure and terminology used for narrative writing, they can also improve their own writing. When they read, listen to, and discuss narratives, students solidify their comprehension and make comparisons and connections to their own stories. After increasing their knowledge of narratives, students learn to skillfully describe characters, plots, techniques, styles, and other story elements during discussions and writing activities. And by focusing on the different elements of stories, students learn to write with confidence.

Writing, reading, comprehending, and analyzing stories are all important academic skills that build on one another.

## Objectives

- Teach students the structure and terminology of narrative writing
- Encourage students to read more
- Increase students' attention to story elements in order to improve writing
- Teach literary terms that students will use to analyze narrative elements

| Strategy | Strategy Description | Page | Tools |
|---|---|---|---|
| **6-1** Introducing Story Grammar and Terminology | Learning and applying terms used in the discussion and assessment of stories | 258 | 6-1a to 6-1d |
| **6-2** Learning Story Elements | Improving understanding of story terminology and the parts of a story by reading, comprehending, and analyzing short stories while using a reading guide | 259 | 6-2a, 6-2b |

## 6-1 Introducing Story Grammar and Terminology

When students understand and can use literary terms, they are better able to self-evaluate their stories and learn from feedback, and they feel more confident in story discussions. Students can use this strategy to learn literary terms and practice applying the terms in discussions and assessments of narratives.

### Before Class

Make overhead transparencies and student copies of *Tools 6-1a* through *6-1d*.

### During Class

1. Introduce narrative terminology using *Tools 6-1a* through *6-1d*.

   • Point out the terms listed along the left side of the Tools.

   • Read and discuss each term, providing and asking for examples from stories students know.

2. Demonstrate how your students will use these Tools with stories they read.

   • Explain that students should use the space in the examples column to write down lines from the text that represent the terms. They could also add notes of explanation.

   • Point out the space for page numbers for each example. Tell students to add the page numbers as soon as they write down the note or quotation to make it easier to find during class discussions. Remind them that whenever using a direct quote or when paraphrasing, it is always good to note the source. Reinforce that they should always protect themselves against plagiarizing—it is just as easy and effective to list the source.

3. Have students work in small groups and give each group a term from the Tools.

   • Using a story the class has read, have students find quotations and write notes that support their group's term.

   • Review and discuss as a class the examples they have found.

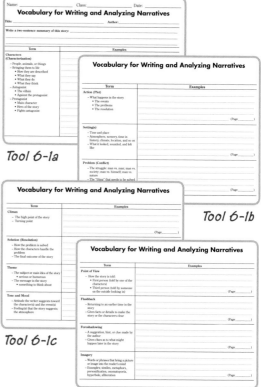

*Tool 6-1a*

*Tool 6-1b*

*Tool 6-1c*

*Tool 6-1d*

### Additional Ideas

   • Encourage students to keep *Tools 6-1a* through *6-1d* in their writing notebooks for quick reference.

- Have students use narrative terminology to label the parts of their own narratives, or have them use the vocabulary study guide to analyze their narratives.

- Challenge students to write narratives that focus on one element of fiction (e.g., setting, theme, or characters).

- During the study of a short story or novel, assign words to individual students. As they find examples, have them write the term, page number, and paragraph references on the board for all students to see. Use their examples in class discussions about the terms.

- Ask students to use the study guide as they read, collecting quotations as they go.

## 6-2 Learning Story Elements

Some students find it challenging to learn and remember narrative elements such as characters, setting, and plot. Have them use this strategy to better understand story or narrative elements by reading, comprehending, and analyzing stories.

### Before Class

- Make an overhead transparency and student copies of *Tool 6-2a* and/or *6-2b*.

- Have available short stories that your students are familiar with, or use *Tools 6-7a* and/or *6-7d*.

*Tool 6-2a*

### During Class

Tell students that different reading guides concentrate on different skills. Explain that when they use a guide, they should write quick notes for each category; fully developed sentences aren't necessary, which is why the guides have limited space for notes.

**Identifying Setting, Characters, Problem, and Climax**

1. Display *Tool 6-2a* and explain that this Tool will help students understand the organization and main components of the story. If your students are not familiar with story terminology, teach them **6-1 Introducing Story Grammar and Terminology.**

2. Distribute copies of *Tool 6-7a* or another short story students have recently read. With your students, review the story and fill out the guide as shown on the following example. Take time to answer questions.

### Short Story Reading Guide

| Title — Author | Theme | Setting — Characters | Conflict | Climax — Resolution |
|---|---|---|---|---|
| The New Gloves | honesty | three boys racing | they find money in a wallet | Good build up to finding the wallet |
| | | new sports store | have to decide to keep it or give it to owner | made tension more believable |
| | | new baseball gloves | | |
| | | | | |

On Tool 6-2a

**Identifying Beginning, Middle, and End**

1. Using *Tool 6-2b*, explain to students that this reading guide will help them identify a story's beginning, middle, and end, and to note facts so they remember stories better.

2. Distribute copies of *Tool 6-7d* or another short story your students are familiar with. With your students, review the story and fill out the guide. Take time to discuss and provide additional models if needed.

### Short Story Reading Guide

| Title — Author | As the story started . . . (Beginning) | Later on . . . (Middle) | The story ended after . . . (End) |
|---|---|---|---|
| | | | |
| | | | |
| | | | |
| | | | |

Tool 6-2b

## Short Story Reading Guide

| Title — Author | As the story started . . . (Beginning) | Later on . . . (Middle) | The story ended after . . . (End) |
|---|---|---|---|
| The Unexpected Package | a package from grandma arrives from UPS | she decides to visit grandma regularly | after she decided to mail a package of memories back to her grandma and head to graduation. |
| | high school girl finds dentures, a letter, and a ring from a gumball machine inside | On her visits learns family history. | |
| | | | |
| | | | |

*On Tool 6-2b*

### Continue to Practice Using a Reading Guide

- Have students work with a partner or in small groups to select another story that they have recently read. Together, they can fill in the boxes on *Tool 6-2a* or *6-2b*. Review their work, offering suggestions for improvement when needed.

- Give students time to practice speaking in front of the class, sharing their insights, and using notes they have made on the reading guide.

- Ask students to keep the guides in their reading folders to use with other stories that they read. *Tools 6-2a* and *6-2b* have space for notes for about four different stories. (Each row is used for a new story.) Provide more copies as needed, or encourage students to remake the reading guides on notebook paper. Tell them the guides will help them remember the stories they've read and feel successful when they realize all that they have read.

## Additional Ideas

Design other guides to fit lessons you teach on other books. Challenge students to do the same. When students remember stories and can easily refer to them, they feel empowered. When they use story terminology in their discussions, they will feel like experts.

# Prewriting and Planning

In *Step Up to Writing*, prewriting and planning are discussed as two separate stages. Prewriting includes any step that writers take to learn and think about a topic before they plan, such as exploring, analyzing, and discussing their topics. From these activities, writers create plans (quick sketches and quick notes) for their stories.

Writers plan in order to focus their thoughts, develop their characters, and decide how to begin, expand, and end their stories. Students need time, instructions, and encouragement to build these skills. Remind students that planning is an important part of all writing.

## Objectives

- Teach students the difference between prewriting and planning
- Develop students' prewriting skills and empower them to think and work quickly
- Instruct students how to plan—how to organize details and sequences of events
- Help students create vivid, interesting characters that change over time

| Strategy | Strategy Description | Page | Tools |
|---|---|---|---|
| **6-3 Prewriting and Planning** | Introducing story mapping and distinguishing prewriting with story maps from planning with quick sketches | 263 | 6-3a |
| **6-4 Prewriting with a Story Map** | Practicing prewriting with story maps | 265 | 6-4a |
| **6-5 Alphabet Soup and Other Ideas** | Using imagination and creativity to find and use topics/ideas for stories | 267 | 6-5a |
| **6-6 Six Steps for Planning and Writing a Narrative** | Introducing students to using a process for writing a first draft | 270 | 6-6a |

*(chart continues)*

| Strategy *continued* | Strategy Description | Page | Tools |
|---|---|---|---|
| **6-7** Quick Sketch and Quick Note Planning | Planning and organizing ideas for a story using quick sketches and quick notes | 272 | 6-7a to 6-7f |
| **6-8** Sequencing Events | Learning to properly describe events that happen in a set order | 275 | n/a |
| **6-9** Creating and Developing Characters | Using a planning grid to develop characters and make them more interesting | 276 | 6-9a |
| **6-10** Planning for Changes/Growth in Characters | Finding ways to plan for changes and growth in characters | 277 | 6-10a |
| **6-11** Showing—Not Telling | Writing sentences that show—not tell— and bring the characters and settings to life | 278 | 6-11a |

Ⓟ Consider using the Posters with the strategies in this section.

## **6-3** Prewriting and Planning

Story mapping is a popular and useful tool for prewriting. This strategy introduces story mapping to students and helps them learn the difference between story mapping for prewriting and developing quick sketches and quick notes for planning.

**Note:** For more information on prewriting, see 6-4 Prewriting with a Story Map and 4-5 The Writing Process.

### Before Class

Make an overhead transparency and student copies of *Tool 6-3a*.

## During Class

- Explain that a story map is a diagram students can use to brainstorm ideas or jot down notes in an organized way. It is appropriate to use words and phrases, complete sentences, and pictures when developing a story map.

- Let students know that story maps may have different forms, but generally they include areas to brainstorm about:

| | |
|---|---|
| the character(s) | the setting(s) |
| the problem/conflict(s) | the solution/resolution |

- Inform your students that in most situations they will have time for prewriting—exploring, analyzing, and discussing their topics. From those activities, they will create plans (quick sketches and quick notes) for writing. However, in timed assessments, they may have little or no time for prewriting. In these situations, planning will be limited to the thinking students do as they analyze the prompt. But it is always important for students to plan a bit before they begin to write.

### Comparing Story Mapping and Quick Sketches

- Using *Tool 6-3a*, tell your students that both story maps and quick sketches can help them as they write a story, but each is used for different purposes. Emphasize that, compared to story maps, quick sketches are more detailed and concrete, and sketch out a picture of the story from beginning to end.

- Lead a discussion about the importance of prewriting and planning. Remind students that story maps and quick sketches are not meant to take a lot of time. Be sure to answer any questions students have.

Tool 6-3a

## 6-4 Prewriting with a Story Map

Story maps come in different shapes. The random arrangement of parts of a story map should remind students that a story map is a prewriting tool, not a planning tool. Use this strategy to give students practice prewriting with story maps.

**Prerequisite:** 6-3 Prewriting and Planning

*Tool 6-4a*

### Before Class

- Make an overhead transparency and student copies of *Tool 6-4a*.

 *Bonus Tool 6-4-1* provides an additional example.

### During Class

1. Introduce students to story maps by having them map a story they all are familiar with. Using *Tool 6-4a*, model mapping the story by writing ideas from the story in the various categories, using suggestions from your class. As they generate ideas, explain and define terms like *tone, atmosphere,* and *mood.* With help from students, complete the map, including phrases that fit the terms in each section.

**Tone**
- little hope of help
- unrealistic expectations

**Mood**
- frustration
- fear
- determination

**Atmosphere**
- rained for days
- crops were ruined
- wagons stuck in deep mud

2. Have students work in pairs or small groups to make another story map. They should begin by thinking about a story they have read and then quickly jot down ideas on the Tool. This activity gets them thinking about the information they would use in a book report or a story, such as setting, character, plot, problem, and solution.

## Using a Story Map for Prewriting

1. Using *Tool 6-4a*, brainstorm ideas for a story with students. As they generate ideas, fill in each area with words and phrases. (For an additional story map, see *Bonus Tool 6-4-1.*)

2. Explain that the space inside each area can be used in any way that shows they are thinking about a possible story. Offer suggestions, embellish ideas students share, and encourage creativity.

3. Have your class work in small groups, pairs, or individually to create their own story maps. Have all of your students work on the same topic or have them use a topic they have chosen. Provide them with support and assistance as they work.

## Going from Story Map to Quick Sketch

1. Use a story map created by the class or one that a student is willing to share in order to show how to transition from a story map to a quick sketch. Use **6-7 Quick Sketch and Quick Note Planning** to build a quick sketch with quick notes. Point out that this step takes the random information from the story map and organizes it sequentially before narrative writing begins.

**Note:** Explain that sometimes they will have limited time to plan and write their stories. In those situations, they should move right into planning and limit the time they spend developing a story map.

2. Discuss the results. Ask students to explain differences by asking questions like the following:

   - How are the story map and the quick sketch alike?
   - How are they different?
   - How do they help each other?
   - How much of your story map did you use in the quick sketch?
   - When it is time to write, why is the quick sketch more helpful?
   - Why are both methods important?

## 6-5 Alphabet Soup and Other Ideas

In some assessment and classroom situations, students must create their own topics for a story. Some students creatively generate ideas, while others struggle to think of characters, settings, problems, and so on. Use the activities in this strategy to help students gain skills and confidence in developing ideas for stories. With this confidence, they will be able (and will want) to write stories.

**Prerequisite:** 6-7 Quick Sketch and Quick Note Planning

### Before Class

- Make an overhead transparency and student copies of *Tool 6-5a*.
- Make student copies of *Tool 6-7c* or *6-7f*.
- Look through the activities that follow and collect any needed supplies.

### During Class

Share the following activities with students as a way to find new ideas for a story.

#### Alphabet Soup

- Use the alphabet soup activity whenever your students need fresh topics and ideas. They can develop an alphabet soup list for topics, settings, and even characters.
- Using *Tool 6-5a*, read the examples and discuss this method for generating ideas. Point out that some phrases focus on characters while others present possible problems/conflicts for a story.
- Ask students to work in small groups to create more alphabet soup ideas. Students can post the ideas or store them in their writing notebooks for use throughout the year.
- Have students create lists of alphabet soup ideas for specific assignments. In history, for example, students might generate several options for writing short historical fiction after having studied a specific period in history.

*Tool 6-5a*

## Thumbprint Stories

- Have students create characters by adding details to their thumbprints. Provide inkpads and paper. Have students incorporate their thumbprint characters into the planning process using the Tools from **6-7 Quick Sketch and Quick Note Planning**. Then ask students to add sketches for the setting, action, and other details of a beginning, middle, and end. The novelty of this activity often encourages students to plan and write interesting stories.

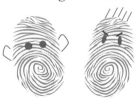

- Elementary school students like seeing and reading stories written by older students. Have older students write thumbprint stories with younger students in mind and then share these stories with students in lower grades.

## A Part of a Picture

- Collect pictures from ads, junk mail, magazines, newspapers, and brochures. Give each student a picture. Rather than writing about the entire picture, ask students to find an artifact or small section of the picture that can be used for a story.

- Tell students to look for something in the picture that shows a specific theme, feeling, or mood that could become the central idea of a story.

## Squiggle

A "squiggle" is any short line that students must use to complete a picture. As more lines are added, whatever setting or character the lines look like to them can become part of a setting or a character in the story. Have your students use their squiggle drawings as part of the planning process using **6-7 Quick Sketch and Quick Note Planning** and then write their stories based on their quick sketches. Encourage students to use their imaginations and have fun with this activity.

*Tool 6-7c*

*Tool 6-7f*

## Stickers

Distribute several stickers of animals, people, places, or objects to your students. Ask them to select a sticker to use in the first block of a quick sketch. Have students add other sketches. The novelty and the challenge of this activity will engage students.

## Music, Poetry, and Art

Share a piece of music, poetry, or art with students. Ask them to write stories based on what they have seen or heard. Or, give students a chance to find music, art, or poetry that generates story ideas for them. Tell them they may write about the entire piece, or they may focus on one particular aspect of it.

## A Specific Setting

Give each student two index cards. On each index card, have students write three words or phrases that describe a setting for a story. Collect all the cards. Have students select a card at random from all of the cards and write a story to fit at least two of the three words on the card.

| street at night | raining | small town |
| --- | --- | --- |
| old barn | rusted sports car | locked doors |

## A News Story

Give students time to select and read a news story. Ask them to select a character, theme, setting, problem, or object in the news item as the focus of a story. Before starting out, explain that they don't have to write on the same topic as the news story—the news story is simply to spark ideas to write about. Encourage students to think outside the box, to use their imaginations, and to be creative in this activity.

## Current Issues

Make a list (on your own or with students) of current issues. Write the current issues on cards. Ask students to select a card and write a story based on that issue or theme.

## Using Ideas from Different Content Areas

Use content from science, history, social studies, music, art, or other subjects to write stories. Create interdisciplinary projects based on content and narrative writing.

### Seasons, Holidays, Special Celebrations, and Special Events

Have students focus on the setting of seasons, holidays, special celebrations, or special events in a writing assignment. Encourage them to write detailed, descriptive paragraphs in this assignment. Provide students with a few examples of events to spark their imaginations, such as rock concerts, sports or dance championships, science fairs, or Cinco de Mayo.

### Animals and Personification

Challenge students to write stories with animals as the characters. Review or introduce the concept of personification—giving human traits to nonhuman subjects. Students will enjoy creating characters that are similar to themselves, their friends, family members, and other people in their community. See *Bonus Tool 9-15-1* for more information about personification.

## 6-6  Six Steps for Planning and Writing a Narrative

This strategy teaches students to use pictures and words to plan before writing. With a quick sketch and quick notes, students can begin and complete a creative, well-organized narrative. This process can be used whether there is only a short period of time or time to work on a narrative for several days, such as in a writer's workshop.

**Handy Pages**

## Before Class

Make an overhead transparency and student copies of *Tool 6-6a*.

## During Class

Read and discuss each of the six steps on *Tool 6-6a*. Have students mark or highlight important words and phrases on their copies as you go. Explain that writing a narrative can be easier if they follow these simple steps.

*Tool 6-6a*

### *Step 1*
### Write a Working Title

Encourage students to give their stories a title right away to give a sense of order and purpose. They may want to improve the title later, but a working title will keep them focused on their topic. Instruct them to consider using an important word or phrase from the prompt in the title, especially when it is part of an assessment.

# Step 2
## Make a Quick Sketch

A quick sketch's purpose is to help students plan and organize their thoughts before writing and to empower students to create stories quickly and confidently. Using a quick sketch will teach students to visualize their stories—beginning, middle, and end—before they start writing. (See 6-7 Quick Sketch and Quick Note Planning for more information.)

Define the quick sketch to students as "drawing pictures for a story; that is, taking an idea for a story and making it concrete." Explain that as they draw, they will imagine the beginning, middle, and end. They also need to:

- Pick a setting.
- Create characters.
- Present a conflict/problem.
- Plan for an ending/resolution.

Clarify that quick sketching is not illustrating; speed is the goal. In a sense, the quick sketch lets students rehearse their story before they write it. Reinforce that the sketches should be meaningful to them and help them as they write their first draft.

# Step 3
## Add Quick Notes

Tell students to jot down notes along the right side of their quick sketches. These notes are not a formal outline, just words and phrases that relate to the story in some way and help with writing. These notes should include names, places, feelings, action verbs, descriptions, moods, weather, sensory details, colors, and any other ideas that come to mind. Encourage your students to be creative as they plan. Especially in the beginning, many students benefit from discussing their stories with a peer. It gives them a chance to add detail and can help them improve diction.

Students who make quick notes gain a second chance to rehearse their stories before they write. Point out that as they write their stories, they are free to change and add to both the quick sketches and the quick notes. But with their completed and detailed sketches and notes, students feel empowered to write immediately; they are less likely to feel overwhelmed by blank pages or to lack ideas for a story.

# Step 4
## Write an Interesting Beginning

Encourage students to use 6-12 Ways to Begin a Story to write a beginning. These methods promote creativity and make getting started much easier and more productive.

## *Step 5*
### Include Narrative Transitions

Explain that narrative transitions, also called signal words or connectors, help both the reader and writer with organization. They indicate a new time or place in the story's action. Writers can choose among hundreds of words and phrases to transition from one event in a story to another. See **6-15 Function and Variety of Narrative Transitions** for more information about narrative transitions.

With practice, students learn to recognize transitions in the stories they hear and read; they also learn how and when to add narrative transitions in their own writing.

## *Step 6*
### Finish with a Memorable Ending

Talk with students about endings. Note that endings pose a challenge because by the time writers reach the ends of their stories, they may be tired or uncertain about what to write next.

Tell students that using quick sketches and quick notes gives them an advantage. By the time they have finished developing their quick sketch and quick notes, they have thought about the ending, jotted down ideas, and rehearsed the ending twice. See **6-17 Options for Writing the End of a Story** for more information about how to end a story.

## 6-7 Quick Sketch and Quick Note Planning

Writing a narrative does not need to be difficult or time consuming. Students who practice with quick sketches and quick notes write and generate ideas more quickly and confidently.

**Handy Pages**

### Before Class

- There are two quick sketch formats in this strategy (*Tools 6-7a, 6-7b*, and *6-7c* or *Tools 6-7d, 6-7e* and *6-7f*). Choose the one that will work best for your students.
- Make overhead transparencies and student copies of *Tools 6-7a, 6-7b*, and *6-7c* or *6-7d, 6-7e*, and *6-7f*.

**Note:** Quick sketches can also be made on notebook paper folded in half lengthwise, either by drawing boxes or by using sticky notes for the quick sketch.

## During Class

1. Review quick sketches and quick notes with your students, if necessary. Inform them of the importance of taking time to plan before writing. In *Step Up to Writing*, planning for a story includes creating a title, making a quick sketch, and adding quick notes.

2. With your students, read and discuss the story on *Tool 6-7a* or *Tool 6-7d*. Take time to answer students' questions.

3. Display and read the plan on *Tool 6-7b* or *Tool 6-7e*. Compare the story to the plan. With your students, review the story again and note how the quick notes summarize the story's details.

4. Choose a story that all of your students are familiar with or have read in class. As a group, develop a quick sketch of this story using *Tool 6-7c* or *Tool 6-7f*. Once students understand the process, have them develop other quick sketches from stories they have read.

**Note:** If you wish to use both quick sketch formats with your students, make sure you provide adequate models and guided practice when introducing the new format.

## Planning a Story Using Quick Sketches and Quick Notes

1. Develop a story with your class using *Tool 6-7c* or *Tool 6-7f*. Point out and have students highlight on their copies the boxes marked "beginning," "middle," and "end."

2. Explain that quick sketching a story works best (at least for their first stories) if they:

   - Show the characters and setting in the first block.
   - Introduce the problem/conflict by the second block.
   - Include action in all middle blocks.
   - Show the characters and setting again in the last (end) block.

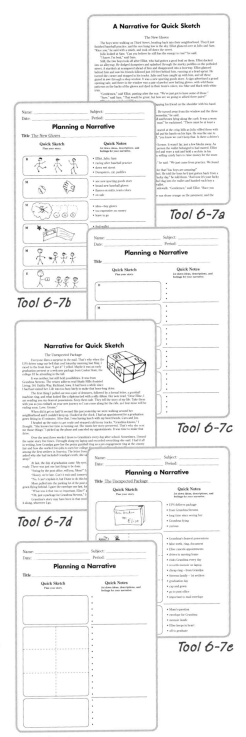

Tool 6-7a

Tool 6-7b

Tool 6-7c

Tool 6-7d

Tool 6-7e

Tool 6-7f

3. Point out that the number of blocks in a quick sketch is not fixed. They should use as many blocks as they need for their story, and no more or less.

4. Remind students that sketches are not illustrations for a story, so it is okay if their quick sketches only make sense to themselves.

5. Create a quick sketch on the overhead. Work quickly, encouraging and prompting students for ideas for the story. Add quick notes, using suggestions from students.

6. Have students work alone to plan a story with a quick sketch—without having them actually complete the entire story. Ask them to try quick sketching the beginning and ending first and add the middle events last.

7. Explain that it is best to quick sketch the entire story first. After the quick sketch is finished, they can add quick notes. This way, they can think about the entire story twice: once by putting it into pictures and symbols and again by adding the notes along the right side.

8. Remind students that quick notes are random, unlike informal outlines, which connect several ideas. Quick notes can be anything—any word or phrase that comes to mind and describes pieces of the story. Stress descriptive words, feelings, action verbs, imagery, and specific details.

**Note:** With a bit of practice, students learn to complete all three parts of the plan—title, quick sketch, and quick notes—in six to ten minutes. This is especially helpful for students in testing situations, where they usually have a limited time to plan their story or essay. Even for class assignments, students often must be able to read directions/prompts and make plans in only a few minutes. Even though students usually do not receive grades or points for their plans, planning saves time, reduces stress, and improves writing.

## Additional Ideas

- Play "beat the clock!" Give students only a few minutes to quick sketch a story. Then ask students to share their stories orally, using their quick sketches as the plans for their stories.

- Practice guides like those on *Tools 6-7c* and *6-7f* artificially limit the number of events in the story. Use these Tools when students are first learning the strategy. As students become more advanced, have them use notebook paper and add as many sketches as they need.

- Help students anticipate the length of their stories. A three-page story is a good length to suggest. Make the length visual for students by asking them to lay three blank pages of notebook paper side-by-side on their desks. When students see these pages and compare them to the length and details in a quick sketch, the task of writing a story seems doable. Three pages keep students focused but provide adequate space for developing a short story. Students who write longer stories should still use a quick sketch to help them stay organized.

- In addition, most students are able to edit and revise three-page stories. Narratives that are well organized, have logical sequencing, make sense, and are entertaining are also easy to grade.
- Test booklets often provide three or four blank pages for narrative writing assessments. If students have written several three-page stories in class, they will have less anxiety when they face a similar task on an assessment.

**Note:** Show students short stories from magazines and short-story collections that are three- or four-pages long but still engage the reader.

# 6-8 Sequencing Events

Students sometimes have trouble describing events in a sequence when they write. Use this strategy to help students learn to sequence events in their narratives.

Explain to your students that sequencing events in a story is similar to explaining a process or giving directions. Remind them that they were sequencing when they created their quick sketches for narrative writing. The events need to be described in order, so that each event helps explain why a later one occurs. The difference is that sequencing focuses on telling about something that happened rather than outlining steps in a process. (See **8-12 Giving a How-To Speech** for more information about describing a process.)

Tell your students to think through the order of a series of events in a logical way before they write. Sometimes it helps to make a list of all the events in the order that they happened. When they do write, they should give accurate and detailed information about each thing that happened and use obvious narrative transitions to help them keep the events in order, such as *in the beginning, as the story begins, at first, then, later, after, while,* and *toward the end.*

You can practice sequencing after students have finished a story or a history lesson. Select several narrative transitions (like the ones in the previous paragraph) and write them on the board. Using these transitions as a frame, have students arrange the events from their story or lesson into a properly sequenced paragraph. If you don't have much time, you can complete this lesson orally as a group. This activity improves student's oral and written skills in retelling (as discussed in **1-30 Four-Step Summary Paragraphs**).

## 6-9 Creating and Developing Characters

Have students use a planning grid to develop ideas and list specific details about their characters before writing their first drafts. Students using this strategy add details to characters to make them more interesting.

### Before Class

- Make an overhead transparency and student copies of *Tool 6-9a*.

 *Bonus Tool 6-9-1* provides additional examples.

*Tool 6-9a*

### During Class

- Using *Tool 6-9a*, introduce the grid for character development. Explain to your students that they should use this grid to add more detail to the characters in their stories. The more details they add, the more readers will understand the characters and the characters' actions.

- With your students, develop characters by brainstorming as you fill out the grid. Each character will be on a different row. Guide and encourage them to add as much detail as they can. Note that the description should be in words and phrases, as in the example that follows (also on *Bonus Tool 6-9-1*):

Name: _____  Class: _____  Date: _____

## Developing the Characters in Your Narrative

How will your readers get to know your characters?

Title _____

| Character's Name | What will he/she say or think? | How will he/she act and treat other characters? | What will other characters say (or think) about this character? |
|---|---|---|---|
| Scruffy | Life is an adventure. Wants to see the world Curious | Helps others along the way Helps lost boy Always happy and full of energy | Always there when you need a friend Unusual Lifts spirits Welcome anywhere |

- Have your class work in small groups or in pairs to develop a character for a story they could write. Give them time to discuss, share, and make adjustments.

## Additional Ideas

Students can also use *Tool 6-9a* to review a story they have read. Instead of the word *will*, substitute the word *did* in the question at the top of the page.

## 6-10 Planning for Changes/Growth in Characters

Use this strategy to encourage students to plan for changes and growth in characters.

### Before Class

Make an overhead transparency and two sets of student copies of *Tool 6-10a*.

### During Class

1. Select a character from a story that all of your students know. Using *Tool 6-10a*, write the name of the character at the top of the page. With your students:

    *Tool 6-10a*

    - Describe the character at the beginning of the story in the first column.

    - Think about the events in the story. List some challenges the character faced in the second column.

    - Describe how this character was different at the end of the story—better/worse, less considerate/more considerate, thankful/ unappreciative, sad/happy, frightened/confident, confused/clear, and so on—and what the character said or did. List those changes in the last column.

2. Have students practice the strategy on their own or with a partner, using characters from stories and movies that they know. Have students share their results. Discuss the activity with students and answer any questions they may have.

3. Once students understand the process, develop a character for a story as a whole-class activity.

    - Encourage students to use their imaginations to help you describe this character at the beginning of the story.

    - Think about the events in the story. Ask students to help you imagine four important events or challenges this character will face in the story.

    - Create the end of the story. Describe how this character will have changed and what the character will say and do.

4. When students are writing their own stories, ask them to complete *Tool 6-10a* for each of the main characters in their stories. Remind them to use this strategy before they write a first draft.

## Additional Ideas

Use *Tool 6-10a* in peer-editing sessions when you want students to evaluate stories they and their classmates have written. (See **10-6 Review/Editing/Revision** for more information.)

## (6-11) Showing—Not Telling

Use this fun and effective strategy to help students bring characters and settings to life in their narratives.

## Before Class

- Make an overhead transparency of *Tool 6-11a*.
- Have notebook paper available for student use.
- *Bonus Tools 6-11-1* and *6-11-2* provide additional examples.

**Bringing the Characters to Life**

| Character | Telling | SHOWING! |
|---|---|---|
| The mailman | Ned the mailman loved his job. | I heard a whistling at the door. I looked at the clock. Yep, noon sharp. It had to be Ned the mailman. He never missed a day of work, come rain, snow, or a chance to go fishing. |
| A clever fox | Clever Fox was happy that he outwitted us again. | A sly smile crossed Clever Fox's face. With hands on hips and head held high, he pranced off like the King of England. |
| Gramps | Gramps looked fragile as he crossed the street. | Steadying himself with his cane, Gramps slowly zigzagged across the street as if he had just gotten off a ride at the amusement park. |

*Tool 6-11a*

## During Class

1. Display *Tool 6-11a*. Review the example and explain that by using more detail, writers bring both characters and settings to life. Many students remember show-and-tell activities from their early years at school. Use this example, if it is helpful, to explain how telling is different from showing.

2. Tell students to use this process after they have written their quick sketches and quick notes, but before they write their drafts. Provide additional examples like the following (also on *Bonus Tool 6-11-1*) or others you have created:

**Bringing the Characters to Life**

| Character | Telling | SHOWING! |
|---|---|---|
| Prudence | Prudence knew her manners. | After their neighbor Mrs. Kinder put the casserole, salad, and cake on the table, Prudence walked across the room, hugged her, and said, "Thank you. I know that Grandma would've appreciated all that you've done for us." |

## Bringing the Characters to Life

| Character | Telling | SHOWING! |
|-----------|---------|----------|
| Mr. Knightly | Tom Knightly could play the piano. | Everyone smiled and kept rhythm with their feet as Tom Knightly's piano music filled the summer air. |

3. Ask students to bring their own characters to life using this strategy. Have them begin by folding a piece of notebook paper lengthwise into three parts— a burrito fold.

4. Instruct them to put the words *Character, Telling,* and *Showing* at the top of each column. Have your students

   - List all the characters in the first column;

   - Make a simple and direct statement about each character in the second column;

   - Bring this statement to life in the third column using action verbs and detailed descriptions.

5. Have your students take a story they have written or are writing and further develop their characters using this process. Give them a chance to share with their peers and make changes.

### Improving Setting Descriptions

Use this activity also when you want students to improve the descriptions for the setting(s) in their stories. Use the following example (also on *Bonus Tool 6-11-2*) to show students how vivid a setting can become with a more detailed description:

## Bringing the Setting to Life

| Setting | Telling | SHOWING! |
|---------|---------|----------|
| Aunt Rosa's house | Aunt Rosa's house was old. | Several slats on the porch needed to be replaced and the front door didn't quite shut, but Aunt Rosa's cottage on Third Street was always a welcome sight. |

# Writing a Narrative

Once students have learned to create plans with quick sketches and quick notes, they are ready to learn how to write a narrative's beginning, end, and transitions, and then write their first draft. The following strategies will give students tools for writing their narratives.

In formal assessments, students often have little time to read a prompt, make a plan, write a draft, and complete a final copy of a narrative. If students learn strong narrative techniques—from quick sketch planning to revision—and practice responding to prompts, they will have greater confidence in their writing abilities and greater success in assessments.

## Objectives

- Teach the different ways to start, end, and improve narratives
- Teach the function and use of narrative transitions
- Teach the connections between a narrative's beginning and its end
- Teach students to write a first draft with skill and confidence
- Teach students to recognize the parts of a prompt
- Teach students how to respond to a prompt in an assessment situation

| Strategy | Strategy Description | Page | Tools |
|---|---|---|---|
| **6-12** Ways to Begin a Story | Learning different strategies for starting a narrative | 282 | 6-12a to 6-12d |
| **6-13** Three-Step Strategy to Write the Beginning | Writing, revising, and improving narrative beginnings | 285 | 6-13a |

*(chart continues)*

| Strategy *(continued)* | Strategy Description | Page | Tools |
|---|---|---|---|
| **6-14** Writing Dialogue | Learning how and when to write effective dialogue in narratives | 286 | 6-14a |
| **6-15** Function and Variety of Narrative Transitions | Learning different narrative transitions, and recognizing how narrative transitions are different from expository transitions | 288 | 6-15a, 6-15b |
| **6-16** Analyzing Transitions | Recognizing narrative transitions in context | 289 | 6-16a |
| **6-17** Options for Writing the End of a Story | Reading, hearing, and analyzing endings for stories/narratives | 290 | 6-17a to 6-17c |
| **6-18** Comparing the Beginning and the End of a Story | Making comparisons between beginnings and endings of stories/narratives | 292 | 6-18a |
| **6-19** Eight Tips for Writing a First Draft | Learning several ways to successfully write a good first draft | 293 | 6-19a, 6-19b |
| **6-20** Working on the Qualities of a Good Narrative | Adding interesting details and descriptions to a narrative | 294 | 6-20a, 6-20b |
| **6-21** Narrative Writing Assessments | Reading, interpreting, and responding to an assessment prompt | 295 | 6-21a to 6-21c |

**P** Consider using the Posters with the strategies in this section.

## 6-12 Ways to Begin a Story

The goal of this strategy is to provide easy-to-use processes that eliminate stress and help students better use their time—not to limit students to these six options. As students practice and perfect their narrative writing, they will become more aware of how narratives start and will develop their own approaches. Use these activities to teach students several different strategies to start a narrative.

**Handy Pages**

**Prerequisite:** 6-7 Quick Sketch and Quick Note Planning

### Before Class

- Make overhead transparencies and student copies of *Tools 6-12a* through *6-12d*.
- Collect short stories to use for modeling and practice.

 *Bonus Tool 6-12-1* provides additional examples.

### During Class

Present each of the following options and give examples from *Tools 6-12a* and *6-12b*. If needed, provide additional examples like the following (also available on *Bonus Tool 6-12-1*).

Tell your students that they can begin a narrative by:

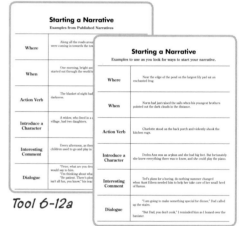

*Tool 6-12a*

*Tool 6-12b*

- **Stressing the where—the setting where the narrative will take place**

> **Near** the park in the center of the village . . .
>
> **Throughout** the dark and crowded room . . .
>
> **Beyond** the city limits . . .
>
> **Just below** the surface of the clear blue water . . .

- **Stressing the when—the time in history, in the day, in the week, and so on**

> **As** my grandmother baked cookies . . .
>
> **By the time** my little brother found his shoes . . .
>
> **At the end** of an unproductive day . . .
>
> **While** the radio blared and the telephone rang . . .

- **Using a strong action verb to grab the reader's attention**

  > Jamal **slammed** on his brakes.
  >
  > Three tall firefighters **formed** a line in front of the door into City Place Bank; two others **smashed** the glass.
  >
  > A gray spaniel **stretched** his small frame out on the antique rug and **blocked** the entry to his master's room.
  >
  > Music **filled** the auditorium.

- **Introducing major or minor characters in the story**

  > One thing about **Coach Sanchez**, he doesn't ever give compliments.
  >
  > **Aaron** fell in love twice in October and three times in November, just before he celebrated his fifth birthday.
  >
  > **Lamar and Agnes** have been married forever, and they own the only laundromat in my neighborhood.
  >
  > My **grandfather** walks fast, and he expects everyone to keep up with him.

- **Making an interesting comment—a comment that makes the reader wonder or draws the reader into the narrative**

  > The surprise birthday party had been a bad idea from the beginning.
  >
  > I have two sisters—one I like and one I can live without.
  >
  > The small black crow landed on the north end of the fence and waited for the others to arrive.
  >
  > It always rains when I need sunshine.

- **Presenting a short dialogue between characters**

  > "The wind seems strange today," said Ned.
  >
  > "And the cattle seem a bit restless," Zach replied as he dipped his biscuit into the gravy.

Explain that some beginnings combine two or more of the six options. Using the short stories you have collected or *Tools 6-7a* and *6-7d*, reread the first paragraphs of the stories. Note the methods that are used to start each story. For instance, "The New Gloves" begins with an Action Verb Sentence and adds dialogue. "The Unexpected Package" starts with an interesting comment: "Everyone likes a surprise in the mail."

Share beginnings—first sentences—from other stories that you find. Ask students to collect beginnings of stories that they find. Have them write these beginnings on paper to post on a "Wall of Beginnings" in the classroom.

## Using the Six Methods

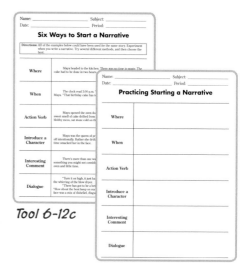

Tool 6-12c

Tool 6-12d

1. Using *Tool 6-12c*, show different ways to start the same narrative. Explain that all six beginnings could be used to start the story "The Unexpected Package," from *Tool 6-7d*. Point out that each beginning has a slightly different tone and meaning, but all could start the same narrative.

2. Read and discuss the examples with students, using the following questions to guide the discussion:

   - Which is the best?
   - How are they alike?
   - How are they different?
   - Why would a writer want to try several different ways to start a narrative?

3. Point out the directions at the top of *Tool 6-12c* and have them note: "Experiment when you write a narrative. Try several different methods, then choose the best."

4. Give your students a topic related to material they have studied in class. Using *Tool 6-12d*, have them practice several different ways to start a narrative on the topic. After they have written several possibilities, have them select the one they like best and encourage them to begin a narrative with it.

**Note:** Whenever students write their first drafts, ask them to experiment with the six methods presented here as well as with other approaches they have noticed as they read.

# (6-13) Three-Step Strategy to Write the Beginning

Most students have little trouble completing the rest of their story once they have written the beginning. Use this strategy to teach students a simple three-step approach to write, revise, or improve their story beginnings.

**Prerequisite:** 6-12 Ways to Begin a Story

## Before Class

- Make an overhead transparency and student copies of *Tool 6-13a*.

 *Bonus Tool 6-13-1* provides an additional example.

## During Class

Explain to your class that the following three-step approach can help them write the beginning of their stories:

> *Step 1* **Use one of the narrative-starter methods from** 6-12 Ways to Begin a Story **to write the first sentence.**
>
> *Step 2* **Imagine what will happen next, then add a second sentence to complement the first.**
>
> *Step 3* **Add more sentences to keep the reader interested and to move the narrative into the next scene or event.**

Display *Tool 6-13a* and read the two examples. Discuss how the sentences follow the three steps.

### Modeling the Three-Step Approach

- Model the three-step approach using chart paper, an overhead projector, or the board. Work slowly, showing students how to layer one sentence after the other.
- Start with one of the methods from **6-12 Ways to Begin a Story**. Use the following example (also on *Bonus Tool 6-13-1*) to model this step, explaining that this story starts with an Action Verb Sentence and an interesting comment.

*Tool 6-13a*

- Model the second step, adding a second sentence to the "Training Chester" example to complement the first and show what happens next.

- Model the third step, adding more sentences with details to keep the reader interested and to move the story into the next scene or event.

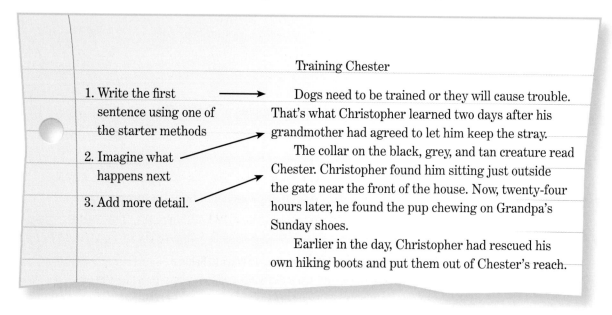

Training Chester

1. Write the first sentence using one of the starter methods

2. Imagine what happens next

3. Add more detail.

Dogs need to be trained or they will cause trouble. That's what Christopher learned two days after his grandmother had agreed to let him keep the stray.

The collar on the black, grey, and tan creature read Chester. Christopher found him sitting just outside the gate near the front of the house. Now, twenty-four hours later, he found the pup chewing on Grandpa's Sunday shoes.

Earlier in the day, Christopher had rescued his own hiking boots and put them out of Chester's reach.

- Give your students several first sentences for a narrative (or use the examples on *Tools 6-12b* and *6-12c*). Challenge students (individually or in pairs) to create interesting beginnings for a narrative. Instruct them to include a title and three to six sentences.

## 6-14 Writing Dialogue

Some students have a hard time writing dialogue. Using this strategy, they will learn how and when to write interesting and effective dialogue.

### Before Class

- Make an overhead transparency and student copies of *Tool 6-14a*.

 *Bonus Tool 6-14-1* provides additional support.

## During Class

1. Introduce students to dialogue writing by showing them a copy of *Tool 6-14a*. Explain each of the rules and examples on the Tool, using other examples from stories students have read in class if necessary.

2. Explain to students that just because they can write dialogue, it does not mean that they should. Review the following tips (also on *Bonus Tool 6-14-1*) for when and how to use dialogue to help students add dialogue to their narratives.

**Tool 6-14a**

- Writers always need a reason for the dialogue they add to their narrative. Dialogue should help readers better understand the characters, setting, or plot.

- When writing dialogue, they should always plan ahead and decide where it will fit the best and make the most sense.

- Writers should use dialogue only for emphasis or to make a point. Too much dialogue can be boring and weigh their stories down. Remind them that they can write good stories without any dialogue.

- Most dialogue should be introduced with the words *said* and *asked*. Writers should use other dialogue words, like *replied, mentioned, begged,* or *called,* only if they have a good reason, such as describing the way a character is talking.

- Remember that *said* can stand alone. It does not need *quickly, excitedly, unhappily, rapidly,* or other adverbs to describe it. Use adverbs like these only once in a while, for very special reasons.

- When writing dialogue—the conversation between the characters—writers start a new paragraph each time a different character speaks.

Once students are familiar with the rules for writing dialogue, have them work in pairs or as a class to write some sample dialogues. If they have a hard time deciding what to say, describe a simple situation, such as two players on a soccer team talking about another player who scored a goal, to spark ideas. Once they are finished, call on volunteers to share their dialogues with the class.

## 6-15 Function and Variety of Narrative Transitions

Use this strategy to review or introduce different narrative transitions and to help students recognize how narrative transitions have a function different from those used for expository writing.

**Handy Pages**

### Before Class

- Make an overhead transparency and student copies of *Tools 6-15a* and *6-15b*.

- Collect short stories to use for modeling and practice.

### During Class

1. Using *Tool 6-15a*, introduce or review the definition and function of transitions in a story. (For more information comparing the transitions used for narrative and expository writing, see **4-2 Comparing Two Kinds of Writing**.)

2. Use the analogy of a road to help reinforce students' understanding of transitions.

   - Explain that narratives, like roads, have many twists and turns. In a narrative, the reader does not know what will happen as the action progresses, much like a driver does not know what to expect at the next bend in the road.

   - Explain that narrative transitions help writers present each new event (twist and turn) without confusing the reader. They serve as markers for the twists and turns in a story.

3. Have students work as a whole group, in pairs, or individually, to look for and highlight transitions using stories you have collected or "The New Gloves" (*Tool 6-7a*) and "The Unexpected Package" (*Tool 6-7d*). Ask students to share their findings with the class. As a group, discuss how the transitions that students have found reflect the tips on *Tool 6-15a*.

4. Display *Tool 6-15b* and inform your students that it would be impossible to make a list of all the possible transitions used in narrative writing. Novels, short stories, feature articles, and news stories are filled with many different words and phrases that act as transitions. Students should use the transitions on *Tool 6-15b* as a starting point, and then find new transitions on their own.

5. Encourage students to keep *Tools 6-15a* and *6-15b* in their writing notebooks as a reference tool to use throughout the year. Encourage them to add more transitions on the back of the list.

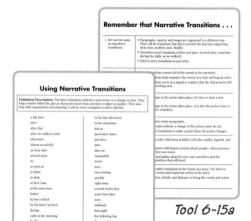

*Tool 6-15a*

*Tool 6-15b*

### Comparing Narrative and Expository Transitions

Remind students that transitions for expository writing are different from and serve a different purpose from those for narrative writing. Take time to review the difference. Review 4-23 Definition and Function of Transitions for more on transitions in expository writing.

## 6-16 Analyzing Transitions

Use this strategy to discuss and review transitions in context and to demonstrate the many ways that writers use transitions.

**Handy Pages**

### Before Class

- Make an overhead transparency of *Tool 6-16a*.
- Make student copies of a story (or part thereof) from a class assignment, student anthology, or magazine.

### During Class

1. Display *Tool 6-16a* and share the examples of transitions from the popular tale *Zlateh the Goat* by Isaac Bashevis Singer. Point out that these transitions include words and phrases as well as description. Explain that including the transitions' page numbers is important for quickly finding the references again in class.

2. Distribute copies of the story you have selected. Have students work in groups to hunt for transitions. Ask them to find and list as many transition words and phrases as they can. Have them note the page number for each transition so that they can share the site of the transition with the class.

*Tool 6-16a*

3. When students have finished their lists, take time to share the transitions they found, listing them on the board or a blank overhead transparency.

4. Discuss the transitions students have collected. Ask:
   - What is the purpose of a transition?
   - What was the most interesting transition that you found?
   - How often did the writer use transitions?
   - How will you apply what you have seen and learned to your own narrative writing?

5. Have students find a short selection in a novel or story that shows good use of transitions. Have them continue to look for examples and share them throughout the year.
   - Ask them to write a short paragraph explaining how transitions are used in the selection.
   - Then have them tell why transitions are an important part of the narrative.

### Using Transitions When Writing

1. Have your students create a short story of their own using transitions they found in their review of published material.
2. Have them review a narrative they have written and change out some of their transitions. Lead a discussion on the different ways you can use transitions.

## 6-17 Options for Writing the End of a Story

Students learn about endings by reading, hearing, and analyzing many story endings. They know that there is more to an ending than writing *The End*, but they are often unsure how to finish their stories. Use this strategy to demonstrate endings for narratives.

**Handy Pages**

## Before Class

- Make overhead transparencies and student copies of *Tools 6-17a*, *6-17b*, and *6-17c*.
- Collect examples of endings from age-appropriate stories, class literature, anthologies, student magazines, or collections of folk tales, myths, and legends.

  *Bonus Tools 6-17-1* and *6-17-2* provide additional examples.

## During Class

### Looking at Endings from Published Stories

1. Using *Tool 6-17a*, point out that the left-hand column lists four good ways to write an ending. Read the excerpts from published stories to reinforce each option with your students.

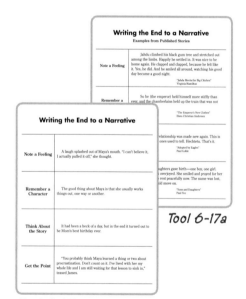

Tool 6-17a

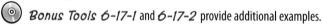

Tool 6-17b

2. Share the endings from other published material you have collected (or use *Bonus Tool 6-17-1*). Talk about how each ending matches one of the four options.

3. After reviewing and discussing a number of different endings, ask students to look for more examples to match each option.

## Looking at More Endings

1. Display and read *Tool 6-17b* with your students and discuss each ending. These are examples similar to endings students might write.

2. Provide your students with additional samples of endings and have them match each one to one of the four methods. Note that an ending may include more than one technique. (The following examples are also on *Bonus Tool 6-17-2*.)

**Get the Point**
The rain ruined my plans, but it did not ruin my life.

**Think About the Story**
The Takeshi family never saw the black puppy again.

**Get the Point**
All of our hard work had paid off.

**Note a Feeling**
No one complained. Everyone celebrated.

**Remember a Character**
Ted and his brother were off to a new adventure.

**Remember a Character and Think About the Story**
Carmen found the watch and she found a new friend.

**Note a Feeling**
The principal was angry with what we had done, but she forgave us.

**Remember a Character**
Manuel is the best librarian in town!

## Additional Ideas

- Use *Tool 6-17c* to model writing different endings for or with students. Have them use the Tool when they are looking for examples to share, practicing writing endings, and drafting possible endings for a narrative.

- Make several overhead transparencies to give to students. Ask them to work in pairs. Using an overhead marker, they can write on the transparency and then share their successes with classmates. Students learn about endings by reading and hearing many endings.

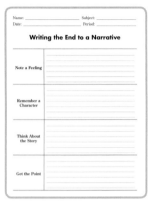

*Tool 6-17c*

## 6-18 Comparing the Beginning and the End of a Story

Use this strategy to note the relationship between the beginnings and endings of narratives.

**Handy Pages**

### Before Class

Make an overhead transparency and student copies of *Tool 6-18a*.

### During Class

1. Using *Tool 6-18a*, read the example and discuss the connection between the beginning and the ending of stories using the following questions:

   - Did the writer make a deliberate effort to connect the story's ending to its beginning?
   - How are the beginning and ending connected in this example?
   - What words and phrases repeat in the ending?
   - Is it necessary to connect the ending to the beginning of a narrative? Why? Why not? Explain.
   - What makes the ending in this example a good ending?

2. Ask students to find other sets of beginnings and endings to share with classmates. Have students write one of these sets on notebook paper.

3. Have students share their discoveries. Describe and analyze the connections orally as a class.

*Tool 6-18a*

##  6-19 Eight Tips for Writing a First Draft

Use this strategy to remind students that to write a good narrative they need to develop a first draft.

**Prerequisite:** 6-7 Quick Sketch and Quick Note Planning

### Before Class

Make overhead transparencies and student copies of *Tools 6-19a* and *6-19b*.

### During Class

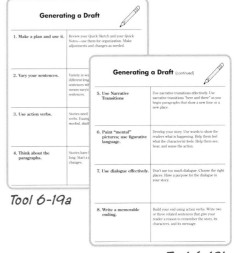

Tool 6-19a

Tool 6-19b

1. Explain to students that a draft is the first attempt at writing a narrative. When they write a draft, they write out a complete story using the plans, beginnings, and endings they have created. A draft is a working version of the story, and will be revised and edited before becoming the final version of the story.

2. Using *Tools 6-19a* and *6-19b*, read and discuss the tips for writing a narrative draft.

3. Give students opportunities to ask questions and clarify expectations. Tell students to use the extra space on the Tools to jot down notes during the discussion.

4. Tell students to keep these Tools in their writing folders and use them for reference when they write. When they write stories or narratives, they can check off each of the hints for writing a draft.

5. Explain to your students that these tips will improve the quality of their first drafts, but even good first drafts need revision to ensure that the narratives are interesting, make sense, and have style and a strong voice. See **6-23 Ten Tips for Revising** for more information.

 For a scoring guide and other support for assessment, see **10-18 Narratives Scoring Guide**.

## 6-20 Working on the Qualities of a Good Narrative

Use this strategy to encourage students to think about ways to add interesting details and descriptions that will improve a draft and create a good narrative.

### Before Class

- Make an overhead transparency and student copies of *Tools 6-20a* and *6-20b*.
- Have available stories that your students have read.

### During Class

#### Modeling the Qualities of a Good Story or Narrative

1. Using *Tool 6-20a*, model the qualities of a good story. Read and discuss each example, using the following questions:

   - What does it mean to include detail? Give examples.
   - When a storyteller "explains," what does that mean? Give examples.
   - What makes a description "vivid"? Give examples.
   - Define "specific." Give examples.
   - How does the last example "appeal to the senses"?

2. Ask students to find qualities of a good story in the narratives you have collected or from *Tools 6-20a*, *6-7d*, and *6-16b*.

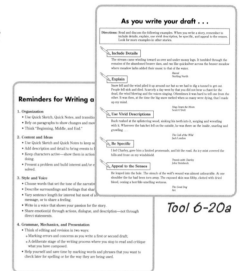

Tool 6-20a

Tool 6-20b

#### Checking for Qualities of a Good Story or Narrative

Display *Tool 6-20b* and tell your students that even as they write their first or second draft, they can review and assess their work and make changes as needed. Review each of the items on the Tool. Encourage them to review their work to make sure they have done their best.

 For a scoring guide and other support for assessment, see **10-18 Narratives Scoring Guide**.

# 6-21 Narrative Writing Assessments

Students need practice writing organized and interesting narratives in short periods of time to prepare for formal, timed assessments. Use this strategy to help students learn how to read, interpret, and respond to prompts for writing assessments.

## Before Class

- Make overhead transparencies and student copies of *Tools 6-21a* and *6-21b*.

- Choose prompts from *Tool 6-21c*. Make copies of the prompts as needed.

## During Class

1. Using *Tools 6-21a* and *6-21b*, read through the tips with your class. Explain that these tips can help students rehearse for narrative-writing assessments. Encourage your students to keep these Tools in their writing folders or notebooks.

2. Using one of the prompts you have selected from *Tool 6-21c*, demonstrate the first three steps with your students. Explain that with practice they will be able to read the prompt, write a title, and make a plan in about six or seven minutes.

3. Using a different prompt, have your students complete Steps 1, 2, and 3 from the tips on *Tool 6-21a*. Give them seven minutes for each prompt, timing them as they work. Afterward, discuss what was easy or challenging.

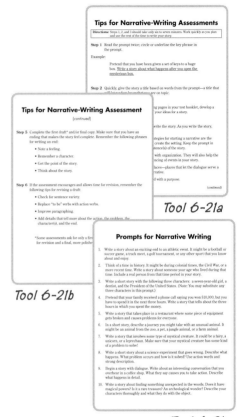

*Tool 6-21a*

*Tool 6-21b*

*Tool 6-21c*

4. Review all of the steps on *Tools 6-21a* and *6-21b*. Give your students a new prompt from *Tool 6-21c*. Have them follow the first five steps and write a narrative. Give them the rest of the period to complete their first draft. Encourage them to refer to the list of tips when necessary.

5. Offer students many opportunities to practice writing narratives by sharing more of the prompts on *Tool 6-21c* or using prompts that you have written or collected.

 For a scoring guide and other support for assessment, see **10-18 Narratives Scoring Guide**.

# Revising and Editing

Story writers revise and edit over and over again. Many student writers often want to avoid these steps; however, when students have a strong plan and strategies for revision, they can attack the revision with more confidence.

## Objectives

- Teach students better strategies for revision
- Challenge students to choose more descriptive language
- Help students develop structured revision methods
- Empower students to revise confidently and to write with style and unique voice
- Teach students the difference between revising, editing, and proofreading

| Strategy | Strategy Description | Page | Tools |
|---|---|---|---|
| **6-22 Writing Drafts and Revising** | Preparing drafts to make revising easier | 297 | 6-22a |
| **6-23 Ten Tips for Revising** | Reviewing and learning strategies for revision | 298 | 6-23a |
| **6-24 Editing and Proofreading** | Teaching the concepts of editing and proofreading and explaining how they are different from revising | 301 | 6-24a |

 Consider using the Posters with the strategies in this section.

## 6-22 Writing Drafts and Revising

Use this strategy to teach a variety of ways to write drafts that make the revision process easier.

**Handy Pages**

### Before Class

Make an overhead transparency of *Tool 6-22a*.

### During Class

#### Using a Two-Column Fold

*Tool 6-22a*

- Display *Tool 6-22a* and explain that the revision of *Mama Bear* on the right brings the narrative to life; it shows the action. The story on the left just tells the story. Tell students that when they revise, they will want to show the action in their narratives. For practice, they may continue the revision shown on *Tool 6-22a*.

- When students are prepared to write, have them fold paper into a two-column fold, like the example on *Tool 6-22a*. Ask students to write their drafts on the left side, leaving space for the revision on the right.

#### Skipping Lines

Tell students that when they write their drafts on notebook paper, they should use every other line. They should also use only the page's front side, so the page doesn't become cluttered and hard to read.

Explain that skipping lines makes revising easier because it leaves space for revising and editing. If students word process their drafts, double spacing will make drafts easier to read and revise.

> Asking students to write their drafts on every other
>
> line will save you time and energy. The drafts are easier
>
> to read, there is room for editing and revision, and
>
> there is space for comments.

 For a scoring guide and other support for assessment, see **10-18 Narratives Scoring Guide**.

## 6-23 Ten Tips for Revising

Review or teach these strategies for revision.

**Handy Pages**

### Before Class

Make an overhead transparency and student copies of *Tool 6-23a*.

### During Class

- Using *Tool 6-23a*, read and explain the ten tips for revising a narrative. Encourage students to highlight important ideas and terms as you read.

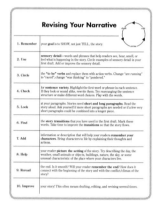

*Tool 6-23a*

- Discuss the circle graphic at the top of the page. Remind students that they may revise, draft, and edit as many times as needed.

- Explain that writers edit best if they focus on only one or two lines at a time as they review their work.

- Include and emphasize the following information on each of the ten tips during the discussion. Tell your students to use the back of *Tool 6-23a* for notes and examples. Encourage them to keep this Tool in their writing notebooks for use throughout the year.

**1. Show; don't just tell.**
   - Explain that good writers make it easy for the reader to see and feel the narrative.
      ▸ First, check the verbs. Do they show action?
      ▸ Next, write phrases that help the reader visualize what is happening.

**2. Use sensory detail.**
   - Remind students to emphasize scenes that appeal to the senses, asking themselves what a character or observer might hear, see, smell, taste, or feel. If their writing does not vividly answer these questions, they should consider revising to portray sensory details.

3. **Avoid *to be* verbs.**

- As a class, list *to be* verbs on the board—*is, am, are, was, were, be, being,* and *been*. Include verbs that are in such phrases as *was walking* and *were screaming*.

- Have students scan their drafts, circle any *to be* verbs, and replace them with strong action verbs.

- Explain that action verbs improve narratives by making sentences more engaging. See **10-4 Revising "To Be" Verbs** for a list of action verbs.

4. **Check for sentence variety.**

- Have students highlight the first few words of each sentence, allowing them to see if they overuse certain words or phrases. As needed, have students remedy this by rearranging sentence structures, adding or removing prepositional phrases, or creating new descriptions for characters (for example, saying "the frisky puppy" instead of "Spot"). Challenge students to find new ways to vary their sentences.

> **Original Sentence**
> Mom was already off to work. I could tell her all about the game later.
>
> **Revised Sentence**
> Mom had already left for work when I slid into the kitchen. I'd tell her all about the game that night, play by play.

- To check sentence length and structure, have students use two colored markers or colored pencils to underline every other sentence with a different color. At a glance, they will see if their sentence lengths vary.

5. **Use paragraphs for emphasis, movement, and rhythm in the story.**

- Explain that paragraphing in a narrative is different from doing so in a report or essay. Narrative paragraphs help move action along, so they are often short. Longer paragraphs in narratives usually contain background details and descriptions.

- Students should check their stories to make sure they have paragraphed properly. Try having them read their stories aloud to themselves or to a partner, listening for changes in voice intensity that might signal paragraph breaks. Have students note where breaks occur.

- Remind students to indent for a new paragraph every time the speaker changes in a dialogue, and when a new dialogue begins.

6. **Make good use of narrative transitions.**

- Reinforce good transition usage. Writers include transitions whenever they create new action, introduce a new character, or move to a new scene. If necessary, review *Tool 6-15a* with students.

- Ask students to keep lists of narrative transitions handy. Remind them that hundreds of transitions exist, and use *Tool 6-15b*, if needed. Encourage them to experiment with different transitions when revising.

7. **Bring characters to life.**

- Students should have sketched out their characters during the planning stage, but they can still improve detail and descriptions. Use activities like those on *Tools 6-9a*, *6-10a*, and *6-11a* to help students think more deeply about their characters.

- Remind students to moderate the amount of dialogue in their narratives. Dialogue should be used deliberately to help readers understand characters' feelings, motives, or actions. Too much dialogue might mean that the narrative lacks adequate action or description. Too little might leave readers struggling to understand the characters and create a narrative that lags.

8. **Help readers visualize settings.**

- Readers need adequate, vivid details and descriptions to help them visualize a story's setting(s). It is important to show the scene, not just tell about it. Have students examine their narratives and then apply what they have learned about descriptive writing. (See Section 9 for descriptive-writing strategies and Tools.)

- Have students select single sentences in their drafts and then help them rewrite these sentences with emphasis on word choice and phrasing. Help them make good choices for other words that bring a setting to life. Provide resources like *The Clear and Simple Thesaurus Dictionary* (Wittels and Greisman). A good thesaurus that is easy to read and provides words that students are likely to use is an important classroom resource.

9. **Write a smooth, memorable end to your narrative.**

Remind students that their ending can be used for a variety of goals. Writers may want their readers to:

- Remember a character;
- Understand the point of the narrative;
- Continue to think about the narrative;
- React with a specific emotion.

Have students review the endings in their drafts to make sure that they meet at least one of these goals.

10. **Repeat the drafting, revising, and editing cycle.**

Whenever possible, give students time and incentive to revise more than once. Encourage them to review these tips during each revision.

 For a scoring guide and other support for assessment, see **10-18 Narratives Scoring Guide**.

# 6-24 Editing and Proofreading

Use this strategy to teach students editing and proofreading concepts and to teach them how these tasks are different from revising.

## Before Class

Make an overhead transparency and student copies of *Tool 6-24a*.

## During Class

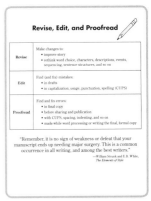

*Tool 6-24a*

1. Display *Tool 6-24a*. Define and clarify the terms as needed. Point out the differences between editing and proofreading.
   ▶ *Editing* is the intensive process that ensures that writing sounds good, makes sense, and follows standard rules of English. In this process, writers decide whether they will fix mistakes or keep them for stylistic purposes or to make a point.
   ▶ *Proofreading* is a careful reading of the final copy for small mechanical errors (such as punctuation and spelling mistakes) and serious errors that were missed during editing.

2. Check for comprehension of the three terms by having students work in pairs to write definitions for *revise*, *edit*, and *proofread*.

3. Explain to your class that editing and proofreading are important but often-neglected steps in the writing process. Remind them that software spell checkers will not catch some errors. Emphasize that mistakes in **c**apitalization, **u**sage, **p**unctuation, and **s**pelling (CUPS) hurt even well-written stories, so all writers need to carefully review their work.

4. Tell students to use the following process (or one similar) when they edit and proofread:

- Read your narrative slowly, focusing on one or two sentences at a time. Keep a dictionary with you, and look up words you aren't sure how to spell or that you have misspelled before.
- Focus on how each sentence sounds; read aloud as needed.
- If a word or phrase sounds strange, make sure you have used the correct words, that the subject and verb agree (see Section 3), and that the sentence makes sense.
- Finally, check for proper capitalization and punctuation.

5. Using *Tool 6-24a*, review the definitions of *revise*, *edit*, and *proofread*. Post a copy of the Tool in your classroom and have students keep a copy in their writing notebooks for future reference. Encourage students to use the correct terms as they write, read, or analyze narratives.

### Editing for Capitalization, Usage, Punctuation, and Spelling (CUPS)

Review and teach editing rules through direct instruction and by giving examples. See **10-7 Editing with CUPS** for more information on teaching this important skill.

Celebrate narrative writing by publishing and sharing the students' work.

# SECTION 7 INTRODUCTION
## Personal Narratives

Personal narrative writing allows students to share an event in their lives that taught them a valuable lesson. To be successful personal narrative writers, students must be familiar with strategies for writing introductions and conclusions (expository writing), and beginnings, middles, and ends (narrative writing).

The personal narrative combines elements of report writing and narrative writing. The personal narrative is framed with an introduction and a conclusion as in a report. The writer states the message of the piece in the introduction and reinforces it in the conclusion. The body of the personal narrative is written like a narrative, with a beginning, middle, and end. The narrative serves as the evidence or illustration of the message's significance, or personal reflection. Personal narrative writing gives students an opportunity to develop an individual style and voice in their writing. Through examination of important events in their lives, they also develop the ability to think critically about specific events. They then make inferences and form opinions based upon those inferences.

Writing personal narratives can also help students analyze themes in literature they read. After having multiple opportunities to find significance and lessons in their own personal experiences, students can more readily transfer insights into literature they are required to read.

Teaching personal narratives, like expository writing, has practical applications. Many colleges require an essay in the form of a personal narrative as part of the application process, just as many school districts and state assessments require a personal narrative at the middle and high school level. Narratives can also be required on applications for special activities or volunteer work. Students are expected to create an expository text about themselves in a narrative form; thus the term—personal narrative. It is important, then, to have the skills for success in crafting personal narratives.

To be successful at writing personal narratives, students need to be introduced to the following skills:

- Understanding the differences between a report, story, and personal narrative
- Analyzing a narrative for its significance or lesson
- Recognizing the organizational pattern of a personal narrative
- Methods of preparation for writing a personal narrative, such as:
  - ▶ Writing an introduction and conclusion
  - ▶ Adding quick sketches and quick notes for the story portion
- Practicing, sharing, and publishing personal narratives

# When Teaching the Personal Narrative

- Have students talk about their notable experiences (such as a time when they encountered a random act of kindness or they made a new friend), and ask them questions that elicit the significance (what they learned, what they would do differently, and so on). Emerging and developing writers often benefit from rehearsing their ideas in speech before committing them to words on paper.
- Find, or have students find, examples of autobiographical incidents written by others, and then write the introduction and conclusion paragraphs to create a personal narrative.
- Provide adequate modeling and reinforcement of the components of a personal narrative before asking students to write independently. Give them plenty of opportunities to practice writing personal narratives, whether in finished or draft form. Students learn to write by writing!

- Have students read their personal narratives aloud in small groups of four or five students, and then have the listening students jot down and share the message of the piece. This activity will also build students' listening skills.

- Teach or reinforce sentence writing and word choice as you teach the personal narrative. Use first drafts to revise for precision in language and sentence variety.

- Practice different leads (the Blues) for personal narratives. (See **4-22** Adding a Lead—the Blues—to a Paragraph and **5-8** Leading with the Blues.)

- Teach narrative strategies: description of specific locations, objects, actions, and characters; dialogue, including punctuation rules for dialogue; sensory imagery and figurative language; variation of pace; and creation of suspense, tension, and surprise. (See Section 6 for more about narrative writing).

## Tips for Using These Strategies Across Content Areas

✓ Read personal narratives of famous people in the content area and identify the parts of the personal narrative using color coding (green for the introduction and conclusion, lilac for the beginning, and purple for the middle and end).

✓ Have students use **9-7** RAFTS: Writing from a Different Point of View and adopt the persona of a content-specific tool, such as photosynthesis, a color wheel, Manifest Destiny, or a basketball, and write a personal narrative from that perspective.

✓ Read autobiographies of famous people in the content area, and have students create the introduction and conclusion paragraphs to frame the narrative.

✓ Have students research a famous person in the content area and then write a personal narrative from that person's perspective. Consider having them write it as a not or e-mail to a friend.

✓ In art classes, have students create and illustrate a personal narrative in comic book or children's book format.

✓ In drama, have students write or convert personal narratives into scripts and act them out.

# CONTENTS
## Personal Narratives

Choose those strategies that best meet the needs of your students.

# Composing Personal Narratives

## Objectives

- Teach students how to organize their ideas for writing personal narratives
- Teach students to use narratives as examples, along with elements of report writing, in their personal narratives
- Provide opportunities for students to demonstrate their insights and observations
- Give students opportunities to write in their own voice and encourage them to share valuable experiences

| Strategy | Strategy Description | Page | Tools |
|---|---|---|---|
| **7-1** Report, Story, or Personal Narrative? | Recognizing the similarities and differences among three common writing genres | 308 | 7-1a to 7-1k |
| **7-2** Recognizing the Personal Narrative Pattern | Recognizing the pattern for personal narratives and understanding the importance of the theme and message | 312 | 7-1a, 7-2a |
| **7-3** Preparing to Write Personal Narratives | Organizing ideas for writing personal narratives | 315 | 7-1h, 7-2a, 7-3a to 7-3d |
| **7-4** Practicing Personal Narratives | Writing personal narratives using practice guides and sample introductions and conclusions | 321 | 7-1a, 7-3a, 7-4a to 7-4e |
| **7-5** Sharing and Publishing Personal Narratives | Sharing personal narratives with others | 324 | n/a |

P Consider using the Posters with the strategies in this section.

## 7-1 Report, Story, or Personal Narrative?

Using this strategy, students learn about personal narratives and how they are similar to and different from reports and stories.

**Handy Pages**

Because a personal narrative uses aspects of both reports and stories, it is important for students to know how the three genres compare with each other. They should be able to describe the purpose of each and create plans for each. After teaching this strategy, your students should know that personal narratives, reports, and stories each have different prompts, writing plans, and writing styles.

## Before Class

Make overhead transparencies and student copies of *Tools 7-1a* through *7-1k* as needed.

## During Class

- Introduce the concept of personal narratives to your students by showing them *Tool 7-1a* and letting them know that the structure of a personal narrative is unique because it has elements of both reports and stories.

- Point out that the introduction and the conclusion are like a report but the structure of the body is like a story.

*Tool 7-1a*

### Reports

1. Inform or remind your students that reports are also called *expository writing*.

2. Explain to your students that reports

    - Give information in an orderly fashion;
    - Have an introduction, body, and conclusion;
    - Have a topic sentence that is supported by key/star ideas and elaboration.

3. Inform students that a report is different from a personal narrative. A report does not tell a story; rather, it simply relates information about the student's experience in a direct but interesting fashion. The information in a report may be personal, but it is not presented as a narrative. (See Section 5, Accordion Essays and Reports, for more information about expository writing.)

4. Using *Tool 7-1b*, point out to students the prompt and the informal outline for a report on the topic "My Summer Vacation," titled "My First Job."

5. Using *Tool 7-1c*, read with students the report "My First Job." On the transparency, mark the topic sentence ("Working a job has taught me a lot about what it is like out in the 'real world,' as they call it.") and the conclusion. Mark the key/star ideas as they are identified on *Tool 7-1b*.

## Stories

1. Inform or remind your students that stories are also called *narratives*.

2. Explain to your students that stories

   - Have a beginning that draws the reader in;
   - Have a middle that reveals a series of events marked by a problem that needs to be solved;
   - Have an end that gives a solution to the problem and a resolution to the story;
   - Have characters with problems that need to be solved.

3. In a story, the message is not stated directly or may even be absent. The reader is free to make guesses about what the writer intended. The main purpose of a story is to entertain. A personal story is simply a story written in the first-person ("I" and "me") voice.

4. Stories are not created with a series of key/star ideas (as reports are), and stories do not have topic sentences (as reports do) or thesis statements (as essays and personal narratives do).

5. Even when a story shares personal information, it is not a personal narrative unless its purpose is to share a message. A personal narrative has an introduction that introduces the topic and sometimes the message and draws the reader in, and a conclusion that supports the topic and states the message or lesson learned from the experience.

6. Using *Tool 7-1d*, point out to students the prompt and the writing plan for the story titled "The Regular." Explain to students that the quick sketch boxes in the left column can be used to organize the story's main points with small drawings. The quick notes in the right column can be jotted down to support the main points. (The quick notes can also include story transitions, descriptions, and dialogue, as needed.)

*Tool 7-1b*

*Tool 7-1c*

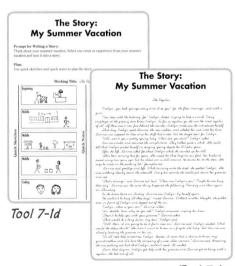

*Tool 7-1d*

*Tool 7-1e*

7. Using a transparency of *Tool 7-1e*, read with students "The Regular." On your transparency, mark the beginning, middle, and end as identified on *Tool 7-1d*. Circle the story transitions in the piece ("After she left," "Lannie said goodbye," "As she drove," "'Evelyn, where is,'" and "From that day on") and discuss their use.

## Personal Narratives

1. Inform or remind your students that personal narratives are also called *personal essays* or *personal experience writing*.

2. Explain that a personal narrative

   - Is a combination of expository and narrative writing;
   - Includes an introduction and conclusion, as a report does;
   - Has a beginning, middle, and end, as a story does;
   - Presents a moral, lesson, or message that gives significance to the experience described;
   - Shares a message that is stated or hinted at in the introduction, reinforced by the story, and clearly stated in the conclusion.

3. Remind students often that the stories they use in their personal narratives need to support the messages they are trying to convey.

4. Explain to your students that they need to tell their personal narratives in a way that will interest readers.

5. Using *Tool 7-1f*, point out the prompt and writing plan for a personal narrative titled "A Sticky Situation." Show students how the quick sketch boxes in the left column of *Tool 7-1f* can be used to organize the story's main points with small drawings. Point out to students that the quick notes in the right column support the main points. (The quick notes can also include story transitions, descriptions, or dialogue.)

6. Using a transparency of *Tool 7-1g*, read with students the personal narrative "A Sticky Situation." On your transparency, mark the introduction, the story, and the conclusion as identified on *Tool 7-1f*. Point out the story transitions ("I just knew," "Then it started," "All day," and "I still miss her") and how they help with organization.

Tool 7-1f

Tool 7-1g

## Compare Writing Samples

Once you have helped students understand the purposes of and plans for personal narratives, reports, and stories, remind students of the similarities and differences among these three genres.

1. Show your students *Tool 7-1h*. This Tool provides a side-by-side comparison of the three genres using the same topic of "My Summer Vacation." Note how personal narratives are similar to and different from reports and stories:

   • A personal narrative has an introduction and a conclusion, as a report does; and a personal narrative tells a story with a beginning, middle, and end, as a story does.

   • A personal narrative has a clear message (a moral or a lesson). Explain that in a story, the writer does not state a message, and in a report, the writer usually does not use a story to reinforce a message.

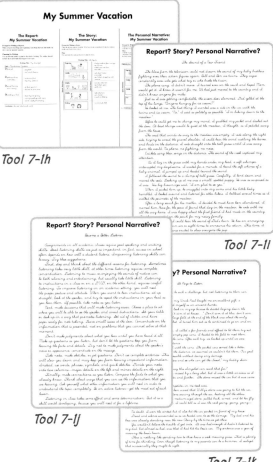

*Tool 7-1h*

*Tool 7-1i*

*Tool 7-1j*

*Tool 7-1k*

2. Show the transparencies of *Tools 7-1c, 7-1e,* and *7-1g* again. With your students, compare the components of each writing genre, pointing out how the three samples are similar and different.

## Practice Identifying Reports, Stories, and Personal Narratives

Using *Tools 7-1i, 7-1j,* and *7-1k*, have your students identify which Tool is a story, a report, and a personal narrative. Then have them mark the appropriate components of each example. You can use these Tools as students work in small groups or individually. Following is the key to the type of genre on each Tool:

• *Tool 7-1i*, "The Sound of a New Friend"—Story

• *Tool 7-1j*, "Become a Better Listener"—Report

• *Tool 7-1k*, "It Pays to Listen"—Personal Narrative

## 7-2 Recognizing the Personal Narrative Pattern

Using this strategy, students develop the framework for writing their own personal narratives and an understanding of the importance of a theme and a message.

**Handy Pages**

**Note:** A good way to define personal narrative is to show how it is different from reports and stories. You may choose to use the **7-1 Report, Story, or Personal Narrative?** strategy to begin instruction on personal narratives. Teaching the information in that strategy first will make teaching personal narratives easier.

### Before Class

Make overhead transparencies and student copies of *Tools 7-1a* and *7-2a* as needed.

### During Class

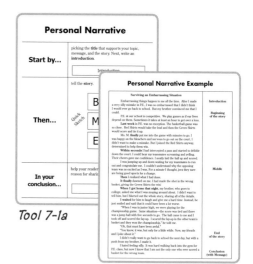

*Tool 7-1a*

*Tool 7-2a*

1. Explain that when students write personal narratives, they are either given a topic, or they need to select an experience of their own. Students must analyze the event or experience about which they are writing and create a plan for the personal narrative. The purpose of the personal narrative is to share a message, which conveys the significance of the event or experience.

2. Using *Tool 7-1a*, tell your students that a personal narrative, in its simplest form, follows the pattern on this Tool.

   • Show them that the plan includes an introduction that sets the audience up to read the story or event and hints at the message or lesson learned.

   • Explain that the event or experience itself is told in a story format, with a beginning, middle, and end (indicated by the B, M, and E boxes on *Tool 7-1a*). This story component of the personal narrative can be completed by using quick sketches for the beginning, middle, and end, and quick notes can be jotted down to support the main points. These quick notes can also include story transitions, descriptions, and dialogue, as needed.

   • Tell students they must add a conclusion that reinforces the theme and clearly states the message or lesson learned from the experience described.

3. Using *Tool 7-2a*, read with your students the personal narrative "Surviving an Embarrassing Situation." Point out the pattern that includes the introduction, story (beginning, middle, and end), and conclusion. Note that the story transitions are in bold print. With your students, discuss the message of this personal narrative.

## Importance of the Message

1. Explain that an important characteristic of the personal narrative is that it always contains a moral, message, or lesson learned from the experience described in the story. Personal narratives can address a variety of general, universal themes. Themes might be light, such as embarrassment, or they might be serious, such as prejudice, anxiety, or failure.

2. The personal narrative is different from a simple story because the personal narrative has an obvious message. A story does not necessarily have a message, and if it does, it is inferred and not stated directly—the reader must guess at the message of the story. The writer of a personal narrative lets the reader know why he/she is sharing the experience.

## Prior Experience

- Students actually have lots of experience with personal narratives, even if they have never written any. Teenagers use personal narratives to tell about their day in conversations when they encounter friends or family members.

### Personal Narrative—Conversations

**Theme** = *learning*

**Introduction** = *You'll never guess what I learned today!*

**The Story . . .**

**Conclusion** = *The stuff we learned about angles and ellipses in geometry is going to be really useful when I build my skateboard ramp. I never knew math could be so much fun, and I'm going to try harder now.*

**Theme** = *success and determination*

**Introduction** = *I made it! I made it!*

**The Story . . .**

**Conclusion** = *I am going to work hard. I wanted this part in the play so badly.*

- Students also write personal narratives on their own long before they are assigned in class. The friendly notes and e-mails that students send each other often follow the personal narrative format. Notice in the following note the introduction, which states the message, the story transitions, and the conclusion, which reinforces the message.

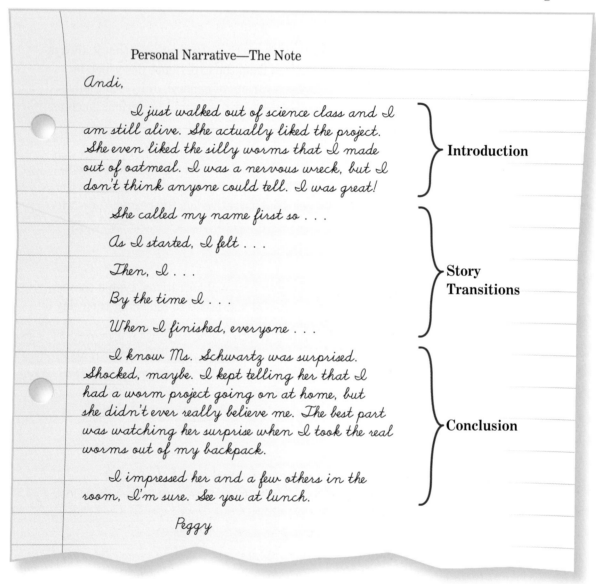

Personal Narrative—The Note

Andi,

    I just walked out of science class and I am still alive. She actually liked the project. She even liked the silly worms that I made out of oatmeal. I was a nervous wreck, but I don't think anyone could tell. I was great!

} **Introduction**

    She called my name first so . . .

    As I started, I felt . . .

    Then, I . . .

    By the time I . . .

    When I finished, everyone . . .

} **Story Transitions**

    I know Ms. Schwartz was surprised. Shocked, maybe. I kept telling her that I had a worm project going on at home, but she didn't ever really believe me. The best part was watching her surprise when I took the real worms out of my backpack.

    I impressed her and a few others in the room, I'm sure. See you at lunch.

} **Conclusion**

Peggy

- Autobiographies of famous people that contain a clear message are actually personal narratives. In these autobiographies, the writers share personal experiences intended to encourage, inspire, or educate others on important and not so important topics.

- Sharing examples has a powerful impact on students who are learning to write personal narratives. Look for personal narratives in the newspaper and in magazines (feature columns and personal narratives submitted by readers). Use these examples to help students when it is their turn to write. Following are two sources of personal narratives that might be appropriate for your students:
  ▸ Actress Whoopi Goldberg shares an event from her life in the collection of personal narratives called *The Right Words at the Right Time—Marlo Thomas and Friends* (Thomas 2004). She recalls an important lesson she learned from her mother.
  ▸ Most *Chicken Soup for the Soul* books are filled with personal narratives.

## 7-3 Preparing to Write Personal Narratives

Using the Preparing to Write Personal Narratives strategy provides students with an organized plan for writing a good personal narrative.

**Handy Pages**

### Before Class

- Make overhead transparencies and student copies of *Tool 7-1h*, *Tool 7-2a*, and *Tools 7-3a* through *7-3d* as needed.
- You may also wish to have colored pencils or markers available for your students. If you have introduced the Traffic Light colors for expository writing (4-1 Introducing Two Kinds of Writing) and purple/lilac for narrative writing (4-6 Color-Coding and the Five Elements of Expository Writing), use them with your demonstration. You can also introduce the colors as you give instructions.

### During Class

1. Explain to your students that the purpose of a personal narrative is to share a message—the moral, message, lesson, or significance of the experience—described by the writer. The topic that you assign should be one that all readers can understand. For example, everyone has been embarrassed at one time for some silly thing.

2. Explain that an experience is an event or occasion that you remember. It can be very minor or quite important. It can be something that happened recently or long ago, one time or many times, and to you or someone else. Share one or two experiences from your life or a well-known story that might generate ideas for a personal narrative. Examples might include occasions when you or someone you know

   - Learned a lesson;
   - Were surprised;
   - Had to work hard to achieve a goal;

- Were excited by some success;
- Had to make an important decision.

3. Using *Tool 7-2a*, read "Surviving an Embarrassing Situation" to the class as an example of a good personal narrative.

4. Explain that this personal narrative started with a topic (getting over being embarrassed); shared a story in the body of the paper; referred to the topic again in the conclusion; and had a message. Personal narratives also have a theme, a general idea that readers can understand. The theme of the personal narrative on *Tool 7-2a* is embarrassment.

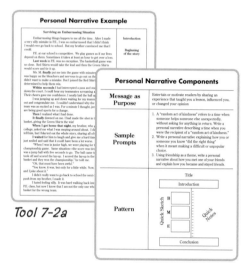

Tool 7-2a

Tool 7-3a

**Note:** If you have already taught the 7-1 Report, Story, or Personal Narrative? strategy, this should just be a quick review. If you have not, spend adequate time to ensure your students know the relationships among these three writing genres and the purpose of personal narratives.

5. Read the top column of *Tool 7-3a* with your students. Tell them that writers of personal narratives do not just tell stories. They also explain how an event has impacted their lives or someone else's life. Reinforce that the purpose of a personal narrative is to share the lesson learned from the experience described in the story—the message. Reread the "Message as Purpose" section on *Tool 7-3a*.

6. Direct students' attention to the Pattern section at the bottom of *Tool 7-3a*. Point out the illustration of the personal narrative pattern. With colored overhead markers, label the parts of a personal narrative as shown in the pattern on the Tool and ask students to do the same. The colors will help students remember that a personal narrative combines narrative writing and expository writing.

   - Mark the introduction in green and point out that the introduction includes the topic and sometimes the message.
   - Color the story blocks in lilac (for beginning) and in purple blocks (for middle and end).
   - Color the conclusion in green and show how it relates to the introduction, states the message, and reminds the reader of the purpose for writing.

7. Remind students that this pattern is actually the basic plan they will use when they write their own personal narratives.

8. Provide additional opportunities to discuss the components of a personal narrative with your class and provide additional models as needed.

## Sample Prompts for a Personal Narrative

1. Using *Tool 7-3a*, direct students' attention to the middle row, Sample Prompts. Read the three prompts with the class. Read them more than once to make sure students understand the prompts. Have students identify the themes that each prompt suggests:

   - Being kind
   - Doing the right thing
   - Making friends

2. Ask your students to think about their own life experiences. Tell them to jot down on the back of *Tool 7-3a* an event or experience from their own lives, or from the life of someone they know, that could be used in response to each prompt. Encourage students to identify three different events or experiences—one for each prompt.

3. Ask your students to select one of their three events or experiences. Working in pairs, give each student a few minutes to share his/her experience with a classmate. Keep the sharing time short.

4. When students have finished sharing, explain that people are naturally good at creating personal narratives. You may choose to use the examples of conversations and notes from the "Prior Experience" subsection of **7-2 Recognizing the Personal Narrative Pattern**. Remind students that they have been creating personal narratives whenever they have shared their experiences with others.

5. Give students a chance to role-play or write a short, made-up note to a friend to make the point. For example, ask them to write a note to a made-up friend that describes a wonderful experience in art class (or some other class). The note should be filled with feeling and passion about what happened. The note needs an introduction and conclusion. The description of the experience becomes the story or body of the note. As students write, create your own example to share. This note activity should take only a few moments.

6. Remind students that the goal in the note activity was to demonstrate the three parts of a personal narrative: the introduction, the story (or body), and the conclusion. Also, point out that notes—even the made-up notes—tend to be filled with feelings, emotions, and descriptions because often notes are intended to share feelings.

## Qualities of a Good Personal Narrative

Using an overhead transparency of *Tool 7-3b*, read and discuss the four qualities of a good personal narrative: voice, feelings, description, and message. Explain that you will be looking for these qualities when you read the personal narratives that the students write. Also, remind your students that as they edit and revise their first drafts they should look for the qualities presented on *Tool 7-3b*.

| Personal narratives have: | |
|---|---|
| Voice | • Evokes feelings<br>• Sets the tone<br>• Shows good word choice<br>• Varies sentence structure |
| Feelings | **PRIDE** **SURPRISE!** **contentment** Anxiety |
| Description | • Vivid<br>• Paints a mental picture<br>• Detailed<br>• Shows, not tells, what happened<br>• Realistic |
| Message | • Insights<br>• Beliefs<br>• Lessons about life<br>• The point you want to share with your reader |

*Tool 7-3b*

- **Voice:** Personal narratives are filled with writing that has voice. For students, this means that they share stories that are important to them. Tell students that good writers put voice into their writing by carefully choosing unique and interesting words, and by varying the kind and length of the sentences that are used. Writing in the first person (using "I" and "me") will help them share their thoughts and feelings.

  Explain that their voice in the personal narrative will set the tone and the mood. That is, what they say and how they say it will change how their readers feel as they read or hear the narrative.

- **Feelings:** A personal narrative is written with strong feelings and engages or pulls in the reader. Because personal narratives are about specific topics and general themes that are familiar to readers, it is easy for readers to connect with the writer. One of the goals of personal narratives is to remind readers of events in their own lives.

  Possible topics for personal narratives that remind readers of events in their own lives are:

  | | |
  |---|---|
  | losing something | not telling the truth |
  | being treated unfairly | hurting someone's feelings |
  | putting up with sisters and brothers | caring about nature |
  | disappointing a friend | loving an animal |

- **Description:** Personal narratives call for writing that gives details and helps the reader picture the event. Their descriptions should show, not tell, the reader what is happening. Remind students of the **3-6 Better Sentences** strategy, if you have taught it already. Have them use strong action verbs and specific, interesting nouns. Warn them that too many adjectives and too many adverbs will weaken their descriptions, and too few will prevent the reader from picturing the story. If you wish, suggest that dialogue can enhance a story if it is used sparingly and for a specific purpose. (See **6-14 Writing Dialogue** for additional information about using dialogue in narratives.)

- **Message:** The message in a personal narrative may be shared in the introduction; moreover, it is a thread that runs throughout the story, and it should be clearly stated in the conclusion. It shares what writers think and what they want their readers to know. Read, reread, and discuss the four message descriptions on *Tool 7-3b* with your students. Discuss messages they have derived from their own experiences and from books, articles, and movies. Tell students to add more message ideas to the back of *Tool 7-3a*.

## Analyzing Examples of Personal Narratives

One way to ensure that your students can write good personal narratives is to have them analyze components of good writing in preselected examples.

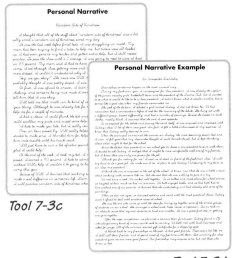

Tool 7-3c

Tool 7-3d

1. With your students, read the personal narratives on *Tools 7-3c* and *7-3d*.

2. Point out and mark in green the introduction and conclusion of each of the three personal narratives.

3. Discuss the story that appears in the body of each narrative. Draw a purple box around the story section to show it is a story.

4. Ask students to explain how the story supports the topic (what the personal narrative is specifically about). How does the story lead the reader to the lesson learned—the message?

**Topic for "*Random Acts of Kindness*" (Tool 7-3c)**

*helping others*

**Topic for "*An Unexpected Friendship*" (Tool 7-3d)**

*making new friends*

**Message for "*Random Acts of Kindness*" (Tool 7-3c)**

*Sometimes people really do commit random acts of kindness, and they can make a real difference in someone's life.*

**Message for "*An Unexpected Friendship*" (Tool 7-3d)**

*People you think are different from you might turn out to be good friends if you just get to know them.*

5. Have students mark or highlight the story transitions in each example. Story transitions are powerful tools for storytellers. Students will want to use story transitions when they write their own personal narratives. Following are examples of story transitions that appear in *Tools 7-3c* and *7-3d*.

| Story Transitions for "*Random Acts of Kindness*" (Tool 7-3c) | Story Transitions for "*An Unexpected Friendship*" (Tool 7-3d) |
|---|---|
| It was the last week . . .<br>At first . . .<br>Over an hour passed by . . .<br>At the end of the week . . . | During my freshman year . . .<br>The week of the election . . .<br>As we prepared . . .<br>When the principal . . .<br>We met twice a week . . .<br>When we did not agree . . .<br>After the ropes competition . . . |

6. Assess and discuss personal narratives using the template shown on *Tool 7-3a* and the description of important qualities on *Tool 7-3b*. Encourage students to ask questions like the following:

- How do the personal narratives fit the pattern at the bottom of *Tool 7-3a*?
- What is the general theme and specific message in each personal narrative?
- How do the stories support the message?
- What feelings are shared?
- Do the personal narratives answer the prompts correctly?
- Where can you find vivid descriptions that really make a situation come to life in the reader's imagination?
- Can you hear the writer's voice? In what way?
- What words and what sentences catch your attention?
- Can you understand the writer's message?

## Preparing for Successful Personal Narratives

Before you ask students to create their own personal narratives, review with them what they have learned about personal narratives.

1. Remind students of the differences among stories, reports, and personal narratives. Use *Tool 7-1h*, which gives examples of report, story, and personal narrative writing. Read and discuss how the three different versions of writing about a summer vacation are different from and similar to one another.

2. Take time to review the informal outline and plan used for the report on "My First Job" and the quick sketch plan used for the story "The Regular."

3. Help students make a connection between the sample plan for the personal narrative "A Sticky Situation" on *Tool 7-1h* and the template for a plan at the bottom of *Tool 7-3a*.

4. Give students time to discuss the differences among the three writing genres and time to ask questions.

5. Use examples from books, magazines, articles, and the Internet for additional practice opportunities.

6. When it is appropriate, ask students to create their own reports, stories, and personal narratives all on the same topic. Choose topics that you think would be of interest to your students or have them pick their own.

*Tool 7-1h*

## 7-4 Practicing Personal Narratives

Using this strategy, students will learn how to write a personal narrative using practice guides and sample introductions and conclusions.

**Handy Pages**

A practice guide helps students develop plans for their first personal narratives. After they have used the practice guides a few times, students should create their practice guides on notebook paper.

### Before Class

- Make overhead transparencies and student copies of *Tool 7-4a* or *Tools 7-4b* and *7-4c*.

- Make overhead transparencies and student copies of *Tools 7-1a*, *7-3a*, *7-4d*, and *7-4e*.

### During Class

1. Reproduce *Tool 7-1a*, which illustrates the components and pattern of the personal narrative, on the board or chart paper. Ask students to make a similar template on notebook paper. Use *Tool 7-1a* to remind students that when they are asked to write a personal narrative, they follow four simple steps:

*Tool 7-1a*

| | |
|---|---|
| *Step 1* | Start by creating a title that fits the theme, topic, and message. |
| *Step 2* | Write an introduction that includes a thesis statement. |
| *Step 3* | Tell a story that supports the theme, topic, and message. |
| *Step 4* | Write a conclusion that reinforces the theme and the message. |

2. Tell students that most of their personal narratives will be about two to three pages long. The students' goals should be to

- Create a short but engaging introduction;
- Relate the stories or events quickly, using strong action verbs and good descriptions;
- Use story transitions to make the story clear and interesting;
- Write a conclusion that helps readers remember the message or lesson of the experience described in the story.

3. Select a prompt from the middle row of **Tool 7-3a**, create a prompt of your own, or use a prompt from the **Bonus Tools CD**. With students, create several options for introductions. One- or two-sentence introductions work best. The introduction is sometimes where the message is first stated, so as a group, think of a message that fits your topic. You can then incorporate the message into the introduction or save it for the conclusion. (For more information about introductions, see **5-4 Creating Two-Sentence Introductions**.)

4. Give students time to write introductions on their copies of **Tool 7-4a** or **Tools 7-4b** and **7-4c**. Students can write their own or borrow ideas from the introductions that the class has created.

5. Using **Tool 7-4a** or **Tools 7-4b** and **7-4c**, have students complete their introductions and quick sketch the main points of their stories in the B, M, and E boxes and add quick notes to the right of the story boxes to support the main points. Students can write their conclusions at the bottom of **Tool 7-4a** or on **Tool 7-4c**. Because story transitions are so important, have students jot them down next to their sketches as a reminder. When students actually write, they may decide to use other transitions that fit better. (See **6-15 Function and Variety of Narrative Transitions**.)

6. Have students write their conclusions. Remind them that the conclusion should tie the story and the theme together and clearly state the message of their personal narrative. (See **5-18 Writing Successful Conclusions**.)

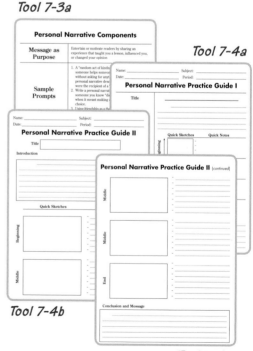

*Tool 7-3a*

*Tool 7-4a*

*Tool 7-4b*

*Tool 7-4c*

7. Have students write their first draft using the plans that they created on their copies of *Tool 7-4a* or *Tools 7-4b* and *7-4c*. Remind them that their final product will be about two to three pages long. Help students and give suggestions as needed to promote success for all.

8. Have students review their first draft by looking for the components of a good personal narrative using *Tool 7-3b*. Have them edit for content, punctuation, capitalization, spelling, and word choice before they revise their first draft and create their final copy. Take time to discuss the process and share successes.

## Using Prompts for Writing Practice

The sample introductions and conclusions on *Tools 7-4d* and *7-4e* can serve as prompts to give students extra support as they learn to write personal narratives. Feel free to make changes as needed, and encourage students to make changes to fit their styles and topics.

The sample introductions and conclusions on *Tools 7-4d* and *7-4e* can be used in several different ways.

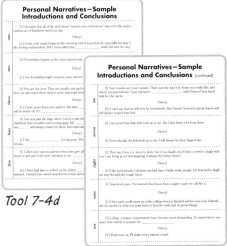

Tool 7-4d

Tool 7-4e

- Begin a discussion about how students can create their own introductions and conclusions.

- Discuss the strengths and weaknesses of using the sample introductions as practice prompts.

- As a group, read all of the introductions or practice prompts. Have students work independently or in pairs to create other practice prompts. This activity helps students develop their skills for writing introductions and conclusions.

- Select a practice prompt or introduction to use each week, or have students select one randomly. Make copies, cut them apart, and distribute the prompt.

- Use the practice prompts or introductions to practice writing personal narratives.

## Additional Ideas

- Personal narratives, like all other kinds of writing, are flexible. The length and complexity will vary depending on the assignment, time available for writing, and the abilities of the students.

- Students may want to experiment by sharing two or three short stories in the body of their papers instead of just one, all of which lead to a single message or lesson.

- As students experiment and as they listen to personal narratives written by their classmates, they discover new topics. They also discover that the basic parts of a personal narrative can be manipulated to meet the goals they have when they write.

## 7-5 Sharing and Publishing Personal Narratives

Students enjoy sharing their personal narratives with others.

**Prerequisite:** 7-4 Practicing Personal Narratives

**Handy Pages**

Students often write on similar topics and have experiences in common with their classmates. They like knowing what their friends think and the significance of the experiences they have had. Students also like to be recognized for the time and effort they put into their work, and sometimes they look for ways to publish their work outside the classroom.

If you are looking for ways to help students share, consider the following suggestions and ask students for other ideas:

- Publish good work in the school paper.
- Give students time to share in small groups. This is less threatening and less time-consuming than if done with the whole class.
- Pass on information for writing contests. These contests often require students to write personal narratives.
- Ask the librarian for space to post student work.
- Create a student booklet filled with good personal narratives.
- Create a collection of personal narratives written by the students on the same theme. Send copies to nearby businesses or senior centers. Give copies to the parent/teacher organization.
- Submit appropriate personal narratives to local newspapers for publication.
- Post student work for parents to read at conference time.
- Ask for student volunteers to read their work at the end of class each day.
- Send personal narratives to students in other schools, states, or countries.
- Look for books or Web sites with suggestions for getting work published.

**Note:** Before sending students' personal narratives to outside sources, be sure to obtain appropriate permission and releases.

# SECTION 8 INTRODUCTION
## Speeches

*T*he ability to express oneself orally is necessary not only for academic success, but also for success in life outside the classroom. In the classroom, students are expected to deliver speeches and oral presentations, to engage in productive discussions, and to be respectful listeners. As they interact with the world at large, students need to have confidence in their abilities to speak in front of others, think on their feet, and present their ideas in a coherent, engaging manner. The strategies and skills in this section help students develop these abilities.

Students will prepare speeches and presentations, applying and practicing the *Step Up to Writing* planning strategies for expository and narrative writing. Students begin to see that blocking out, informal outlines, and quick sketches have applications for more than writing and can be adapted and used in several areas. Also, because students have already learned how to plan and organize thoughts, they can concentrate on the content and delivery of their speeches.

This section also presents lessons that improve students' abilities to participate in productive discussions and be considerate listeners who are respectful of diverse opinions. These skills improve the feeling and tone of the classroom and provide students the opportunity to learn from each other as they listen to and discuss information and ideas. These skills set the stage for success in oral communication.

Students give better speeches when they are introduced to the following:

- What a good speech looks, sounds, and feels like
- Planning strategies, such as blocking out and creating a "train of thought"
- Different types and purposes of speeches:
  - ▸ Introductions
  - ▸ Informational
  - ▸ Impromptu
  - ▸ Demonstration (how-to)
  - ▸ Persuasive
  - ▸ Book reports
- Considering the audience for a speech
- Improving listening skills

## When Teaching Speeches

- Keep in mind that speaking in front of a group is intimidating to most students. Encourage their efforts and celebrate their successes. Allow plenty of opportunities to practice, and remind them that public speaking becomes easier the more that it is practiced.
- Be a consistent example of appropriate and effective posture, gestures, and expression for students. Reinforce instruction about speeches before expecting students to remember it independently.
- Have students review the informal outline and quick sketch strategies.
- Begin with one- to two-minute speeches using familiar topics such as favorite foods, best books or movies, or reasons for having or not having a pet.
- Provide time for students to practice with partners or in small groups before presenting to the whole class. Their rehearsals will help them get over nervousness and will add to their skills in collaboration and peer review.
- Have students save the plans or outlines of their speeches and, as their skills develop, have them choose and revise an existing speech.
- Practice listening skills frequently, and have students use their note-taking strategies (Section 1).
- Have students sit and observe discussions, then report what they saw and heard to offer constructive feedback.

- Debrief after small group discussions: What worked? What needs to be worked on?
- Stop during lectures or readings and ask students to evaluate their active listening at that time.

IDEA BANK

## Tips for Using These Strategies Across Content Areas

✓ Use **8-8** Impromptu Speeches to review the key ideas of a lesson or reading assignment.

✓ Use **8-9** Giving a How-To Speech in activities and electives such as art, P.E., or drama for students to demonstrate processes or the creation of products.

✓ Have students read and present historical speeches, and then deliver the speech as they imagine the writer would have done in that period.

✓ Have students present **8-10** Persuasive Speeches on an issue in the content area or to evaluate a work of art or music, a recipe, and so on.

✓ Have student write scripts to demonstrate effective and noneffective discussion.

✓ Have students listen carefully for a content-area "word of the day" (especially in world languages); recognize or reward students who raise their hands when they hear it spoken.

# Speeches

Choose those strategies that best meet the needs of your students.

# Organizing and Planning a Speech

These strategies help students think about effective ways to organize material for oral presentations. Students may lack confidence when presenting a poorly organized speech. The strategies in this section help students build confidence through simple but effective techniques for planning and memorizing speech content.

## Objectives

- Teach students the qualities of a good speech
- Enable students to visualize and quickly plan a speech

| Strategy | Strategy Description | Page | Tools |
|---|---|---|---|
| **8-1** Components of a Good Speech | Learning the basic elements of a good speech | 330 | 8-1a |
| **8-2** Speech Planning | Using an informal outline to organize a speech | 330 | 8-1a, 8-2a, 8-2b |
| **8-3** Blocking Out a Speech | Blocking out a speech as a way to plan and see its basic parts | 334 | 8-3a, 8-3b |
| **8-4** Including Stories in a Speech | Including narratives in a speech as a way to make a point or make the speech more interesting | 335 | n/a |

P Consider using the Posters with the strategies in this section.

## 8-1　Components of a Good Speech

This strategy teaches students the basic elements of a good speech. Students use it to learn what is needed to prepare and deliver a good speech.

### Before Class

Make overhead transparencies and student copies of *Tool 8-1a*.

### During Class

- Using *Tool 8-1a*, review and discuss the attributes of a good speech. Discuss each component and answer any questions your students might have. Explain that some students (and adults) dread presentations and try to avoid public speaking whenever possible. But assure them that with practice and by keeping these components in mind, they will be successful.

*Tool 8-1a*

- Show students what good posture, eye contact, voice volume, and animation look and sound like. Discuss the other attributes on *Tool 8-1a*, give examples as needed, and connect each idea to the goal of keeping the audience's attention. Have students practice in small groups.

- Discuss ways to increase confidence and organization when presenting. Reinforce the usefulness of referring to an informal outline; memorizing the introduction, conclusion, or the whole speech; presenting evidence and/or using props that support the topic; and other ideas that will help make the speech more interesting, organized, and on topic.

- Remind your students to keep their copies of *Tool 8-1a* handy as they work on other speech assignments.

## 8-2　Speech Planning

This strategy uses an informal outline to help students organize and prepare for speeches of any length. Using this planning tool will keep them organized so that they can become enthusiastic and effective speakers.

**Handy Pages**

**Prerequisite:** 4-7 Planning with an Informal Outline

### Before Class

- Make overhead transparencies and student copies of *Tools 8-1a*, *8-2a*, and *8-2b*.
- Have ready a topic to use for modeling the development of an informal outline.

## During Class

### Introducing the Informal Outline

- Display *Tool 8-2a* and point out the components of an informal outline. If students have already been introduced to informal outlining, remind them that this is the same process used for planning an expository paragraph, essay, or report. Discuss each component as you present the example.
  - ▸ Introduction—Includes a topic sentence and what you plan to prove or explain
  - ▸ Key/Star Ideas—How you plan to support or prove your topic; the categories that you will use
  - ▸ Elaboration and Explanation—What you will use as specific proof or what specific examples you will share to support the key/star ideas
  - ▸ Transitions—How you plan to move from one key/star idea to the next
  - ▸ Conclusion—How you plan to help the audience remember your message

- Demonstrate and have students mark the Traffic Light colors on their copies of the Tool. Mark the introduction and conclusion in green, the key/star ideas and transitions in yellow, and elaboration and explanation in red.

- Explain that using an informal outline is a great way to plan before making a speech, and it is also a good memory helper to use when giving a speech. Emphasize how easy it is to read the page at a glance and that you use only brief words and phrases for the key/star ideas and elaboration.

*Tool 8-2a*

*Tool 8-2b*

### Steps to Writing an Informal Outline

- Explain that there are six basic steps to writing an informal outline.

- Using *Tool 8-2b*, model the development of an informal outline based on a topic that is familiar to your students. Have students copy your outline on notebook paper using the two-column fold, or have them use their copies of the Tool. Show *Tool 8-2a* again if it will help them visualize what a finished informal outline looks like.

| Step 1 | Write the topic and a draft of the introduction. |
|---|---|
| Step 2 | Select key/star ideas. |
| Step 3 | Elaborate on key/star ideas (the E's, the Reds, the dashes and dots). Explain that the E's carry any speech and that, ultimately, they are the parts that count the most. |
| Step 4 | Add transitions. In speeches, it is especially important for transitions to be obvious. Transitions help the audience follow the speaker's key/star ideas. |
| Step 5 | Consider adding some Blues to the introduction. As students give more speeches, they will need or want to add leads or hooks. See 4-22 Adding a Lead—the Blues—to a Paragraph or 5-8 Leading with the Blues for more information. Have students note (in just a word or two) the lead they want to use, and place it in the margin next to the introduction. |
| Step 6 | Write the conclusion. When students become more skilled, encourage them to enhance their conclusions in the same way they add leads to an introduction. |

- Display *Tool 8-1a* again. Read through the features of a good speech. Inform your students that they will be successful when they are organized and confident.

**Note:** You may wish to introduce the Quick Check for Speeches, *Tool 10-13a*, and compare it to *Tool 8-1a*.

## Practice Using an Informal Outline for Speech Planning

- With your class, create a "What Bugs You?" speech or use a similar topic of your choice. The "things that bug you" topic hits home with most students. Give students two options:
  ▸ Choose one thing that bugs them and give two reasons (key/star ideas) with lots of evidence or examples, or
  ▸ Choose two things (each becomes a key/star idea) that bug them and give a few examples to demonstrate and/or explain each frustration.

Topic suggestions:

| | |
|---|---|
| friends who share secrets | bad manners |
| bad sports and sore losers | Mondays |
| shopping with parents | silly rules |
| no time to finish an art project | being told what to do |
| siblings who borrow your things | long tests |

*A Good Speech Needs . . .*

| Topic = | - message to share<br>- point to make<br>- information to explain |
|---|---|
| | - organization (a plan)<br>• blocking out<br>• an informal outline |
| | - enthusiasm<br>• strong voice<br>• good word choice<br>• appropriate tone and mood |
| | - evidence<br>- examples<br>- visuals |
| | - eye contact<br>- good posture<br>- gestures |
| Conclusion = | - restate the message<br>- end on a positive note |

*Tool 8-1a*

- Once the informal outline is completed, demonstrate how easy it is to present the information, and how helpful the plan really is, by giving a speech to the class.
- Remind students to keep their copies of *Tool 8-2b* handy as they work on other speech assignments.

### Making a Good Speech

- Give students time to plan a brief, informal outline for a "What Bugs You?" speech of their own. Guide them, giving hints and suggestions as needed.
- To save time and ensure success, have students present their ideas in small groups (three or four students). Ask group members to listen for the topic sentence, the key/star ideas, the transitions, and the conclusion in each speech. This will encourage students to stick to their plans and stay organized.
- Circulate to visit as many groups as possible to hear what students have to say and how confident they are when making their speeches.
- Let them know that once they learn how to plan and organize speeches, and have some experience giving speeches, they will have an opportunity to focus on improving their posture, eye contact, enthusiasm, and so on.
- When students are initially learning to give speeches, it is best for them to keep both the introduction and the conclusion short. It is also good for them to memorize these two parts of the speech. These are the two places where they will be the most nervous and forgetful. When your students give strong introductions and conclusions, they will feel confident and willing to try another speech assignment.

## Additional Ideas

- If the technology is available, let students record their speeches. This will give everyone more opportunities to practice giving speeches, and your students will enjoy the challenge and novelty of recording a speech.
- **Teleprompter**—Set up an overhead projector so it will reflect on the back wall of the classroom. If a blank wall is not available, create one using bulletin board paper. Give students blank overhead transparencies and overhead markers. Ask students to put their outlines on a transparency. The outline reflects on the back wall while the student is in the front of the room. It serves as a prompt that only the speaker can see, leaving their hands free for demonstration and/or sharing visuals. You can achieve the same effect if students write their outlines on large pieces of chart paper.
- **Group Outline**—Ask small groups of students to develop an introduction and an informal outline. The outline will need as many key/star ideas as the number of students in the group. Each student will then present one of the key/star ideas. Group members help each other complete all parts of the outline. A conclusion to the speech is created by the entire group.

- **Teacher Outline**—Create the topic, the introduction, and the conclusion of a speech for your students. Have students then add the other pieces of the informal outline on their own. This activity can be used to review for an exam, to direct students as they read a textbook section, or to help students learn about themes in a novel. Your framed speech outlines can also be used for students who need extra support and guidance. When you provide the frame for a speech, give students three options:
  - ▸ Use the framed informal outline as it is.
  - ▸ Improve it; add their own touch.
  - ▸ Use it only as an example; make their own speech on the same topic.

## 8-3 Blocking Out a Speech

This strategy helps students identify their key/star ideas and visualize where and how they fit into speech planning. It takes only a few minutes, but it will help them focus on their key points and stay on topic while planning.

**Handy Pages**

### Before Class

- Make overhead transparencies and student copies of *Tools 8-3a* and *8-3b*.
- Have ready a topic to use for modeling.
- Have available black overhead markers and green and yellow highlighters and overhead markers.
- Review **5-5 Blocking Out Essays and Reports** and **8-6 Informational Speeches and Oral Reports** for more information about blocking out.

### During Class

1. Using *Tool 8-3a*, introduce the Blocking Out a Speech strategy by explaining that this strategy will help students plan their speeches. Tell them that the blocks indicate the different parts of the speech and will help them visualize their speeches. Point out the blocks used for the introduction (I), conclusion (C), and key/star ideas, which will make up the body (B) of the speech.

2. Point out the Traffic Light color coding on the left and explain that it will also help them to visualize their speeches. Have them color the outline of the blocks that will contain the key/star ideas in yellow and the blocks for the introduction and conclusion in green.

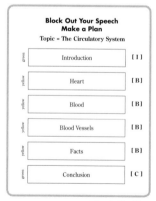

**Block Out Your Speech**
**Make a Plan**
Topic = The Circulatory System

| | | |
|---|---|---|
| green | Introduction | [ I ] |
| yellow | Heart | [ B ] |
| yellow | Blood | [ B ] |
| yellow | Blood Vessels | [ B ] |
| yellow | Facts | [ B ] |
| green | Conclusion | [ C ] |

*Tool 8-3a*

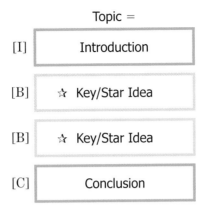

Topic =

[I] Introduction

[B] ☆ Key/Star Idea

[B] ☆ Key/Star Idea

[C] Conclusion

**Note:** Blocking out can be done with the blocks going vertically, as shown here, or horizontally, as shown in Sections 4 and 5. Use a consistent format with your students.

3. With your students, read *Tool 8-3a* and then ask them if they have a good idea of what the speech will be about. Discuss the value of blocking out.

4. Using *Tool 8-3b*, block out a draft with your students on the topic you have chosen.

   • Ask them to write the word "Introduction" in the first block and the word "Conclusion" in the last block.

   • With your students, determine the key/star ideas they plan to cover and write them in the middle blocks.

5. After students have blocked out their speeches, have them create an informal outline. (More information on using informal outlines can be found in 8-2 Speech Planning.)

*Tool 8-3b*

8-4 **Including Stories in a Speech**

Review the **6-7 Quick Sketch and Quick Note Planning** strategy with your students to remind them how to write a story/narrative. Then have them use quick sketches to add short stories to their speeches as examples or evidence to support their topics.

A quick sketch of a story to be used in a speech does not need a separate plan. Simply include the beginning, middle, and end (with small illustrations) in the right-hand column of the informal outline, along with the other examples or explanations.

**Note:** Some speeches with stories as proof work well with the personal narrative planning guides in Section 7.

# Giving Speeches

"The chief cause of your fear of public speaking is simply that you are unaccustomed to speaking in public."
—Dale Carnegie, *Effective Speaking*

The implication of Dale Carnegie's advice is important. The more we help students become accustomed to speaking in front of a group, the more they are prepared for public speaking. The Giving Speeches strategies are used for a variety of oral presentations and informal speaking opportunities. These strategies can help students organize their thoughts and present them with confidence whenever they are called on to speak.

## Objectives

- Teach students to speak with confidence in both formal and informal situations
- Help students communicate clear, persuasive ideas
- Enable students to organize and present thoughts quickly

| Strategy | Strategy Description | Page | Tools |
|---|---|---|---|
| **8-5** Making Introductions | Learning to introduce speakers in a clear, organized manner | 338 | 8-5a |
| **8-6** Informational Speeches and Oral Reports | Giving an information speech; telling about a person, product, item, or event | 338 | 8-3a, 8-3b, 8-6a |
| **8-7** Asking and Answering Questions | Answering questions on a topic a speaker has shared | 341 | n/a |
| **8-8** Impromptu Speeches | Organizing ideas quickly and presenting these ideas with confidence | 342 | 8-8a |

*(chart continues)*

| Strategy (continued) | Strategy Description | Page | Tools |
|---|---|---|---|
| **8-9** Giving a How-To Speech | Explaining a series of steps and teaching a procedure; giving process, demonstration, and instructional speeches | 344 | 8-9a |
| **8-10** Persuasive Speeches | Winning over an audience by organizing an oral presentation with a clear topic/thesis and believable support | 346 | 8-10a to 8-10d |
| **8-11** Stand Up and Sound Off | Arguing a point on a topic by organizing ideas quickly and providing specific evidence and examples | 348 | 8-11a, 8-11b |
| **8-12** Focus on Your Audience | Taking the audience into consideration when planning | 349 | n/a |
| **8-13** Oral Book Reports | Identifying main ideas and/ or key themes in books; presenting these ideas and themes in an organized way using visuals | 350 | n/a |
| **8-14** Planning Longer Presentations | Preparing speeches that are long and include several key/ star ideas | 351 | 8-14a |

P Consider using the Posters with the strategies in this section.

## 8-5 Making Introductions

Students use this strategy to feel comfortable introducing others. Most students welcome the chance to introduce a guest or a speaker. If, however, they are not organized, they may feel frustrated and their introductions may not be effective.

**Handy Pages**

### Before Class

Make an overhead transparency and student copies of *Tool 8-5a*.

### During Class

- Explain to your students that making an introduction is actually quite simple once they know the formula. Using *Tool 8-5a*, model and review the goals and format for an introduction. With your students, write an opening sentence and the key/star ideas for a sample introduction.

- Practice introductions frequently using characters from books that the class is familiar with, people in the news, sports stars, scientists, mathematicians, artists, and/or musicians. Have your students keep a copy of *Tool 8-5a* in their notebooks for quick reference.

*Tool 8-5a*

## 8-6 Informational Speeches and Oral Reports

This strategy teaches students how to organize information in an engaging manner. Students use it when they need to tell about a person, product, item, or event.

**Prerequisites:** 8-2 Speech Planning and 8-3 Blocking Out a Speech

**Handy Pages**

Students may find that the toughest part of giving a report is not sounding as if the information they present came straight from encyclopedias or other reference material. This strategy will help students intentionally plan and organize the content of informational speeches and reports.

### Before Class

- Make overhead transparencies and student copies of *Tools 8-3a*, *8-3b*, and *8-6a*.
- Have available green, yellow, and red overhead markers and highlighters.

(⊚) *Bonus Tool 8-6-1* provides additional support.

## During Class

1. As you display *Tool 8-6a*, remind students that a report should

   - Be focused and give detailed information;
   - Address only the most important key/star ideas;
   - Contain rich examples, vivid explanation, and accurate evidence.

2. Point out that a report with these elements will be much more helpful to the audience than a long report with numerous key/star ideas and little explanation. Explain to your students that they will still need to do extensive research on their topics, but they probably will not use all of it in their speeches.

3. Explain that preparation for informational speeches begins by collecting information. Good reports are the result of good research and careful reading. Emphasize that when taking notes, it is best for students to put the ideas into their own words. That will make the material more memorable and they won't have to worry about plagiarism. Remind them that if they write something down exactly as it was written in their source material, they should be sure to use quotation marks. (See **1-17 Easy Two-Column Notes** and **1-21 Research Note Cards** for more information.)

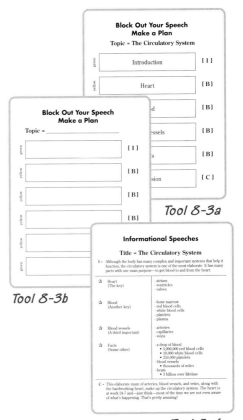

*Tool 8-3a*

*Tool 8-3b*

*Tool 8-6a*

4. After students have completed their research, they are ready to determine what their key/star ideas are going to be. This means that they may need to narrow their topics to select the most important ideas. Those selected will become the key/star ideas for their speeches.

5. Once they have selected their key/star ideas, it is time to block out their speeches. Using *Tool 8-3b*, review the blocking-out process with your students. Note that I, B, and C on the right stand for Introduction, Body, and Conclusion. Have them color the blocks using the Traffic Light colors.

6. Display *Tool 8-3a* and show the example of blocking out a speech about the circulatory system. Then display *Tool 8-6a* and point out how this informal outline relates to what was blocked out on *Tool 8-3a*. Have students highlight their informal outlines. The highlighting, like the blocking out, will help them learn and remember the information in their speeches. It will also make it easy to show how blocking out and informal outlining relate to each other.

7. Review the introduction and conclusion on *Tool 8-6a*. Remind students that the introduction and conclusion provide an opportunity to focus attention on the main objectives of the speech. For additional information about creating introductions and conclusions, see Sections 4 and 5.

8. When students prepare their own information speeches, ask them to block them out and make informal outlines on their copies of *Tools 8-2b* and *8-3b*, on 5" × 8" cards or notebook paper. If using cards or paper, have them use the front for blocking out and the back for their informal outline.

9. In the empty space to the right of the elaboration and evidence notes (the dashes) in the informal outline, have students make sketches, symbols, or notes to remind themselves about any visuals props they will use at each point in their speeches.

## Additional Ideas

- Have students prepare their informal outlines on 5" × 8" cards. They are easy for students to hold and glance at as they are giving their speeches. For an example, see *Bonus Tool 8-6-1*.

- Collect short informational books from the school library or books your students have brought from home. These books are often around 80 pages long and should be on subjects such as science, animals, travel, outer space, music, art, painting, or fashion. Read one of the books to your class and with their assistance develop an informal outline. Model giving a speech based on the outline. Keep the speech short, select only a few key/star ideas, and add transitions. Have each of your students select a book to read and develop an informal outline from. If there isn't time for all students to give their speeches to the whole class, have them give their speeches to a partner or to other members of a small group.

- Challenge students to read as many books as they can. Have them prepare cards for each book, even if there is not enough time in class to share all of the speeches from the cards. Students often have books at home that they can use. Magazine articles and news items also work well for this strategy. Use these as alternate assignments for the 5" × 8" speech.

- Use *Tool 8-3b* and informal outlines like the one on *Tool 8-6a* with students for other kinds of reports: news, sports, health, community, school, the arts, social studies, and so on. The blocks and the outline can be used to organize reports in the standard *who, what, where, when,* and *why* format for news reporting.

- Consider having your students use visual aids for their presentations. The visual aid could be graphs, pictures, posters that your students have made, or some other type of prop.

**Asking and Answering Questions**

This activity prepares students to anticipate questions and answers after informational speeches (oral reports). Students use it to improve their listening skills and practice asking and answering questions about a report.

**Prerequisite:** 1-35 Great Short Answers

When your students give informational speeches, take time to practice the skill of asking and answering questions. Let your students know that they might be called on to ask questions after listening to a speech or report. Tell them that the questions they ask should

- Show that they listened;
- Demonstrate their ability to ask good questions.

## Before Class

- Have available notebook paper or 4" × 6" index cards.
- Review 1-36 Responses to Essay Questions and 1-38 Levels of Questioning for more information on asking and answering questions.

## During Class

### Before the Speech

- Give each listener a half sheet of paper or a 4" × 6" index card. Students can save paper and cards by using each side for a different report. The small piece of paper will not seem overwhelming and will make the task feel doable for your students.

- Have students fold the paper/card into three parts and add the following headings:

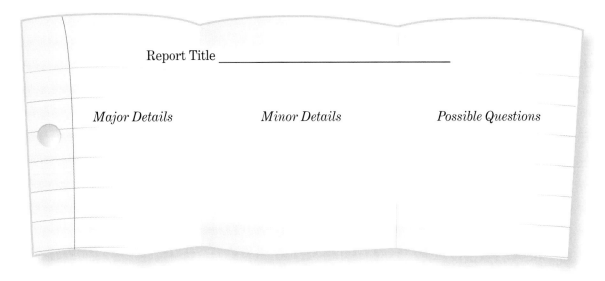

Report Title _____

*Major Details*      *Minor Details*      *Possible Questions*

### During and After the Speech

1. Have a student present a short speech based on *Tool 8-6a* (The Circulatory System) or a topic that has been used in other activities.

2. Tell the rest of the class to take quick notes on the prepared notebook paper or index cards while their classmate presents the report. Let students know that this quick note-taking assignment will help them prepare questions and will improve their listening skills. Have students refer to their notes as they prepare questions about the report.

3. Call on students to ask questions and have the speaker provide answers, using **1-35 Great Short Answers**. Remind the speaker to use part of the question in the answer. The following is an example:

> Q = In your report you mentioned the arteries, the capillaries, and the veins. Is there a big size difference—widthwise—in these three passageways that transport blood?
>
> A = *Yes, the width of the arteries, capillaries, and the veins are different sizes because of their functions. Let me give an example…*

## 8-8 Impromptu Speeches

This strategy helps students quickly organize thoughts and present them with confidence.

**Handy Pages**

Impromptu speeches are short. They are great because they do not take much time from regular class activities. They can be on any topic, and they provide a perfect opportunity for students to practice speaking in public. Impromptu speeches should be fun; make success the goal for everyone.

## Before Class

- Make an overhead transparency of *Tool 8-8a*.
- Have available index cards for student use.

  *Bonus Tool 8-8-1* provides additional support.

## During Class

*Tool 8-8a*

1. Display *Tool 8-8a* and explain that *impromptu* means something that happens quickly, with little or no time for planning, or something that hasn't been rehearsed.

2. Point out the prompt above the index card on *Tool 8-8a*. Discuss how the prompt has been turned into the introduction for the speech. Advise students to use key words from a prompt to create the topic sentences for their own speeches. (See prompts on the *Bonus Tools CD*.)

3. Explain that an impromptu speech is more than just giving a list, a one-word answer, or a sentence. Because the speech is short, it is important for students to present their topic and key/star ideas in a well-organized format.

4. Pass out index cards. Tell students they will practice taking notes for an impromptu speech using the format on *Tool 8-8a*, but they will not use the card when they speak. This short, informal outline will help them organize and remember their thoughts.

5. Give your students a prompt like one of the following, and have them practice giving their speeches in small groups or as a whole class. For additional prompts, see *Bonus Tool 8-8-1*.

> What time should curfew be for students your age and why?
>
> What would be the toughest thing about being President of the United States?

## Additional Ideas

- Write a variety of prompts on pieces of paper and put them into a bag or box. Have each student pick a prompt randomly and give a speech based on the prompt.
- Play "beat the clock," giving students only a minute to prepare a speech.

## 8-9 Giving a How-To Speech

How-to speeches are oral presentations that explain a topic through a series of steps. Students use them to explain a procedure, demonstrate a skill, or give instructions.

**Prerequisite:** 8-2 Speech Planning

## Before Class

Make an overhead transparency of *Tool 8-9a*.

## During Class

*Tool 8-9a*

- Display *Tool 8-9a* and explain that the expectations for each type of speech—process, demonstration, or instructional—might be slightly different, but the planning and organization for each kind of speech will be the same.

- Review the small triangles at each corner of the larger triangle. Read and discuss the meaning of each type of speech. Point out the triangle in the center and review the similarities of all three kinds of how-to speeches.

- Review the possible topics for each type of speech on the bottom of *Tool 8-9a* and brainstorm additional topics with your class.

- Discuss how the presentation for each type of speech will be different.

### Modeling How-To Speeches

1. Have students select the type of how-to speech they want to give from the samples on *Tool 8-9a* or ideas of their own, and then begin planning their speeches by developing an informal outline. Either the Tool or the two-column fold on notebook paper is an ideal vehicle for organizing their topic.

2. Have students put their key/star ideas in the left column and their elaborations in the right column.

3. Stress the importance of using the right combination of transitions in this type of speech. The following sets of transitions help students be organized, sequential, and explicit:

> - First, second, third, fourth
> - To begin, next, then, later, finally
> - Start by, after that, when, then, stop when
> - First of all, the second, the third, the fourth, the fifth and last

See the transition lists on *Tools 4-24a* and *4-25a* for more ideas and examples.

4. Encourage students to highlight transitions and make them obvious in their speeches. Adding the transitions to charts and other visuals will help the students recall the organization of their speech. Transitions help the audience comprehend the steps of a process.

5. Remind students that the best conclusion for this type of speech is a quick review of the process, steps, or instructions.

6. Place the students in small groups and have them practice their speeches. Discuss whether the transition sets aided the audience in understanding the material.

## Additional Ideas

Informal outlines written on notebook paper can be difficult for students to use and may be a distraction. Suggest these options to your students:

- Use large index cards.
- Use heavy stock paper.
- Tape the outline to the table so it can be seen at a glance but not picked up.
- Memorize key/star ideas and transitions and use hands-on visuals as reminders.
- Use a teleprompter (see **8-2 Speech Planning**).

## 8-10 Persuasive Speeches

A persuasive speech encourages an audience to rethink a position or to take action.
**Prerequisite:** 8-2 Speech Planning

**Handy Pages**

### Before Class

- Make overhead transparencies and student copies of *Tools 8-10a* through *8-10d*.
- Review **9-1 Persuasive Writing** for additional ideas.

### During Class
#### Considering Both Sides of an Issue

1. Display *Tool 8-10a* and read the second row together with your class. Explain that students must learn and think about both sides of a topic before they begin planning and that a good persuasive speech acknowledges and shows respect for opposing points of view but presents evidence and facts to refute those views. (When students are just learning to give persuasive speeches, it is difficult for

| **Persuasive Speech** | |
|---|---|
| Topic = | • Your clear, stated opinion<br>*"I have something important to say."* |
| ⚖ | • Acknowledgment of and respect for opposing views, with facts to refute them<br>*"I have studied my topic and know how others might feel."* |
| ☰ | • Clearly organized (with powerful transitions) support for your topic/opinion<br>*"I can prove it. I want to convince the audience."* |
| 🏛 | • Believable examples and explanations<br>*"This makes sense. My information is accurate. The audience will listen to me."* |
| 🔊 | • Convincing voice, good eye contact, and correct posture<br>*"My eyes and the way I talk prove that I am serious and have something important to say."* |
| Conclusion = | • A conclusion that people will remember<br>*"I want the audience to think about my topic and take action when my speech is finished. I want to motivate them."* |

*Tool 8-10a*

them to incorporate both sides of an argument into a speech. They will learn this skill as they practice, listen to, and read more persuasive speeches.)

2. To provide practice for your students in considering the two sides of an issue, have them list both sides of an argument.

*Wearing Seatbelts*

| For | Against |
| --- | --- |
| - safety | - uncomfortable |
| - law | - takes time |
| - no injuries | - don't feel free |
| - save lives | |

3. Let them know that in their audience (even if the audience is very small) there may be people who will have different opinions and ideas. That is what persuasive speeches are all about.

4. Explain that although students will be expected to address the opposing point of view, they do not need to state the opposing point of view directly. If they wish, it is fine to briefly mention how others feel about their topic, but remind them that they will want to focus on their own opinions, defend their positions, and win their arguments with good examples, evidence, and explanation.

## Staying Organized and Backing Your Position with Evidence

1. Read the first row *Tool 8-10a* with your class, and explain that the topic of a persuasive speech always addresses issues that
   ▸ Have two sides;
   ▸ Can be debated;
   ▸ State a problem with more than one solution;
   ▸ Are specific and require the audience to form an opinion.

2. Point out the last row and discuss the importance of a strong conclusion that connects to the topic, reminds the audience of the facts, and summarizes their position.

3. Point out the third row and explain how important it is to plan a speech. Remind students that an informal outline will help them stay organized when they make their speeches.

**Hints for Presenting Your Evidence**

- Present **facts** in short, clear sentences. Be prepared to verify your sources if questioned, but mention them only if it seems necessary.
- Generally, save **the most important** and most convincing information for the end of the speech. As the speech progresses, briefly mention facts that you have already stated as you introduce new facts.
- Use **statistics**, but use them sparingly, and make them visual by presenting charts, showing the statistics on a screen, or writing them on a board.
- Speak in a way that paints pictures for the audience. Choose **words and phrases** that will help listeners picture your examples in their heads.
- Use **pictures that illustrate** your point whenever possible.
- Consider reading short passages (a few lines) from **sources** that support your argument. Have your lines well marked and easy to find when it is time to read. Use **quotations** from well known and/or respected sources that support your position.
- Use the acronym LEE to help you check your evidence and judge the strength of your argument. You can reach (or lose) your audience with **logic, evidence**, and **emotions**.

   **L** – Logic (Is your speech presented in an organized and logical manner? Is your topic/thesis logical? Does it make sense? Have you selected evidence that really fits your key/star ideas?)

   **E** – Evidence (Is your evidence believable? Is it easy to explain? Will your audience understand your point? Have you given the audience enough information? Have you made things confusing by giving too much?)

   **E** – Emotions (What emotional response do you want from the audience? How will you need to adjust your speech to reach them? What have you done to prepare for your audience and how will you touch their emotions in order to get them to believe what you are saying?)

*Tool 8-10b*

4. Read through the third and fourth characteristics (rows) of a persuasive speech and lead a discussion with your students on the importance of using accurate facts (key/star ideas) and of backing them up with believable, easily understood evidence that makes sense (the E's).

5. Display *Tool 8-10b* and share the hints for selecting and presenting evidence. Also consider using one of the "either/or" ideas from **9-1 Persuasive Writing**.

6. Share your own ideas for selecting evidence and ask students for suggestions. Remind students that they will not use all of the suggestions—just the ones that fit their speech.

## Comparing Persuasive Speeches

1. Display *Tools 8-10c* and *8-10d*. With your students, read through the informal outlines. Take time to point out the introductions, key/star ideas, evidence and examples, transitions, and conclusions. Ask students to label the speeches and add the Traffic Light colors.

2. Ask your students if a speech using these notes would persuade an audience. Lead a discussion on how the notes attempt to address the need for logic, evidence, and an emotional response. Have your students make suggestions for changing and/or improving the speeches on *Tools 8-10c* and *8-10d*.

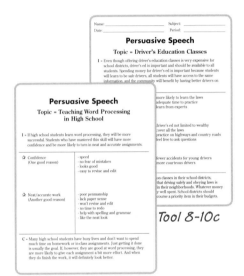

*Tool 8-10c*

*Tool 8-10d*

3. Remind them that the success of any persuasive speech depends on the audience. That means that it is always important to think about the audience when it is time to prepare a persuasive speech. Use one or more of the activities from **8-12 Focus on Your Audience** to help your students gain this perspective.

## 8-11 Stand Up and Sound Off

This activity prompts students to take a position on a topic and deliver a speech on it. It can be used with any kind of speech, but can be especially useful as students perfect their persuasion skills.

### Before Class

- Make an overhead transparency and student copies of *Tools 8-11a* and *8-11b*.

- *Bonus Tool 8-11-1* provides additional examples and support.

### During Class

- Explain to your students that Stand Up and Sound Off speeches are short—no more than two minutes—and will give them experience talking in front of a group and putting their thoughts into words.

- Inform them that their goal is to quickly convince their listeners that an opinion is true, valid, or correct. Some topics might require them to persuade an audience to perform a specific action or to change their way of thinking.

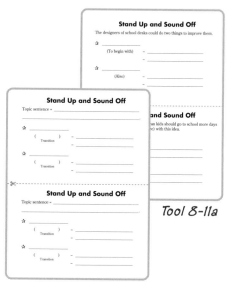

*Tool 8-11a*

*Tool 8-11b*

- Model the Stand Up and Sound Off strategy by completing with your class one of the examples on *Tool 8-11a*. It is important that your speech follows the plan you set up on the Tool and that your opinion on the topic is clear. Have students fill out their copy of *Tool 8-11a* with their opinions. Then give them a chance to share their opinions. Students can share with the entire class or in pairs and small groups.

- Have them practice by giving them a topic or having them choose topics of their own. Have students use notebook paper or *Tool 8-11b* when planning. At first, you may want students to offer opinions on general/generic topics such as the ones that follow. (For additional sample topics, see *Bonus Tool 8-11-1*.)

| | |
|---|---|
| Smoking | School uniforms |
| Class schedules | Shorter school days |

### Additional Ideas

- After your students practice with generic topics, ask students to stand up and sound off on content-area topics.
  - ▸ In social studies, students might sound off about living in different climates, protecting the environment, or being a good member of the community.
  - ▸ In science, students might sound off about eating right, space travel, saving water and energy, or new discoveries.

  ▸ After reading short stories or novels, students might sound off about the actions of a character or characters.

- Eventually, you will want to ask students to sound off on topics they read about in newspapers or magazines. This activity encourages them to form and support opinions on important topics. Use local newspapers or student news magazines. When students sound off on topics from the news, expect them to

  ▸ Have a copy of the article(s) they want to discuss;

  ▸ Read the entire article first and both highlight and make reading notations (Section 1) as they read;

  ▸ Back up opinions with specific examples and lines from the text.

## 8-12 Focus on Your Audience

Whenever students are making a speech, they should keep their audience in mind.

## Before Class

Have available six 4" × 6" index cards per student.

## During Class

### Learning to Consider the Audience

1. Lead a whole class discussion about reaching different audiences and the importance of considering the audience when students prepare for a speech.

2. List some possible audiences on the board. Next to each audience, list ideas for reaching that group. Possible audience members could include:

   parents

   middle and high school students

   members of the city council or school board

   educators—teachers and principals

   representatives of local temples, synagogues, and churches

   police officers

   retired (but active) citizens

   doctors and nurses

   business owners in the neighborhood

3. On a set of cards, write some possible audiences for a speech. Have students draw a card, take a stand on an issue, and prepare their speech outlines to fit their audience.

4. Use one of the following scenarios as prompts, or develop additional prompts, and assign students (individually or in small groups) a specific audience.

- All district schools should become community schools that are open in the evenings and on Saturdays to offer special classes for families, business professionals, and students. The special classes would help people master basic skills in math, reading, and writing. The classes would also focus on health, art, music, and technology.
- The city has money to build a new park. Some community members want a pool and skateboarding area in the park, but others want a quiet park with lots of walking trails, places to sit and read, and beautiful scenery.

### Sell-It! Activity

1. Ask students to select (or invent) a product or a service and sell it to the class.
2. Give each student six index cards. On the cards, ask students to write how they will
   - Get their audience's attention;
   - Show the audience why they (or someone they know) need it;
   - Describe how happy/satisfied they will be when they own it and use it;
   - Help them see (visualize) themselves using it, playing with it, and looking at it;
   - Explain how their friends and family will feel when they see that they have it;
   - Get them to buy it.
3. Once students have put their cards in the order that makes the most sense to them, have them use the backs of the cards to create quick, informal outlines complete with introductions and conclusions as they prepare to make their sales pitch.
4. Discuss how a salesperson who wanted to sell the product or service would arrange and use the cards.

## 8-13 Oral Book Reports

Review 9-5 Responding to Literature with your class. This strategy will help your students plan well, stay on topic, and produce more interesting book reports. Use it to prompt students to analyze what they have read, and to think critically and creatively.

All too often, when students are asked to give oral book reports, they try to do too much. Many want to retell the entire story or cover all of the key points. These kinds of reports can become long and tedious. Let your students know that this strategy will help them produce better, more interesting book reports because it helps them to think about the theme of a book rather than just retell it; they must sort major ideas and minor ideas and share their own insights. When they give a speech, this strategy provides them with a visual aid that will keep their presentations more focused and interesting.

# 8-14 Planning Longer Presentations

Presentations are longer, more involved speeches. When creating a presentation, students' biggest challenge is organizing the vast amounts of information they will gather. Students can use this strategy as a way to get started.

## Before Class

Make an overhead transparency and student copies of *Tool 8-14a*.

*Tool 8-14a*

## During Class

1. Use *Tool 8-14a* and a general topic that the students recognize or have studied in order to model this strategy.

2. Complete the "What do you know?" section (a listing of all the possible ideas they know about the topic) and the "What do you want your audience to know?" section (a shorter list of those things they most want the audience to know about the topic) sections with your students. Explain that this will help them be clear about all of the ideas they want to cover in their speeches.

3. Ask students to think about how they would complete the question "How will you connect both sides?" Share the following list of suggestions for ways to connect the "What do you know" and "What do you want your audience to know" lists. Add ideas of your own to the list.

   - Facts, statistics, testimonies
   - Charts, pictures, props
   - Stories or narratives, quotations
   - Interview responses, rhetorical questions
   - Music, news reports, primary sources

4. Discuss the options and complete the diagram, reminding students to keep their audiences in mind when they begin planning their own presentations.

5. Work with your students as they complete their own diagrams using their own topics. Remind them to apply the active reading, note-taking, organizing, and writing strategies they have used for shorter assignments, and encourage them to ask for help and to share ideas with each other.

6. When students are finished, have them create informal outlines and use blocking out to create a specific, useful plan for their presentations.

# Improving Listening and Discussion Skills

The abilities to listen and to discuss are important academic and life skills. These skills are used in all content areas, as well as outside school. When students practice listening and discussion skills, they build their confidence in their ability to participate.

## Objectives

- Develop students' active listening skills
- Increase students' active participation in discussions

| Strategy | Strategy Description | Page | Tools |
|---|---|---|---|
| **8-15** Good Listening Skills | Evaluating listening skills and setting goals for improving them | 353 | 8-15a, 8-15b |
| **8-16** Participating in a Discussion | Listening, asking questions, sharing insights, and taking responsibility for the success of a small-group or whole-class discussion | 356 | 8-16a |

**Good Listening Skills**

These activities teach and encourage good listening, and help students master this skill.

## Before Class

Make an overhead transparency and student copies of *Tools 8-15a* and *8-15b*.

## During Class

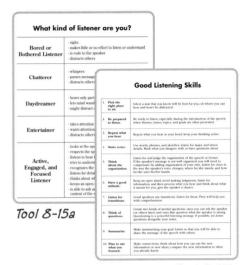

*Tool 8-15a*

*Tool 8-15b*

1. Display *Tool 8-15a* and read through the characteristics and descriptions of different kinds of listeners. Ask students to add more descriptors in the right-hand column. Encourage them to think about what kind of listeners they are.

2. Remind students that there are different reasons for listening. Explain that the goal in a school setting is to improve listening skills needed for learning and that to learn, students know they must become the active, engaged, and focused listener as described on *Tool 8-15a*. Discuss why good listening skills are important.

3. Begin a discussion with your class by asking them for reasons and ways people listen. On the board, draw two columns. At the top of the first column, write the heading "Reasons and Ways People Listen." At the top of the second column, write "Skills Needed for This Kind of Listening." As students share their perspective, add their thoughts to the chart.

4. Using *Tool 8-15b*, discuss with your students ways that they can be proactive and improve their listening skills.

5. Use this activity and ones you create to teach and encourage good listening skills. Let students know that you will be assessing their listening skills and that you will provide strategies to help them master good listening skills.

# Additional Ideas

## What's in it for me? The WIIFM Theory

The thinking behind the WIIFM (pronounced *wiff em*) theory is that people will be more motivated to change bad habits or try new things if they see a purpose or a value for themselves.

- Introduce the "What's in it for me?" question.
- Give students time to make a list of reasons why they will be better off if they spend time and energy on listening skills. Refer to the chart on *Tool 8-15a* for a list of the attributes of poor and good listeners.
- Consider offering points or grades for listening if it helps some students with motivation.

## Doormat Theory

The thinking behind the Doormat Theory (Dove 1995) is that people who carry issues and problems into a class will learn less and listen less than those who arrive with an open mind and a desire to learn.

- Explain the Doormat Theory to students. Share your interest in wanting to know about things that are important to students, but also describe how it is important to establish a system in the classroom that ensures the best use of class time.
- Put a doormat (real or imaginary) at the classroom door.
- Ask students to leave all small issues and concerns at the door. This includes things like disagreements with friends, after-school activities, assignments due later in the day, and so on.

**Note:** Most students will understand (and many will appreciate) the Doormat Theory. Young people, like adults, want to make the best use of their time and they like learning. Assure students that they should always approach you about serious problems and emergencies.

## "I Was Thinking. . . . What Were You Thinking?" Activity

Use the "I was thinking. . . . What were you thinking?" activity to keep all students involved in a class discussion.

- Start a discussion by sharing your insights. State an opinion, using language like "I was thinking that the school vending machines should sell more fruit juice and less soda."
- Pull a student into the discussion by saying, "I was wondering what you were thinking."

When you use this activity, students are aware that they can and will be called on randomly. They will learn that it is their responsibility to be ready to offer insights and new ideas. Instead of asking for volunteers to answer your questions or to comment on the lesson, start a discussion by sharing your insights.

## Whole Class Informal Outlines Activity

When students brainstorm and create informal outlines, they identify topics and the supporting key/star ideas.

When creating the informal outline becomes an oral activity, students are forced to listen. In this activity, the teacher calls out the topic. Instead of writing the main concepts (key/star ideas), a student lists them orally. Other students listen and then add the evidence and examples (the E's). See Section 4 for more details and for examples.

## Audiobook Activity

Use this activity with recordings of books or short stories.

- Listen to the audio version of the story before you share it with your students.
- Write down words and phrases from the text in sequential order while listening, being sure to choose words and phrases from the beginning to the end.
- Prepare a list of these words and phrases for students and give each student a copy and a highlighter.
- Have students listen to the story. Ask them to mark the words or phrases on the list that they hear in the story.

Since your list will be in sequential order, students will not get lost. Make the list "not too short and not too long"—just enough to keep students listening and active.

If time permits, follow up this activity with **1-34 The 12-Word Trick**.

## Repeat the Teacher's Directions Activity

Make a habit of having your students repeat your directions. When directions are given, call on a student to repeat them. This helps to reinforce listening and ensures that all students understand the directions.

If directions are in writing, have students underline and/or highlight main points as the teacher reads them aloud.

## Happy Face Activity

Use **1-35 Great Short Answers** strategy with this activity. Ask students questions and require answers that could receive a "happy face" rating. To get a top rating for their answers, students must use parts of the question in their answers. Continue this expectation throughout the day.

## Read-Aloud Activity

Practice classroom listening skills with read-aloud activities. Read stories, poems, or news items to students. Have students give you a summary of what you read, have them share with a partner, or discuss in a small group. At times you will want to read the entire piece; at other times read only the first part, and make the rest of the assignment independent reading.

## 8-16 Participating in a Discussion

This strategy stresses the importance of maintaining standards for classroom discussions and helps students understand that different kinds of discussions may follow different formats. Student can use it to improve their ability to participate in small- and whole-group discussions.

The success of small- and whole-group class discussions depends on several factors:

- The students arrive prepared.
- The teacher has modeled, monitored, and mentored discussion skills.
- The teacher and students evaluate discussion skills.
- The teacher and students expect success.

### Before Class

- Make an overhead transparency and student copies of *Tool 8-16a*.
- Create open-ended, leading questions to share if extra guidance or examples are needed. (See **8-7 Asking and Answering Questions** for additional examples and information.)

### During Class

- Prepare students for discussions about literature, art, music, history, and so on by asking them to use the active reading and listening strategies they've learned (Section 1). Discussions are successful only when students have actually read (or listened) and comprehended.

- Expect students to come to discussion groups with text in hand. The text should be marked (sticky notes, highlighting, and so on) so that students can refer to the text in the midst of a discussion.

- Ask students to create questions to bring to a discussion. Use the questions you prepared to share if students need extra guidance or examples. See **1-38 Levels of Questioning** for additional ideas.

*Tool 8-16a*

#### Modeling a Discussion

- Model and point out the key behaviors needed for a good discussion.
  - ▸ Show how you listen attentively when someone else is speaking, waiting for a speaker to finish before making your own point, and starting your question or comment by acknowledging what the previous speaker said. Point out that these are the same behaviors you would use when having a polite conversation.
  - ▸ Demonstrate how to politely disagree with something another person said.
  - ▸ Demonstrate how one comment during a discussion leads to another.
  - ▸ Remind students to stay on topic in their discussions.

- Using *Tool 8-16a*, lead a discussion on your expectations of discussion groups. Use ideas from the following list (and expectations of your own) as you complete *Tool 8-16a* with your class. Discuss how these may be different depending on the type of discussion and the size of the group.

> **Getting Started**
>> What kind of task is to be tackled? How difficult is it?
>> How long do you have to do it? Do you need to make a timeline?
>> What roles should each person have? Who is going to be the leader?
>> What are the short-term and long-term goals for the task?
>
> **Being the Leader**
>> What is your role?
>> What is your responsibility?
>> Does this role get passed to others?
>> How and/or when will you delegate tasks?
>
> **Doing Your Part**
>> What can all members do to promote active listening?
>> How can all group members show respect for ideas and other participants?
>> How can members and the group as a whole respond, participate, and complete the task on time?
>> How can members of the group encourage each other?
>
> **Reporting Back**
>> Who will rephrase the task and clarify directions?
>> Who will share key points of the discussion? How will key points be shared?
>> Who will sum up what was discussed? Issues? Discoveries? Great comments?
>> How will all members of the group get credit for good ideas and sharing?

### Monitoring a Discussion

Monitor small-group discussions by

- Visiting each group and listening to and for interesting insights and comments;
- Offering suggestions and answering questions when students ask for help;
- Complimenting success.

Monitor whole-class discussions by

- Summarizing or repeating questions and comments to make sure all students have heard them;

- Asking leading questions if students seem unsure of what to say;
- Taking students back to the text in order to stay on topic;
- Encouraging (not frustrating or embarrassing) reluctant students:
  - Send leading questions in their direction.
  - Ask them to follow up on someone else's comment.
  - Ask them to summarize comments that have already been shared.
  - Ask them to read a line or extremely short passage and then make a comment.
- Using discussion cards to make sure that all students participate in whole-class discussions. Discussion cards are colored index cards that students place at the front of their desks after they have contributed to a discussion.

In general, the idea is to pull in everyone. This means preventing a few people from controlling the discussion, plus developing successful ways for reluctant students to share. It is important to monitor your students' discussion skills and prompt them to use the skills they have been taught, because skills that you don't demonstrate as being important enough for you to expect and monitor will probably not be learned.

## Mentoring a Discussion

- Mentor small groups as they participate in discussions. When it is obvious that a group is struggling, confused, and unproductive, join the group for several minutes. Mentor the group using positive, direct, and explicit language. Clarify the task if needed. Dictate and have students copy questions for the group to use to restart their discussion.

- If it is clear that most group members have not completed the necessary reading or research to carry on a discussion, rephrase and narrow the task. Find one page or a very short selection for the group to read. Tell the group to use that selection only for their discussion. This will make the task doable. Congratulate them on their success.

- Expect success and participation. Approach every discussion activity with high expectations. Remember that planning and preparation on your part will help prevent poor performance.

# SPECIFIC WRITING ASSIGNMENTS
## Writing to Improve Reading and Listening Comprehension

*T*hrough an ongoing, integrated use of a variety of reading and writing strategies, the writing process, and writing for a variety of purposes, students begin to see themselves as independent learners and confident writers.

Once students have learned how to use the *Step Up* writing process to create both expository and narrative compositions, they are ready to use those skills to write for a variety of purposes, such as narrating, informing, and persuading. Because each category of writing has numerous subgenres, students need to have experience in many types of specific writing assignments.

In addition, a variety of specific writing opportunities occur in our school, work, and personal lives. The purpose directs the type of composition we need to create. Therefore, students need to understand the requirements of a variety of writing situations.

This section provides students with the tools to use for specific writing genres, whether poetry or science lab reports, business letters or newspaper articles, book reports or math word problems. It also provides the tools to help students prepare for success on local, state, and national assessments when they are asked to compare and contrast, for example, or show how to address an envelope, or to write an imaginative description.

Success with specific writing assignments occurs when students are introduced to the following:

- Specific strategies for each type of writing

- Applying generalized strategies from Sections 1 through 8 to specific types of writing

- Skills in acquiring, analyzing, and prioritizing information, then organizing it into an appropriate format

- Using precise language and a variety of sentence types

- A broad array of illustrative examples of the many types of writing assignments, from analyzing cause and effect in a science report to writing letters for business or personal reasons

# When Teaching These Strategies

- Provide direct instruction and models for each type before having students write independently. Repeated demonstration and practice are keys to effective writing instruction.

- Keep in mind that proficiency in one genre does not necessarily transfer to others, so teach the components of each type separately. Introduce each type of writing as a paragraph to teach the structural requirements of that type of writing.

- Review and practice related strategies learned in other sections of *Step Up to Writing* as you introduce new writing genres.

- Use the same topic to write in a variety of genres, reinforcing the structural differences among the types of writing. Have students write on the same or different topics for a variety of audiences and purposes.

- Have students practice writing in a variety of time frames—those that allow only a first draft and those that permit multiple revisions.

- Teach **9-5** Responding to Literature in conjunction with the strategies used in Section 1 about making connections (for example, **1-12** Text to Self, Text to Text, and Text to World). When students use active reading strategies, they have an easier time comprehending and responding to what they read.

- Use informal formats—learning logs, journals, preparations for discussion, or warm-ups—as well as formal compositions for specific writing assignments.

When students write across disciplines, they are not only learning to write, they are also writing to learn—exploring ideas, synthesizing information, forming opinions, and expressing and supporting those opinions in a coherent and sustained fashion. Use specific writing assignments to teach and review content-specific concepts. These are just a few ideas:

*IDEA BANK*

## Tips for Using These Strategies Across Content Areas

✓ Section 9 is rich with ideas for student writing. Guarantee your students' success by using **1-17** Easy Two-Column Notes regularly to make sure that students have comprehended information before they have to write about it. Add **1-20** Three- and Four-Column Notes as often as possible to move students beyond basic comprehension. The three column note plus a summary (**1-2** Three-Column Notes with Summaries) is especially effective because it will help students with content and elaboration.

✓ Use **9-3** Writing to Compare or Contrast to have students analyze eras in history, forms of government, or characteristics of different species. Using Tools 9-3b through 9-3g will make compare and contrast writing faster and clearer. When there is not time to have students write out their paragraph or essay, use just the tools. They give students a chance to show their thinking.

✓ Have students write a letter (**9-10** Writing Letters) to favorite authors, favorite celebrities, prominent politicians, local government or civic leaders, scientists, and so on to present issues, ask questions, or to suggest topics that need attention. Letters, like other forms of expository writing, should be organized with informal outlines (**4-7** Planning with Informal Outlines).

✓ Have students write a persuasive essay (**9-1** Persuasive Writing) and take a position related to a time in history they have studied or a controversy such as the effects of reintroducing wolves to a wilderness area. Use informal outlines and **4-13** Practice Guides for Accordion Paragraphs to save time and to help students organize their ideas.

✓ Use **9-5** Response to Literature to have students write a multiparagraph essay demonstrating their understanding and opinion of a literary work.

Choose those strategies that best meet the needs of your students.

# Creating Specific Writing Assignments

Unlike other sections in *Step Up to Writing,* the strategies presented in Section 9 are not always stand-alone. They often rely on concepts and strategies presented in previous sections. For this reason, it is strongly recommended that these strategies be taught after or in conjunction with the strategies in Sections 1 through 8.

| Strategy | Strategy Description | Page | Tools |
|---|---|---|---|
| **9-1 Persuasive Writing** | Proving to readers that something is true; convincing readers to agree with a belief; making a claim and moving readers to believe it; motivating readers to action | 366 | 9-1a to 9-1k |
| **9-2 Supporting an Opinion with Facts** | Sharing personal beliefs about things encountered in daily life, events, art, and/or books | 371 | 9-2a, 9-2b |
| **9-3 Writing to Compare or Contrast** | Explaining how two people, places, creatures, objects, ideas, or feelings are alike or different | 373 | 9-3a to 9-3k |
| **9-4 Creating Biographical and Autobiographical Sketches** | Telling the story of a person's life; discussing the person's characteristics, life events, and view of life; describing events in students' own lives | 378 | 9-4a, 9-4b |

*(chart continues)*

| Strategy *(continued)* | Strategy Description | Page | Tools |
|---|---|---|---|
| **9-5** Responding to Literature | Writing short and long responses to literature; writing about themes, elements of fiction, style, content, and personal insights; writing formal and informal book reports | 379 | 9-5a to 9-5h |
| **9-6** Writing to Show Cause and Effect or Problem and Solution | Identifying a cause—a problem, outcome, or circumstance—and writing about the effect it has on someone or something; presenting a problem and offering a solution; describing a problem and explaining how it was solved | 385 | 9-6a to 9-6c |
| **9-7** RAFTS: Writing from a Different Point of View | Writing as someone else, such as a character, animal, plant, rock, or another person | 387 | 9-7a to 9-7f |
| **9-8** Descriptive Writing | Developing descriptions using creative narrative and factual topics; being factual, specific and technical | 389 | 9-8a to 9-8e |
| **9-9** Using Writing Frames | Creating writing frames to aid writing, assess comprehension, and/or build writing and thinking | 391 | 9-9a |
| **9-10** Writing Letters | Writing letters for a variety of purposes; writing clear memos, e-mails, and messages | 393 | 9-10a to 9-10h |
| **9-11** Applying for a Job | Responding to advertisements; writing résumés; completing a job application | 396 | 9-11a to 9-11e |

*(chart continues)*

| Strategy *(continued)* | Strategy Description | Page | Tools |
|---|---|---|---|
| **9-12** Writing in Math | Explaining problem-solving processes; describing their own problem-solving processes; writing about graphs | 397 | 9-12a to 9-12l |
| **9-13** Writing Reports on Science Experiments | Writing a science lab report that includes a conclusion section | 400 | 9-13a to 9-13d |
| **9-14** Technical Writing | Writing pieces that are factual, accurate, and direct; explaining a process; giving instructions; giving directions | 402 | 9-14a |
| **9-15** Poetry | Comparing prose and poetry; experimenting with words and phrases to create poems; analyzing poems | 403 | 9-15a to 9-15g |
| **9-16** Writing a Skit | Writing a short sketch or play; preparing for Reader's Theater | 405 | 9-16a |
| **9-17** Writing About the News | Completing current event reading assignments; reading and analyzing a news item; creating news stories; planning for and writing about interviews | 407 | 9-17a to 9-17i |
| **9-18** Personal Writing | Making journal entries and keeping learning logs; using freewriting to generate ideas for writing topics | 410 | 9-18a to 9-18c |

P Consider using the Posters with the strategies in this section.

**Persuasive Writing**

Using this strategy, students write persuasive paragraphs, reports, or essays.

Persuasive writing can take many forms. Assignments that ask students to *convince, argue, write an editorial,* or *create an advertisement* are forms of persuasive writing. The various forms of persuasive writing should be taught one at a time. Choose the type that is right for your students.

## Before Class

Make overhead transparencies and student copies of *Tools 9-1a* through *9-1k*.

## During Class

1. Discuss *persuasion* with your class. Explain that the purpose of persuasive writing is to convince the reader. The writing tries to prove to readers that something is true, or attempts to motivate readers to change or take action by appealing to the readers' intellect and/or emotions. In persuasive writing, there is always a call to action—to buy something, join something, do something, and so on. Effective arguing and persuading relies on reasoning and clear logic to influence others. It pushes the audience to think about an issue.

2. Inform your students that the process used for persuasive writing is the same used for any other type of expository writing. Direct them to follow the same writing process as noted in Section 4 or Section 5. Inform or remind them that good persuasive writing needs

    • Research that shows understanding of the topic;

    • Clear, concise organization, as is planned using an informal outline;

    • A topic sentence that clearly explains the topic in a way that fits the audience;

    • Respect for and knowledge of opposing opinions;

    • Interesting, accurate, and engaging key/star ideas that support the topic sentence;

    • Elaboration that is clear, makes sense, and engages the reader;

    • Strong word choices that engage the reader's attention;

    • A conclusion that gives the reader a final reason to consider the topic and the purpose for the essay.

3. Read aloud the example persuasive paragraph on *Tool 9-1a*.

- Ask students to look for the topic sentence and supporting key/star ideas by highlighting the paragraph with the Traffic Light colors. Show students how the informal outline was used for organization—topic, key/star ideas, transitions/elaboration/conclusion. Discuss the importance of organization in persuasive writing.

- Help your students find and evaluate the facts used as proof and/or evidence.

- Point out to your students that persuasive writing is often enhanced by good word choices that make it easy for the reader to follow the logic of the writing. Encourage students to bury these terms for smooth flow and stronger impact. Persuasive writing often includes words and phrases such as:

*Tool 9-1a*

| | | |
|---|---|---|
| should | must | ought |
| since | because | for that reason |

- The conclusion in persuasive writing often includes words and phrases such as:

| | | |
|---|---|---|
| certainly | clearly | for these reasons |
| definitely | therefore | in fact |

4. Read with your students *Tool 9-1b* and explain that there are a number of techniques they can use to frame their writing and make it more persuasive. Have students mark their copies as you read, explain, and answer questions about each entry. Read through the examples; ask students which examples are most persuasive. Give them a chance to add a few ideas that they would use if they had to persuade students to learn more science.

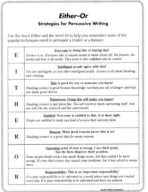

*Tool 9-1b*

5. Point out that the words *EITHER* and *OR* are a good memory hook for some of the common strategies used for persuasive writing. Display *Tool 9-1a* and have students determine which approaches were used in the example paragraph. Following are the persuasive strategies used in "Turn Classrooms into Gyms!" (*Tool 9-1a*):

**T**—This is good for you (lose weight, get in shape)

**R**—Many good reasons (blood to brain, won't fall asleep)

**I**— Intelligent people agree (experts say kids not getting enough exercise)

6. In guided lessons, have students practice writing persuasive paragraphs using your topics or ones suggested on the *Bonus Tools CD*. As a class, develop a position to take on the topic and write a quick informal outline before writing.

7. Explain to students that when preparing for persuasive writing, they will often need to research or gather facts and details to support their topic, but after gathering the information they should narrow their key points down to the strongest few and provide supporting evidence and examples for each key/star idea.

   • Remind them that there are a variety of strategies they can use to write the topic sentence. (See **4-18 Topic Sentence Variety** for more information.)

   • Note that, in the conclusion, they should appeal directly to the reader and restate their goal and reason for writing.

8. Have students work independently to develop persuasive paragraphs using a topic you have provided or one they want to share with others. Give feedback on their writing.

9. When students are ready, have them move from writing paragraphs to persuasive essays. The process is similar to the concept of stretching a paragraph into a multiparagraph essay, as outlined in Section 5. Begin by displaying and reading *Tool 9-1c*.

   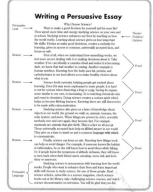

   *Tool 9-1c*

   • Using the Traffic Light colors, highlight the organization of the essay.

   • Help students find what persuasive strategies listed on *Tool 9-1b* have been used. Writers often use more than one. Following are the persuasive strategies used in "Why Choose Science?" (*Tool 9-1c*):

   > **T**—This is good for you (more secure; good choices; knowledge; safety)
   >
   > **I**—Intelligent people agree (people who want to enhance lives)
   >
   > **R**—Many good reasons
   >
   > **R**—Responsibility (to be informed and stay safe)

   • With input from students, judge the effectiveness of the essay.

10. Create or select a prompt from the *Bonus Tools CD*. As a group, write a persuasive essay, or allow students to work independently or with a partner. Use *Tool 9-1b* and the example on *Tool 9-1c* to help complete the essay.

## Noting the Opposing Position

- Explain to your students that a good way to make their persuasive writing more effective is to provide a rebuttal to the opposing point of view.

- Read with your students *Tools 9-1d* and *9-1e* and note how writers address the opposing position along with their own perspectives.

- Point out that in these examples, the writers mention the opposing positions but focus primarily on their own beliefs. Explain that in a multiparagraph essay, the writer's position might be in one paragraph, the position of others in the next paragraph, followed by a rebuttal paragraph. Writers acknowledge opposing opinions in different ways.

## Writing an Argument

1. Tell students that well-written arguments win over the reader by presenting strong evidence and by being logical. Tell them that even though a written argument is filled with emotion, the emotion is expressed in a clear, well-organized manner. Remind them that writing an argument is not about engaging in a fight, but rather winning the reader through logic and the strength of evidence.

2. With your students, read and discuss the examples on *Tools 9-1f* and *9-1g*. Together list the reasons presented.

3. Use *Tools 9-1h* and *9-1i* to model writing an argument. Read and discuss the chart on *Tool 9-1h*. Explain that this is a good prewriting strategy for sorting ideas to use—or not use—in a final essay. With students, read the matching essay on *Tool 9-1i*. Discuss and evaluate its effectiveness.

4. Give student volunteers a chance to present both sides of an argument orally. Use topics related to content that students have studied. Keep the sharing light and fun—but know that each time students practice orally, they are building the foundation for good writing.

*Tool 9-1d*

*Tool 9-1e*

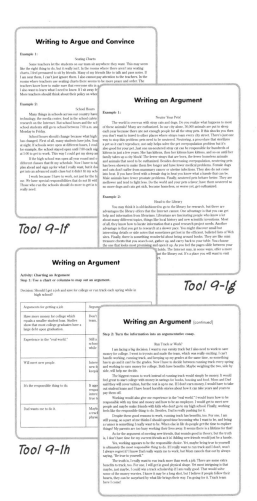

*Tool 9-1f*

*Tool 9-1g*

*Tool 9-1h*

*Tool 9-1i*

### Writing Editorials and Letters to the Editor

1. With your students, read through *Tool 9-1j* and/or additional grade-appropriate examples you have found in newspapers and magazines.

2. Explain that, along with stating personal reasons, good editorials give information and facts to back up the writer's claims and statements. Besides trying to convince readers of their viewpoint, editorials may name the "who, what, where, when, why, and how" of a problem and/or ways readers can get involved. Often, editorials use humor to make their point.

3. Have students write their own editorials using the same writing process they would use for any other form of expository writing. Give them feedback and opportunities to share their best work. Encourage your students to submit editorials on issues that are important to them to a local newspaper or the school newsletter.

*Tool 9-1j*

*Tool 9-1k*

### Writing an Advertisement

1. Explain that although many advertisements may look different from a formal paragraph or essay, they need to be organized and developed like other forms of persuasive writing so that the reader can follow the writer's logic and point.

2. Share with your students advertisements from many different sources and formats. Ask families to help collect ads. Focus on the sentences in these ads.

   - Stress the importance and strength of action verbs and catchy words or phrases. Discuss how they help get the audience's attention.

   - Ads sometimes include sentence fragments. Explain to students that sometimes advertisements break the rules to make a point, for emphasis, or to save space.

3. Display *Tool 9-1k* and discuss these examples of advertisements. Point out that the two examples are written for the same product, but one is written for radio and the other for a newspaper. Discuss how the format is different depending on how it will be used.

4. Working as a class, individually, or in pairs, have students pick a product to write an advertisement for. The product can be real or imaginary. They should choose whether their ad will be in print, on the radio, on TV, or another medium.

## Additional Ideas

- Write two persuasive paragraphs on the same topic—one from each opposing point of view.

- Write a persuasive essay from the point of view of the person you are trying to persuade.

- Write a persuasive essay for younger students; organize a class visit so students can read their essays with and to the younger students.

- Write persuasive essays about content-area subjects to demonstrate mastery of content and concepts.

- Write a persuasive essay that could be read on a radio program; create a "pretend radio station" as a way to practice. Another suggestion is to use a digital voice recorder to record students reading their essays, and then upload them to a free Internet radio station or the school's Web site.

# 9-2 Supporting an Opinion with Facts

Students use this strategy to share and support their opinions in writing.

**Prerequisite:** 9-1 Persuasive Writing

## Before Class

- Make overhead transparencies and student copies of *Tools 9-2a* and *9-2b*.

- Have available 5" × 8" index cards and two colors of highlighters.

## During Class

1. Display *Tool 9-2a* and read the examples aloud to your students. Explain to your students that opinion writing

   - Is often very open-ended and less structured than other forms of expository writing;

   - Includes statements of personal belief about ideas, objects, events, food, and so on, or about situations encountered in life;

   - Is validated by knowledge of a subject, life experiences, likes, and dislikes.

2. Use this opportunity to teach or review the difference between facts and opinions by creating a simple two-column chart. Choose a topic and write a topic sentence at the top; write the word *facts* at the top of one column and the word *opinion* at the top of the other. Ask your students to help you fill in the two columns with information from the examples—always stopping to ask students to justify their choices. Later, when students write their own opinion paragraphs or reports, ask them to identify their facts and their opinions by highlighting them each in a different color.

3. Ask students to look for the topic sentences and the key/star ideas that explain or prove the topic, as well as the E's that provide additional evidence and examples to support the opinion.

**Tool 9-2a**

4. In a whole-group guided lesson, help students create an opinion paragraph using an informal outline and one of the topic sentence strategies found in Section 4. Remind students that it is always best to start by identifying the key/star ideas, and then adding the dashes and dots needed for elaboration. Use a prompt from the *Bonus Tool CD* or ask students for suggestions.

5. Writing, speaking, and listening to classmates are important ways to share opinions. Use this time to help students learn how to respect the opinions of others without necessarily agreeing with them.

## Writing a Critique

Like opinion paragraphs and reports, critiques give writers an opportunity to rely on personal observations, insights, and knowledge of a genre to pass judgment on architecture, plays, movies, art, music, video games, poetry, and so on.

1. Read and discuss the two examples of critiques on *Tool 9-2b*.

2. Practice writing critiques with students as a whole-class activity before asking them to work on their own.

*Tool 9-2b*

- Show students a picture, have them listen to a piece of music, read an article or other text, or watch a movie on a subject related to something they are studying.

- Give students questions (or help them create questions) to help them make judgments and form opinions. For example:
  ▶ Does the organization of the piece make sense?
  ▶ Is it trying to make a point, and does it succeed?
  ▶ How powerful are the graphics and illustrations?
  ▶ Does the piece surprise me or disappoint me?
  ▶ How does it compare to similar works?
  ▶ Is it better or worse than other pieces, and in what way?
  ▶ What are others saying or writing about this?
  ▶ Is it worth reading, seeing, buying, and so on?

- Tell students that it is important to elaborate on the personal impressions that they share—not to just make a statement about how they feel. They should support their judgments with references to the text or to their personal experiences.

3. Have students develop critiques while working in small groups, with partners, and individually. Critiques can be a fun way to encourage discussion.

4. Consider developing a classroom bulletin board about movies, books, articles, poems, songs, and plays. Make critiquing a regular class activity. Keep 5" × 8" index cards handy. On the card's back, students can write informal outlines and drafts for short paragraphs that critique movies, books, songs, artists, and so on. On the front, students write a polished version of their critiques. Display good critiques for all to enjoy, and submit them to the school newspaper for publication.

## 9-3 Writing to Compare or Contrast

Using this strategy, students write paragraphs or reports that compare or contrast two or more people, places, things, or ideas.

### Before Class

- Make overhead transparencies and student copies of *Tools 9-3a* through *9-3k*, as needed. There are two sets of Tools for prewriting—*Tools 9-3b*, *9-3c*, and *9-3d*; and *Tools 9-3e*, *9-3f*, and *9-3g*. Choose a set based on the needs of your class and on the number of items to be compared or contrasted (if more than two, use *Tools 9-3e*, *9-3f*, and *9-3g*). Eventually, you may wish to use both prewriting options, but present only one set at a time.

- Have available green, yellow, and red markers.

 *Bonus Tools 9-3-1* through *9-3-5* provide additional support.

### During Class

1. Explain to students that in school and on tests, *compare* almost always means explaining how subjects are alike and *contrast* means explaining how they are different. But also show students that *compare* can mean examining likenesses and differences. Have students read definitions of compare and contrast in their dictionaries or use *Bonus Tool 9-3-1*; discuss the definitions.

2. Tell students that when they write to compare or contrast, they will look for similarities or differences in people, places, things, or ideas and then select categories to demonstrate how they are alike or different.

3. Remind students of the Compare or Contrast Topic Sentence (**4-18 Topic Sentence Variety**). Explain that there are many terms and phrases to use for completing compare and contrast assignments. Provide examples of terms and phrases for comparing and contrasting. (The following are also on *Bonus Tool 9-3-1*.)

| | | | | | |
|---|---|---|---|---|---|
| alike | similar | similarities | compare | either | better |
| best | worse | in common | same | resemble | alike |
| contrast | differ | differences | different | variations | vary |
| varied | opposite | unlike | diverse | dissimilar | reminds me of |

4. Read aloud the examples on *Tool 9-3a*. (*Bonus Tool 9-3-2* provides additional examples.) Ask students to look for topic sentences, compare-or-contrast words, transitions, and other elements of expository writing.

*Tool 9-3a*

**Writing to Compare or Contrast**

**Example 1 (Compare):**
Presidential Candidates Alike

The two leading candidates and their two running mates in the 1996 presidential campaign had four things in common. First, all four men had experience in politics. Clinton was governor of Arkansas in 1978 and served four terms. Al Gore had a seat in Congress. He served for several years as a U.S. senator. Bob Dole served 34 years in Congress and 27 of them were in the Senate. Jack Kemp was elected to the U.S. House of Representatives and served from '71 to '89.

In addition, all four of these men were athletes and honor students in high school. Bill Clinton was a super student in high school, running for office in every club and organization he could find. Al Gore was a top student who played basketball and football. Bob Dole was a football, track, and basketball star. Jack Kemp became the first-string quarterback in high school and went on to a professional football star.

Third, these four men vowed to make the country better. Clinton and Gore wanted to improve health care and clean up the environment. Dole and Kemp wanted to cut taxes and get rid of the budget deficit.

Last, Clinton and Dole both had a strong desire to be president. Clinton wanted to be president since he was four. Dole ran for the presidency three times. Even though these men were in different political parties, they all had things in common.

**Example 2 (Contrast):**
Planet Mars versus Planet Venus

My parents are proof that men and women are from different planets. Take school, for instance. They have totally different opinions about what school success means. My mom believes that while grades are important, making friends and being a good school citizen is most important. She thinks getting involved in clubs and teams and having good friends gives kids vital life skills, like how to cooperate, negotiate, share, and support each other emotionally. "Getting along with others is what success in life is really about," she says. Across the galaxy in my dad. He agrees that people skills are important, but he doesn't think they will land you that high-paying job like good grades will. "Good grades are the passport to the good things in life," he says. He says good grades get you into a good college, which gets you a good job. Wow! It gets tiring traveling between these two distant planets."

5. Show students how each example is different and yet follows the same simple pattern (topic sentence, key/star ideas, elaboration, and conclusion) used in an informal outline. Color-code the examples using the Traffic Light colors.

6. Help students identify the categories of comparison used in each example on *Tool 9-3a*. Tell them that the key to success in compare-or-contrast writing is selecting the categories for comparison. Encourage them to select interesting and insightful categories when they write. The categories become the key/star ideas.

1. *Presidential Candidates Alike*
   ☆ *experience*
   ☆ *athletes and honor students*
   ☆ *want better country*
   ☆ *desire to be president*

2. *Planet Mars versus Planet Venus*
   ☆ *Mom*
   ☆ *Dad*

## Prewriting and Planning for Compare-and-Contrast Writing

1. Explain to your students that compare-and-contrast writing follows the same process as any other form of expository writing. The main difference is that they will spend time during prewriting to determine how the people, places, things, or ideas are similar or different and how they will categorize the elements of comparison.

2. Graphic organizers can help your students determine the categories and specifics of what they are comparing. Review *Tools 9-3b* and *9-3e* and choose a graphic organizer for your students to use. Only after students have developed some success with one format should you introduce them to the other. (Also consider using *Tool 1-28f*.)

3. Explain to your students that the goal before they begin to write is to determine the categories for comparing or contrasting, so that the finished paragraph will be well organized.

   • For the graphic organizer on *Tool 9-3b*, tell your students that it can be used to list descriptions of two items and possible categories for comparison. Explain that as they use the Tool, they will brainstorm several possible categories and then select the ones that will work best, using only those as they write.

   • Explain that the graphic organizer on *Tool 9-3e* can be used for *two or more* items or categories for comparison. The grid shown is for describing two items, but extra columns can be added to the center of the Tool by drawing additional "Describe!" areas as needed. (See *Bonus Tools 9-3-3, 9-3-4,* and *9-3-5* for a third graphic organizer option.)

   • Display and read through the examples on *Tool 9-3c* or *Tool 9-3f* as well as the finished paragraphs on *Tool 9-3d* or *Tool 9-3g*, depending on the graphic organizer you are demonstrating.

4. Use *Tools 9-3b* or *9-3e* and their matching examples to help students visualize and think about how things compare or contrast, and to demonstrate how the graphic organizer will help them develop an informal outline and then a paragraph. Remind students they still need the planning stage (informal outlining) before writing their paragraphs.

5. Tell students that it is best in a single paragraph to show either how things are alike or how they are different. In a single stand-alone paragraph, they should focus on one direction only.

6. Model using the graphic organizer you have selected in a whole-group guided lesson and give students opportunities to work in groups before asking them to work on their own. Taking students slowly—step by step—through the process will help them learn how to complete compare-or-contrast assignments on their own.

7. Use *Tools 9-3b* and *9-3e* across content areas for compare-and-contrast writing.

## Writing Paragraphs that Compare or Contrast

1. To give students the support they need to write paragraphs that compare or contrast, review **4-13 Practice Guides for Writing Accordion Paragraphs**. Introduce the following process through whole-group instruction, then have students practice in small groups or pairs before they work independently.

2. Select one student's completed prewriting plan from *Tool 9-3b* or *Tool 9-3e*, or create a new one as a class to compare or contrast a topic that is familiar to everyone. Remind students that, for now, the writing will focus on either similarities or differences, but not both.

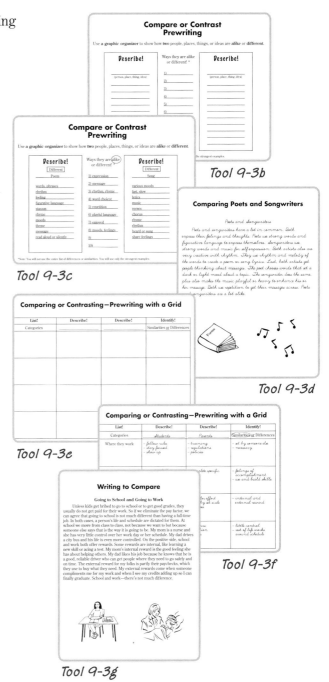

Tool 9-3b

Tool 9-3c

Tool 9-3d

Tool 9-3e

Tool 9-3f

Tool 9-3g

3. Write out a topic sentence, convert the categories into key/star ideas, and use the "Describe!" notes to provide evidence and elaboration—the E's. Draft a concluding sentence. Explain that, like Accordion Paragraphs, compare-or-contrast paragraphs can accommodate various lengths by modifying the number of key/star ideas and E's they use. (Consider using the practice guides for writing Accordion Paragraphs found on *Tools 4-13a* and *4-13b*.)

## Both Comparing and Contrasting in One Writing Assignment

1. Explain to your students that when they are asked to compare *and* contrast in one assignment, they generally will want to write a multiparagraph report. Tell them to use a four-paragraph format, as shown on *Tools 9-3h, 9-3i,* and *9-3j*.

2. Explain that they will use *Tool 9-3b* or *Tool 9-3e* to develop their thoughts during prewriting. Display *Tool 9-3i* and discuss the informal outline for the four short paragraphs that explain how the subjects (grandmother and me) are alike and different. Discuss the following:

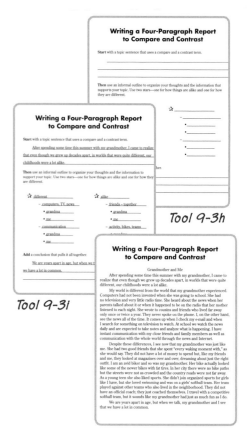

Tool 9-3h

Tool 9-3i

Tool 9-3j

**Paragraph 1**
*Introduction*—be concise; can be a one-sentence introduction; will include both a **compare** and a **contrast** word in the topic sentence, as shown in the following examples:

> *My cousin's new bicycle and my bicycle look **similar**, but they have two important **differences**.*

> *Spaghetti and lasagna may look **different**, but when you eat them, they really taste a lot **alike**.*

**Paragraphs 2 and 3**
*Paragraphs that show the similarities and the differences*—place the paragraphs in the same order that the compare-and-contrast words are placed; be specific and give details in each.

**Paragraph 4**
*Conclusion*—reinforce the topic sentence; give the reader a reason to remember the comparison.

3. Display and read the final product on *Tool 9-3j*.

4. Using *Tool 9-3h*, develop a report in a whole-group guided lesson using content from subjects like science, history, art, and math. Have students plan and write additional reports in pairs or small groups before they practice independently.

## Making an Analogy

*Tool 9-3k*

1. Explain to your class that an analogy describes a likeness between two things that might otherwise be different; it compares two things that ordinarily might not be compared but that share a common similarity, difference, or characteristic. For example, wheels on a car are like feet on a person: they help them to move.

2. Use *Tool 9-3k* to introduce analogies. Explain that when planning to write analogies, students can use an informal outline, just as they would when planning to write compare or contrast paragraphs and reports. However, to write an analogy, the writer makes inferences about how the two things being compared are alike. The ways they are alike become the categories for the comparison and key/star ideas in the informal outline.

3. Read both examples on *Tool 9-3k* with your students. Have students underline (or highlight in green, using the Traffic Light colors) the topic sentences that state the comparison. Point out to students that both topic sentences use the same phrase: "is like." Students will do the same when they write analogies.

4. Then show students the categories that were used for comparison. Have them underline (or highlight in yellow, using the Traffic Light colors) the words that note the categories.

| **Example 1:** | **Example 2:** |
| --- | --- |
| ☆ a spreading web | ☆ words that bring a picture to life |
| ☆ possible dangers | |
| ☆ overuse sucks out life | ☆ images that are hard to forget |

5. Finally, model the steps in writing an analogy using a prompt from the *Bonus Tool CD* or a prompt that you have selected or created.

6. Keep the analogies simple; two comparisons (key/star ideas) work well when students are first learning to write analogies.

7. Create analogies with the whole class frequently; help students with their thinking; encourage them to stretch their imaginations; celebrate their efforts!

## 9-4 Creating Biographical and Autobiographical Sketches

A biographical sketch tells the story of one person's life. Information is usually presented in chronological order explaining major events, characteristics, and other people's viewpoints of the person.

**Prerequisites:** 4-7 Planning with an Informal Outline and 5-22 Moving from a Paragraph to an Essay or Report

### Before Class

Make overhead transparencies and student copies of *Tools 9-4a* and *9-4b*.

### During Class

1. Inform or remind students that *biography* means writing about another person's life, and *autobiography* means writing about one's own life. Explain to students that biographies are usually written about real people, but can be written about story and movie characters, as well. (These might also be called character sketches.) Let them know that biographies can be a paragraph, an essay, a report, or even a book.

2. Read or ask for student volunteers to read the examples on *Tool 9-4a* aloud. As you read, stop and ask students to point out facts and details that have been included in each biographical sketch.

3. Show students how to plan a biographical sketch with an informal outline. Explain that it often follows a chronological order or the sequence of events, or it can sketch the important qualities of a person's life. Point out the key/star ideas in each of the examples on *Tool 9-4a*.

**Writing a Biographical Sketch**

**Example 1:**

Ella Fitzgerald

To make it in the music business you need to have a little luck, meet the right people, and of course, have talent. Ella Fitzgerald had it all. Born in 1917, she was a shy and insecure girl. At the age of 17 she found herself singing in front of a tough crowd on amateur night at the Apollo. The crowd's cheers proved she was headed for stardom. At first, she sang in New York night clubs with a band, working her way up to play at Harlem's famous Savoy Ballroom. Shortly after getting her first gig she made her first album. Ella's unique art form included scat singing, a way of using the voice to make the sounds of instruments, and put Ella Fitzgerald in the record books. Her career really took off in 1938, when she did a scat version of "A Tisket A Tasket." That song hit number one and stayed there for 17 straight weeks. Ella continued to travel and tour, but this time across the nation. A popular Hollywood club hired her after hearing that Marilyn Monroe said she would pay for a table up front for every one of Ella's performances. Such fame launched her onto the television screen and radio shows. By the time she died in 1996, Ella had made over 200 albums and received numerous awards including a National Medal of Arts presented by Ronald Reagan. Ella had everything it takes, and more, to become a famous musician.

**Example 2:**

Laurens, a Modern-Day Scientist

A family friend of ours from Holland has taught me a lot about the atmosphere and about success. Laurens is an atmospheric scientist. To become a scientist, he had to study very hard. In Holland, kids only get to go to the best high schools if they perform well. Then, only the best of the best are chosen to go on to college and have the government pay for it. Laurens is very smart, but he is also a hard worker. He went as far as he could in the Dutch education system and got his PhD. Most of his life work has been creating a computer model that shows how actions we take on earth affect our atmosphere. What is really great about what he does is that he doesn't look at just one piece of the puzzle, like carbon monoxide. Instead, he looks at everything that affects our environment, including many types of pollutants, mining, drilling, and cutting down trees in the rain forest. Laurens has been working on his model for almost 20 years. He never gives up. I think he has a chance of really making a difference in helping the environment and changing the way we humans treat it. I have learned a lot from Laurens about life and the environment.

*Tool 9-4a*

| Example 1 | Example 2 |
|---|---|
| *Ella Fitzgerald* | *Laurens* |
| ☆ *young girl at the Apollo* | ☆ *scientist* |
| ☆ *first album* | ☆ *growing up in Holland* |
| ☆ *career takes off* | ☆ *creating a computer model* |
| ☆ *television* | ☆ *working for 20 years* |
| ☆ *special honors* | |

4. Read the autobiographies on *Tool 9-4b* aloud and discuss. Point out that autobiographies are always written in the first person, using pronouns such as "I," "my," or "our."

5. Create a biographical sketch as a whole class. Select a person or character the class has studied. Pick one or two important elements in the life of the person or character to write about. Show students how to be objective and accurate when telling this person's life story.

**Tool 9-4b**

## Additional Ideas

- Use **1-17 Easy Two-Column Notes** or **1-18 One Idea per Paragraph Note Taking** when students do research for a biographical sketch.

- Make a class chart labeled "Terms for a Biographical Sketch." Add words like *courageous, determined, intelligent, foolish, infamous, creative, kind, clever,* and so on.
    - ▶ These words (and others that you and your students find) will build thinking skills when students write biographical sketches. Instead of listing key/star ideas that are obvious and simply factual, students will select terms that tell more about the person's character.
    - ▶ Instead of limiting their description of a person to a label such as a president, scientist, astronaut, or explorer, students learn to think beyond the obvious, make inferences, and form opinions: president, for example, can be replaced with *strong leader, world leader, unpopular leader,* or *responsible leader.*
    - ▶ Display the chart, add new words to it often, and encourage students to use it.

## 9-5 Responding to Literature

Students will use this strategy to write well thought-out and organized responses to literature they have read or heard, and to support their judgments with examples and details from the text or from their own personal knowledge or experience.

**Prerequisite:** 1-30 Four-Step Summary Paragraphs

## Before Class

- Make overhead transparencies and student copies of *Tools 9-5a* through *9-5h.*
- Have available green, yellow, and red markers.
- ⊙ *Bonus Tools 9-5-1* through *9-5-5* provide additional support.

## During Class

1. Inform your students that the process used for writing a response to literature is the same used for any other type of expository writing. Direct them to follow the same writing process found in Section 4 or Section 5.

2. Explain to your students that *response to literature* is an umbrella term referring to their reaction to what they have read. Responding to literature refers to showing their understanding, insights, and judgments about what they read. These insights relate to the theme of the literature, such as courage, strength, adversity, determination, growing up, and so on, through a discussion of elements such as content, clarity, impact, or style.

3. Tell your students that when they write a response to literature, they will present the theme or topic and a few strong key/star ideas that support the theme or topic in the topic sentence and then elaborate with specific text-based examples and/or quotes. Remind students of strategies from "Responding to the Text," Section 1.

4. Introduce your students to responding to literature using the examples on *Tools 9-5a* and *9-5b*. Point out that a response to literature can be a single paragraph, as in the first example on *Tool 9-5a*, or a multiparagraph essay, as in the second example. Explain that the length of the response will depend on the teacher's directions or a test prompt and on how much time students have to write.

5. After reading *Tools 9-5a* and *9-5b* as a group, show students that all of the responses have strong, focused topic sentences. Highlight the topic sentences in green (using the Traffic Light colors).

*Tool 9-5a*

*Tool 9-5b*

- Example 1: *A Long Way from Chicago* is a hilarious book written by Richard Peck.

- Example 2: McCourt tells his life story in this stunning memoir about living in severe poverty in Ireland.

- Example 3: "The Dinner Party" by Mona Garner is very short and yet it packs a powerful punch.

- Example 4: "Those Three Wishes" illustrates the consequences of the misuse of personal power.

6. Next, point out on *Tools 9-5a* and *9-5b* the examples where the writers refer directly to specific details and facts. These text-based examples can be either key/star ideas or elaboration (E's).

7. A response to literature sometimes includes connections to personal experiences. They may be made throughout the essay or in the final paragraph. When students make personal connections, they should

   - Make the connection specific;
   - Keep the connections short with clear, concise writing—in other words, limit the detail;
   - Use an example only once;
   - Stay on topic.

8. Display and read *Tool 9-5c* with your students. Have them mark, highlight, and make notes as you explain and answer questions.

9. Display *Tool 9-5d* and explain that writing a response to literature uses the same writing process as writing an expository paragraph or essay. Discuss how the planning guide on *Tool 9-5d* is used just like an informal outline, with key/star ideas and specific examples from the text that prove the topic sentence.

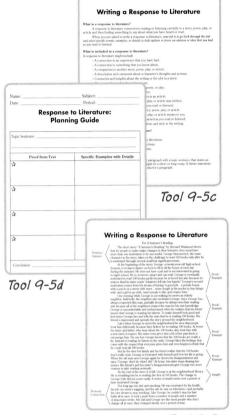

*Tool 9-5c*

*Tool 9-5d*

*Tool 9-5e*

**Note:** Students will need lots of guided practice as they learn to support their positions with examples from the text.

10. Read the example on *Tool 9-5e*. With help from students, identify the key/star ideas used to support the topic and highlight them in yellow (for the Traffic Light colors).

   **Topic** = *motivation comes in small steps*

   ☆ *boredom, sister's reading, dream*

   ☆ *elderly neighbor*

   ☆ *people notice*

   ☆ *disappointment of the neighbor*

   ☆ *library scene*

   ☆ *my dad*

11. Have students point out the place that shows personal connections and personal insights. Ask them to evaluate the effectiveness of the response. Since these are examples (the E's) to support the key/star ideas, highlight them in red. Remind students that personal connections can be placed anywhere in the essay.

12. With your students, develop a response to literature based on a book that the class has read or that everyone is familiar with.

    • Review the IVF topic sentence with your students (**1-30 Four-Step Summary Paragraphs**). It works best for writing responses. The theme or topic should be included and emphasized in the third part of the sentence.

| The story *A Summer's Reading* by Bernard Malamud | shows | that for people to make major changes in their behavior, they must have more than one motivation to be successful. |
|---|---|---|

    • Using *Tool 9-5d*, model creating an informal outline for a response. Have students make copies of the Tool. Uses dashes and dots for the elaboration.

    • After completing the informal outline, develop a response to a text. Guide students as they write their topic sentences.

13. Give your students many chances to write short and extended responses to literature using the form on *Tool 9-5d*. As often as appropriate, have them write paragraphs or multiparagraph essays based on their outlines.

**Note:** Use *Tool 9-7f*, for a list of feeling words and *Tools 2-11c* and *2-11d* for a list of abstract nouns to help students master the concept of theme. Abstract nouns like *honesty*, *courage*, and *determination* can become a part of the students' topic sentences for a response to literature.

### Using Practice Cards and Prompts to Initiate Responses to Literature

Students need direct instruction and modeling as they learn to write responses independently. Students might want to say something about what they have read, but do not always have the language to start a response. Using cards and prompts can help them experiment with and learn concepts that are often used for responses. Make copies of *Bonus Tools 9-5-1* through *9-5-5*. Cut cards apart and use the prompts on them for practice, discussion, and exam rehearsal. Add cards with your own prompts to meet your own response goals and expectations.

## Writing a Book Report

**1.** Use *Tools 9-5f* and *9-5g* to introduce the differences between a book report written on nonfiction and fiction. Note that in a standard book report, students are expected to reflect on and write about:

| Nonfiction | Fiction |
|---|---|
| • content | • character |
| • usefulness | • setting |
| • accuracy | • plot (events) |
| • interest | • conflict (problem) |
| • relevance | • theme |
| • author's style | • author's style |

**2.** Read the two examples with your class and discuss both reports using questions such as:

- What is the topic sentence in each report?

- What is the goal or purpose for each report?

- How are the reports organized?

- How can you tell that the writer of the report actually read the book?

- How would you imitate either of the reports? What strategies would you use?

**3.** Book reports are responses to literature, written in many different forms and for different purposes.

- Have students use **9-7 RAFTS: Writing from a Different Point of View** when you want them to use their imaginations and take the role of a character, object, famous person, and so on in their reports. For example, students might tell about a book of fiction from the author's point of view or from the main character's point of view. Or, they might take the point of view of an animal or an animal trainer if they were reporting on a nonfiction book about a specific animal.

- See **9-1 Persuasive Writing** in this section if you want students to write a book report that is meant to convince the reader to share the opinion of the writer.

- See **9-3 Writing to Compare or Contrast** if you want students to compare a book to its movie version or another book.

- See **9-2 Supporting an Opinion With Facts** if you want students to share personal opinions about and reactions to a book, its character(s), content, topic, or theme.

*Tool 9-5f*

*Tool 9-5g*

- See **1-30 Four-Step Summary Paragraphs** if you want students to stick to the facts and demonstrate their comprehension of the text.

- Use activities from **9-8 Descriptive Writing** (narrative description) or **6-8 Sequencing Events** for assessments or reports that demonstrate comprehension of the *beginning, middle,* and *end* of a story.

## Oral Book Reports with Posters

Tool 9-5h

1. Show *Tool 9-5h* and explain that it is important for students to consider the following when they present their reports:

   - Introduction—Includes a topic sentence and a brief preview of the key/star ideas they will be covering.

   - Informal outlines—Push students to be specific and to select examples to support their topic sentences and key/star ideas; also push them to think critically and creatively and show analysis of what they read.

   - Illustrations—Each represents a key/star idea and reinforces the whole plan.

2. Show your students how to use the poster on *Tool 9-5h* by making a short speech based on *The Adventures of Tom Sawyer.*

3. Have students create their own posters in preparation for making a speech. Tell them to write their introduction on the front side of the poster. The introduction should include a topic sentence. Their lettering should be neat and large enough to be seen from a distance.

4. Have them add an informal outline to the back of their posters. Remind them to include transitions that will help them move from one key/star idea to the next and to use only words and phrases in the outline rather than to write out complete sentences so that they will be less likely to read the report verbatim.

5. Finally, have them add to the front of their posters the drawings, pictures, or illustrations that reflect the key/star ideas. Explain that pictures will be a great visual aid for the audience and a memory aid for them. They might also add a border that reinforces the topic.

6. Explain that even though they will have the poster to refer to, they should memorize the introduction and conclusion. That way, they can concentrate on adding enthusiasm to their presentation and sharing information the audience will remember.

7. Model and have students practice holding the poster where they can see their outlines. Tell them that if they plan to read lines from the book itself as a part of a report, they should add the page numbers to the outline. Demonstrate how they can then set the poster down, read from the book, and then return to the poster.

8. Encourage your students to keep their reports short but interesting by being specific and sharing the examples they included on their outline. Remind them that they won't be retelling the book but will share insights and reactions.

9. Have students practice making book reports often. Be sure to give them support, encouragement, and feedback.

## 9-6 Writing to Show Cause and Effect or Problem and Solution

Students can use this strategy to show cause and effect or problem and solution.

### Before Class

Make overhead transparencies and student copies of *Tools 9-6a, 9-6b,* and *9-6c.*

### During Class

**Cause and Effect**

1. Explain to your students that cause-and-effect writing emphasizes the connection between a topic (cause) and the results or impact this topic has on someone or something else. The goal for cause-and-effect writing is to encourage the reader to think about something that happens and its effect on specific people or the world at large.

2. Read the examples on *Tool 9-6a* with your class. Make a two-column chart on the board (or use *Tool 1-17b*). Above the left column, write the word *cause*. Above the right column, write the word *effect*. Reread Example 1. In the left column list the cause—the topic of the paragraph—and on the right list all of the effects. Ask students to explain the cause and the effects in their own words. (Also consider using *Tool 1-28g*.)

**Writing to Show Cause and Effect**

Example 1:

Too Much Violence on Television

Most people enjoy television, but unfortunately, many shows are filled with violence. Watching too much violence on television can have many negative effects. One negative effect is that watching a lot of violence has been shown to desensitize people to violent acts. When murder and death are seen on a regular basis, it gives a person a sense that life isn't valuable. One other way it desensitizes the viewer is that they don't see the perpetrators of violence receiving appropriate consequences. In one study, 73 percent of all violent acts on television had no consequences. Without consequences, viewers can develop the idea that they can solve their problems with violence, without fear of the consequences. Another negative effect of watching too much violence is that it gives the viewer a misconceived notion of the real world. Viewers develop a sense that the world is a violent place and they no longer feel safe. They aren't able to get a sense of where the world of make-believe ends and the real world begins. An additional effect of watching too much violence on television is that it can increase aggression in its viewers. Studies have shown that children and young adults who have spent many hours watching violence on television have increased episodes of hitting, impatience, and disobedience. All in all, the effects of watching too much television, especially shows that include a lot of violence, are quite negative.

Example 2:

Study Tips

Even when you think you know all the answers on a test, using study strategies ensures that you are truly ready for the test. Making index cards with the questions and the answers is helpful because it makes you think out clear, concise answers to possible test questions. Another study strategy that works is typing up your notes. Rewriting or retyping your notes is much more effective than simply reading them over. The strategy I find most helpful is to go over all the questions at the end of the chapter and write out the answers. Since tests are weighted more than regular assignments, it is important that you do well on them; using study strategies is the surest way to do well.

*Tool 9-6a*

| Cause | Effect |
|---|---|
| *Too much television* | - *desensitize people* |
| | - *violence* |
| | - *wrong notion of the world* |
| | - *increased aggression* |

3. Working in pairs or individually, have your students reread and make a cause and effect chart for Example 2. Discuss their findings.

4. Explain to students that when they write to show cause and effect, they will need to identify a cause—a problem or circumstance. This will become the topic sentence in the paragraph or report. The Occasion/Position Topic Sentence **4-18 Topic Sentence Variety** works well for writing that shows cause and effect.

> *If you often forget to brush your teeth, you may discover some serious problems when you visit the dentist's office.*

5. With your students, choose a topic that includes a cause and effect and develop it into a topic sentence. (See the *Bonus Tools CD* for ideas or develop one of your own.) For example, the door was left open (cause). My dog ran away (effect).

6. With your students, develop key/star ideas for an informal outline as they create a plan for writing and add evidence, examples, and statistics to support the claimed effects. Add notes for the conclusion by restating the cause and its effect(s). Reinforce the importance of making a plan with an informal outline to organize ideas and save time.

7. Develop a paragraph or report from the informal outline. Give students several opportunities to practice and perfect this skill.

*Tool 9-6b*

*Tool 9-6c*

## Problem and Solution

- Explain to your students that planning for and writing about problems and their solutions is much like writing to show cause and effect. (Consider using *Tool 1-28h*.)

- Informal outlines make this kind of writing easy and successful. The problem (the topic or subject) is stated in the topic sentence. The *And, But, So,* and *Or* Topic Sentence strategy (**4-18 Topic Sentence Variety**) works well for problem-and-solution writing assignments.

> *Having a friend hurt your feelings is never fun, but there are some good ways to get over those hurt feelings quickly.*
>
> *Last summer my brother broke our aunt's favorite vase, but he found a good way to make things right and solve the problem.*

- Explain to students that there are two ways to write about a problem and a solution.

  1. Present a problem and offer a solution of your own.

  2. Describe a problem and explain how someone else solved the problem.

- Read the examples on *Tools 9-6b* and *9-6c*. As you read aloud, ask students to help you identify the topic sentence, the key/star ideas, elaboration, and the conclusion.

- Select a topic or use a prompt from the *Bonus Tools CD* to model an informal outline for problem-and-solution writing.

- Give students several opportunities to perfect their skills at showing a problem and solution.

## 9-7  RAFTS: Writing from a Different Point of View

Students using this strategy write from the perspective of another person, a character in a book, an animal, or almost anything. This strategy not only supports creativity but can also be used in content-area classes to see information from new perspectives.

### Before Class

- Make overhead transparencies and student copies of *Tools 9-7a* through *9-7f*.

- *Bonus Tools 9-7-1* through *9-7-5* provide additional examples and support.

### During Class

1. Explain to your class that writing from a different role, or perspective, means that instead of writing as themselves, they will write as if they are someone else—a character in a book, an animal, a plant, a rock, or almost anything. In other words, they choose a *role*. They decide who or what they will be as they write.

2. Writing from another point of view can be a powerful way to make a statement and grab a reader's attention. Explain that using different roles often makes it easier and more fun to read and learn new information.

3. Begin by sharing the examples on *Tool 9-7a*. Explain to students that in the first example, the writer is pretending to be a soldier writing to another soldier. In the second example, the author pretends to be a girl who has moved into the town where Tom Sawyer lives. Explain that, in both cases, the writers are imagining they are someone or something else.

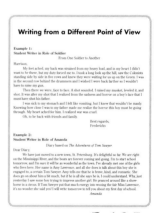

*Tool 9-7a*

4. Review *Tool 9-7b* with your students and provide the following information to help them understand each step. Help students keep in mind their purpose—what they want the reader to do or to feel—so they have a sense of direction while they write.

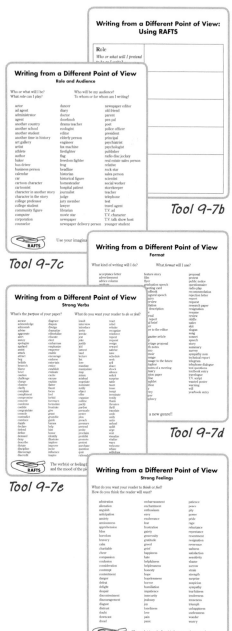

Tool 9-7b

Tool 9-7c

Tool 9-7d

Tool 9-7e

Tool 9-7f

- **Role**—Who or what will they pretend to be as they write? Emphasize that, no matter what perspective they use, they must use it throughout the piece.

- **Audience**—To whom or for whom will they write? Help students select an audience that fits the purpose of their writing.

- **Format**—Pick a format that will fit their purpose and audience. Explain that they could write a poem, letter, speech, play, advertisement, dialogue, cartoon, e-mail, or even a joke.

- **Topic**—What, specifically, will they write about? One good way to narrow the topic is to write their purpose in a complete sentence. This will help them organize and focus their writing.

- **Strong verb or feeling**—What do they want the reader to do, or how should the reader feel? Choose a strong verb or feeling to show the tone, mood, and voice for the writing. The verb or feeling word does not need to show up in the actual text, but may serve just to give the writer a sense of direction as he or she writes.

5. Display *Tools 9-7c* through *9-7f* to provide students with starter ideas for considering the role, audience, format, topic, and strong verb or feeling (RAFTS) they want to write about.

6. With students in a whole-class guided lesson, use *Tool 9-7b* to create a plan for writing from a different point of view following the RAFTS approach. Use content from subject areas that students are studying, such as science, math, or history. Push students to use their imaginations!

7. Have students keep RAFTS forms as a packet to use throughout the year. Use this strategy frequently in all subject areas.

## Additional Ideas

- Select books, advertisements, editorials, articles, and songs that are written from different roles. Have students identify the role, audience, format, topic, and strong verb/feeling for the story.

- Use the RAFTS form on *Tool 9-7b* as part of a class discussion after reading a story or a chapter in a book. Have students brainstorm possible RAFTS even when they lack time to write the developed piece. The thinking that goes into creating RAFTS makes this activity worthwhile.

- Look for RAFTS assignments (i.e., writing from a different role) in math, science, and social studies textbooks. Work with students to complete these assignments. Ask students why the textbook authors give these kinds of assignments.

- Use *Bonus Tools 9-7-1* through *9-7-5* for additional examples and ideas for RAFTS.

## 9-8 Descriptive Writing

Students use this strategy to write descriptions in four different ways.

### Before Class

Make overhead transparencies and student copies of *Tools 9-8a* through *9-8e*.

### During Class

1. Explain to your class that descriptive writing takes many forms. Description is used in narrative writing as well as in factual, specific, and technical writing. It can be done in a number of different ways:

    - **Imaginative description**—writing that lets readers use their imaginations; feels and sounds a bit like poetry; uses figurative language; appeals to the senses

    - **Factual description**—writing that shares facts and not opinions; objects and processes are described clearly and orderly with words that fit the topic; includes content vocabulary that fits the object, place, creature, and so on

    - **Narrative description**—writing that describes a sequence of events; uses action verbs and descriptive phrases to paint a scene and share emotions; seems like a short movie

    - **Realistic description**—tells about one quick event or situation that really happened; describes things as they really were or as they happened so others can understand; uses colorful but specific language

2. Inform your students that descriptive writing helps readers learn and understand more about topics. With all four forms of description, the writer creates sentences that help the reader sense, feel, and understand what the writer knows about the topic.

3. Tell them that all four forms of descriptive writing can be serious or unserious. The voice, tone, and mood of each piece change to match the purpose and audience for the writing. Also explain that a description's length depends on the amount of elaboration needed and the complexity of what it describes.

4. Using *Tool 9-8a*, read and discuss the definitions for imaginative and factual descriptions with your students and show what an informal outline would look like for those two forms of descriptive paragraphs on clouds.

5. Display *Tool 9-8b*. Read and discuss the definitions for narrative and realistic descriptions with your students and review the informal outlines. Have students place their copies of both Tools on their desks. Discuss how the informal outlines are different and similar.

6. Using *Tools 9-8d* and *9-8e*, read the paragraphs that go with each informal outline on *Tools 9-8a* and *9-8b*. Highlight the paragraphs using the Traffic Light colors to make it easy for students to see how the organization in the informal outlines was used in the paragraphs. Discuss the similarities and differences between the paragraphs.

7. Your goal is to teach students that there are different ways to write a descriptive paragraph, depending on its purpose. One way to do this is by having students write descriptions of the same thing in each of the four forms.

8. Select a general topic that students know (soup, a test, a movie, a pet, a touchdown). Have students work as a whole class or in small groups to develop informal outlines for descriptions written in each of the four styles. They can develop their outlines on copies of *Tool 9-8c* or on notebook paper.

9. Remind your students that even though *Tool 9-8c* has space for only two key/star ideas, they may use two, three, four, or even five key/star ideas. The number of key/star ideas is determined by what they are trying to describe, not by the Tool.

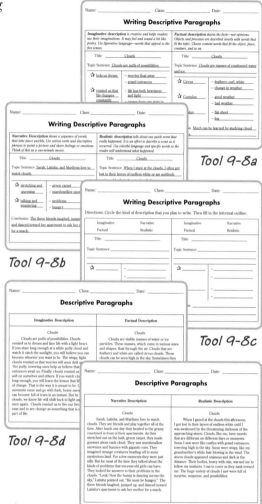

*Tool 9-8a*

*Tool 9-8b*

*Tool 9-8c*

*Tool 9-8d*

*Tool 9-8e*

> *Soup*
>
> *Imaginative*—describing soup by focusing on the five senses
>
> *Factual*—describing contents, appearance, and purpose
>
> *Narrative*—three friends select, carry, and slurp soup during lunch at school
>
> *Realistic*—making and eating soup with your family for lunch at home on a cold rainy day

10. Have students, alone or in pairs, write the paragraphs using the outlines that the class created.

11. Explain that in each paragraph, they should focus on only one form. Throughout the year, remind students to consider what type of description they will use in their writing.

12. Have students keep *Tools 9-8a* through *9-8c* for reference throughout the year. Use *Tool 9-8c* frequently for descriptive-writing practice.

## 9-9 Using Writing Frames

Students can use this strategy often to support their progress during scaffolded writing instruction and for a number of other purposes.

As their name implies, writing frames provide a ready-made *frame* for students to follow—a very bare frame of a paragraph that already has in place a title, most of a strong topic sentence, and good transitions. The key/star ideas and examples that support the topic sentence are left blank for the students to complete with their own thoughts and words. The best framed paragraphs cause students to think about the content and make good word choices.

### Before Class

- Make an overhead transparency and student copies of *Tool 9-9a* and/or develop your own framed paragraphs and reports to meet the needs of your students.

⊙ *Bonus Tools 9-9-1* through *9-9-6* provide additional support.

## During Class

1. Framed sentences, paragraphs and reports can be used for a variety of activities and in any content area. When presenting a writing frame to your students, explain the purpose for using the frame.

2. Using *Tool 9-9a*, review the frame at the top and then show students what it would look like after being filled in. Answer any questions they might have.

3. Use writing frames throughout the year. Monitor student work and provide timely feedback. Remember that writing frames are flexible, like all *Step Up to Writing* strategies. Make changes and help students make changes as needed. If you use the frame as a scaffold for paragraph or report writing, support students as they move to the next stage (writing good, formal copies on notebook paper).

4. Develop writing frames to support the acquisition of information in content-area classes and to improve writing skills. Develop frames like the following or like those contained on *Bonus Tools 9-9-1* through *9-9-6*. Provide frames to students by writing them on the board, chart paper, or a transparency. Students can then copy and complete them on notebook paper.

**Framed Paragraph Examples**

Example for a how-to paragraph:

Title _____

Learning how to _____ is an important skill. You can learn this skill in ___ steps. First, _____ The reason you do this is because _____ Second, you must _____ This is important because _____ Next, _____ [Add other steps here, if needed.] As a final step _____ This will ensure that _____ Now that you know how to _____, you will be able to do it more easily if such a need arises.

Rescue Breathing

Learning how to *perform rescue breathing or mouth-to-mouth resuscitation on someone who has choked or nearly drowned* is an important skill. You can carry out this skill in *four* steps. First . . .

*Tool 9-9a*

---

*Physical Education*

*Climbing Skills*

During P.E. class this week, my classmates and I practiced many climbing skills on our school's rope course. One of the easiest skills was _____. Another skill _____. The most important skill _____.

---

**Note:** Bonus Tools in this strategy are, in general, for teacher use, not as handouts for students.

## Additional Ideas

- Writing frames can also be used for
  ▸ Sentence writing—see *Bonus Tools 9-9-4* and *9-9-5*;
  ▸ Respond to films and videos—see *Bonus Tool 9-9-6*;
  ▸ Explain a math process—see *Tool 9-12g*;
  ▸ Other content areas—see *Bonus Tools 9-9-1*, *9-9-2*, and *9-9-3*.

- Create framed paragraphs by
  - ▸ Selecting a title;
  - ▸ Writing a topic sentence;
  - ▸ Using transitions to start key/star ideas sentences that support the topic sentence;
  - ▸ Leaving space for students to complete key/star idea sentences and add elaboration;
  - ▸ Framing a conclusion sentence that will help students stay focused.
- Writing frames can be a good addition to teaching plans left for substitute teachers.
- Simple writing frames can help English language learners with fluency.

**Note:** Writing frames should support instruction but should not be the primary tool used to teach skills or strategies.

# 9-10 Writing Letters

Students can use this strategy to write informal and business letters, e-mails, and messages.

## Before Class

- Make overhead transparencies and student copies of *Tools 9-10a* through *9-10h* as appropriate.
- ◉ *Bonus Tools 9-10-1, 9-10-2,* and *9-10-3* provide additional support and examples.

## During Class
### Writing Informal Letters

1. Explain to your class that letters can be a formal or informal way to communicate with a person or organization. They can make inquiries, announce events, thank people, and share news. Tell students that informal letters are sometimes called personal letters or friendly letters.

2. Display *Tool 9-10a* and point out the terms used for the parts of an informal letter. Explain to students that informal letters have six parts: return address, date, salutation (greeting), body, complimentary close, and signature line. Point out the punctuation after the salutation and close.

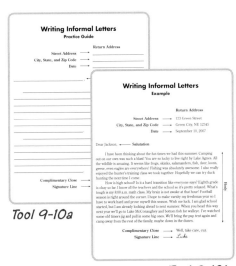

*Tool 9-10a*

*Tool 9-10b*

3. Acknowledge that when writing to very close friends or family members, the header (location and date) may not be required. But emphasize that use of a header is generally the correct format. They should master it to help deal with state assessments and job applications.

4. Read *Tool 9-10b* with your students. Have them mark each of the six parts as you point them out and explain their purposes. Review the punctuation used for the city, state, and the date.

5. Using a transparency of *Tool 9-10a*, develop an informal letter to someone known to your class. Then have students write their own informal letters. Provide them guidance and feedback as needed. Students can write letters to family members, friends, or characters from books.

## Writing Business Letters

1. Display *Tool 9-10c* and point out the terms used for the parts of a business (formal) letter. Explain how business letters are different from informal letters in that they have seven parts: sender's full name and address; date; recipient's name and title, company name and address (inside address); greeting; body; complimentary close; signature line.

2. Read *Tool 9-10d* with your students. Have them mark each of the seven parts as you point them out and explain their purpose. Remind your students of the punctuation used for the city and state and the date. (For additional example letters, see *Bonus Tools 9-10-1, 9-10-2,* and *9-10-3.*)

3. Point out that the punctuation for a business letter's salutation is different from that used in informal letters. Also, point out that in a business letter, the date, inside address, and closing are all on the left side, but in informal letters, they are on the right.

4. Using a transparency of *Tool 9-10c*, develop a business letter to someone associated with something your class has recently studied. Then have students write their own business letter. Provide them guidance and feedback as needed. Students can write letters to political figures, heads of companies, or members of the school system.

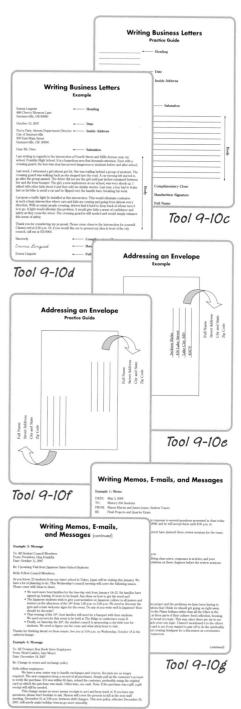

Tool 9-10c

Tool 9-10d

Tool 9-10e

Tool 9-10f

Tool 9-10g

Tool 9-10h

5. Explain to students that in formal or business letters, it is sometimes appropriate to quickly get to the point about why you are writing, keeping the information brief. The recipients usually are busy people and want to read letters quickly. Explain that informal letters to friends, pen pals, and family can be about any topic. Discuss with students reasons why people might write informal letters.

6. In a small- or whole-group guided lesson, have students use the blank letter form on *Tool 9-10c* and the example on *Tool 9-10d* as guides. The more students see and work with letter formats, the more comfortable they will become with letters' terminology and punctuation.

## Persuasive Letters

One of the purposes for writing informal or business letters is to persuade a friend or someone in authority to do or believe something. Use **9-1 Persuasive Writing** for persuasive strategies.

## Practice Addressing Envelopes

Use *Tools 9-10e* and *9-10f* to give students instructions about addressing envelopes. Explain the process using *Tool 9-10e*. Practice often with *Tool 9-10f* and with blank envelopes.

## Writing Memos, Emails, and Messages

1. Memos and e-mails are used to share information as quickly and clearly as possible. They include only pertinent information, usually on one subject. Using *Tool 9-10g*, point out that traditional memos include the following for headings and body paragraph(s).

> To:
>
> From:
>
> Date:
>
> Subject: (or Re:)

Discuss with your class how the information is spread out with bullets and short paragraphs so that it is easy to read and understand. Point out the use of Power (Number) Statements in the memo. These kinds of statements help a writer organize important information.

2. Display *Tool 9-10g* again and read the e-mail example. Discuss the clarity and detail in it. Ask students to explain why and when it is important to write clear messages like those on *Tool 9-10g*. Compare the purpose and content of e-mails and paper memos. Discuss with students the use of paper memos, like the one on *Tool 9-10g*, which are usually posted on bulletin boards for a wide audience, and e-mails, which are often faster and more direct.

3. Use *Tool 9-10h* to teach your students to write clear and accurate informal messages. Explain that we often write informal notes to people we know well. Although the notes are informal, they usually contain important information, so those who write them must make them neat and accurate. The recipient will need all details (especially any directions and phone numbers) to be clear. Discuss what might happen if the information in either of the messages on *Tool 9-10h* was wrong or incomplete.

## 9-11 Applying for a Job

Students can use this strategy to review or acquire some skills needed to look and apply for jobs, scholarships, and/or extracurricular opportunities.

### Before Class

Make overhead transparencies and student copies of *Tools 9-11a* through *9-11e*.

### During Class

1. Read *Tool 9-11a* with the class and discuss its contents. Ask students to identify the skills they would need for the job. Compare this ad with others from newspapers. Have students work in pairs to create similar ads for jobs suited to middle level and high school students.

2. Display, read, and discuss the résumé on *Tool 9-11b*. Have students create their own résumés following the example on this tool or other examples that you have collected. Explain the purpose and importance of a résumé.

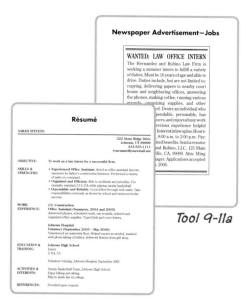

*Tool 9-11a*

*Tool 9-11b*

3. With the class in a guided lesson, complete the job application on *Tools 9-11c, 9-11d,* and *9-11e.* Ask students to describe job applications that they have completed. Stress the importance of neatness and accuracy. Give students time to assess the job application and to ask questions.

4. Tell students that employers often require applicants to print legibly as they complete the forms. See **10-2 Cursive Writing** for information and description of the importance of mastering handwriting.

*Tool 9-11c*

*Tool 9-11d*

*Tool 9-11e*

## (9-12) Writing in Math

Writing for math requires a variety of strategies for different tasks. Students can use this strategy to write about math for schoolwork and assessments.

### Before Class

- Make overhead transparencies and student copies of *Tools 9-12a* through *9-12l* as appropriate.

*Bonus Tool 9-12-1* provides additional support.

### During Class
#### Writing to Explain a Solution

1. Explain to your students that in some classes or assessments, they will need to explain in paragraph form how they solved a math problem.

2. Display *Tool 9-12a* and read the first paragraph. Emphasize that they can manage the process more easily if they visualize the steps they took to solve the problem. Tell them that the goal is to identify all of the steps by recalling their solution process thoroughly.

3. Point out the six boxes for steps and explanations and have your students fold a piece of notebook paper into six parts as shown.

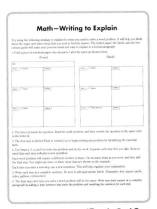

*Tool 9-12a*

4. Read the next two instructions with your students and have them label all of the parts on the front and back of their papers as described.

5. Tell students that they will use a new box for each step—each new operation—they used to solve the problem. Their goal is to show each step individually—not to combine steps. Inform them that even though there are spaces for six steps on their paper, they might have solved the problem in more or fewer steps, and they should add more boxes or use fewer boxes, as needed.

6. Read the fourth instruction on *Tool 9-12a* with your students. Point out that in the right column they explain each step in complete sentences, and that each sentence will begin with a transition. Explain that there are certain rules for writing about numbers, such as not starting a sentence with a number unless it is spelled out, spelling out small numbers (usually one through nine), and using hyphens to join the parts of a fraction (*two-thirds, one-half*). See **Bonus Tool 9-12-1** for more information.

7. Display *Tool 9-12b* and read the word problem with your students.

8. Using *Tools 9-12c* and *9-12d*, walk them through each step. Have your students copy the example on their folded notebook paper. Point out transition words such as *first, next,* and *finally,* and discuss the importance of using transitions in explaining a process. Remind students that they will always write the answer as a complete sentence, using math terms and labels as needed.

9. Explain that the final step is to write a complete paragraph explaining how they solved the math problem, but that most of the work is already done. They need to write a topic sentence that explains the problem and then rewrite the sentences they just created.

10. To illustrate how to write the topic sentence, display *Tool 9-12e*. With your students, read the examples and discuss. Using *Tool 9-12f*, show them how the information from their folded paper will become a complete, organized paragraph. Point out the topic sentence that starts the paragraph on *Tool 9-12f*.

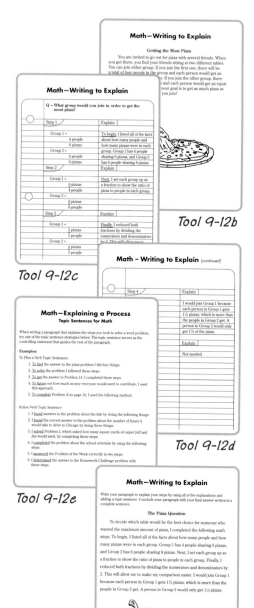

Tool 9-12b

Tool 9-12c

Tool 9-12d

Tool 9-12e

Tool 9-12f

11. Guide the whole group through the strategy again. Have them use easy problems when first learning this strategy. Help them create topic sentences and write paragraphs. Move to more challenging, grade-appropriate problems once they understand the process.

## Using Framed Paragraphs to Promote Writing for Math

Writing frames can be a good way to help students focus and write about math processes and concepts. Use *Tool 9-12g* to create more framed paragraphs and as a model for students. Use *Tool 9-12h* with students as they try this strategy. (See **9-9 Using Writing Frames** for additional ideas for using writing frames and for directions on how to make your own.)

## Reading and Solving a Word Problem

The two-column strategy for reading and solving a math word problem gives students a practical method to follow as they solve and explain word problems in math. Read *Tool 9-12I* with your students and discuss the word problem at the bottom, "Earning an Income." Then display *Tool 9-12j* to illustrate how this strategy was used to solve the word problem. Ask students to follow your steps using their own notebook paper. Practice the strategy several times. While students are learning the strategy, use simple problems that are easy to solve. Then move to more challenging, grade-appropriate problems.

## Writing About Graphs

1. Students can apply the three-part IVF sentences strategy for summary writing (**1-30 Four-Step Summary Paragraphs**) to write about what they read on graphs.

2. Guide students as they read through the example on *Tool 9-12k*, which shows results from a hypothetical survey to answer the question, "How have magazine sales changed?" Discuss the information, verb, and finish of the IVF sentence. Point out the fact outline at the bottom of the page. Tell students that when they are asked to write about a graph, they should write an IVF sentence and a fact outline by asking themselves:

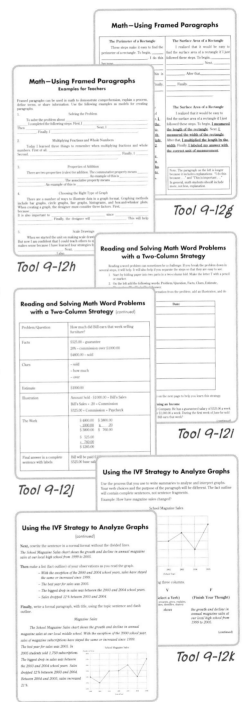

*Tool 9-12g*

*Tool 9-12h*

*Tool 9-12I*

*Tool 9-12j*

*Tool 9-12k*

*Tool 9-12I*

- What is the purpose of the graph? How does it answer the question?
- What are the important facts to tell the audience?
- What trends can be seen from the facts?
- Are there extremes that don't really represent the average or norm?
- Are there facts to combine or to compare in an interesting way? If so, be sure to explain what figures were combined or compared.

3. Help students see how *Tools 9-12k* and *9-12l* are connected. Explain that the IVF sentence becomes the topic sentence and the fact outline helps with the body of the paragraph.

4. Review with students the rules for writing about math terms, such as spelling out small numbers, using numerals for larger numbers, and not starting a sentence with a numeral. (See *Bonus Tool 9-12-1* for additional information.)

5. Instruct students to use complete sentences when filling in fact outlines and write about information on graphs. It will make their observations clearer and easier to assess. Also, math teachers will probably find time to have students write fact outlines, even if they do not always have time for students to write out full, paragraphed responses.

## 9-13 Writing Reports on Science Experiments

Students can use this strategy to write clear, well-organized science lab reports.

### Before Class

- Make overhead transparencies and student copies of *Tools 9-13a* through *9-13d* as appropriate.
- *Bonus Tools 9-13-1* and *9-13-2* provide additional support.

### During Class

1. Explain to your students that a science lab report has two parts. Each part is discussed in a separate paragraph.

   - Lab Process—Summarizes the process used to complete the science experiment.
   - Lab Conclusion—Explains observations made as the experiment was conducted; explains how successful or unsuccessful the experiment was.

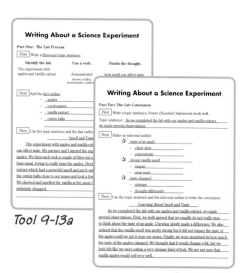

*Tool 9-13a*

*Tool 9-13b*

2. Display *Tool 9-13a*. Read and discuss "Part One: The Lab Process" with your students. Note that the lab process follows a strategy similar to the summary strategy in **1-30 Four-Step Summary Paragraphs**. Review the IVF topic sentence and remind students that a fact outline uses only facts—not key/star ideas or the E's—and that a summary paragraph does not need a conclusion statement because they will write a separate conclusion paragraph.

3. Explain to your students that the lab process portion is a straightforward account of what they did to complete the experiment. When they write their experiment process, they will summarize the experiment and the steps in the procedure. The experiment process may include results but does not include opinions or conclusions about what happened.

4. Review the following steps for writing a summary. Explain that they will use these steps to write their lab process paragraph.

## Step 1
**Write a topic sentence using the IVF sentence strategy.**

Identify the lab. | Select a verb. | Finish the thought.

(Verb choices for science reports might include: *shows, verifies, demonstrates, confirms.*)

## Step 2
**Create a fact outline with four to six dashes outlining steps taken or facts about the experiment. Use complete sentences for each fact.**

These facts will become sentences for the lab report.

## Step 3
**Write up the lab process using obvious transitions (*first, next, then, finally,* and so on).**

It is important to write a clear topic sentence and use the facts from the fact outline.

5. Display *Tool 9-13b* and discuss "Part Two: The Lab Conclusion." Point out that the lab conclusion uses the same components as an Accordion Paragraph (informal outline and conclusion). Reinforce that a fact outline, which contains only the facts of the experiment, is used to write lab reports, as in Part One: The Lab Process, but informal outlines, which include details and the students' own thoughts, are used to write lab conclusions.

6. Tell students that Power (Number) Statements make good topic sentences for lab conclusions. (See **4-18 Topic Sentence Variety** for more information.)

> *When we completed Lab 27 and mixed water with oil, we noticed three changes in the liquid mixture.*

7. Explain to students that in the lab conclusion, they will share results, comment on what happened, make conclusions, and assess the success of the experiment. In short, they will mix observations with facts. This means that they will recount observations and hypothesize on why, why not, or how something happened. It also means that they will list possible problems with the experiment that might have affected the outcome, and what kind of further research/exploration the experiment might inspire.

*Tool 9-13c*

*Tool 9-13d*

8. After students have completed a science lab or you have demonstrated a science experiment, use *Tools 9-13c* and *9-13d* to develop a science experiment report. Model the process often and have students work in pairs or small groups to develop their reports. Have students develop reports independently once they have numerous guided-practice opportunities. See *Bonus Tools 9-13-1* and *9-13-2* for more examples.

## 9-14 Technical Writing

Students can use this strategy to learn a variety of forms of technical writing.

### Before Class

- Make an overhead transparency and student copies of *Tool 9-14a.*
-  *Bonus Tools 9-14-1* through *9-14-5* provide additional support.

## During Class

1. Inform your students that technical writing includes informational paragraphs or reports that tell about a technical or scientific topic or process. Technical pieces are factual, emphasize accuracy, and are direct and to the point, but they don't have one particular length or format.

2. Explain to your students that the goal in technical writing is to imagine that the reader knows nothing about the subject and then to describe it thoroughly. For technical pieces, it is important to consider the audience, the role of the writer, the purpose, and the choice of format.

3. Review with your class *Tool 9-14a* and discuss these different forms of technical writing. Discuss how different formats and styles (bullets or in-text lists, complete sentences or sentence fragments) may be used. Collect additional examples and add them to your discussion. Show students that all technical writing is factual, accurate, and written with short phrases, clauses, or sentences that are easy to read.

4. Assign writing that requires students to explain a process, give directions, enumerate, classify, or list characteristics as a way for students to practice the basic organizational skills needed for technical writing. Whenever introducing a new form of technical writing, use an example you have collected (or *Bonus Tools 9-14-1* through *9-14-5*) as you discuss and model. Emphasize the need for organization, clarity, and accuracy in technical writing. Provide your students with numerous opportunities for guided practice before they work independently.

## Additional Ideas

Help students recognize technical writing in its many forms. Start a collection of examples by asking families for help. Give parents a chance to share the work they do or hobbies they enjoy. Encourage them to send samples of lists, directions, brochures, labels, and so on. Make your own collection by watching the mail, visiting businesses, and searching through magazines. For fun, collect an array of technical-writing items that your school district uses or has created.

## 9-15 Poetry

Students can use this strategy when they are first introduced to poetry and for additional information and practice opportunities. Use 2-12 Poetry Pieces along with this strategy to help students gain confidence writing poetry.

These strategies provide the structure that most beginning writers need, open doors to creativity, and give opportunities to experiment with style, voice, and themes. More importantly, they give student poets a chance to write freely and feel successful.

## Before Class

- Make overhead transparencies and student copies of *Tools 9-15a* through *9-15g*.

 *Bonus Tool 9-15-1* provides additional support.

## During Class

1. Tell students that when people write poems, they want to make an impact and bring forth strong reactions or emotions in readers. A poet might share experiences, describe scenes, pass along insights, make observations, or write about interesting topics or issues.

2. Remind students that poetry comes in many forms; poets use many different writing methods to help them express themselves on paper, but all poems have some traits in common.

3. Use *Tool 9-15a* to demonstrate some of these traits.

4. In a whole group or in small-group discussions about poetry, display and read *Tool 9-15a*. Have students highlight key words and phrases on their copies of the Tool as you guide the discussion about "What does a poet do?" Encourage questions and comments.

5. Tell students that they can use the same methods when they write their own poems.

**What Does a Poet Do?**

*Tool 9-15a*

### Writing Poems from Prose

The Writing Poems from Prose strategy teaches students to write freely on any topic in a paragraph form. Then, from these paragraphs, students grab interesting ideas, phrases, and information to create poems.

1. Use *Tool 9-15b* to remind students about the difference between prose and poetry. Display and read the short selection from William Wordsworth's poem "To a Butterfly." Then read the prose version at the top of the page. Explain that writers can express themselves on the same topic in a paragraph format, but that poets look for ways to share their message in a more condensed, powerful fashion.

2. Read the poem and the paragraph a second time; in an oral discussion give students a chance to explain the similarities and differences in their own words.

3. Display and share the example on *Tool 9-15c*. Explain to students that this is what you will be asking them to try. Point out the topic in the circle at the top right corner; read the prose paragraph; share the poem. Discuss the poem and the strategy.

**Writing Poems**

*Tool 9-15b*

*Tool 9-15c*

4. Create a paragraph and a poem with the class. Choose a general topic that all students recognize (music, a difficult class, a family member, the classroom, a friendship, and so on). Write the paragraph using ideas from the class.

5. Guide students as they change their ideas into a short poem. Welcome new ideas and words. Use what the paragraph provides—add what comes naturally and makes sense.

6. Have students use *Tool 9-15d* to practice individually or in pairs.

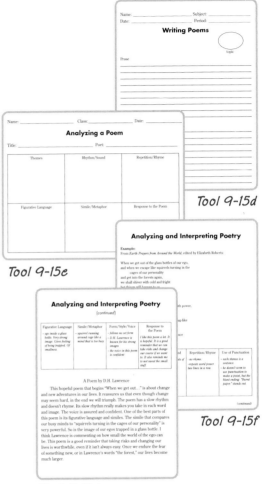

Tool 9-15d

Tool 9-15e

Tool 9-15f

Tool 9-15g

## Analyzing Poems

1. Explain to your class that they will sometimes need to analyze and/or interpret what is in a poem or what it means to them. To do so, they will first think about the different elements of the poem.

2. Display *Tool 9-15e* and tell students to use this grid to support their prewriting. Review the terms on the grid. (Use the definitions on *Bonus Tool 9-15-1* if needed.) Explain that the grid has space for their comments as well as for words or lines from the poem they are analyzing. The grid will then help with the key/star ideas for their informal outlines.

3. Display *Tools 9-15f* and *9-15g* and show how information from the grid on *Tool 9-15e* was used to develop an informal outline and write an essay.

4. Practice this approach several times in whole- or small-group guided lessons using poems that students read as a part of their literacy instruction.

5. Have students use the grid as they work in pairs to analyze their own poems or poems of their choice.

## 9-16 Writing a Skit

Students can use this strategy to write a skit. Writing a skit reinforces many of the sentence-writing skills introduced in Section 3.

## Before Class

Make an overhead transparency and student copies of *Tool 9-16a*.

## During Class

1. Explain to your class that a skit is a short sketch or play. Skits can be spoofs, satires, or parodies that poke fun at somebody or something. They can also tell short stories and share information.

2. Tell students that, as with narrative writing (Section 6) they will need to develop characters and setting, create problems and solutions, and plan endings. They will also need to write dialogue. (See **6-14 Writing Dialogue** for more information.)

3. Remind students of the power of action verbs. These verbs help readers (and actors) picture the facial expressions, tone of voice, and body movements of the characters as they speak.

4. Tell students that skits are effective when the writer

   • Exaggerates to add emphasis but still makes characters believable;

   • Describes each scene and makes each one advance the plot;

   • Gives details between many lines of dialogue, describing actions the actors take, clothing, things happening on stage, music, lights, and so on. These details are set apart with parentheses or brackets;

   • Keeps the audience in mind. The writer thinks about what reaction he or she wants and creates characters, scenes, and situations that will get that reaction;

   • Considers not just the story, but the stage, costumes, and actions as well;

   • Keeps it simple and limits the skit to one or two scenes.

5. Share the example on *Tool 9-16a*. Display and read the beginning of *Turn a Fiend into a Friend*. As you share and discuss, have students mark the features of a skit: characters, setting, scenes, information in brackets, use of dialogue, colons after characters' names, and use of punctuation in dialogue. With help from the students, write several more lines for the skit.

*Tool 9-16a*

6. Ask students to work in pairs to create a one-page skit of their own using a book or story from class reading as a model. Review rules for writing dialogue (**6-14 Writing Dialogue**) as needed, Give students one of the following prompts, or use prompts that you or they have created.

   • Write a short skit about what would happen if you worked in a restaurant and had to calm an unhappy customer.

   • Write a short informational skit about a group of friends working as a team to solve a problem.

7. Take time to share.

8. Discuss with students how writing skits forces writers to focus on details, form, word choice, and sentence structure (including fragments).

### Reader's Theater

- Reader's Theater activities are a great way for students to get a feel for writing skits.

- Many reading series and magazines for students include skits or short plays for your use. Ask the school librarian for help in locating books of short plays. Assign parts or ask for volunteers. Review all of the previously listed elements of a skit: description of characters and scenes, dialogue, and so on. Look for action verbs. Discuss the descriptions and hints for actors that appear inside brackets. Have fun as you read part or all of the skit together.

## 9-17 Writing About the News

Reading and writing about current events is one way that students learn to form opinions about local, national, and world issues. Students can use this strategy both to respond to published news articles and to write their own news articles.

## Before Class

Make overhead transparencies and student copies of *Tools 9-17a* through *9-17l*.

## During Class
### Writing About Current Events

Tool 9-17a

1. Explain to students that when they are writing about current events (not just summarizing particular articles) they should share not only facts but also personal reactions, insights, and thoughts about their news sources and the events themselves.

2. Read and discuss the two examples on *Tool 9-17a*.

3. Point out that these paragraphs include not only facts, but also personal reactions and insights.

4. On the board or chart paper, make two columns: one labeled *facts* and the other labeled *opinions*. As you reread and discuss the two examples, list the facts and opinions in the correct columns. Have students mark the facts and opinions on their copies by underlining facts and circling opinions.

5. Reread the two examples on *Tool 9-17a* for further practice and to encourage discussion.

6. With your students, read an article from a student magazine or a local newspaper. Develop a response by creating an informal outline.

   - First, decide on a focus and write a topic sentence.

   - Next, add key/star ideas to the outline using information from the news item.

   - Add dashes and dots to the outline with details and facts.

   - Complete the outline with a phrase that reinforces the class's opinion or insight.

7. Try having students create oral responses to current events using the information from the outline. If time permits, have students each write out a paragraph following the class outline.

8. Have your students write about current events often, especially after class discussions. This may increase their ability to form and write their insights. Provide support and guidance as needed.

## Additional Ideas

- Have students and their families collect news items that are upbeat and share a message. Use these for activities about current events.

- When you read articles with students, help them recognize the different elements that are in almost all news articles, and increase comprehension by creating current events charts. Make a T-chart on the board or chart paper. Write labels for the following in the left column: Headline, Who, What, Where, When, How, and Why. With help from students, fill in the right column with information from the articles.

- Give students simple number-statement topic sentences to use as they write three- to four-sentence responses about current events and specific news items. Encourage students to add illustrations.

> 1. The news article explained two facts about _____.
>
> 2. The article from _____ gives three important pieces of information about _____.

- Keep copies of news magazines available for students, and ask teaching colleagues to share old copies. Cut off address labels and store the magazines in your classroom for independent reading.

## Writing a News Article

1. Use *Tools 9-17b* through *9-17f* to help students write news articles. Writing news articles helps students learn about the news as well as gain important skills for focusing their writing.

2. Read the news items on *Tool 9-17b*, pointing out that newswriting answers the "who, what, when, where, why, and how" about an event. Explain that it is concise and specific, but does not overtly try to entertain—it just gives well-written information. News articles give just the facts about local, regional, or world events. There is no room for opinions; in fact, the goal of journalism is to present the information in as neutral a way as possible. If there are two sides to an issue, reporters cover both.

*Tool 9-17b*

*Tool 9-17c*

3. Note how the active voice and short paragraphs help readers get information quickly.

4. Display *Tool 9-17c* and inform your students that a reporter collects information to answer the "five W's and the how" before writing, and they can do the same to ensure that they have all the information they need to write. Use *Tool 9-17c* (or a T chart created on the board) as you read each of the news articles on *Tool 9-17b*. With input from students, complete the chart on *Tool 9-17c* for both articles.

5. Review that in news articles, the most important details are mentioned first, followed by less important information. Display *Tool 9-17d* and explain how the inverted triangle helps to organize information for the article. This triangle shows that the most important information is given first.

6. Use *Tool 9-17e* as an example of notes a reporter might have collected before writing a news article on a new park.

7. Read *Tool 9-17f* with your students. It is the completed article based on the notes. Ask students to locate the "five W's and the how" and to assess the news article itself. Ask students to show how the reporter presented information in the inverted triangle format, from most important to least important.

8. Have students collect additional examples of news articles and have them identify the five Ws and the how.

9. When it is time for students to write an article of their own, have them use *Tools 9-17c* and *9-17d* as well as the sample news items for models.

*Tool 9-17d*

*Tool 9-17e*

*Tool 9-17f*

## Interviews

1. News reporters often include information from interviews in their news stories. Students can develop good interviewing skills to become better reporters. They can also use these skills for writing reports or research papers and for writing and giving speeches.

2. Use *Tools 9-17g*, *9-17h*, and *9-17i* to help students learn about interviewing.

3. Tell students that the success of an interview almost always depends on the quality of the

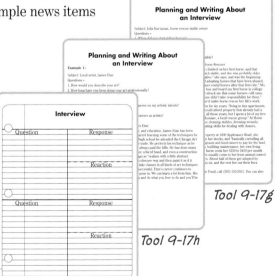

*Tool 9-17g*

*Tool 9-17h*

*Tool 9-17i*

questions that are asked. (See Section 1 for question-writing strategies.) Read the interview questions on *Tool 9-17g* and the paragraphs that follow. Help students see how the answers to the questions show up in the writing.

4. Have students interview a family member, school staff member, or reputable local business person. Give students a chance to write their own interview questions using *Tool 9-17i* or notebook paper created to mimic the Tool. Explain that the real work in an interview may not be the answer itself, but rather what the person doing the interview thinks, sees, and observes during the interview.

5. When students have completed the questions and the interview, give them time to write about the experience and share their results with classmates.

6. Use *Tool 9-17h* for an additional example. Ask students to evaluate the questions and the paragraphs on this Tool and on *Tool 9-17g*.

## 9-18 Personal Writing

Activities like journaling, completing learning logs, and freewriting give students opportunities to express their ideas, opinions, and inner experiences, and to reflect on what they have learned in school, read, and heard.

If used as the primary or sole source of student writing, freewriting, learning-log writing, and journaling do not provide the direct instruction and guidance that students need in order to master the skills that good writers possess. However, when used correctly and for specific purposes, they are great ways for students to become better thinkers and writers, and for students to learn to enjoy writing for its own sake.

## Before Class

Make overhead transparencies and student copies of *Tools 9-18a, 9-18b*, and *9-18c*.

## During Class

### Journaling

1. Explain to students that journaling is the act of writing down reflections, thoughts, and questions that come to mind on a topic or a experience. School journals give students time to practice expressing thoughts and to write.

2. Have students use journals to record reactions to in-class topics. For example, have students keep open-ended science journals to record any questions about science they may have. Or, have students write journal entries in response to prompts related to current in-class content or readings. Consider having students generate lists of topics to use for journaling.

3. Try having students write for a set amount of time each day. Then collect the journals and respond to entries on a regular basis. Have students date each entry at the top of the page.

4. Try providing words and phrases as prompts for journal writing:

When . . .                          In math today I finally . . .
I have a question about . . .       I'm excited about . . .
I wonder . . .                      I want to . . .
I'm confused about . . .            In science today I discovered . . .
I think . . .                       Using the computer this week . . .
If only . . .                       During the (lecture, film, and so on) I learned . . .
Whenever . . .                      I would like to get good at . . .
I don't think I'll ever . . .       I like . . .
I appreciate . . .                  I am grateful for . . .
I wish . . .                        I have mastered . . .

5. Display *Tool 9-18a*. Read the entries and discuss the contents. Tell students that journals sometimes help writers discover what they want to write. Ask them to point out possible writing topics in the sample journal entries.

6. Occasionally use journaling as a prewriting activity. (See *Bonus Tool 4-5-1* for more information on prewriting.)

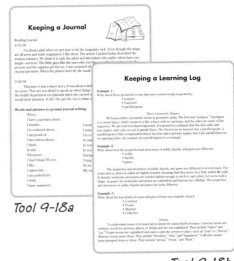

*Tool 9-18a*

*Tool 9-18b*

## Learning Logs

1. Explain to your class that, unlike journal writing, learning logs have a specific purpose or goal. Tell them that in their logs they will record thoughts about what they learned in a focused way. When writing in their learning logs, they start by generating a quick plan and then write a short, organized paragraph synthesizing a lesson or activity. For example, you might put a Power (Number) Statement on the board and ask students to use it as they write a very short paragraph about a subsection in a history textbook.

2. Learning logs give students the chance to practice recording content, creating topic sentences, and reviewing or summarizing main ideas. Most of all, they give students time to reflect on and process what they know about specific topics.

3. Read the examples on *Tool 9-18b*. Discuss how the writer has turned the prompt into a topic sentence. Point out how the writer has used the list of key/star ideas to write an organized response. Also, note the use of transitions like *first, also,* and *the third* in the first example. In the second example, the prepositional phrases *in liquids* and *in gases* help organize the material. The transitions in the third example are *common nouns, proper nouns,* and *abstract nouns.*

## Freewriting

1. Explain that freewriting is free of limitations, formalities, structure, and rules. It means putting pencil to paper and writing without stopping. It is like brainstorming—writing thoughts and ideas instantly as they come to mind. It means not making judgments about what is written; it is writing without worry about subject matter, organization, spelling, or pausing to think.

2. Let your students know that this unrestrained style can flush fresh ideas to the surface as the mind wanders from one topic to another. It often brings up vivid images or thoughts, providing good fodder for future creative writing projects, and can be a way to combat writer's block.

3. Tell them that when freewriting, they will write continuously for a short amount of time—two, five, or ten minutes—and just let the ideas and words flow.

4. Explain that when they freewrite, they:

   - Take a moment, with pencil in hand, to close their eyes and clear their heads.
   - Write down the first thing that pops into their heads. Pretend that the pencil is a faucet that they keep flowing.

5. When a class needs a boost:

   - Ask a class member to retell a funny event. Everyone writes!
   - Think about something that happened during the day. Tell students to get a picture of it in their minds and then just start writing.
   - Share something that makes you mad (sad, excited, determined, motivated). Have students then put pencil to paper and write.

6. Once students have written for a few minutes, ask them to stop and try "looping." When students "loop," it means they discover a new idea from the freewriting and now want to write about that topic. Looping lets students write and explore ideas.

7. Use *Tool 9-18c* to show students that ideas for freewriting can come from many sources—their own thoughts, stories, music, and art. Together, list other places, items, or events that could be a source for freewriting. Sometimes it helps to start with one subject or word to act as a launching pad.

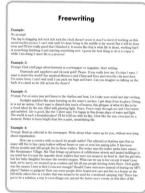

*Tool 9-18c*

# SECTION 10 INTRODUCTION
## Assessment and High Standards

*T*he purpose of assessment and high standards is to develop writers who are skilled and confident in their abilities to produce high-quality writing on demand in a variety of situations, from timed writings to multiple-draft compositions.

To perfect writing skills, students need to learn the skills of editing and revising. These skills should be taught directly and students given adequate practice before they can be expected to revise and edit on their own. Many students feel that when they have written the last sentence of a composition their work is done, but adequate reinforcement can make revising and editing a natural part of their writing routine. When students edit and revise, they can move their writing to proficient and advanced levels.

When teachers communicate clear expectations for writing with exemplary models, students understand what is required of them. However, in order to improve, students also need continued direct instruction in specific skills and continual, constructive feedback about skills they have mastered, as well as skills that need improvement.

*Step Up to Writing* provides the means for teachers and their students to use ongoing assessment to improve achievement in writing. As with all other skills, students need direct, explicit training in the purposes and uses of scoring guides and quick checks. Also, students need to see examples of each performance level to compare to their own writing and to see what they must do to improve to the next level.

Scoring guides help students understand the hallmarks of exemplary writing and the high expectations and standards set for them as writers. The frequent use of scoring guides allows students to track their progress as they improve and develop their writing skills to meet those expectations and standards.

Scoring guides with parallel, detailed descriptions of levels of achievement (rubrics) provide the feedback needed for students to understand the strengths and weaknesses of their own writing. When they understand what improvements need to be made, they can target those skills during revision. In effect, scoring guides encourage revision by making the task smaller and more manageable.

Students will have success with assessments and high standards when they are introduced to following:

- Rules for neat presentation and handwriting
- The process for revising and editing, including specific methods for improving word choice
- Rules for capitalization, usage, punctuation, and spelling
- Scoring guides and quick checks for self-evaluation of skills
- Definitions and descriptions used on scoring guides and quick checks
- Examples of writing at each level of achievement (below basic, basic, proficient, and advanced)
- Ways to monitor their own progress as well as to receive regular feedback that is effective but not time-consuming

## When Teaching These Strategies

- Communicate and frequently remind students of the expectations for quality work. Provide students a means to receive frequent feedback from you (consider **10-23** Labels to Use with Scoring Guides, for example).
- Have students use checklists during the composing process, prior to submitting their compositions, and during the revision process.

- Teach students the criteria of each level of achievement and show models that meet those criteria. Students need to see models at each achievement level for a concrete illustration of writing expectations.

- Teach students how to use the scoring guides to assess their peers' and their own writing (**10-6 Peer Review/Editing/Revision**).

- Use anonymous student compositions to practice using the scoring guides as a whole class and in small groups.

- Revise the scoring guides to meet your needs and those of your students.

- At times, have students practice revising using only one or two skills at a time, or focusing on only a single paragraph in a multiparagraph composition.

- Provide constructive feedback and positive reinforcement, but don't hesitate to point out mistakes to students when they consistently repeat them. Students need to learn from their mistakes. Use the strategies found in Sections 1 through 9 to review and address particular areas of weakness.

- Use **10-7 Editing with CUPS** and teacher-created handouts to address specific, high-frequency errors.

- Use the **10-8 Perfect Three-Sentence Paragraphs** strategy as a ticket out at the end of class or before students move on to a preferred activity. It will remind them of the importance of high-quality work.

Choose the strategies that best meet the needs of your students.

# Setting High Standards and Clear Expectations

It is important to set high standards and clear expectations. Unless students know what is expected of them, they will not be able to reach the goal of being proficient or advanced writers. Having clear expectations and the tools to revise and edit their work provides students with a framework for success.

## Objectives

- Understand the importance of neatness
- Learn how to edit and revise

| Strategy | Strategy Description | Page | Tools |
|---|---|---|---|
| **10-1 Neat Paper Rules** | Learning practical guidelines for improving the presentation of written work | 418 | 10-1a |
| **10-2 Cursive Writing** | Learning clear guidelines for cursive writing | 419 | 10-2a |
| **10-3 Checklists for Revision** | Using checklists to help focus revision | 420 | 10-3a, 10-3b |
| **10-4 Revising "To Be" Verbs** | Improving writing by limiting "to be" verbs, using action verbs, and assessing fluency | 421 | 10-4a |

*(chart continues)*

| Strategy *(continued)* | Strategy Description | Page | Tools |
|---|---|---|---|
| **10-5** **Improving Word Choice with the ABC Activity** | Reviewing writing and improving word choice during revision | 422 | 10-5a |
| **10-6** **Peer Review/Editing/Revision** | Helping classmates improve their writing through quick feedback from peers | 423 | n/a |
| **10-7** **Editing with CUPS** | Following basic rules for capitalization, usage, punctuation, and spelling | 424 | 10-7a to 10-7d |
| **10-8** **Perfect Three-Sentence Paragraphs** | Writing an interesting, error-free paragraph with a clear topic sentence and two supporting sentences as a way to demonstrate mastery of important writing skills | 427 | 10-8a to 10-8c |
| **10-9** **Analyzing a Paragraph** | Using a grid to focus attention on parts of a paragraph; revising and improving writing | 429 | 10-9a |

## **10-1** Neat Paper Rules

Using this strategy, students learn that readers appreciate organized, attractive writing because it is easier to read, understand, and grade.

### Before Class

Make an overhead transparency and student copies of *Tool 10-1a*.

## During Class

1. Display *Tool 10-1a* and read through the guidelines for neat, acceptable work. Alter to fit your own expectations for your class. Have students use the back of the page to take notes and to add your personal "neat paper" expectations.

2. Don't rely on lecture alone; show students what each guideline looks like. Lead a discussion and answer all questions.

3. Have students practice each guideline. Give them feedback and encouragement on all writing assignments.

4. Have students keep the Neat Paper Rules in their writing notebooks for frequent reference.

5. Let your students know that these guidelines should be followed in all subject areas. Congratulate and encourage them as they strive to meet these expectations.

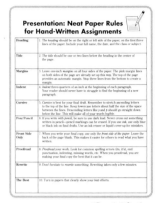

*Tool 10-1a*

## 10-2 Cursive Writing

All students can and should learn to word process, print neatly, and write in cursive. Being able to write quickly and accurately using cursive writing is an important but often neglected skill.

Research by Baker, Graham, Harris, Fink and many others reinforces the importance of good handwriting and describes problems caused by a lack of handwriting skills. This research shows a strong connection between self-concept, quality of completed writing assignments, the number of spelling and grammatical errors, overall academic success, and good cursive writing skills.

Most secondary students have been introduced to cursive, but many stop using cursive when no one requires it.

### Before Class

- Make an overhead transparency and student copies of *Tool 10-2a*.
- Have available a blank transparency of lined notebook paper.

### During Class

1. Boost your students' cursive writing skills with these three steps:
   - Give specific instruction on how to write in cursive.
   - Provide copies of cursive letters for them to use as models.
   - Require several short assignments each week written in cursive.

2. Explain to your students the importance of writing cursive legibly and quickly.

- Cursive improves the appearance of handwritten assignments.
- Papers written in clear cursive are easier (and faster) to read.
- Students who write in cursive take more pride in their work.
- It is important for students to be able to read notes or instructions written in cursive, and they learn to read cursive as they learn to write in cursive. (Students often admit that they cannot read cursive. No student should graduate from high school unable to read cursive.)
- Learning to write in cursive is rewarding. Students want to and need to develop a sense of pride about what they write and provide for others to read.
- Assessments (formal and informal) require speed and legibility.

### Improving Handwriting

1. Display *Tool 10-2a* and introduce your students to the methods for improving handwriting. Discuss and demonstrate writing in cursive on a transparency of lined notebook paper.

2. Inform your students that the methods will give them the flexibility to develop their own style and yet produce neat, easy-to-read handwriting. Remind them that the purpose of writing is to communicate ideas and share information. This will happen only if writing is neat and readable.

3. Give students a chance to explore cursive as an art form. Read and try the suggestions for teaching cursive as an art form in *Drawing on the Right Side of the Brain* by Betty Edwards. Encourage art teachers to include calligraphy in their curriculum and show how writing can be a form of artistic expression (Edwards 1999).

*Tool 10-2a*

## 10-3 Checklists for Revision

Checklists can help students review their writing and check for things that may need revision. Checklists are not used for grading; instead, scoring guides are used as a part of the grading process.

### Before Class

Make overhead transparencies and student copies of *Tools 10-3a* and/or *10-3b*.

## During Class

1. Review the checklists found on *Tools 10-3a* and *10-3b* and decide which would be best for your students to use. *Tool 10-3a* is a checklist that students can use often with almost any kind of writing. *Tool 10-3b* should be used when students write paragraphs.

2. Using either *Tool 10-3a* or *Tool 10-3b*, explain that the checklist is intended to help them review their writing and make sure they have done all that they need to do in order to organize their materials and make schedules for completing assignments. Remind students that checklists are not grading sheets. They are reminders of the steps that need to be taken to ensure success and a high score.

*Tool 10-3a*

*Tool 10-3b*

3. Model how you would use the checklist. Lead a discussion and provide an opportunity for students to ask questions.

4. Have students use a checklist as they work on a writing assignment and during the revision process. Give your students reinforcement as they use the checklist. Use the checklist with them in the beginning and before they hand in their work.

5. Students should use scoring guides along with checklists to ensure they reach the proficient level in all of the categories that you will use to assess their work.

## Additional Ideas

Some of the Tools included in Sections 1 through 9 could also be used as checklists. Good examples include *Tools 5-1a*, *5-2a*, and *4-5a*. Create checklists of your own for specific assignments.

## 10-4 Revising "To Be" Verbs

One way that students can improve their writing is by using more powerful verbs. This strategy helps students use more vivid action verbs.

**Prerequisite:** 3-13 Recognizing Parts of Speech

## Before Class

• Make an overhead transparency and student copies of *Tool 10-4a*.

🔘 *Bonus Tool 10-4-1* provides additional support and examples.

## During Class

1. Using *Tool 10-4a*, read the lists in the left and right columns and remind your students of the power of action verbs. Discuss the power and descriptive value of the action verbs compared to the "to be" verbs. Explain that it is not practical or necessary to eliminate all "to be" verbs, but their writing will improve if they include more action verbs.

2. Have your students keep a copy of *Tool 10-4a* in their writing notebooks and tell them to use the list as a reminder. Encourage them to add their own action verbs to the A–Z list by listing the alphabet on the back of the page. Next to the letters, have them add lines so they can easily write down additional action verbs as they discover them.

3. When students are working with specific topics and content, have them brainstorm verbs that might be helpful before they begin writing.

"To Be" and Action Verbs

*Tool 10-4a*

### Active and Passive Voice

> The habitual use of the active voice … makes for forcible writing.
>
> by William Strunk and E.B. White
>
> —from *Elements of Style*

Remind your students that the terms *active* and *passive* refer to the subject and verb used in a sentence. Writing in active voice means that the subject of a sentence is performing the action. Active voice is more powerful, direct, bold, and lively. In passive voice, the subject receives the action. Share the following examples with students, as well as other examples of active and passive voice that you collect. Additional support and examples are available on *Bonus Tool 10-4-1*.

> Mice <u>were chased</u> by the arctic wolf.     (Passive)
> The arctic wolf <u>chased</u> mice.     (Active)

## 10-5 Improving Word Choice with the ABC Activity

Students can use this strategy to improve sentence variety, make better word choices, and prove to themselves and others that they can, in fact, revise and improve their writing, even when they claim they lack ideas and cannot think of other ways to write their sentences and paragraphs.

## Before Class

Make an overhead transparency and student copies of *Tool 10-5a*.

## During Class

1. Explain to your students the importance of good word choice and sentence variety. Tell students that for this activity they will write a paragraph where the first word for each sentence is in alphabetical order.

2. Students can start with any letter. As they start new sentences, they must use the next letters in alphabetical order. Tell them they may skip letters, as long as they stay in alphabetical order.

3. Let students know that the goal for this activity is not for them to complete regular assignments this way. Rather, the goal is for them to play with words in order to write more interesting sentences. Students will try new sentence structures and look for new ways to begin sentences.

4. Display *Tool 10-5a* and read through both paragraphs. Point out that in the second paragraph, the first letter of each sentence begins with a different letter of the alphabet and the letters are in alphabetical order. Discuss which paragraph has better sentence structures, more sentence variety, and better word choices. Ask them which one is more interesting to read.

5. Next, give students a topic sentence, remind them about transitions for the sentences that introduce key/star ideas, and help them quickly write a simple but well-organized paragraph. Have them write this draft without regard to the alphabetical order of the first letters in each sentence.

6. After students have completed their paragraphs, ask them to improve their paragraphs by using the alphabet technique. As they revise, they start each sentence with another letter that keeps all sentences in alphabetical order.

*Tool 10-5a*

## 10-6 Peer Review/Editing/Revision

Students want and need constructive comments from their teachers; however, comments and guidance from classmates can also be beneficial for both the writer and the reviewer. Students can use this strategy to make peer editing a positive way to give and receive feedback.

After students have mastered strategies like those presented in Sections 1 through 9 and have developed a common language, introduce them to peer editing as a way of giving timely feedback. Students help each other revise and improve their writing and broaden their own skills as they analyze and read the writing of others.

Peer review, editing, and revision will be effective only if students

- Share a clear understanding of what is expected for specific writing assignments;
- Are motivated to help each other;
- Have strategies and methods that make the process go quickly;
- Have strategies and methods to share with each other;
- Have been taught how to give feedback in a constructive, nonevaluative manner.

Teach and have students practice giving their peers feedback by sticking to the observable elements of writing and not just their opinions. Remind them about the "no arguments" rule during peer editing. They should back up their criticisms with reasons better than just "I don't like it," and always include positive statements in their feedback.

Great Tools for peer review/editing/revision include:

- The Writing Process (*Tools 4-5a* and *5-2a*)
- Strategies for specific skills like paragraph, essay, and narrative writing (*Tools 5-1a* and *5-1b*)
- Neat Paper Rules (*Tool 10-1a*)
- Quick checks (*Tools 10-10a, 10-11a, 10-12a*, and *10-13a*)
- Scoring guides (*Tools 10-14a, 10-15a, 10-16a, 10-17a, 10-18a, 10-19a*, and *10-20a*)
- Samples for student writers found in strategies **10-15 Expository Paragraphs Scoring Guide** through **10-20 Summary Writing Scoring Guide**
- The CUPS booklet (*Tools 10-7a* through *10-7d*)

**Note:** When students share a common language and common strategies for writing, they can help their peers, and they also can become good tutors to younger or new students who need to learn the strategies.

## 10-7 Editing with CUPS

Students can use this strategy to develop good basic editing skills, focusing on writing conventions and word usage.

### Before Class

- Make overhead transparencies of *Tools 10-7a* through *10-7d*.
- Make student copies of the four Tools as reference booklets to keep in their writing notebooks. If the copies are single-sided, they can use the backs of the pages for more notes and examples. Copy the booklets on brightly colored paper to make them easy to locate. Make extra copies for class use or to share in writing labs.
- Enlarge and laminate a set of the Tools to post in the classroom.

*Bonus Tool 10-7-1* provides additional examples.

## During Class

1. Introduce CUPS to your class. Explain to your students that the term *CUPS* serves as a reminder about what it means to edit a piece of writing. Students will need to look for and fix errors in:

**C**apitalization

**U**sage

**P**unctuation

**S**pelling

2. With your class, introduce or review the rules and examples on *Tools 10-7a* through *10-7d*.

   • Use a series of mini-lessons and direct instruction to teach or review each Tool.

   • Add more examples for each rule.

   • Teach students to make the pages their own by marking the text, highlighting rules that they need help remembering, and adding their own examples for each rule.

   • Refer to these pages throughout the year whenever students are writing or editing.

   • Have students begin their own set of examples for each rule.

## Additional Ideas

Just reading the rules on the page will have minimal impact. Students will learn the rules best if they make them their own. Students could

   • Copy the rules onto index cards and add their own examples;

   • Create a booklet or set of mini-posters called *CUPS Rules to Remember*;

   • Participate in active, teacher-guided lessons;

   • Look for other ways to demonstrate mastery of the rules.

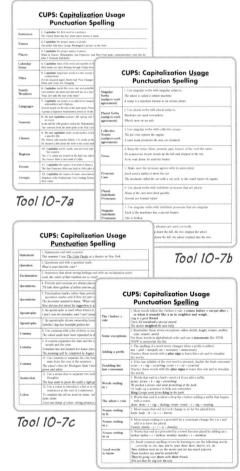

Tool 10-7a

Tool 10-7b

Tool 10-7c

Tool 10-7d

## Improving Spelling

- Spelling can be difficult for many students. Tell students that the first step for improving their spelling is to know their spelling strengths and weaknesses. The second step is to make every effort to compensate for their weaknesses.

- Students have different learning styles and different spelling needs. To improve their spelling, most students need a vast collection of strategies and resources. Add the strategies and suggestions below to strategies you already share with students.

  ▶ Give students lists of frequently misspelled words. Make the lists visible and easy to access. Call them "no excuse" words and hold students accountable for correct spelling.

  ▶ Show students books (or create booklets of your own) with long lists of commonly used and frequently misspelled words. These books should not have definitions, just alphabetized lists of words. Students can highlight the words that cause them problems. When they go back to the lists, they will easily find the correct spellings. Tell students to use the space in the margins to add other words that they frequently misspell.

  ▶ Make lists of spelling/vocabulary words that students can use when you introduce new content. This is especially helpful for content in history, science, math, geography, and social studies. Expect students to keep the lists. Hold them accountable for spelling the words correctly when they write.

  ▶ Create outrageous stories to help students master tough words. Make the story visual and hard to forget. (For an example, see *Bonus Tool 10-7-1*.)

  ▶ Teach students to write and memorize sentences that help them learn and remember how to spell a word. (For an example, see *Bonus Tool 10-7-1*.)

  ▶ Show students how to find and use small words inside difficult or challenging words. Seeing the small word will help when it is time to spell the challenging word. (For an example, see *Bonus Tool 10-7-1*.)

  ▶ Encourage students to make lists of words that relate to their report or research projects. This way they will not have to look them up a second time.

  ▶ Ask students to share hints or tricks that they have learned or developed themselves for spelling certain words. One idea that helps many students is to spell the word backward, then forward, from memory.

- Make spelling a priority and remind students that the saying "spelling counts" is true in school, but even more so in business and social activities outside of school.

## 10-8 Perfect Three-Sentence Paragraphs

Students can use this strategy to apply what they have learned about sentence writing and to practice writing short, organized responses. It directs students to edit, revise, and copy a three-sentence paragraph.

**Prerequisites:** 3-6 Better Sentences and 3-11 Sentence Variety

The goal of the Perfect Three-Sentence Paragraphs strategy is for each student to write and then rework a paragraph until it is perfect. This means that the paragraph is well written and free from capitalization, usage, punctuation, and spelling errors. Teachers can assess three-sentence paragraphs quickly and give students the guidance they need to edit, revise, and perfect their writing.

## Before Class

- Make overhead transparencies and student copies of *Tools 10-8a, 10-8b,* and *10-8c.* Cut the sections apart on student copies of *Tool 10-8c.*
- Have available blank overhead transparencies and overhead markers.

## During Class

1. Display *Tool 10-8a*. Review and discuss the Ten Expectations for Writing a Perfect Three-Sentence Paragraph. Explain to students that the primary goal for this activity is that they practice and master important language skills.

2. Using *Tool 10-8b*, read through the five steps on the left side and the examples on the right. Use content-area information to provide additional examples on the board or a blank overhead transparency.

3. Model the planning process for Perfect Three-Sentence Paragraphs on a blank transparency. (See Section 4 for more information about topic sentences, key/star ideas, and transitions.)

   - Choose a topic using content-area information. When students use content they are learning or have learned, it is easy for them to add detail and meaning to each sentence.
   - Choose a working title.
   - Write a topic sentence.
   - Identify two key/star ideas.

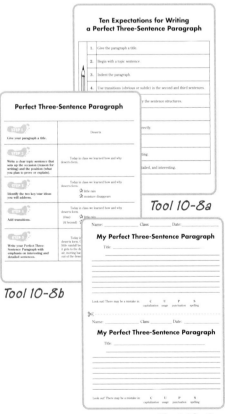

*Tool 10-8a*

*Tool 10-8b*

*Tool 10-8c*

- Explain that transitions are words and phrases that connect ideas in a paragraph or report. Select transitions that best fit your topic. Put the transitions in parentheses as shown on *Tool 10-8b*.

4. With input from your students, demonstrate writing more Perfect Three-Sentence Paragraphs on a transparency of *Tool 10-8c* or on half sheets of paper.

5. Give students half sheets from *Tool 10-8c*. Assign a topic or theme or have them choose one.

6. Have your students use the back of *Tool 10-8c* to draft their topic sentence and two key/star ideas. If students have not learned or mastered topic sentences, give them one. If they have learned topic sentences, give just the topic.

7. On the lined side of the sheet, have students write their own Perfect Three-Sentence Paragraphs.

8. Have students hand in their paragraphs. When you score the paragraphs, circle any mistakes or use another technique to point out any errors.

9. When you return their paragraphs, include a new copy of *Tool 10-8c*, or have students use blank notebook paper. Have them staple the new sheet on top of the old. Have students use the new sheet to revise their paragraph, again aiming for a perfect paragraph.

**Note:** Using the Perfect Three-Sentence Paragraphs strategy on a regular basis sets high standards for all writing assignments. Each time students write these paragraphs, they learn and master important writing skills. Because they rewrite until they have perfect paragraphs, their scores should always improve their overall grades. Initial instruction will take time and guidance, but once students have practiced the Perfect Three-Sentence Paragraphs strategy a few times, it can become a quick and easy activity.

## Additional Ideas

- Give each student a 9" × 12" envelope for storing his or her paragraphs. Keep the envelopes in class or have students put them in their writing notebooks. Students enjoy seeing their progress and sharing their successes with others. You could also have students write their paragraphs in a spiral notebook that can be stored in the classroom. These writing samples are good to share at student-parent-teacher conferences.

- Turn the Perfect Three-Sentence Paragraphs strategy into a five- to seven-minute review once or twice a week.

- When students tackle longer writing assignments, they should be expected to apply the same high standards they used for writing their Perfect Three-Sentence Paragraphs. Review *Tool 10-8a* as needed.

- Expect interesting paragraphs from all students by assigning content-based topics. This allows students to show off what they know, use content vocabulary and concepts, and include interesting details in their short paragraphs.

- Add variety to paragraph assignments by using pictures, art, quotations, and special events. Ask students for creative suggestions.

## 10-9 Analyzing a Paragraph

Using this strategy helps students learn to quickly see the strengths and weaknesses in a short piece of writing. This information will help them to focus on what needs to be revised.

### Before Class

- Make an overhead transparency and student copies of *Tool 10-9a*.
- *Bonus Tool 10-9-1* provides additional examples.

*Tool 10-9a*

### During Class

1. Display *Tool 10-9a* and explain to your students that they will use this form to help them quickly take a paragraph apart so they can see what works and what doesn't. Tell them they will not use the grid for every writing assignment, but only occasionally as a part of a class discussion or assignment, or as a way to get a clearer picture of their own writing.

2. Review *Tool 10-9a* with your class and point out each column. Give examples as needed.

3. Tell your class that a paragraph is weak if
   - Several sentences start with the same word(s);
   - Many sentences are short (five to eight words per sentence);
   - Many sentences are very long (fifteen or more words per sentence);
   - The list for verbs contains lots of "to be" verbs;
   - There are no strong vocabulary words used for description;
   - There is no appropriate content vocabulary used to elaborate or explain.

4. On the other hand, the paragraph is strong if sentences are varied, contain action verbs, and share interesting and detailed content.

5. As a group, use the grid on *Tool 10-9a* to analyze a basic paragraph (see *Bonus Tool 10-9-1* for an example) that has very simple short sentences, few action verbs, and little or no description.

6. With your students, rewrite the basic paragraph creating a strong, descriptive paragraph. Then re-evaluate the new paragraph. Have students analyze other paragraphs such as those in Sections 4 and 9 and discuss their strengths and weaknesses.

7. Have students assess their own paragraphs using the grid. Encourage them to look carefully at their own writing, and support them as they try to make improvements.

# Using Quick Checks for Self-Evaluation

Quick checks can be a wonderful way for students to evaluate their own work. It gives them a frame of reference and provides a clear understanding of what's expected of them. For students to improve their writing, they need to know what is expected of them and receive feedback regarding their successes in meeting those expectations.

## Objectives

- Learn how to evaluate writing
- Learn what is expected

| Strategy | Strategy Description | Page | Tools |
|---|---|---|---|
| **10-10** Quick Check for Sentences and Topic Sentences | Self-evaluating sentences and topic sentences | 431 | 10-10a to 10-10h |
| **10-11** Quick Check for Short Answers | Self-evaluating short answers | 432 | 10-11a to 10-11d |
| **10-12** Quick Check for Note Taking | Self-evaluating notes | 433 | 10-12a |
| **10-13** Quick Check for Speeches | Self-evaluating speeches | 433 | 10-13a |

# 10-10 Quick Check for Sentences and Topic Sentences

Students can use this strategy to set their own goals and evaluate their general sentences and topic sentences. It also gives teachers an easy method to assess student progress.

**Note:** You may present quick checks for topic sentences and general sentences individually or together. These instructions are for presenting them separately.

## Before Class

- Make overhead transparencies and student copies of *Tools 10-10a* through *10-10d* for checking most types of sentences.

- Make overhead transparencies and student copies of *Tools 10-10e* through *10-10h* for checking topic sentences.

## During Class

1. With your class, review *Tool 10-10a* for general sentences or *Tool 10-10e* for topic sentences. Discuss the descriptors for below basic, basic, proficient, and advanced levels. Note that the levels are given as a continuum. Tell students this Tool can be used for evaluating sentences in any writing assignment, and for evaluating topic sentences in an expository writing assignment.

2. Share the examples on *Tools 10-10b* and *10-10c* for general sentences, and *10-10f* and *10-10g* for topic sentences. Compare the sentences to the descriptors on *Tool 10-10a* or *Tool 10-10e* and continue to discuss why each example earns the rating shown.

3. Use *Tool 10-10d* or *Tool 10-10h* to demonstrate writing sentences or topic sentences at advanced through below basic levels, and/or have students write sentences at all four levels.

4. Have students keep copies of *Tools 10-10a* and *10-10e* for reference.

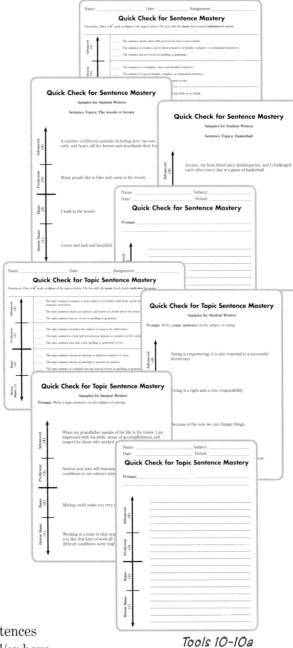

*Tools 10-10a through 10-10h*

## 10-11 Quick Check for Short Answers

Students can use this strategy to set their own goals and evaluate their short answers (Section 1). Teachers can also use it as an easy method for assessing student progress.

## Before Class

Make overhead transparencies and student copies of *Tools 10-11a* through *10-11d*.

## During Class

1. With your class, review *Tool 10-11a* and discuss the descriptors for below basic, basic, proficient, and advanced levels. Note that the levels are given as a continuum. Tell students they can use this Tool to evaluate their own short answers.

2. Share the examples on *Tools 10-11b* and *10-11c*. Compare the short answers to the descriptors on *Tool 10-11a* and continue to discuss why each answer earns the rating shown.

3. Use *Tool 10-11d* to demonstrate writing short answers that illustrate below basic through advanced ratings and/or have students write answers at all four levels.

4. Discuss the importance of being able to give a great short answer orally or in writing in a variety of settings, such as school, home, or a workplace.

5. Have students keep a copy of *Tool 10-11a* for reference throughout the year.

6. Expect great short answers—oral and written.

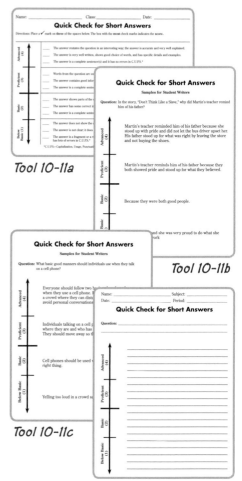

Tool 10-11a

Tool 10-11b

Tool 10-11c

Tool 10-11d

# 10-12 Quick Check for Note Taking

Students can use this strategy to set their own goals and evaluate their note taking. Teachers can also use it as an easy method to give feedback and assess student progress.

## Before Class

Make an overhead transparency and student copies of *Tools 10-12a*.

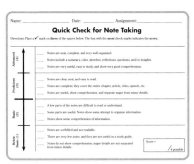

*Tool 10-12a*

## During Class

1. Review *Tool 10-12a* and discuss the descriptors for below basic, basic, proficient, and advanced levels. Note that the levels are given as a continuum. Discuss with your students what examples of each level of note taking would look like.

2. Have students keep a copy of *Tool 10-12a* for reference throughout the year, and encourage them to use it to evaluate their own notes.

# 10-13 Quick Check for Speeches

For students to improve their presentation skills, they need to know what is expected of them and receive feedback regarding their successes in meeting those expectations. Students can use this strategy to set their own goals and evaluate their speech and presentation skills (Section 8). Teachers can also use it as an easy method for assessing student progress.

## Before Class

Make an overhead transparency and student copies of *Tool 10-13a*.

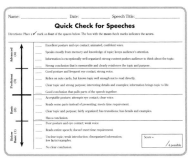

*Tool 10-13a*

## During Class

1. Review *Tool 10-13a* and discuss with your class the descriptors for below basic, basic, proficient, and advanced levels. Note that the levels are given as a continuum. It is not unusual for a speaker to be at a proficient level on one attribute and at a basic level for another.

2. Give students a model of what good posture, eye contact, voice volume, and animation looks and sounds like. Discuss how these are important ways to keep the audience's attention. Have students practice in small groups. Discuss the other attributes and explain and give examples as needed.

3. Discuss ways to increase confidence when presenting, such as memorizing parts of the speech, using an informal outline, and taking notes as methods for staying organized and keeping on topic.

4. Reinforce that a good speech

   - Is well organized—uses an informal outline for planning;
   - Has a clear introduction in which the topic is clearly stated;
   - Has a strong conclusion that makes the topic memorable and the purpose of the speech clear (to persuade, describe, inform, and so on;
   - Contains sufficient details, facts, and examples that reinforce the topic.

5. Inform your students that a good way to prepare for a speech is to review the quick check found on *Tool 10-13a* and make sure that they have covered all the appropriate components of a speech. Have students keep a copy of *Tool 10-13a* for reference throughout the year.

**Note:** On your own or with help from students, design more detailed and specific quick check tools for different types of speeches that students give for you or for other teachers. Use *Tool 10-13a* as a guide. See Section 8 for various types of speeches and presentations.

# Practical, Effective Assessment

Students need targeted and focused feedback so they know when their performance is on track and when it needs to be improved. The following six scoring guides and the matching samples for student writers address the most frequently assigned types of writing.

Frequent formal and informal assessments help students improve their writing, especially when they understand how their work will be scored and when they feel empowered about earning the final score that they receive. The purpose of having standards and assessments is to take the "guesswork" out of grading, and to help students know exactly what they need to do to rise to their best level of performance.

## Objectives

- Develop a better understanding of what constitutes good writing
- Provide a consistent format and forms and processes for giving feedback

| Strategy | Strategy Description | Page | Tools |
|---|---|---|---|
| **10-14** Definitions and Descriptions for Using Scoring Guides | Learning background information about the four areas evaluated on the scoring guide | 436 | 10-14a to 10-14d |
| **10-15** Expository Paragraphs Scoring Guide | Using rubrics, assessment forms, and student samples to assess paragraph writing | 441 | 10-15a to 10-15c |
| **10-16** Expository Essays and Reports Scoring Guide | Using rubrics, assessment forms, and student samples to assess essay and report writing | 442 | 10-16a to 10-16c |

*(chart continues)*

| Strategy *(continued)* | Strategy Description | Page | Tools |
|---|---|---|---|
| **10-17** **Persuasive Writing Scoring Guide** | Using rubrics, assessment forms, and student samples to assess persuasive writing | 443 | 10-17a to 10-17c |
| **10-18** **Narratives Scoring Guide** | Using rubrics, assessment forms, and student samples to assess narrative writing | 445 | 10-18a to 10-18c |
| **10-19** **Personal Essays Scoring Guide** | Using rubrics, assessment forms, and student samples to assess personal essay writing | 446 | 10-19a to 10-19c |
| **10-20** **Summary Writing Scoring Guide** | Using rubrics, assessment forms, and student samples to assess summary writing | 448 | 10-20a to 10-20c |

# **10-14** Definitions and Descriptions for Using Scoring Guides

In this strategy, students become familiar with scoring guides. Make the guides an important part of your writing instruction. Include them as a part of the common language that students and teachers share as they work together to improve writing skills.

The frequent use of scoring guides is an excellent way to provide students with feedback. When they understand how their work will be scored and therefore have control over the final score that they receive, their writing skills will improve.

This 16-point scoring guide format with its four categories can be used for all kinds of writing. Its simplicity makes it appealing to students, helpful to teachers, and easy to understand for family members.

## Before Class

- Make overhead transparencies and student copies of *Tools 10-14a* through *10-14d*.

- Make a set of transparencies of the various scoring guides (*Tools 10-15a, 10-16a, 10-17a, 10-18a, 10-19a,* and *10-20a*), and make student copies into a booklet.

## During Class

1. Use the phrase "welcome to success" when introducing scoring guides. Explain to students that they will be using scoring guides that will show them exactly what to fix, improve, or change to be successful in their writing. As they make these changes, students will see their scores improve—and eventually they will see scores that are consistently proficient or advanced.

2. Using *Tool 10-14a*, explain these are the four main areas that will be used to evaluate and score writing: organization, content, style, and grammar/mechanics/presentation (G.M.P.). The questions themselves help students see what each of the four categories used on their scoring guides means. Explain that they can also use these questions to monitor their own work.

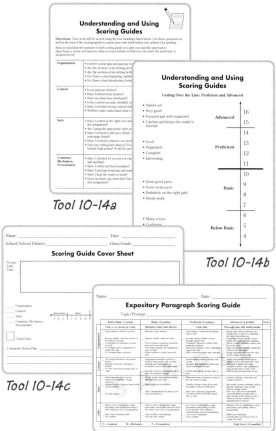

*Tool 10-14a*

*Tool 10-14b*

*Tool 10-14c*

*Tool 10-14d*

3. Display *Tool 10-14b* to introduce the 16-point continuum that shows the four different levels of success (advanced, proficient, basic, and below basic). Explain that the continuum is important because it a strong visual of where they are with a particular piece of writing and what point on the line they want or need to reach. Point out that *Tool 10-14b* also contains general descriptors for each level, but students will also use a scoring guide that will help determine the number of points they receive.

   - Explain that this continuum uses a 16-point scale. The better their writing, the more points they will receive.

   - Tell your students that 16 points are used because it is easy for teachers, students, and others to manipulate. In other words, it is easy to add, subtract, and multiply all parts of 16.

   - The 16-point scale can, of course, be translated into percentages, but the continuum is not meant to replace grades that teachers give. The teacher determines how and what criteria are used for final grades.

4. Point out the dark horizontal line in the center of *Tool 10-14b* and let your class know that the continuum presents the concept of "getting over the line" (to proficient or advanced). Tell students that the goal for all writing assignments is to get scores that are over the line. Assure students that you will teach the strategies and skills that they need, and that you will give guidance as they revise and edit.

## Introducing Scoring Guides

1. Display a transparency of *Tool 10-14d* and explain that this is a sample of a scoring guide. Help students follow along as you read the scoring guide by placing a blank piece of paper under the line that starts with "Below Basic (1 point)" to cover up the descriptions of each category. As you read through the categories, gradually reveal the next lines of text.

2. Remind students that *below basic*, *basic*, *proficient*, and *advanced* are the terms used on the continuum. Next, remind students about the importance of planning.

3. Tell students that they will receive 1, 2, 3, or 4 points for each of the four categories listed along the left: organization, content, style, and grammar/mechanics/presentation (G.M.P.).

   - The points received for each category match the box with the most check marks. In organization, for example, if there are three check marks under proficient and two under advanced, the score would be 3, or proficient. Write the score (3) in the "Score" column to the right.

   - If there are two check marks under proficient, two under basic, and one under below basic, the score would be 2 for basic. If there are two check marks under advanced, two under proficient, and one under basic, the score would be 3.

   - It is best to score low as a way to help students see what needs to be fixed. It is always better to show students what can be improved. Points for effort alone defeat the purpose.

4. Keep in mind, and remind students, that the goal is improvement through revision, and the ultimate goal is success based on meeting a standard.

5. Read through all descriptors for the remaining categories at all four levels. Define and explain terms as needed. Point out the fact that the descriptors that run across the page are parallel to each other and easy to read. Demonstrate this by setting a blank piece of paper along a line of descriptors on your transparency. Have students do the same with their copies. Assure your students that in just a little time they will become very familiar with the scoring guides and, after using them two or three times, they will have memorized many of the descriptors. As they use the guides, they quickly become familiar with what is needed to reach various levels of success.

6. Finally, explain to your students that although the sample scoring guide is for paragraph writing, all of the other scoring guides have the same categories and levels of success. Only the descriptors change.

7. Demonstrate how the individual scores for each category go along the right side and total points are recorded at the bottom of the page.

8. Take time for questions and practice using a scoring guide with a sample that you have written or with the samples provided in the Tools for each writing style. (There are additional writing samples on Bonus Tools for each writing type.)

9. Ask students to keep *Tool 10-14a* and a copy of each of the scoring guides in their writing notebooks for reference throughout the year.

## A Baseball Analogy for the Scoring Guides

As you score student work, consider the following analogy.

While you read their work, picture a student writer who is eager to play baseball. Like baseball players, some writers will have strong skills, while others will need extra help and more practice. As the coach, you will want all "players" to become strong team members. This means having a plan for improvement. The scoring guide will be that plan. The check marks on the grid give students a clear message about what to do; the marks make revision and editing seem doable. More importantly, the time and effort they put forth will seem worthwhile.

The message to give students with the scoring guide is that all students can and will succeed. The coach will help make it happen!

**Below Basic: Some players (writers) might be in the park but not on the field; not ready to play.**

Pieces of writing described as below basic are easy to recognize. Content is not logical—it is difficult to read and understand. The assigned task is not addressed at all or in a very minimal way. The writer is clearly not ready to take his or her place on the field.

The game plan for improvement includes two parts. Part one is presenting frequent, short writing assignments in a way that guarantees success. This means increasing practice time with teacher-guided lessons, framed assignments, and practice guides. The second part is to present frequent, short lessons to improve specific language skills and to build confidence.

**Basic: Many players (writers) are working to join the team. They are players who spend lots of time on the bench, but they hope to improve and may even get an occasional hit.**

A piece of writing with a basic score shows clear signs of organization and logical content. It is obvious that the writer understands the task. The content of the piece, however, is not developed. The writer needs guidance and encouragement during practice sessions to develop skills that will move him or her off the bench and onto the field more often.

The game plan includes lots of modeling and guided instruction to improve skills. The plan also includes writing with the student to make sure he or she sees and hears the correct message. Just like coaches who sometimes help hold the bat as a batter learns to connect with the ball, teachers give student writers the support they need to succeed. Teachers, like coaches, also increase the practice time by requiring writing in all subjects, every day.

**Proficient: Strong team players (writers) are those who have good skills and consistently get hits.**

When a piece of writing has a proficient score, it is because the clarity, organization, and content of the piece are impressive. There is a clear sense of direction and an obvious understanding of the writing task. The readers feel good about what they are reading. The writer has a definite hit, but the piece needs more work to become a home run.

The game plan for improvement is to help each student hit a home run. Teachers use the scoring guides to provide directions for earning more points. The guide gives students specific, practical, and helpful hints for editing and/or revising. Teachers coach proficient writers, explaining and modeling as needed. They provide many examples that show the fine line between proficient and advanced writing.

Teachers also remind student writers that proficient means good. Writers, like baseball players, cannot expect to hit a home run each time they get up to bat. The fun challenge is trying to make the big hit.

**Advanced: If players (writers) have advanced skills, they frequently hit home runs. They are also able to coach others, giving them tips about their performances.**

A piece of writing rated advanced shows that the writer could actually coach others. The piece demonstrates mastery of many skills and insights about writing that can be shared with classmates.

The game plan for enrichment of advanced writers is to provide challenging assignments, encourage risk taking, and promote independence. Teachers and coaches know that even top-quality players appreciate the opportunity to discuss their performances and are anxious to learn more.

# 10-15 Expository Paragraphs Scoring Guide

Use this scoring guide and writing samples with the paragraph-writing strategies presented in Section 4 and with specific paragraph assignments suggested in Section 9.

**Prerequisite:** 10-14 Definitions and Descriptions for Using Scoring Guides

Encourage success by modeling and expecting students to make plans for their paragraphs using informal outlines.

## Before Class

- Make overhead transparencies and student copies of *Tools 10-15a, 10-15b,* and *10-15c.*

  *Bonus Tools 10-15-1* through *10-15-4* provide additional examples.

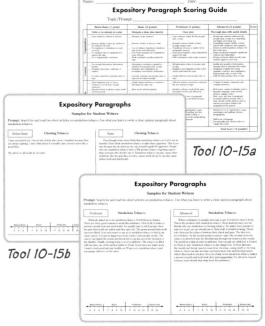

*Tool 10-15a*

*Tool 10-15b*

*Tool 10-15c*

## During Class

1. Tell or remind students that you will use a scoring guide to rate their writing assignments below basic, basic, proficient, or advanced. Reinforce that the scores will help them learn what they're doing right and what they need to improve for successful writing, and that it takes practice to write at the advanced level.

2. Review the scoring guide for expository paragraphs on *Tool 10-15a.*

3. Display transparencies of *Tools 10-15b* and *10-15c.* With your students, use the "Smokeless Tobacco" paragraphs on *Tools 10-15b* and *10-15c* to identify and explain the differences in the four levels of writing and to promote the power of revision. (For an additional group of example paragraphs, see *Bonus Tools 10-15-1* through *10-15-4.*)

### Below Basic "Smokeless Tobacco"

The score for this piece is very low because the information is confusing and there is no clear purpose for the writing.

### Basic "Smokeless Tobacco"

The score for this piece is basic. The thesis statement or topic sentence is clear and shows a clear purpose for writing, but there is no conclusion. There are some facts but they are not well organized. Transitions are missing. The paragraph needs to be developed.

### Proficient "Smokeless Tobacco"

The score for this piece is proficient. The paragraph has a clear purpose. Information is well organized and transitions are clear. There is a strong connection between the topic sentence and the conclusion. Fixing the spelling errors and developing a more engaging style would make it advanced.

### Advanced "Smokeless Tobacco"

The score for this piece is advanced because it has an interesting lead, an engaging thesis statement, and well-thought-out arguments with good elaboration. The conclusion restates the thesis in a new way. The piece has style—good word choice and variety in sentences and sentence structures.

## 10-16 Expository Essays and Reports Scoring Guide

Use this guide with the essay- and report-writing strategies presented in Section 5 and with the specific writing assignments suggested in Section 9.

**Prerequisite:** 10-14 Definitions and Descriptions for Using Scoring Guides

Encourage success by modeling and expecting students to make plans for their essays and reports by using the **5-5 Blocking Out Essays and Reports** and **4-7 Planning with an Informal Outline** strategies.

## Before Class

- Make overhead transparencies and student copies of *Tools 10-16a, 10-16b*, and *10-16c*.
-  *Bonus Tools 10-16-1* through *10-16-4* provide additional examples.

## During Class

1. Tell or remind students you will use a scoring guide to rate their writing assignments as below basic, basic, proficient, or advanced. Reinforce that the scores will help them learn what they're doing right and what they need to improve for successful writing and that it takes practice to write at the advanced level.

2. Review the scoring guide for reports and essays on *Tool 10-16a*.

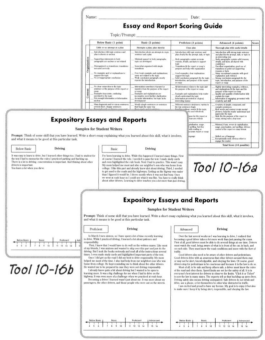

*Tool 10-16a*

*Tool 10-16b*

*Tool 10-16c*

3. Display transparencies of *Tools 10-16b* and *10-16c*. With your students, use the "Driving" essays on *Tools 10-16b* and *10-16c* to identify and explain the differences in the four levels of writing and to promote the power of revision. (For an additional group of examples, see *Bonus Tools 10-16-1* through *10-16-4*.)

**Below Basic "Driving"**

The score for this piece is very low because the information is confusing and there is no clear purpose for the writing. The text is not long enough to be considered an essay. The comments are random and incomplete. The writer should rewrite using a plan.

**Basic "Driving"**

The score for this piece is basic. There is some attempt at a thesis statement and some attempt to organize information. Some explanation supports the key/star ideas. Simple but effective transitions help with organization. The text looks like a paragraph (although it is not indented) but it contains enough information to be developed into an essay. It should be rewritten with subtler transitions and more varied and effective word choice and sentence structures.

**Proficient "Driving"**

The score for this piece is proficient. It follows a clear plan. The thesis statement in the introduction is clear and effective. Information is well organized with good transitions. Key/star ideas are elaborated with good examples. There is a strong connection between the introduction and the conclusion. It has a few mechanical errors, and it uses appropriate, but ordinary, words and sentence structures. This piece could be improved with more creative word choice and sentence structures.

**Advanced "Driving"**

The score for this piece is advanced because the writer takes a simple topic and develops the thesis with interesting examples and explanations. Supporting information is very well organized. Using the football analogy and the reminder to "Click it or Ticket" make it easy to think about the act of driving. The essay fully addresses the prompt with style and a strong voice.

# 10-17 Persuasive Writing Scoring Guide

Use this guide when students write persuasive essays from Section 9.

**Prerequisite:** 10-14 Definitions and Descriptions for Using Scoring Guides

Encourage success by modeling and expecting students to make plans for their essays by using the **5-5 Blocking Out Essays and Reports** and **4-7 Planning with an Informal Outline** strategies as well as the Tools for persuasive writing from Section 9.

## Before Class

- Make overhead transparencies and student copies of *Tools 10-17a*, *10-17b*, and *10-17c*.

 *Bonus Tools 10-17-1* through *10-17-4* provide additional examples.

## During Class

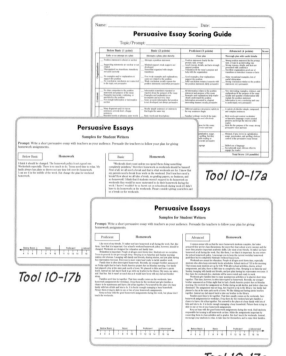

*Tool 10-17a*

*Tool 10-17b*

*Tool 10-17c*

1. Tell or remind students you will use a scoring guide to rate their writing assignments below basic, basic, proficient, or advanced. Reinforce that the scores will help them learn what they're doing right and what they need to improve for successful writing and that it takes practice to write at the advanced level.

2. Review the scoring guide for persuasive essays on *Tool 10-17a*.

3. Display transparencies of *Tools 10-17b* and *10-17c*. With your students, use the "Homework" essays to identify and explain the differences in the four levels of writing and to promote the power of revision. (For an additional group of examples, see *Bonus Tools 10-17-1* through *10-17-4*.)

### Below Basic "Homework"

The score for this piece is very low. There are some hints at developing a position, but the information is confusing and there is no clear purpose for the writing. The text is not long enough to be considered an essay. The comments are random and incomplete. Some good ideas are scattered throughout. Creating and using a detailed informal outline based on some of these random thoughts could produce a good essay.

### Basic "Homework"

The score for this piece is basic. There is some attempt at a position statement and some attempt to organize information. Some explanation supports the key/ star ideas. The language is simple and often too casual to be effective in this context. Obvious transitions help with organization. The text, however, looks like a paragraph. The piece needs elaboration and explanations in order to be developed into an effective persuasive essay.

### Proficient "Homework"

The score for this piece is proficient. The position statement in the introduction is clear and effective. Information is well organized with good transitions. Key/star ideas are elaborated with good examples. There is a strong connection between the introduction and the conclusion. There are a few mechanical errors. The mechanical errors should be fixed, and the piece could be improved with more creative sentence structures and word choice.

### Advanced "Homework"

The score for this piece is advanced because the writer goes beyond trying to convince the audience; the writer takes a clearly stated position and offers suggestions for improving the homework policy. A powerful position statement that is supported by logical reasons is convincing. Information is very well organized. Transitions, made by repetition and emphasis, help make the writer's point. The essay begins with a strong lead and a clear introduction. The topic is reinforced by a well-stated conclusion.

## 10-18 Narratives Scoring Guide

Use this guide with the narrative-writing strategies presented in Section 6 and with specific writing assignments suggested in Section 9.

**Prerequisite:** 10-14 Definitions and Descriptions for Using Scoring Guides

Encourage success by modeling and expecting students to make plans for their narratives by using the quick sketch strategy.

### Before Class

- Make overhead transparencies and student copies of *Tools 10-18a, 10-18b,* and *10-18c*.

- *Bonus Tools 10-18-1* through *10-18-4* provide additional examples.

### During Class

1. Tell or remind students you will use a scoring guide to rate their writing assignments below basic, basic, proficient, or advanced. Reinforce that the scores will help them learn what they're doing right and what they need to improve for successful writing and that it takes practice to write at the advanced level.

2. Review the scoring guide for narratives on *Tool 10-18a*.

3. Display transparencies of *Tools 10-18b* and *10-18c*. With your students, use the "Student Director" samples to identify and explain the

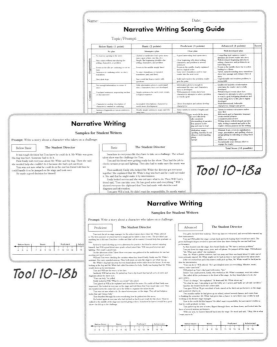

*Tool 10-18a*

*Tool 10-18b*

*Tool 10-18c*

differences in the four levels of writing and to promote the power of revision. (For an additional group of examples, see *Bonus Tools 10-18-1* through *10-18-4*.)

**Below Basic "The Student Director"**

The score for this narrative is very low because the sentences are confusing and there is no clear purpose for the writing. The text is not long enough to be considered a complete narrative. The simple sentences list some events but they are not connected. The writer needs to create a plan with details and notes that could lead to good description.

**Basic "The Student Director"**

The score for this piece is basic. There is some attempt to create a narrative with a beginning, middle, and end. The narrative is somewhat organized, but effective transitions are missing. The narrative is flat; it tells the events but does not describe mood or feelings.

**Proficient "The Student Director"**

The score for this piece is proficient. The narrative is told in a clear, organized fashion with good use of transitions. There is an obvious attempt to include details and descriptions; action verbs like "glared" and "thumbed" help the reader picture the events. Smoother transitions and a more developed, engaging style would make this piece advanced.

**Advanced "Student Director"**

The score for this piece is advanced because a strong, active voice is used in this narrative. The writer builds the events to a climax with good description and word choice. The writer helps the reader understand the main character by learning about the character's thoughts and about his past. The narrative shows what is happening rather than just telling the story.

## 10-19 Personal Essays Scoring Guide

Use this guide with the personal essay writing strategies presented in Section 7.

**Prerequisite:** 10-14 Definitions and Descriptions for Using Scoring Guides

Encourage success by modeling and expecting students to make plans for their essays by using the personal narrative planning strategy which incorporates Accordion Essay organization (**5-1 Elements of Accordion Essays and Reports**) and quick sketches for narrative writing (**6-7 Quick Sketch and Quick Note Planning**).

## Before Class

- Make overhead transparencies and student copies of *Tools 10-19a*, *10-19b*, and *10-19c*.

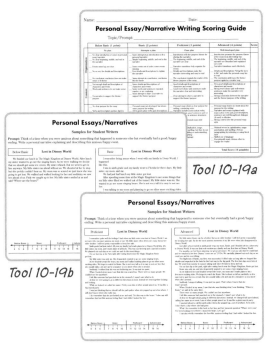

  *Bonus Tools 10-19-1* through *10-19-4* provide additional examples.

## During Class

1. Tell or remind students you will use a scoring guide to rate their writing assignments as below basic, basic, proficient, or advanced. Reinforce that the scores will help them learn what they're doing right and what they need to improve for successful writing and that it takes practice to write at the advanced level.

2. Review the scoring guide for personal narratives on *Tool 10-19a*.

*Tool 10-19a*

3. Display transparencies of *Tools 10-19b* and *10-19c*. With your students, use the "Lost in Disney World" personal narratives to identify and explain the differences in the four levels of writing and to promote the power of revision. (For an additional group of examples, see *Bonus Tools 10-19-1* through *10-19-4*.)

*Tool 10-19b*

*Tool 10-19c*

**Below Basic "Lost in Disney World"**
The score for this piece is below basic because it does not demonstrate understanding of the personal essay style or format. The information that is shared has the makings of a personal essay, but it needs to be developed. The writer needs to make (or remake) a plan that includes an introduction and a conclusion as well as a narrative for the body of the paper.

**Basic "Lost in Disney World"**
The score for this piece is basic. It is a clear retelling of an important event in the writer's life. It also tells how the writer was impacted by this event. The narrative, however, is flat. The narrative needs to be revised to add descriptions, feelings, and details.

**Proficient "Lost in Disney World"**
The score for this piece is strong proficient. The writer shows knowledge of and control over the personal essay style. The essay has a good, clear introduction. The narrative is retold in an interesting way. Narrative transitions help with organization and enhance the story. A good conclusion shares the writer's feelings. The sister's statement used in the conclusion helps share the point of the narrative.

The essay clearly answers the prompt, but there are a few mechanical errors. The writer should correct the mechanical errors and focus his effort on improving sentence structures and word choice.

**Advanced "Lost in Disney World"**
The score for this piece is advanced because the writer takes a simple episode in his life to show what it means to be anxious about someone else. Small details enhance the narrative. Descriptions like "tall as a yardstick" and "giant search party" work well. Good word choice and sentence fluency make the writer's voice and feelings clear.

## 10-20 Summary Writing Scoring Guide

Use this guide with the summary writing strategy presented in Section 1.

**Prerequisite:** 10-14 Definitions and Descriptions for Using Scoring Guides

Encourage success by modeling and expecting students to make plans for their summaries by using the IVF topic sentence and fact outline strategy. (See the **1-30 Four-Step Summary Paragraphs** strategy.)

### Before Class

- Make overhead transparencies and student copies of *Tools 10-20a, 10-20b,* and *10-20c.*

- ⊚ *Bonus Tools 10-20-1* through *10-20-4* provide additional examples.

### During Class

1. Tell or remind students you will use a scoring guide to rate their writing assignments below basic, basic, proficient, or advanced. Reinforce that the scores will help them learn what they're doing right and what they need to improve and that it takes practice to write at the advanced level.

2. Review the scoring guide for summary writing on *Tool 10-20a.*

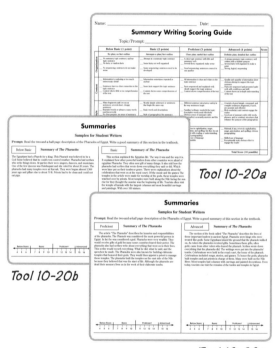

*Tool 10-20a*

*Tool 10-20b*

*Tool 10-20c*

**3.** Display transparencies of *Tools 10-20b* and *10-20c*. With your students, use the "Summary of *The Pharaohs*" examples to identify and explain the differences in the four levels of writing and to promote the power of revision. (For an additional group of examples, see *Bonus Tools 10-20-1* through *10-20-4*.)

**Below Basic "Summary of *The Pharaohs*"**
The score for this piece is very low because the paragraph is a collection of random facts from the selection about pharaohs. There is no topic sentence. The sentences are not well sequenced. The paragraph does not show good language skills or an understanding of summary style of writing.

**Basic "Summary of *The Pharaohs*"**
The score for this piece is basic. There is some attempt at a topic sentence, however, it does not give the title of the piece being summarized. The sequencing of facts is weak and sometimes hard to follow. There is some sense of summary style.

**Proficient "Summary of *The Pharaohs*"**
The score for this summary is proficient. The summary starts with a topic sentence; however, it is somewhat awkward since it mentions only "luxuries and responsibilities." It is not clear and focused. The body of the summary is fairly well sequenced. Facts and explanations are clear and cover the scope of the article. The summary could be improved with more creative word choice and sentence structures as well as with more clarity about the article's information.

**Advanced "Summary of *The Pharaohs*"**
The score for this piece is advanced because the writer demonstrates a strong sense of summary style. The topic sentence is clear and focused. Facts to support the topic sentence are well written and informative. Sentences are also well sequenced. The summary, overall, is well written.

## Additional Ideas

- All of the Tools and Bonus Tools showing samples for student writers give students guidance as they write. Display transparencies of them periodically to inform or remind them of what is expected in their writing.

- Create samples on topics of interest and content that students must master.

- Challenge students (or groups of students) to make their own sets of samples to demonstrate their mastery of specific kinds of writing.

**Note:** When scoring guides are used regularly, all students have the guidance they need to master important academic skills. Students appreciate the timely, practical, and specific tips for revision. Students like knowing that they can control their own success and final score on their writing.

# Recording and Using Assessment Scores

Use the following forms to monitor student work and to guide students as they monitor their progress.

## Objective

- Understand process for monitoring progress
- Build confidence for improving success

| Strategy | Strategy Description | Page | Tools |
|---|---|---|---|
| **10-21** Students Record and Monitor Progress | Recording and keeping lists of writing assignments and working toward writing that is consistently proficient and advanced | 451 | 10-21a |
| **10-22** Teachers Record and Monitor Progress | Using forms to document improvement in writing and to document scores for specific kinds of writing | 451 | 10-22a, 10-22b |
| **10-23** Labels to Use with Scoring Guides | Learning timely, helpful information about a piece of writing; revising and improving writing | 453 | 10-23a |
| **10-24** Check Marks and CUPS for Grading Papers | Editing independently; receiving specific, timely feedback about writing | 453 | n/a |

## 10-21 Students Record and Monitor Progress

Students who are aware of their progress and can see their scores increasing are more motivated to strive for better work.

**Prerequisite:** 10-14 Definitions and Descriptions for Using Scoring Guides

1. Give students copies of *Tool 10-21a* to keep in their writing notebooks. Each time they receive final scores on writing assignments, ask them to record the score on the form in the appropriate place on the continuum.

2. Explain how to use the writing assessment record on *Tool 10-21a* with the following example. If, on September 15, a student earned 10 points on a writing assignment about the water cycle, she would write "Water Cycle Paragraph, September 15" near the number 10 on the grid.

3. If on her next assignment, she earned 12 points on a report about the space shuttle, she would add "Space Shuttle Report, September 28" near the number 12.

*Tool 10-21a*

4. Explain that as they track their own progress and see improvement into the proficient and advanced levels like this student did, they should realize that they should no longer turn in work that earns basic or below basic scores. In other words, they will see that they have the skills and know what they need to do to make their work proficient or above.

5. Tell students that the form is a good way to see how much work they have done and to celebrate their own successes.

## 10-22 Teachers Record and Monitor Progress

Track students' successes from the beginning to the end of the year. Students will enjoy comparing their work from the beginning of the year to the proficient or advanced work they complete at the end of the year.

**Prerequisites:** Strategies 10-14 Definitions and Descriptions for using Scoring Guides through 10-20 Summary Writing Scoring guide

Use *Tool 10-22a* to track a student's successes throughout the school year. Make enough copies for each of your students. If possible, staple copies of the student's work to the form. Students will enjoy being able to see how their skills have improved.

You can use *Tool 10-22a* in different intervals. If it would better meet your needs, change it to say beginning, middle, and end of the month, quarter, or semester. Frequent assessments of student writing promote success. Use regular class assignments rather than making the assessments elaborate and time-consuming.

## Using Multiple Graders to Assess Writing

It is sometimes advantageous to have a number of graders evaluate and score the same student writing sample. This provides an unbiased evaluation of the writing.

*Tool 10-22a*

*Tool 10-22b*

Use *Tool 10-22b* to have a group of teachers assess the same writing samples.

1. Collect writing samples from your students. Give each student a code number. Tell them to write their code number and not their names on their papers.

2. Give the evaluation team copies of the scoring guide that fits the type of writing being assessed (narrative, persuasive, summary, etc.), as found on *Tools 10-15a, 10-16a, 10-17a, 10-18a, 10-19a,* and *10-20a*. Read and discuss the scoring guide with all the members of the evaluation team to ensure that everyone has the same understanding of each element. If this is the first time some team members have participated in a group evaluation, have them first evaluate samples of student writing for practice. (Working in pairs or groups of three is also an option.)

3. Display a copy of *Tool 10-22b* with an overhead projector, or recreate a copy on the board or chart paper. Have one additional copy for each piece of student writing the team is evaluating. At the top of *Tool 10-22b*, put the name of the writing sample and the student code number. Explain there are enough rows on the Tool for each member of the team to pass around one scoring sheet for each writing example they will be evaluating, or you can choose to provide copies for each team member and then compile the scores onto one sheet later.

4. Assign a code number between 1 and 10 to each team member (or team) of the evaluation teams. Have them place the score for each writing sample in the row designated by their number. For example, team member 2 will fill in scores only in row 2.

5. Give each member of the evaluation team copies of the same writing samples.

6. Ask them to read and score the writing samples independently. Tell them to check the appropriate descriptors and make decisions about what points will be given for organization, content, style, and grammar/mechanics/presentation (G.M.P.). Give them time to discuss the scores they have given. Tell them they will need to share specific examples and reasons for their scores.

7. Have each team member report his or her scores as you record them on a transparency of *Tool 10-22b*. This makes it easy to see scores and to show how scorers agreed or disagreed. If there are large differences in scoring, discuss them as a team and allow scorers to make changes if appropriate. Take time to discuss the activity and the results.

8. Remind members of the evaluation team that information about each student sample is confidential and should not be discussed with anyone outside of evaluation meeting.

## 10-23 Labels to Use with Scoring Guides

Pages of blank address labels and/or a grading stamp from an office supply store can save time for teachers faced with lots of writing assignments to score and return to students.

Teachers must be creative and use their imaginations when it comes to scoring written work. In an ideal setting, teachers would have time to read and reread student work. They would have time to make friendly and helpful comments in the margins and at the end of a paper.

Unfortunately, that time and that world often do not exist. But students need (and deserve) more than a percentage or letter grade at the top of the page.

They also want and need to have papers returned as quickly as possible. Immediate feedback helps students keep their interest in the assignment and motivates them to revise and improve their work for a higher score.

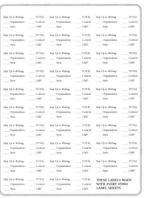

*Tool 10-23a*

As an alternative to using the full-page scoring guide cover sheet for each assignment, use the labels on *Tool 10-23a* or have a self-inking stamp made. This way, you can quickly give students important information about the organization, content, style, and grammar/mechanics/presentation (G.M.P.) of the piece they have written.

Once students have used and become familiar with the full-page scoring guides, the labels and the stamps will make sense to them. They will recognize the terms and will understand which areas of their papers to revise and edit papers.

Continue using the scoring guides for more formal assessments, but try the labels and stamps for everyday assignments.

## 10-24 Check Marks and CUPS for Grading Papers

Try these methods for noting errors in capitalization, usage, punctuation, and spelling on student papers. These tips and the following CUPS method for scoring papers save a great deal of time.

**Prerequisites:** 10-14 Definitions and Descriptions for Using Scoring Guides

### The "Check, Check, Check" Method

This technique is as easy as it sounds. At the end of any line on the page that has errors, make one check mark to denote each error. In the following example, there are four check marks at the end of the first line and one check mark at the end of the second line.

> On November 3 2005 my famly went to the amusememt park ✓✓✓✓
> with my Uncle and our cousins. We all had a very good time. ✓

This method pushes students to find and fix their own mistakes. Ask them to find the errors. The first line needs a comma after 3 and after 2005. Family and amusement are misspelled. In the second line, uncle should not be capitalized.

### CUPS Method

The CUPS method for noting errors (see **10-7 Editing with CUPS**) is just like the "Check, Check, Check" approach. The only difference is that students receive stronger hints about mistakes they may have made. Instead of check marks at the end of a line of writing, students see letters.

> **C** stands for **C**apitalization
>
> **U** stands for **U**sage
>
> **P** stands for **P**unctuation
>
> **S** stands for **S**pelling

Lines from a graded paper might look like this:

> Every time I try to right my name on the list somthing strange    **U S**
> happens my pencil breaks or another studant bumps into me    **P C S P**

The U and the S at the end of the line point out errors in usage (*right* instead of *write*) and in spelling (*something*).

The letters P C S P stand for four errors in the second line: a period after *happens,* a capital letter for *my*, an *S* for the misspelling of *student*, and a *P* for the final punctuation mark. With practice, you will be able to quickly add these marks in the margins of student papers, and students will know exactly what they need to improve.

## Additional Ideas

- Personalize your scoring method by adding notes, messages, or stickers. Circle or highlight errors to help students find them quickly. Be creative. Ask students for suggestions and insights about what kind of (and how much) feedback will help them the most.

- There is not one perfect or easy way to give students feedback. The goal is to eliminate stress and save time when it comes to scoring their papers. If teachers have scoring methods that save time, they are more likely to give students more opportunities to write.

- It is also helpful to remind students of ways to eliminate errors in their writing by setting high standards for the work that they turn in. Using Tools like Neat Paper Rules (*Tool 10-1a*) and the CUPS packet (*Tools 10-7a* through *10-7d*) will help.

# Glossary

### abstract noun
A noun signifying a quality or idea that cannot be observed with any of the five senses. (*courage, identity, condolence*)

### Accordion Essay
An essay that is expanded by adding elaboration to support the key/star ideas.

### Accordion Fold
Notebook paper folded "accordion style" into at least four sections from top to bottom. See T32 in the introduction.

### Accordion Paragraph
A paragraph that is expanded by adding elaboration to support the topic sentence or key/star idea.

### Accordion Report
A report that is expanded by adding elaboration to support the key/star ideas.

### active reading
Engaging with a text being read by employing certain strategies to increase comprehension and retention, such as taking notes, flagging important passages with sticky notes, making connections, and pausing to think about what the text is saying.

### active voice
A sentence in which the subject carries out the action. (*He kicked* the ball.)

### Action Verb Sentence
A declarative sentence with a strong action verb. (Cheyenne *hit* the ball.)

### adjective
A word that adds description to a noun. (*red* ball, *awesome* time, *fast* bike)

### adverb
A word that adds description to a verb, describing a manner of action, a place of action, or a time of action. (ran *quickly*, played *here*, called *yesterday*)

### adverbial clause
A clause that contains a subject and a verb, but one that adds description to another verb as an adverb would. (I waited *until after they left*, he ran *because he could*, she waited *until they were quiet*)

### alliteration
The repetition of consonant sounds at the beginning of words. (The *fickle fox frolicked* in the *flax*.)

### analogy
A sentence or more in writing that describes a likeness between two things that might otherwise be different.

### And, But, So, and Or Sentence
A sentence of two independent clauses that includes a comma followed by a coordinating conjunction. (*and, but, so, or, yet*)

### antagonist
The villain of a story. The villain works against the protagonist.

### appositive
A word or phrase that means the same thing as, or describes, the word that came before it. (Malik, *my brother*, is a great kid.)

**argument**
A set of facts or opinions designed to support a conclusion.

**article**
A word that comes before a noun to limit or describe the noun as definite or indefinite. (*a, an, the*)

**autobiography**
A nonfiction narrative that details portions of the writer's life story.

**big idea**
The main idea in a report or paragraph.

**biography**
A nonfiction narrative that details portions of a person's life story.

**blocking out**
A planning process using rectangles to represent each paragraph in an essay or report, creating a visual plan for a paper. The rectangles contain notes that will later guide the writer in drafting.

**Blues**
The beginning of a piece of writing that both introduces the topic of the writing and tries to capture the reader's interest. Also known as the **lead**.

**burrito fold**
Notebook paper folded into thirds vertically or horizontally. See T32 in the introduction.

**characters**
People, animals, or things about whom a story is written.

**clause**
A group of words that contain a subject and a predicate and are part of a larger sentence.

**climax**
The high point and/or turning point in a story.

**clincher**
A statement made at the end of a piece of information writing that has a friendly tone, shares emotion, and tends to motivate. See **conclusion**.

**closing statement**
A statement made at the end of a piece of information writing that is direct, has a specific tone, offers a clear statement, and expresses an opinion. See **conclusion**.

**collective noun**
A noun that refers to a group of people, animals, or things. (*group, class, family*)

**compare**
To note how facts and ideas are similar.

**Compare/Contrast Sentence**
A sentence about how two people, places, things, or ideas are alike or different. (Makayla and I look a lot *alike*.)

**complex sentence**
A sentence made up of at least one independent clause and at least one dependent clause. (*He waited for his sister when she yelled, "Stop!"*)

**compound sentence**
A sentence made up of at least two independent clauses. (*She ran like a cheetah, so it was hard to keep up with her.*)

**compound verb**
A simple predicate with two or more verbs showing different actions or conditions. (The man *bent* and *picked* up the paper.)

**compound–complex sentence**
A sentence made up of at least two independent clauses and at least one dependent clause. (*While Jaron stood panting on the sidewalk, Haley waited for him to catch his breath, so they could continue their jog.*)

**concept map**
A visual representation of the facts in a piece of information writing. Shows related facts connected by lines to form a map of the information from the piece.

**conclusion**
A statement made at the end of a piece of information writing that is formal and offers food for thought.

**conflict**
The struggle within a story, often the "thing" that needs to be solved or fixed. Also known as a **problem**.

**conjunction**
A word that connects two other words, phrases, or clauses. (*and, but, after, although*)

**conjunctive adverb**
An adverb that connects two clauses. (*also, however, otherwise*)

**contrast**
To note how facts or ideas are different.

**conventions**
The rules of a language including common patterns of grammar, spelling, punctuation, paragraphing, and capitalization.

**counterargument**
A set of facts or opinions that contradict or otherwise cast doubt on an argument. Also known as a **rebuttal**.

**CUPS**
An editing technique focused on mastering the rules of Capitalization, Usage, Punctuation, and Spelling.

**declarative sentence**
A sentence that makes a statement. (*The sun is shining today.*)

**dependent clause**
A clause that cannot stand alone as a sentence, but which adds meaning to, or receives meaning from, the independent clause to which it is attached. (*when she stopped running*)

**dialogue**
Speech between two or more characters or people.

**draft**
A preliminary or early version of a piece of writing that is not final.

**E's**
Elaboration (examples, evidence, and explanation) supporting key/star ideas. Also known as the **Reds**.

**editing**
Fixing mistakes in writing, often according to the rules of capitalization, usage, punctuation, and spelling (CUPS).

**elaboration**
Rich detail added to a report or paragraph that makes the writing more interesting or compelling. Also known as the **E's** or the **Reds**.

**essay**
A short literary composition in which the writer takes a particular position or stresses a point.

**exaggeration**
The intentional enlargement of a statement beyond the truth or what is normally said; an overstatement.

**exclamatory sentence**
A sentence that shows emotion. (*The snake just crawled onto the rake!*)

**expository writing**
Writing to give an audience information. Also known as **information writing**.

**fact outline**
A simple list of the facts in a piece of writing; used to write a summary.

**fiction**
Imaginative story writing. Tends to follow a beginning–middle–end organizational pattern.

**figurative language**
Colorful or imaginative language that paints a mental image for or stirs emotions in readers.

**first person**
A point of view in which the narrator or speaker describes his/her own thoughts and actions and uses words like *I*, *me*, and *myself*.

**flashback**
A section in a story in which the plot moves to an earlier time, often an earlier time in one or more characters' lives.

**foreshadowing**
A suggestion or hint in the text about possible events to come in a story.

**four-part sentence**
A basic sentence composed of four parts: who is doing the action, what the action is, where the action takes place, and when the action takes place. (*I finished my art project yesterday.*)

**fragment**
A phrase or group of words lacking the grammatical structure of a sentence; a subject or verb is missing. (She continued to run. *Quick as a fox.*)

**framed paragraph**
A paragraph form that provides starter words and phrases with "blanks" for students to fill in to complete the paragraph.

**framed response or report**
A paragraph or report organized by a teacher that is incomplete because it has many "blanks" left empty. Students fill in the blanks to complete the paragraph or report.

**free response**
An unstructured, brief, written or oral response to a text.

**gerund**
A verb that functions as a noun. Often ends in –ing. (*Walking* is good exercise.)

**grammar**
The set of rules governing language.

**hamburger fold**
Paper folded in half so the top edge is brought down to the bottom edge of a vertical page, unlike a hot dog fold. See T32 in the introduction.

**Handy Pages**
Reference pages that students use as an aid for a variety of writing tasks.

**happy face answer**
An answer to a question that is written in a complete sentence, is grammatically correct, uses words from the question, and demonstrates understanding of the topic.

**homographs**
Words that are alike in spelling but are different in pronunciation and meaning. (*bass* guitar, *bass* fish)

**homonyms**
Words that are identical in spelling and pronunciation but have different meanings. (The *bat* flew in the night. He swung the *bat*.)

**homophones**
Words that are alike in pronunciation but are different in meaning and sometimes in spelling. (*bass* guitar, home *base*)

**hot dog fold**
Paper folded in half lengthwise. See T32 in the introduction.

**imagery**
Words or phrases including, but not limited to, similes, metaphors, and personification that bring pictures to the mind of the reader.

**imperative sentence**
A sentence that gives a command. (*Don't litter.*)

**impromptu speech**
A speech given with little to no time to plan the speech beforehand. Impromptu speeches are often brief.

**independent clause**
A clause in a sentence that has both a subject and a verb and that expresses a complete thought. It could stand alone as a complete sentence. (*She threw the ball to Deandre* just as the bell rang.)

**infinitive**
A verb form that includes the word "to" in front of it. (*to run, to fall, to fly*)

**informal outline**
An outline for a report or paragraph. It is composed of a title, topic sentence, key/star ideas, elaborations, and conclusion. The key/star ideas and elaborations are written in brief words and phrases next to stars, dashes, and dots.

**information writing**
Writing to give an audience information. Also known as **expository writing**.

**interjection**
A word or phrase used as an exclamation. (*Wow!*)

**interrogative sentence**
A sentence that asks a question. (*Have you seen the blue pen?*)

**IVF topic sentence**
A topic sentence that stresses a strong verb and sends a clear message. IVF stands for Identify the item, select a Verb, and Finish your thought.

**key/star ideas**
Main points in a report or paragraph that support the topic. Key/star ideas are also supported by elaboration.

**lead**
The beginning of a piece of writing that both introduces the topic of the writing and tries to capture the reader's interest. Also known as the **Blues**.

**meaningful sentence**
A sentence containing a new or unusual vocabulary term that is written in a way that demonstrates understanding of the meaning of the word without just reciting the word's definition.

**mechanics**
The components governing good writing: the parts of speech, the rules of grammar, and accurate punctuation.

**message**
The lesson a writer attempts to teach a reader through a story or information writing.

**metaphor**
An implied comparison between two otherwise unrelated objects or actions. (David likes to play jokes. *He is a real clown.*)

**money summary**
A summary sentence in which a student has a fixed amount of imaginary money to "spend" on words to create a summary. The goal is either to "spend" as much or as little of the capital as possible while writing the summary, depending on teacher directions.

**mood**
The feeling that a story suggests; the story's atmosphere.

**narrative**
A work of writing also known as a story that includes characters, a plot, a conflict, and a resolution. Narratives have a beginning, middle, and end.

**nonfiction**
Writing about real people, places, and things. Often, content follows an introduction–body–conclusion organizational pattern.

**noun**
A word that refers to a person, place, thing, or idea. (*Maria, mouse, California*)

**Number (Power) Statements**
A sentence that includes a number word to help organize anticipated information. (I have *two* pets.)

**occasion**
The reason for writing.

**Occasion/Position Sentence**
A sentence or topic sentence in which the writer first states his or her occasion, or reason for writing, and then follows with his or her position, or what will be proved or explained.

**onomatopoeia**
The use of a word that represents a sound. (He dropped the rock, *kerplunk*, into the pond.)

**paraphrasing**
Taking the words of others and reworking them in writing, giving credit to the original author or speaker.

**passive voice**
A sentence in which the subject receives the action. (The ball *was kicked*.)

**personal narrative**
Writing that entertains or motivates readers by sharing a personal experience and explaining the lesson learned.

**personification**
A form of figurative language that gives human traits to something that is not human. (The sun *awoke* and *smiled* on the prairie below.)

**phrase**
A group of words that work together as a single unit in a sentence.

**plagiarism**
Taking the words of others and presenting them as one's own, giving no credit to the original author or speaker.

**plan sentence**
A sentence that provides structure for a report by presenting key/star ideas near the beginning of the report. Used with a topic sentence, it creates an easy-to-understand introduction.

**planning**
The process of organizing one's thoughts in writing prior to composing a first draft.

**plot**
The action of a story, including events, problems, and the resolution.

**poem**
Writing composed in lines or stanzas, not in prose sentences or paragraphs.

**poet**
A person who writes poems.

**poetry**
Writing, usually in stanzas or verse, that uses metaphoric language, rhyme, rhythm, and/or sound to convey meaning.

**point of view**
The position from which a story is told or an information piece is written, either first, second, or third person.

**position**
What a writer plans to prove or explain in a piece of writing.

**Posters**
Posters displaying helpful information and reminders about various writing topics that students can use as a reference. Posters for *Step Up to Writing* are available separately or in the classroom set.

**Power (Number) Sentence**
A sentence that uses a number word or phrase to organize ideas and information and help the reader anticipate key/star ideas in the text.

**predicate**
One of the two main components of a sentence; it contains the verb. (The cat *went out.*)

**preposition**
A word usually placed before a noun or noun phrase that shows its connection to another noun or phrase. (*on, beneath, against*)

**presentation**
A longer and more involved speech or report, often including visual props, music, news reports, or narratives.

**prewriting**
Assorted activities to help students brainstorm approaches or ideas before writing, including, but not limited to, sketching, free writing, and role playing.

**problem**
The struggle within a story, often the "thing" that needs to be solved or fixed. Also known as a **conflict**.

**prompt**
A statement or passage that directs students to create a response orally or in writing.

**pronoun**
A generic word used in place of a noun or noun phrase. (*he, she, it*)

**proofreading**
Checking a final written draft to catch small mistakes before turning in the work.

**prose**
The ordinary language used in sentences and paragraphs.

**protagonist**
The main character of a story. Often has a conflict with the antagonist.

**purpose**
The stimulation for writing; the reason a student wants to share his or her topic with an audience.

**Question/Statement Sentence**
A rhetorical question followed by a declarative sentence that answers the question. (*Do you like squid? I sure do.*)

**quick check**
A frame of reference that provides a clear understanding of what is expected in writing. Students can use it to evaluate their own work.

**quick notes**
Random notes and phrases jotted down next to a quick sketch. Quick notes are not a formal outline. They are words that show scenes, details, feelings, and so on.

**quick sketch**
A drawing of the beginning, middle, and end elements for a story idea that makes the plan for the story more concrete.

**RAFTS**
A prewriting strategy that encourages writers to write from a perspective other than their own. RAFTS stands for Role, Audience, Format, Topic, and Strong verb or feeling.

**reading notation response**
A variation of free responses made in the margin of a handout or text.

**rebus sentence**
A sentence in which one or more of the words has been replaced with a picture showing the meaning of the word.

**rebuttal**
A set of facts or opinions that contradict or otherwise cast doubt on an argument. Also known as a **counterargument**.

**Reds**
Elaboration supporting key/star ideas. Also known as the **E's**.

**report**
A composition in which the writer disseminates facts about a particular subject; though the writer may express some opinions, he or she does not make the position the purpose for writing.

**resolution**
The final outcome of a story, often including how characters solve a problem.

**revising**
Changing words, sentences, and paragraphs to make them better.

**rhyme**
An occurrence in writing when the ending sounds of two or more words are the same or similar. (bl*ock*, sm*ock*, kn*ock*)

**rhythm**
The timing and beat of words and phrases as they are read.

**scoring guide**
A list of the criteria used to evaluate different types of writing. Four different areas are evaluated for each type of writing, rated from below basic to advanced.

**second person**
A point of view in which the speaker is directly addressing the reader using words like *you*, *your*, and *yours*.

**sentence**
A complete thought with a subject and a verb.

**sentence strips**
Long, thin strips of paper on which teachers or students write sentences. Sentence strips emphasize that though sentences can be "chunked" into separate elements, they are also singular in and of themselves.

**setting**
The time and place in which a story is set, often composed of what the place looked, sounded, and smelled like.

**simile**
Making a comparison between two otherwise different objects or actions by using the words "like" or "as." (Arturo had *muscles* that were *as hard as steel*.)

**simple sentence**
A sentence that has one independent clause and no dependent clauses. (*Keiko caught the ball.*)

**speech**
A spoken version of an essay or report.

**story**

A work of writing that includes characters, a plot, a conflict, and a resolution. Stories have a beginning, middle, and end. They are also known as **narratives**.

**story map**

A prewriting tool for placing and organizing rough ideas for a story.

**style**

The way a writer puts together words, sentences, and paragraphs in his or her writing.

**subject**

One of the two main components of a sentence; it is the noun in which the predicate is interested.

**subordinating conjunctions**

Conjunctions that introduce a dependent clause. (*although, if, because*)

**summary without words**

A summary created using no written language but by using drawings that convey comprehension and help as a memory aid.

**symbol**

A place, object, or being in a poem that stands for or suggests something else.

**synonyms**

Two or more different words that share the same meaning.

**text structure**

The way a composition is written, which varies depending on the purpose of the writing. For example, compare/contrast writing has a different text structure than descriptive writing.

**text to self**

A response in which the reader makes a connection to the text in relation to their own life.

**text to text**

A response in which the reader makes a connection to the text in relation to another text.

**text to world**

A response in which the reader makes a connection to the text in relation to the larger world.

**theme**

The subject or main idea of a story and/or the message of the story.

**thesis statement**

A type of topic sentence used in information writing in which the writer expresses an opinion, takes a position, or makes an argument.

**third person**

A point of view in a story in which the speaker is an all-knowing observer who describes the thoughts and actions of all characters, or the point of view in an essay in which the writer explains facts and shares information using only third-person pronouns like *she, he, it,* and *they.*

**three-part sentence**

A sentence composed of three parts: who is doing the action, what the action is, and where the action takes place. (*I finished my art project.*)

**ticket out**

An exercise in which students hand the teacher a "ticket" on which is written an error-free sentence (or anything else assigned by the teacher) before leaving class or moving to a preferred activity.

## tone

The attitude the writer suggests while writing about the characters and events in a story or the attitude a writer shares about a topic in information writing.

## Tools

Overhead transparencies and student handouts that are used to support the strategies in *Step Up to Writing*. Some Tools contain examples, whereas others provide a framework to help students take notes, write outlines, and complete other writing tasks.

## topic

The main idea of a report or paragraph. The topic of a report about lions, bears, and giraffes might be "zoo animals."

## topic sentence

A sentence near the beginning of a report or paragraph that tells the reader what the writer will be discussing in the text.

## Traffic Light colors

Green, yellow, and red markings that each signify a different aspect of information writing, relative to the "speed" at which the writing is produced. Green signifies both the topic sentence and the conclusion of a report or paper; the theme is "Go! Get to your point." Yellow signifies transitions and key/star ideas; the theme is "Slow down! Present support for your topic." Red signifies elaborations; the theme is "Stop! Take time to provide details to support your key/star ideas."

## Train of Thought

A visual learning aid in which the cars of a train (engine, boxcar, and caboose) visually represent the parts of an information paragraph.

## transition

A word or phrase that lets the reader know the writer is moving from one key/star idea or situation to another.

## transition set

A group of transitions that work well together in the same piece of writing. (*one, another, finally*)

## transition topic sentence

The first sentence in most body paragraphs of a multiparagraph report. It moves the writing from the previous topic to a new one and tells the reader what the key/star idea of the paragraph is. Only paragraphs that consist entirely of elaboration for a previous key/star idea do not have a transition topic sentence.

## Two Kinds of Writing

A term that refers to the two basic patterns in text: information writing and story writing.

## two-column fold

Notebook paper folded lengthwise so that the left-hand side of the page is one-third of the writing area and the right-hand side is two-thirds of the writing area. See T32 in the introduction.

### two-column notes

Notes taken on paper folded with a two-column fold. The main ideas for each paragraph go on the left-hand side, and detail notes supporting the main ideas go on the right-hand side of the paper.

### verb

A word that shows an action. (*run, make, read*)

### vocabulary map

A learning aid for vocabulary that is composed of a word's definition, any available synonym, a personal connection to the word's meaning, a sentence using the word, and a visual representation of the word's meaning.

### voice

The distinct tone or style of writing produced by each individual writer; voice is the "heart and soul" of writing and includes elements such as lively word choice, feeling, and topic choice.

### Where or When Plus What's Happening Sentence

A sentence that begins with an indication of where or when action takes place. (*On our trip* I ate fish.)

### writing frame

An incomplete form of writing that a teacher creates. The teacher leaves blanks in the text to be filled in by students. See **framed paragraph** and **framed response or report**.

# Bibliography

Act-Two. *Under the Sea.* Princeton, NJ: Two-Can, 2002.

Adams, Gail N., and Sheron M. Brown. *The Six-Minute Solution: Secondary.* Longmont, CO: Sopris West, 2007.

Adil, Janeen. "The River Otter." *Ladybug* May 2001: 27.

Adler, David A. *A Picture Book of Amelia Earhart.* New York: Holiday House, 1998.

Ahlberg, Janet, and Allan Ahlberg. *The Jolly Postman, or Other People's Letters.* Boston: Little, Brown and Company, 1986.

"AIDS at 25/Global Connections (A Global Menace)." *Newsweek* May 15, 2006.

Allen, Roberta. *Fast Fiction: Creating Fiction in Five Minutes.* Cincinnati, OH: Story Press, 1997.

Allison, Christine, ed. *365 Bedtime Stories.* New York: Broadway Books, 1998.

Amole, Gene. *The Last Chapter: Gene Amole on Dying.* Denver: *Rocky Mountain News*, 2002.

Andersen, Hans Christian. *The Steadfast Tin Soldier.* Georges Lemoine, illus. Mankato, MN: Creative Editions, 2002.

Annan, Kofi. "Black Dots and Earmuffs." *Highlights for Children* July 2003: 20.

*Angela's Ashes.* Dir. Alan Parker. Based on book by Frank McCourt. Paramount Pictures, 1999.

Angelfish, Christopher. *The Fish Book.* Racine, WI: Golden Books Pub., 1997.

Angelou, Maya. *Poems.* New York: Bantam Books, 1997.

Anglund, Joan Walsh. *The Brave Cowboy.* Kansas City, MO: Andrews McMeel Pub., 2000.

Arnold, Tedd. *Even More Parts: Idioms from Head to Toe.* New York: Dial Book for Young Readers, 2004.

———. *Super Fly Guy.* New York: Scholastic, 2006.

Ash, Russell, and Bernard Higton, comps. *Aesop's Fables: A Classic Illustrated Edition.* San Francisco: Chronicle Books, 1990.

Atwell, Nancie. *In the Middle: Writing, Reading, and Learning with Adolescents.* Upper Montclair, NJ: Boynton/Cook Publishers, 1987.

Avi. *The Good Dog.* New York: Atheneum Books for Young Readers, 2001.

Baker, Sheridan. *The Practical Stylist.* 7th ed. New York: Harper & Row, 1990.

Ballard, Lois. *Reptiles.* Chicago: Children's Press, 1982.

Barrett, Judi. *Cloudy With a Chance of Meatballs.* New York: Simon & Schuster, 1978.

Beal, Carole R. (1993). Contributions of developmental psychology to understanding revision: Implications for consultation with classroom teachers. *School Psychology Review* 22 (4): 643–655.

———. (1996). The role of comprehension monitoring in children's revision skills. *Educational Psychology Review 8* (3): 219–238.

*The Bear.* Dir. Jean-Jacques Annaud. Tri-Star Pictures, 1989.

Belasco, James A., and Ralph C. Stayer. *Flight of the Buffalo: Soaring to Excellence, Learning to Let Employees Lead.* New York: Warner Books, 1993.

Bennett, William J., ed., with commentary. *The Book of Virtues: A Treasury of Great Moral Stories.* New York: Simon & Schuster, 1993.

Berenstain, Stan, and Jan Berenstain. *The Berenstain Bears Get In a Fight.* New York: Random House, 1982.

Berger, Melvin. *From Peanuts to Peanut Butter (a MacMillan Early Science Big Book).* Northborough, MA: Newbridge Educational Publishing, 1992.

Bergman, Carol Ann, and J. A. Senn. *Heath Grammar and Composition (Fifth Course).* Teacher's Edition. Lexington, MA: D. C. Heath and Company, 1986.

Berninger, Virginia Wise. *Reading and Writing Acquisition: A Developmental Neuropsychological Perspective* (Developmental Psychology Series). Boulder, CO: Westview Press, 1996.

Berninger, Virginia Wise, Robert D. Abbott, Diane Whitaker, Leihua Sylvester, and Susan B. Nolen. (1995). Integrating low- and high-level skills in instructional protocols for writing disabilities. *Learning Disability Quarterly* 18 (4): 293–309.

Berninger, Virginia Wise, and H. L. Swanson. (1994). Modifying Hayes and Flower's model of skilled writing to explain beginning and developing writing. In Butterfield, E. (Ed.), *Children's Writing: Toward a Process Theory of the Development of Skilled Writing* (57–81). Greenwich, CT: JAI Press.

*Big River: The Adventures of Huckleberry Finn.* Dir. Des McAnuff, chor. Janet Watson, Eugene O'Neill Theatre on Broadway, 1985.

Blake, William. "To Spring." In Untermeyer, *The Golden Treasury of Poetry,* 271.

Boscolo, P., & Ascorti, K. (2004). Effects of collaborative revision on children's ability to write understandable narrative texts. In Allal, Linda, Lucile Chanquoy, and P. Largy (Eds.), *Revision: Cognitive and Instructional Processes* (157–170). Boston, MA: Kluwer Academic Publishers.

Bower, Lois. "Squirrel School." *Highlights for Children* April 2002: 22.

Bower, Sharon A. *Painless Public Speaking.* Stanford, California: Confidence Training, Inc., 1994.

"Bowling for Bugs." *US Kids* Sept./Oct. 2004: 17–19.

Boyer, Paul. *The American Nation.* Austin, TX: Holt, Rinehart and Winston, Inc., 1995.

Brett, Jan, adapt. and illus. *The Mitten: A Ukrainian Folktale.* New York: Putnam, 1989.

Brewster, Cori, and Jennifer Klump. (2004). Writing to Learn, Learning to Write: Revisiting Writing Across the Curriculum in Northwest Secondary Schools. Portland, OR: Northwest Regional Educational Laboratory.

Briggs, Raymond. *The Snowman Storybook.* New York: Random House, 1990.

Brown, Margaret Wise. *The Important Book.* New York: HarperCollins Publishers, 1949.

———. *The Runaway Bunny.* Revised ed. New York: HarperCollins Publishers, 2005.

———. *The Sailor Dog.* New York: Random House, 2005.

Brown, Margaret Wise, and Felicia Bond. *Big Red Barn.* New York: Rayo, 2002.

Brushaw, Charles T., Gerald J. Alfred, and Walter E. Oliu. *The Business Writer's Handbook.* 3rd rev. ed. New York: St. Martin's Press, 1987.

Burns, M. Susan, Peg Griffin, and Catherine E. Snow, eds.; National Research Council. *Starting Out Right: A Guide to Promoting Children's Reading Success.* Washington, DC: National Academy Press, 1999.

Burtis, P., C. Bereiter, M. Scardamalia, and J. Tetroe. (1983). The development of planning in writing. In Wells, C. G. and B. Kroll (Eds.), *Explorations of Children's Development in Writing* (pp. 153–174). Chichester, England: Wiley.

Calkins, Lucy McCormick. *The Art of Teaching Writing.* Portsmouth, NH: Heinemann, 1986.

Calmenson, Stephanie. Rosie: *A Visiting Dog's Story.* New York: Clarion Books, 1994.

Canfield, Jack, comp., et al. *Chicken Soup for the Kid's Soul: 101 Stories of Courage, Hope, and Laughter.* Deerfield Beach, FL: Health Communications, Inc., 1998.

Canfield, Jack, Mark Victor Hansen, and Kimberly Kirberger, comps. *Chicken Soup for the Soul: 101 Stories to Open the Heart and Rekindle the Spirit.* Deerfield Beach, FL: Health Communications, 1993.

———*Chicken Soup for the Teenage Soul: 101 Stories of Life, Love, and Learning.* Deerfield Beach, FL: Health Communications, 1997: 298.

———. *Chicken Soup for the Teenage Soul II: 101 More Stories of Life, Love, and Learning.* Deerfield Beach, FL: Health Communications., 1998: 237.

Cannon, Janell. *Stellaluna.* Orlando, FL: Harcourt, Inc., 2007.

Caplan, Jeremy. "Word Wizards." *Time for Kids* April 9, 2004: 4–5.

Carlson, Nancy. *Bunnies and Their Hobbies.* Minneapolis, MN: Carolrhoda Books, 1984.

———. *How to Lose All Your Friends.* New York: Penguin Group, 1997.

———. *Life Is Fun!* New York: Viking, 1993.

Carson, Rachel. *Silent Spring.* Boston: Houghton Mifflin Company, 1962.

Cherry Creek School District Reading Workshop. "Cooperative Integrated Reading and Composition (CIRC)—Reading." Englewood, CO, 1987. Meg Ascencio, Instructor.

Chevallier, Chiara. *The Secret Life of Trees.* New York: DK Pub., 1999.

Churchman, Deborah. "From Trash to Toys." *Ranger Rick,* December 2004: 11–13.

———. "New Dogs in Town." *Ranger Rick,* December 2004: 22–28.

Chute, Marchette. *An Introduction to Shakespeare.* New York: Scholastic, Inc., 1979.

Cleary, Beverly. *Muggie Maggie.* New York: Morrow Junior Books, 1990.

Cohn, Amy L., comp. *From Sea to Shining Sea: A Treasury of American Folklore and Folk Songs.* New York: Scholastic, Inc., 1993.

Collodi, Carlo. *The Adventures of Pinocchio.* New York: Grosset & Dunlap, 1946.

Cormier, Robert. *Eight Plus One: Stories.* New York: Pantheon Books, 1980.

Cosby, Bill. *Fatherhood.* Garden City, NY: Doubleday, 1986.

Cowley, Joy. "A Reading Lesson." *Highlights for Children* Jan. 2002: 24.

Crane, Stephen. *The Red Badge of Courage.* Reader's Digest Best Loved Books for Young Readers. New York: Choice Publishing, Inc., 1989.

Cronin, Doreen. *Click, Clack, Moo: Cows That Type.* New York: Simon & Schuster Books for Young Readers, 2000.

Davis, Kenneth C. *Don't Know Much About Geography.* New York: William Morrow & Company, Inc., 1992.

Dewey, Jennifer Owings. *A Night and Day in the Desert.* Boston: Little, Brown and Company, 1991.

———. *Rattlesnake Dance.* Honesdale, PA: Caroline House, 1997.

DiCamillo, Kate. *Because of Winn-Dixie.* Cambridge, MA: Candlewick Press, 2000.

Dickinson, Emily. "I'm Nobody! Who Are You?" In Untermeyer, *The Golden Treasury of Poetry,* 91.

Dorros, Arthur. *Ant Cities.* New York: Crowell, 1987.

Douglass, Frederick. *Narrative of the Life of Frederick Douglass.* New York: Dover Publications, 1995.

Dove, Mary. "Special Education Workshop for New Teachers." Eaglecrest High School, Aurora, CO, 1995.

Drohan, Michele and Caroline M. Levchuck. *An Environment Q&A Book: When Is It Great to Turn Green?* New York: Kidsbooks, Inc., 2001.

Duke, Kate. *Aunt Isabel Tells a Good One.* New York: Dutton Children's Books, 1992.

Edwards, Betty. *The New Drawing on the Right Side of the Brain.* 2nd rev. ed. New York: Jeremy P. Tarcher/ Putnam, 1999.

Elder, Scott. "The Incredible Dolphin Rescue: How Humans Helped After Hurricane Katrina." *National Geographic Kids* June/ July 2006: 27–31.

*E.T., The Extra-Terrestrial.* Dir. Steven Spielberg. Universal Pictures, 1982.

"Everyone pays for slackers." Editorial. *USA Today,* March 7, 1996: A11.

Evslin, Bernard. *The Adventures of Ulysses.* New York: Scholastic, Inc., 1969.

Finton, Nancy. "The Beat Goes On." *National Geographic Explorer* Jan./Feb. 2003: 4–8.

Fleischman, Paul. *Seedfolks.* New York: HarperCollins, 1997.

Fontes, Justine, and Ron Fontes. *How the Turtle Got Its Shell.* New York: Golden Books Pub., 2000.

Foote, David, Margaret Grauff Forst, Mary Hynes-Berry, Julie West Johnson, Basia C. Miller, and Brenda Pierce Perkins. *Contemporary Short Stories.* Evanston, IL: McDougal Littell, 1993.

Ford, Roberta. "Language Arts Training for Teaching Parts of Speech." Cherry Creek School District. Englewood, CO (Fall, 1995).

Frank, Anne. *The Diary of a Young Girl.* New York: Globe Book Co., 1988.

Freedman, Russell. *Franklin Delano Roosevelt.* New York: Clarion Books, 1990.

Friedrich, Elizabeth. *Leah's Pony.* Honesdale, PA: Caroline House, Boyds Mills Press, Inc., 1996.

"The Future of Energy." *Time for Kids* 11, no. 11 (Nov. 18, 2005).

Garner, Mona. "The Dinner Party." In Safier, *Impact, Fifty Short Short Stories.*

Garrison, Kelly. "A Very Special Program." *Occasions 1990.* Boulder, CO: University of Colorado Writing Program, 1990. N.p.: University of Colorado at Boulder, 1990. 25–26.

Geisel, Theodor Seuss. *I Can Lick 30 Tigers Today! and Other Stories.* New York: Random House Books for Young Readers, 1969.

———. *Yertle the Turtle, and Other Stories.* New York: Random House, 1958.

Gendler, J. Ruth. *The Book of Qualities.* New York: Perennial Library, 1988.

Gersten, Russell, and Scott Baker. (2001). Teaching Expressive Writing to Students with Learning Disabilities: A Meta-Analysis. *The Elementary School Journal* 101 (3): 251–272.

Goble, Paul. *Adopted by the Eagles: A Plains Indian Story of Friendship and Treachery.* New York: Aladdin Paperbacks, 1998.

Gollub, Matthew. *The Twenty-Five Mixtec Cats.* Santa Rosa, CA: Tortuga Press, 2004.

Goodman, Roger B. *75 Short Masterpieces: Stories from the World's Literature.* Reissue ed. New York: Bantam Books, 1985.

"Good Night, Little Bear." In *Sleepytime Tales: A Little Golden Book Collection.*

Gorog, Judith. "Those Three Wishes." In Trelease, *Read All About It!*

Graham, Steve, Karen R. Harris, Charles A. MacArthur, and Shirley Schwartz. (1991). Writing and writing instruction for students with learning disabilities: Review of a research program. *Learning Disability Quarterly* 14 (2): 89–114.

Graham, Steve, Karen R. Harris, and Barbara Fink. (2000). "Is handwriting causally related to learning to write? Treatment of handwriting problems in beginning writers." *Journal of Educational Psychology* 92 (4): 620–633.

Graham, Steve, and Dolores Perin. (2007). *Writing next: Effective strategies to improve writing of adolescents in middle and high schools—A report to Carnegie Corporation of New York.* Washington, DC: Alliance for Excellent Education.

Graves, Donald H. *Writing: Teachers and Children at Work.* Exeter, NH: Heinemann Educational Books.

Greenfield, Eloise. *Africa Dream.* Carole Byard, illlus. New York: John Day Co., 1977.

Hakim, Joyce. *A History of US.* 2nd ed. New York: Oxford University Press, 1999.

Hakim, Rita. *Martin Luther King, Jr. and the March Toward Freedom.* Brookfield, CT: Millbrook Press, 1991.

Hamilton, Virginia. *The All Jahdu Storybook.* San Diego: Harcourt Brace Jovanovich, 1991.

———. *Many Thousand Gone: African Americans from Slavery to Freedom.* New York: Knopf, 1993.

Harcourt Brace Jovanovich. *A Book of Short Stories 1.* 2nd ed. Orlando, FL: Harcourt Brace Jovanovich, 1983.

Harth, Ann. "My Mom Hates to Cook." *Highlights for Children* Oct. 2003: 12–14.

Hartigan, Patti. "Asian Imports. The Academy of the Pacific Rim transports Eastern practices to Boston with impressive results." *Teacher Magazine* 13, no. 4 (Jan. 2002), 12–15.

Haskins, James. *Colin Powell: A Biography.* New York: Scholastic, Inc., 1992.

Hayes, J. R., and Flower, L. S. (1980). Identifying the organization of writing processes. In Greeg, L. W., and Steinberg, E. R. (Eds.), *Cognitive Processes in Writing* (31–50). Hillsdale, NJ: Lawrence Erlbaum Associates, Inc.

Hendra, Sue, illus. *My First Big Book of Creepy-Crawlies.* The Book Studio, 2003.

Herman, Linda. "Horsing Around." *Highlights for Children* July 2002.

Highbridge Company. *Prairie Home Companion Pretty Good Joke Book.* Saint Paul, MN: HighBridge Co., 2000.

Hilton, James. *Goodbye, Mr. Chips.* Boston: Bantam Books, 1986.

Hirsch, E. D., Jr., ed. *What Your 1st Grader Needs to Know: Fundamentals of a Good First-Grade Education* (The Core Knowledge Series). New York: Doubleday, 1991.

———. *What Your 5th Grader Needs to Know: Fundamentals of a Good Fifth-Grade Education* (The Core Knowledge Series). New York: Doubleday, 1993

Hoppey, Tim. *Tito, the Firefighter / Tito, el Bombero,* illus. Kimberly Hoffman, trans. Eida de la Vega. Green Bay, WI: Raven Tree Press, 2006.

Hughes, Langston. *Thank You, M'am.* Mankato, MN: Creative Education, 1991.

Hutcheson, Ron. "Bush Assures Troops on Iraq." *Denver Post,* December 16, 2006: 2A.

Hyde, Dayton O. "The Dangers of Bird Watching." *Highlights for Children* Dec. 2002: 32.

"Jack and the Beanstalk." In Allison, *365 Bedtime Stories,* 259–261.

Jacobsen, Karen. *China.* Chicago: Children's Press, 1990.

Jay, Lorraine A. "A Sea Turtle's Quiet Miracle." *Highlights* Jan. 2003: 36.

Johnson, Carl, Lois Kline, Karen Krupay, Lyn Hutchins, and Robert Ross. *Choices: Decision-Making Processes for Speakers.* Dubuque, IA: Kendall/Hunt Publishing Co., 1992.

Jones, Charlotte Foltz. *Mistakes That Worked.* New York: Doubleday, 1991.

Kantrowitz, Barbara and Pat Wingert. "Curing Senioritis," *Newsweek,* December 11, 2000.

Kennedy, John F. "Address at Rice University on the Space Effort, September 12, 1962." Papers of the Presidents of the United States, v. 1, 1962, 669–670, http://www.rice.edu/fondren/woodson/speech.html (accessed April 2, 2007).

King, Coretta Scott. "Why We Still Can't Wait." *Newsweek* Aug. 1976.

"King Looie Katz." In Geisel, *I Can Lick 30 Tigers Today! and Other Stories.*

King, Martin Luther, Jr. "Ways of Meeting Oppression." *Models for Writers.* Eds. Alfred Rosa and Paul Eschholz. New York: St. Martin's Press, 1986.

King, Stephen. *On Writing—A Memoir of the Craft.* New York: Scribner, 2000.

King-Smith, Dick. *Babe: The Gallant Pig.* New York: Random House, 1983.

Kirby, Dan and Tom Liner, with Ruth Vinz. *Inside Out: Developmental Strategies for Teaching Writing.* 2nd ed. Portsmouth, NH: Boynton/Cook Publishers, 1988.

Kodak. "Composing your pictures." 24 July 2006. http://www.kodak.com/ (accessed April 3, 2007).

Kraske, Robert. *The Twelve Million Dollar Note: Strange but True Tales of Messages Found in Seagoing Bottles.* Nashville, TN: T. Nelson, 1977.

Kreikemeier, Gregory Scott. *Come with Me to Africa: A Photographic Journey.* Racine, WI: Western Publishing Company, 1993.

Langer, Judith A., and Arthur N. Applebee. (1987). *How writing shapes thinking: A study of teaching and learning.* NCTE Research Report No. 22 (Study 3). Urbana, IL: National Council of Teachers of English.

Lee, Harper. *To Kill a Mockingbird.* New York: Perennial, 2002.Lehmann, Ruth P. M. *Beowulf: An Imitative Translation.* Austin, TX: University of Texas Press, 1988.

Leonhardt, Alice. *Ocean Life: Tide Pool Creatures.* Austin, TX : Steck-Vaughn, 2000.

Levine, Ellen. *I Hate English!* New York: Scholastic, Inc., 1989.

Levy, Elizabeth. *If You Were There When They Signed The Constitution.* New York: Scholastic Inc., 1987.

Lin, Grace. *The Ugly Vegetables.* Watertown, MA: Charlesbridge, 1999.

Lincoln, Abraham. "A Letterfrom Abraham Lincoln to His Stepbrother." In Bennett, *The Book of Virtues*, 402–404.

Lobel, Arnold. *Days with Frog and Toad.* New York: HarperCollins, 1979.

———. *Fables.* New York: HarperCollins, 1980.

London, Jack. *The Call of the Wild.* New York: Tom Doherty Associates, LLC, 1986.

Lopate, Phillip. *The Art of the Personal Essay: An Anthology from the Classical Era to the Present.* New York: Anchor Books, 1994.

Lovell, Patty. *Stand Tall, Molly Lou Melon.* New York: G. P. Putnam's Sons, 2001.

Lowe, Steve. *The Log of Christopher Columbus: The First Voyage, Spring, Summer, and Fall 1492,* illus. Robert Sabuda. New York: Philomel Books, 1992.

Lowry, Lois. *Gooney Bird Greene.* New York: Dell Yearling, 2002.

Malamud, Bernard. "A Summer's Reading." In Foote et al, *Contemporary Short Stories*, 198–203.

*The March of the Penguins.* Dir. Luc Jacquet. Warner Independent Pictures, 2005.

Markle, Sandra. "Koalas: Can They Hang On?" *National Geographic Explorer* Mar. 2003: 12–17.

Marzano, Robert J. *A Handbook for Classroom Instruction that Works.* Alexandria, VA: Association for Supervision and Curriculum Development, 2001.

Mayer, Mercer. *Just Big Enough.* New York: HarperFestival, 2004.

Macdonald, Maryann, and Lynn Munsinger, illus. *Hedgehog Bakes a Cake.* New York: Bantam Books, 1990.

McCutchen, Deborah, and Charles A. Perfetti. (1982). Coherence and Connectedness in the Development of Discourse Production. *Text 2*, 113–139.

McMullan, Kate. *Dinosaur Hunters.* New York: Random House, 1989.

———. *Dragon Slayers' Academy 1: The New Kid at School.* New York: Grosset & Dunlap, 2003.

"Medio Pollito." In Hirsch, *What Your 1st Grader Needs to Know.*

Miller, Ned. *Emmett's Snowball.* New York: Holt, 1990.

Milne, A. A. *Winnie-the-Pooh.* New York: Penguin Putnam, 1992.

Mollel, Tololwa M. *The Princess Who Lost Her Hair: An Akamba Legend.* Mahwah, NJ: Troll Associates, 1993.

Murray, Donald M. *A Writer Teaches Writing.* 2nd ed. Boston: Houghton Mifflin Co., 1985.

*The Music Man.* Dir. Morton DaCosta. Warner Bros. Pictures, 1962.

Muth, John J. *The Three Questions.* New York: Scholastic Press, 2002.

National Council of Teachers of English. *Standards for the English Language Arts.* Hillsboro, OR: Blue Heron Publishing, 1995.

National Reading Panel. (2000). *Teaching children to read: An evidence-based assessment of the scientific research literature on reading and its implications for reading instruction.* Washington, DC: National Institute of Child Health and Human Development.

Nelson, Vaunda Micheaux. *Almost to Freedom.* Minneapolis, MN: Carolrhoda Books, 2003.

Newman, Aline Alexander. "Bear-y Generous." *Ranger Rick* March 2004.

Nicholas, J. B. "A Prehistoric Mystery." *Highlights for Children* May 2002: 12–13.

"Night Senses." *Your Big Backyard* Oct. 2004: 19–27.

Nixon, Joan Lowery. *If You Were a Writer.* New York: Simon & Shuster, 1995.

North, Sterling. *Rascal.* New York: Penguin Books, 1963.

Numeroff, Laura Joffe. *Why a Disguise?* Illus. David McPhail. New York: Simon & Schuster Books for Young Readers, 1996.

*Occasions 1993.* Boulder, CO: University of Colorado Writing Program, 1993. N.p.: University of Colorado at Boulder, 1993.

O'Dell, Scott. *Sing Down The Moon.* New York: Dell Publishing, 1970.

Paschen, Elise, ed. *Poetry Speaks to Children.* Naperville, IL: Sourcebooks, 2005.

Paulson, Gary. *The Quilt.* New York: Wendy Lamb Books, 2004.

Peck, Richard. *A Long Way from Chicago.* New York: Scholastic, 1998.

Phelan, Glen. "First Flight." *National Geographic Explorer* Apr/March 2003: 5–11.

"The Pied Piper of Hamelin." In Bennett, *The Book of Virtues.*

"Porcupines." *Your Big Backyard* Feb. 2000: 18.

Powers, Joan. *Eeyore's Gloomy Little Instruction Book.* Inspired by A. A. Milne, with decorations by Ernest H. Shepard. New York: Dutton Books, 1996.

Pressley, Michael, and Ruth Wharton-McDonald. (1997). Skilled comprehension and its development through instruction. *School Psychology Review* 26 (3): 448–467.

Raphael, Taffy, and K. H. Au. "QAR: Enhancing Comprehension and Test Taking Across Grades and Content Areas." *The Reading Teacher* 59 (3) (Nov. 2005), 206–221.

Ratliff, Jennifer A. "Zaaaaaaaap!" *Odyssey* April 4, 2004.

Renner, Mark. "Techniques for Avoiding Bear Attacks." *Occasions 1989.* Boulder, CO: University of Colorado Writing Program, 1989.

Rhodes, Michelle. "The City Mouse and the Country Mouse." In *3-Minute Stories: Best-Loved Tales.*

Riley, Richard. "The Power of Arts Education." *Teaching K–8,* May 1998.

Rivers, Reggie. "Real-Life Tragedy Shouldn't Be a Spectator Sport." *Rocky Mountain News* 5 May 1998.

Roberts, Elizabeth, and Elias Amidon, eds. *Earth Prayers: From Around the World: 365 Prayers, Poems, and Invocations for Honoring the Earth.* San Francisco: HarperCollins, 1991.

Robertson, Matthew. *Bugs: The Encyclopedia of Creepy-Crawlies.* New York: Smithmark Publishers, 1999.

Rylant, Cynthia, with decorations by S. D. Schindler. *Every Living Thing: Stories.* New York: Macmillan, 1985.

Safier, Fannie. *Impact, Fifty Short Short Stories.* Orlando, FL: Harcourt Brace Jovanovich, 1986.

Saltzberg, Barney. *Phoebe and the Spelling Bee.* New York: Hyperion Books for Children, 1996.

Sandburg, Carl. "Fog." In Untermeyer, *The Golden Treasury of Poetry*, 255.

Santa, Carol Minnick, et al. *Content Reading Including Study Systems.* Dubuque, IA: Kendall/Hunt Publishing Company, 1988.

Schleichert, Elizabeth. "Hey, It's Frog Time—Hop to It!" *Ranger Rick* March 2005: 21.

———. "Marvin's Marvelous Meerkat Tours" *Ranger Rick* July 2005: FC, 3, 22–27.

Scieszka, Jon, and Lane Smith. *Science Verse.* New York: Viking/Penguin, 2004.

Sebranek, Patrick, Verne Meyer, and Dave Kemper. *Writers INC: A Student Handbook for Writing and Learning.* Lexington, KY: D. C. Heath and Company, 1996.

"Seeing Double." *3-2-1 Contact*, January/February, 1999.

Seinfeld, Jerry. *Seinlanguage.* New York: Bantam Books, 1993

Seligmann, Judith, with Karen Springen and Jeanne Gordon. "Going Under the Light." *Newsweek* Oct. 2 1995.

Sewell, Anna. *Black Beauty. Great Illustrated Classics.* New York: Waldman Publishing Corp., 1977.

Shaw, John. *The Nature Photographer's Complete Guide to Professional Field Techniques.* New York: American Photographic Book Publishing, 1984.

Shore, Kenneth. "The ABCs of Bullying Prevention: Understanding School Bullying." *Education World*, 2005, http://www.education-world.com/a_curr/shore/shore063.shtml (accessed March 30, 2007.)

Silverstein, Shel. *Falling Up: Poems and Drawings.* New York: HarperCollins, 2005.

———. *The Giving Tree.* New York: Harper & Row, 1964.

———. *A Light in the Attic.* New York: Harper & Row, 1981.

Singer, Isaac Bashevis. *Zlateh the Goat, and Other Stories.* Singer, Isaac Bashevis and Elizabeth Shub, trans. New York: Harper & Row, 1966.

Simmons, R. "Confessions of a Teenage Bully." *Scholastic Scope* 6 (Sep. 2004): 16–18.

Simon, Charnan. "Seasons of the Amazon." *Click* May/June 2001: 8–11.

Simon, Seymour. *Our Solar System.* New York: Morrow Junior Books, 1992.

*Sleepytime Tales: A Little Golden Book Collection.* New York: Random House, 2004.

Smith, MaryLou M. *Grandmother's Adobe Dollhouse.* Santa Fe, NM: New Mexico Magazine, 1984.

Sparks, J. E. *Read for Power.* Los Angeles: Designline, 1987.

———. *Write for Power.* Manhattan Beach, CA: Communications Associates, 1996.

Speed, Toby. "The Spider's Lullaby." *Highlights for Children*, February, 2001.

Spinelli, Eileen. *Sophie's Masterpiece: A Spider's Tale.* New York: Simon & Schuster Books for Young Readers, 2001.

Steinbeck, John. *Of Mice and Men.* New York: Covici-Friede, 1937.

———. *Travels with Charley: In Search of America.* New York: Penguin Books, 1962.

Strunk, William, Jr., and E. B. White. *The Elements of Style.* New York: Penguin Press, 2005.

Swanson, H. L. (1999). Reading research intervention for students with LD: A meta-analysis of intervention outcomes. *Journal of Learning Disabilities* 32 (6): 504–532.

Swanson, H. Lee, Maureen Hoskyn, and Carole Lee. *Interventions for students with learning disabilities: A meta-analysis of treatment outcomes.* New York: Guilford Press, 1999.

Talbott, Hudson. *The Lady at Liberty: Memoirs of a Monument.* New York: Avon Books, 1986.

Thomas, Keltie. *How Hockey Works.* Toronto: Owl Books, 2002.

Thomas, Marlo. *The Right Words at the Right Times—Marlo Thomas and Friends.* New York: First Atria Books, 2002.

*3-Minute Stories: Best-Loved Tales.* Lincolnwood, IL: Publications International, 2003.

"The Three Bears." In *Sleepytime Tales: A Little Golden Book Collection.*

Tildes, Phyllis Limbacher. *Animals in Camouflage.* Watertown, MA: Charlesbridge Publishing, 2000.

Trelease, Jim, ed. *Read All About It! Great Read-Aloud Stories, Poems, and Newspaper Pieces for Preteens and Teens.* New York: Penguin Group, 1993.

Twain, Mark. *The Adventures of Tom Sawyer.* West Berlin, NJ: Townsend Press, 2004.

Untermeyer, Louis, selected and with a commentary by. *The Golden Treasury of Poetry.* New York: Golden Press, 1959.

U.S. Dept. of Education, National Center for Education Statistics. (2003). *The Nation's Report Card: Writing 2002* (NCES 2003-529). Washington DC: U.S. Government Printing Office.

van Allen, Lilyanne. 1991. The Effect of Writing Across the Curriculum Programs on Student Writing Improvement: A Study of Selected Middle Schools in Texas. PhD diss., University of Texas at Austin, 1991. Abstract in *Dissertation Abstracts International,* publ. nr. AAT 9200741, DAI-A 52/07 (Jan. 1992): 2398.

Vaughn, Sharon, Russell Gersten, and David J. Chard. (2000). The Underlying Message in LD Intervention Research: Findings from Research Syntheses. *Exceptional Children* 67 (1): 99–114.

Wallner, Alexandra. *Betsy Ross.* New York: Holiday House, 1994.

Weiss, Michael J. "Adventures of a Country Doctor." *Readers Digest* July 2005: 70–74.

"Why Do Animals Have Tails?" *Your Big Backyard* Mar. 2004: 20.

Williams, Joanna P. (1998). Improving the comprehension of disabled readers. *Annals of Dyslexia* 68: 213–238.

Williams, Margery. *The Velveteen Rabbit.* New York: Avon Books, 1975.

Wittels, Harriet, and Joan Greisman. *The Clear and Simple Thesaurus Dictionary.* Ed. William Morris. New York: Grosset & Dunlap, 1996.

Woods, Ralph Louis, ed. *A Treasury of the Familiar.* Chicago: Consolidated Book Publishers, 1944.

Writing Across the Curriculum Clearinghouse, The. (2007). "An Introduction to Writing Across the Curriculum (WAC): What Makes a Good Writing Assignment?" http://wac.colostate.edu/intro/pop2i.cfm (assessed April 5, 2007).

Wymore, Peggy Wilgus. "Instruments Old and New to Pick or Strum." *AppleSeeds* Jan. 2000: 26–28.

Yee, Paul. *Tales from Gold Mountain: Stories of the Chinese in the New World.* New York: Macmillan Publishing Company, 1989.

Yolen, Jane. *Color Me a Rhyme: Nature Poems for Young People.* Honesdale, PA: Wordsong/Boyds Mills Press, 2000.

Zinsser, William. *Writing to Learn.* New York: Harper and Row, 1988.